S·O·U·R·C·E·S

NOTABLE
SELECTIONS IN
Psychology
Third Edition

About the Editor

TERRY F. PETTIJOHN is a professor of psychology at the Ohio State University at Marion, where he has been teaching introductory psychology for more than two decades. As an undergraduate, he attended Alma College and Michigan State University, where he earned his B.S. in 1970. He obtained his M.A. in 1972 and his Ph.D. in experimental psychology in 1974 from Bowling Green State University. He is the author of a number of teaching publications for the introductory psychology course, including *Psychology: A ConnecText*, 4th ed., (Dushkin/McGraw-Hill, 1999), as well as the accompanying teaching and testing materials. He has served as editor of *MicroPsych Computer Network Newsletter*, and he currently serves on the Advisory Board for *Annual Editions: Psychology* (Dushkin/McGraw-Hill). In addition to introductory psychology, he teaches social and experimental psychology, learning and memory, motivation, adjustment, psychobiology, and research methods. Dr. Pettijohn has been recognized for his teaching efforts, including being a recipient of the Ohio State University Distinguished Teaching Award three times. His current research interests include the study of human emotion, memory, and animal social behavior. He is a member of the American Psychological Society, the Psychonomic Society, the Animal Behavior Society, the Society for Computers in Psychology, and the American Psychological Association, where he is affiliated with the Society for the Teaching of Psychology.

S·O·U·R·C·E·S

NOTABLE SELECTIONS IN

Psychology

Third Edition

EDITED BY

TERRY F. PETTIJOHN
Ohio State University

Dushkin/McGraw-Hill
A Division of The McGraw-Hill Companies

Manufactured in the United States of America

Third Edition

123456789FGRFGR3210

Library of Congress Cataloging-in-Publication Data
  Main entry under title:
    Sources: notable selections in psychology/edited by Terry F. Pettijohn.—3rd ed.
    Includes bibliographical references and index.
    1. Psychology. I. Pettijohn, Terry F., *comp.*

                                                          150
  0-07-303187-9   96-85797

 Printed on Recycled Paper

Preface

Although barely a century old as a formal discipline, the study of psychology has revolutionized how we look at ourselves and others. Psychology is the science of behavior and cognition; it is a rigorous brain science and, at the same time, it seeks to help people. Psychologists study behaviors, such as eating, talking, writing, running, or fighting, precisely because they can be directly observed and recorded. But psychologists also study mental processes, such as dreaming, thinking, remembering, and problem solving, which are not directly observable and are often studied through reports provided by human research subjects.

Psychologists are also interested in the physiological processes that often accompany both overt behavior and cognition. Finally, some psychologists are concerned with applying psychological principles to help people.

Most introductory psychology textbooks cover the important topics in psychology, but are not able to go into the depth required for complete understanding of the discipline. Textbooks summarize results of research studies, but the richness of the original sources is not available. The selections in this book supplement the textbook by providing the original sources for some of the landmark studies in our discipline. They allow students to obtain a "behind the scenes" look at how the leaders in psychology think, feel, conduct research, and develop theories.

Many instructors want students to develop critical thinking skills in their courses. One excellent opportunity is to provide original articles and chapters written by the prominent psychologists who carved out psychology as we currently know it. Some of these writers are of historical significance, while others are on the cutting edge of research and knowledge today. Through reading what these psychologists have to say, students can truly appreciate what psychology is and where it is going. In many ways, being able to read original selections provides a "behind the scenes" glimpse of the making of psychology.

As a discipline, psychology has evolved its own history of ideas and thinkers, research methods, and theories. In this volume I have put directly into your hands those researchers and writers whose works are essential to the study of psychology.

Sources: Notable Selections in Psychology, 3rd ed., brings together 47 selections of enduring intellectual value—classic articles, book excerpts, and research studies—that have shaped the study of psychology and our contemporary understanding of it. The book includes carefully edited selections from the works of the most distinguished psychological researchers and practitioners, past and present, from Sigmund Freud and B. F. Skinner to Mary D. S.

Ainsworth, Richard S. Lazarus, and Elizabeth F. Loftus. These selections allow you to obtain a behind-the-scenes look, so to speak, at psychology in the making.

Sources represents over 100 years of psychological thought and application. The actual dates of publication range from 1890 to 1998. I have made every effort to portray psychology as a dynamic and changing discipline. Obviously, new research has modified our understanding of some of the ideas covered in some of the selections; nonetheless, using these original sources will enrich your understanding of psychology and its elemental concepts.

Glancing over the Table of Contents should convince you that many of the people most frequently cited in psychology textbooks are included here. These widely recognized psychologists have made major contributions to the field and are well-respected researchers and writers. Care has been taken to provide something representative of each person included. Of course, not everyone who made major contributions to psychology was able to be included in the final Table of Contents. I believe the rich diversity of psychology is captured by the final selections.

REVISION PROCEDURE   The challenge of revising this book was carefully considered. In the first edition, I paid great attention to finding those classic works that could best communicate the excitement of psychology. Readability was the top priority, and each selection was carefully edited so that the essence of the original work could be readily understood. Students were able to experience firsthand many of the greatest thinkers in psychology. The descriptions in their textbook came alive through the actual writings of these highly influential people. These goals also guided the development of the third edition.

I wanted to ensure that the third edition continued to be truly representative of the breadth of psychology, both in terms of the distinguished people and of the important issues. I began by reviewing the hundreds of sources that were not included in the first edition, as well as the most historical and contemporary influential articles. Computer searches allowed me to identify writings by some of the most well respected names in psychology. The first edition was reviewed by current users, and their evaluations of each selection were extremely valuable in making decisions about which ones to replace. I also asked my students to provide feedback on the most effective selections as well as the ones that were not quite as informative. Unfortunately, much of the feedback I received was extremely positive on almost all of the selections, so the process of replacing selections was a very difficult one. Although not everyone will agree with the final decisions on individual selections, I believe that with the advice of many people I was able to significantly strengthen the book through inclusion of some of the best work of the past century.

New to the third edition are 13 selections from some of the most distinguished researchers, theorists, writers, and practitioners in psychology. Care was taken to include gender and cultural diversity issues as they relate to the discipline of psychology. In many ways, the most difficult task was deleting articles, many of which are extremely interesting and important. I am confident that the final compilation of writings will challenge students to think about and discuss the core issues that make up psychology today. Some of the selections provide theories that have shaped our discipline; some discuss crucial issues that have confronted psychologists during the past century; and many present the results of original research studies. Together the selections compose a snapshot of psychology as it currently exists, including important landmarks in its development.

ORGANIZATION OF THE BOOK   The selections are organized topically around the major areas of study within psychology: Part 1 includes selections on the Foundations of Psychology; Part 2, Perceptual Processes; Part 3, Learning and Cognitive Processes; Part 4, Motivation and Emotion; Part 5, Personality and Adjustment; Part 6, Psychological Disorders; and Part 7, Social Processes. The selections are organized so as to parallel most introduction to psychology textbooks. This means that these original sources, these classic works that underlie the key psychological concepts covered in the textbooks, can be easily read along with any textbook. But each selection is independent and can be read in any order and used in any way an instructor deems appropriate.

SUGGESTIONS FOR READING EACH SELECTION   As you read these original writings, it is important to keep in mind that ideas and standards have changed over the last century. In particular, changes in ethical concerns and in how language is used need to be mentioned here. Currently, there are very strict ethical guidelines for conducting human and animal research. Today researchers must submit proposals to committees that ensure that ethical standards are met. Some of the studies carried out in the past would not be approved now. As you read these selections, consider how the research contributed to psychology and whether or not the benefits outweighed the potential harm to the subjects.

Each selection is representative of the time in which it was written. Just as psychologists have become more sensitive to ethical considerations over the years, so too have they become more aware of the issue of gender, particularly as regards language. Many of the older articles use the masculine pronoun *he* when referring to both men and women, and many of the early studies had only male subjects. I recommend that you view each selection in the context of when it was written and focus on the psychological issues it reveals. These classic studies have had a major impact on the development of psychology as a discipline and should be read from that perspective.

Each selection is preceded by an introductory headnote that establishes the relevance of the selection, provides biographical information about the author, and includes a brief background discussion of the topic. I have also provided suggestions for understanding statistical tests and thought questions designed to guide critical thinking. It is important to read the headnote before beginning the selection itself.

As you read these selections, you will experience firsthand the ideas of some of the most important and influential psychologists. Remember that in most cases they are writing not to students but to other professionals in their field. This means that some of the selections will be more challenging to read, but it also means that you will gain a rare behind-the-scenes experience of how psychologists think and write.

Try to take an active approach when reading each selection. For example, when reading an experiment, determine what the research hypothesis is, identify the independent and dependent variables, and analyze the research methodology. Does the experiment raise ethical considerations? Do the conclusions follow from the results? Are there any extraneous variables or alternative explanations for the results? When reading a theoretical or summary article, organize the main themes, identify the conclusions, evaluate the relevance of the theory, and question the applications to everyday situations.

Let me make a couple of suggestions to help you get the most out of each selection. First, be sure to read the headnote to gain background information on the topic and on the author. Recognize that some of these selections are easy to read and understand, whereas others may have more challenging language, theories, or statistical concepts. Try to focus on the main ideas and important concepts in each selection. Remember that journal research articles include an introduction to the problem, a description of the research methods, a presentation of the results, and a discussion of the significance of the results. When you finish reading a selection, reread the headnote to make sure that you focused on the important concepts. Finally, take notes on the selection and reflect upon the importance of the writing to your understanding of psychology.

PSYCHOLOGY RESOURCES ON THE INTERNET Each part in *Sources: Notable Selections in Psychology,* 3rd ed., is preceded by an "On the Internet" page. On these pages, I have provided several Internet links that should be of interest to you as you investigate the topics presented in the book. I have tried to include links that were focused and relevant to the specific selections in each part.

There are many resources available on the Internet to help you learn about psychology. In addition to the ones included for each part, here are some general sites that contain information and additional links to other resources:

Psychology: A ConnecText — my Dushkin/McGraw-Hill textbook Web site that contains many resources and activities for students studying psychology.
    `http://www.dushkin.com/connectext/psy/`

American Psychological Association—This APA site provides numerous resources in all areas of psychology.
    `http://www.apa.org`

American Psychological Society—This APS site provides resources for teaching and research in scientific psychology.
    `http://www.psychologicalscience.org`

PsychWeb—This Georgia Southern University site provides numerous psychology resource links in all areas.
    `http://www.gasou.edu/psychweb/psychweb.htm`

Psyc Site—This Nipissing University psychology site provides extensive resource links.

    http://www.unipissing.ca/psyc/info.htm

Psych Central — Site maintained by Donna Stuber of Friends University with links to numerous resources in psychology.

    http://www.psych-central.com

Yahoo Psychology Search—This is a general psychology search site.

    http://www.yahoo.com/Science/Psychology/

A WORD TO THE INSTRUCTOR An *Instructor's Manual With Test Questions* (including multiple-choice and essay questions) is available for instructors using *Sources: Notable Selections in Psychology*, 3rd ed., in the classroom.

ACKNOWLEDGMENTS I was extremely excited when I was first approached with the idea for *Sources: Notable Selections in Psychology*. For a long time I had wanted to be able to introduce my students to original writings in psychology. I was thrilled to be able to share with students the excitement of learning directly from some of the most influential figures in psychology.

This project is very much a joint effort. Although my name as editor is the only one on the cover, I had lots of help from many people. Whenever I had a question about the readability or relevance of an article, my psychology students provided comments and suggestions. I thank the many students who used the first edition of the book and took the time to provide evaluative feedback. I appreciate the feedback from students, including Peggy Reeves, Tonya Samsel, and Brenda Thompson. I especially appreciate the efforts of head librarian Betsy Blankenship and her assistants, who provided outstanding library research. I sincerely want to thank the reviewers of the second edition, especially:

Lynn Davey
St. Joseph College

Dan Dunlap
Blue Mountain Community
College

Brad Olson
Northern Michigan University

Charles Peyser
University of the South

Professor Price
California State University–
Fresno

Ross Seligman
Chaffey College

Doug Wessel
Black Hills State University

They provided many suggestions on potential sources and specific direction for the third edition. My father, Don, provided suggestions for important topics in everyday life. My wife, Bernie, typed the materials and provided much emotional support. And my family, Terry and his wife Shelley, Karen and her husband Kenny, and Tommy, were patient as I worked on this project.

Sources: Notable Selections in Psychology, 3rd ed., is designed particularly to meet the needs of those instructors who want to convey to students the richness of the psychological perspective through original writings. I have worked hard to produce a valuable resource, and I would very much appreciate any comments or suggestions you might have on the book. Although I feel that these selections represent some of the most significant studies in psychology, not everyone will agree with all of the particular selections. I promise to carefully consider all of your suggestions as the book goes through the revision process (my email address is `Pettijohn.1@osu.edu`). I hope you find this collection useful in your teaching.

Terry F. Pettijohn
Ohio State University

Contents

"The discussion of these [research] findings develops the thesis that questions asked about an event shortly after it occurs may distort the witness' memory for that event."

"Our view is that creativity in children—and in adults—involves six resources: intelligence, knowledge, thinking style, personality, motivation and environmental context. Consider each of these resources in turn."

"How much of the improvement in intellectual performance attributed to the contemporary educational programs is due to the content and methods of the programs and how much is due to the favorable expectancies of the teachers and administrators involved?"

"During the 1st year of life, long before uttering his or her first words, an infant makes remarkable progress toward mastering the sound structure of the native language. The biases and proclivities that allow the neonate to detect regularities in the speech stream are, by 1 year of age, exquisitely tuned to the properties of the native language."

"It is quite true that man lives by bread alone—when there is no bread. But what happens to man's desires when there *is* plenty of bread and when his belly is chronically filled?"

PART ONE

Foundations of Psychology

On the Internet . . .

Sites appropriate to Part One

A description of and information on the divisions of the American Psychological Association (APA) is included on this site.

    http://www.apa.org/division.html

This is Emory University's site on William James and includes biographical information and excerpts from his writings.

    http://www.emory.edu/EDUCATION/mfp/
        james.html

A tutorial on brain structures by Dr. John H. Krantz, Hanover College, is found on this site.

    http://psych.hanover.edu/Krantz/
        neurotut.html

Drugs, Brain, and Behavior, a Web book by C. Robin Timmons and Leonard W. Hamilton, is outlined on this site.

    http://www.rci.rutgers.edu/~1wh/drugs/

The Jean Piaget Archives site contains biographical and scientific achievement information.

    http://www.unige.ch/piaget/presentg.html

CHAPTER 1 Introducing Psychology

1.1 WILLIAM JAMES

The Scope of Psychology

The American psychologist William James's *Principles of Psychology,* published in 1890, marked a major milestone in the history of psychology. In it, James asserts that psychology should focus on the functions of consciousness, an idea that helped establish the school of functionalism and that continues to be important to the study of psychology today.

James (1842–1910) obtained his M.D. from Harvard University in 1869 and accepted a teaching position in psychology there three years later. During his lifetime, he wrote on a variety of topics, including consciousness, emotion, personality, learning, and religion.

This selection is taken from James's most famous work, the two-volume *Principles of Psychology.* In it, James argues that psychology is the "science of mental life." Although he includes feelings and cognitions in his definition of psychology, he emphasizes the role of the brain in behaviors that serve the function of survival. His book formed the cornerstone of many early psychology courses, and it encouraged psychologists to take a broad view of their discipline. This book is still very much read and studied today.

Key Concept: an early definition of psychology

APA Citation: James, W. (1890). *Principles of psychology: Volume 1.* New York: Holt.

*P*sychology is the Science of Mental Life, both of its phenomena and their conditions. The phenomena are such things as we call feelings, desires, cognitions, reasonings, decisions, and the like; and, superficially considered, their variety and complexity is such as to leave a chaotic impression on the observer....

[R]eflection shows that phenomena [experience in the outer world] have absolutely no power to influence our ideas until they have first impressed our senses and our brain. The bare existence of a past fact is no ground for our remembering it. Unless we have seen it, or somehow *undergone* it, we shall never know of its having been. The experiences of the body are thus one of the conditions of the faculty of memory being what it is. And a very small amount of reflection on facts shows that one part of the body, namely, the brain, is the part whose experiences are directly concerned. If the nervous communication be cut off between the brain and other parts, the experiences of those other parts are non-existent for the mind. The eye is blind, the ear deaf, the hand insensible and motionless. And conversely, if the brain be injured, consciousness is abolished or altered, even although every other organ in the body be ready to play its normal part. A blow on the head, a sudden subtraction of blood, the pressure of an apoplectic hemorrhage, may have the first effect; whilst a very few ounces of alcohol or grains of opium or hasheesh, or a whiff of chloroform or nitrous oxide gas, are sure to have the second. The delirium of fever, the altered self of insanity, are all due to foreign matters circulating through the brain, or to pathological changes in that organ's substance. The fact that the brain is the one immediate bodily condition of the mental operations is indeed so universally admitted nowadays that I need spend no more time in illustrating it, but will simply postulate it and pass on....

Bodily experiences, therefore, and more particularly brain-experiences, must take a place amongst those conditions of the mental life of which Psychology need take account....

Our first conclusion, then, is that a certain amount of brain-physiology must be presupposed or included in Psychology.

In still another way the psychologist is forced to be something of a nerve-physiologist. Mental phenomena are not only conditioned ... by bodily processes; but they lead to them.... That they lead to *acts* is of course the most familiar of truths, but I do not merely mean acts in the sense of voluntary and deliberate muscular performances. Mental states occasion also changes in the calibre of blood-vessels, or alteration in the heart-beats, or processes more subtle still, in glands and viscera. If these are taken into account, as well as acts which follow at some *remote period* because the mental state was once there, it will be safe to lay down the general law that *no mental modification ever occurs which is not accompanied or followed by a bodily change*. The ideas and feelings, *e.g.,* which these present printed characters excite in the reader's mind not only occasion movements of his eyes and nascent movements of articulation in him, but will some day make him speak, or take sides in a discussion, or give advice, or choose a book to read, differently from what would have been the case had they never impressed his retina. Our psychology must therefore take account not only of the conditions antecedent to mental states, but of their resultant consequences as well.

William James

But actions originally prompted by conscious intelligence may grow so automatic by dint of habit as to be apparently unconsciously performed. Standing, walking, buttoning and unbuttoning, piano-playing, talking, even saying one's prayers, may be done when the mind is absorbed in other things. The performances of animal *instinct* seem semi-automatic, and the *reflex acts* of self-preservation certainly are so. Yet they resemble intelligent acts in bringing about the *same ends* at which the animals' consciousness, on other occasions, deliberately aims. Shall the study of such machine-like yet purposive acts as these be included in Psychology?

The boundary line of the mental is certainly vague. It is better not to be pedantic, but to let the science be as vague as its subject, and include such phenomena as these if by so doing we can throw any light on the main business in hand. It will ere long be seen, I trust, that we can; and that we gain much more by a broad than by a narrow conception of our subject. At a certain stage in the development of every science a degree of vagueness is what best consists with fertility. On the whole, few recent formulas have done more real service of a rough sort in psychology than the . . . one that the essence of mental life and of bodily life are one, namely, 'the adjustment of inner to outer relations.' Such a formula is vagueness incarnate; but because it takes into account the fact that minds inhabit environments which act on them and on which they in turn react; because, in short, it takes mind in the midst of all its concrete relations, it is immensely more fertile than the old-fashioned 'rational psychology,' which treated the soul as a detached existent, sufficient unto itself, and assumed to consider only its nature and properties. I shall therefore feel free to make any sallies into zoology or into pure nerve-physiology which may seem instructive for our purposes, but otherwise shall leave those sciences to the physiologists.

Can we state more distinctly still the manner in which the mental life seems to intervene between impressions made from without upon the body, and reactions of the body upon the outer world again? Let us look at a few facts.

If some iron filings be sprinkled on a table and a magnet brought near them, they will fly through the air for a certain distance and stick to its surface. A savage seeing the phenomenon explains it as the result of an attraction or love between the magnet and the filings. But let a card cover the poles of the magnet, and the filings will press forever against its surface without its ever occurring to them to pass around its sides and thus come into more direct contact with the object of their love. . . .

If now we pass from such actions as these to those of living things, we notice a striking difference. Romeo wants Juliet as the filings want the magnet; and if no obstacles intervene he moves towards her by as straight a line as they. But Romeo and Juliet, if a wall be built between them, do not remain idiotically pressing their faces against its opposite sides like the magnet and the filings with the card. Romeo soon finds a circuitous way, by scaling the wall or otherwise, of touching Juliet's lips directly. With the filings the path is fixed; whether it reaches the end depends on accidents. With the lover it is the end which is fixed, the path may be modified indefinitely.

Such contrasts between living and inanimate performances end by leading men to deny that in the physical world final purposes exist at all. Loves and desires are today no longer imputed to particles of iron or of air. No one supposes now that the end of any activity which they may display is an ideal purpose presiding over the activity from its outset.... The end, on the contrary, is deemed a mere passive result, ... having had, so to speak, no voice in its own production. Alter the pre-existing conditions, and with inorganic materials you bring forth each time a different apparent end. But with intelligent agents, altering the conditions changes the activity displayed, but not the end reached; for here the idea of the yet unrealized end co-operates with the conditions to determine what the activities shall be.

The pursuance of future ends and the choice of means for their attainment are thus the mark and criterion of the presence of mentality in a phenomenon. We all use this test to discriminate between an intelligent and a mechanical performance. We impute no mentality to sticks and stones, because they never seem to move for *the sake of* anything, but always when pushed, and then indifferently and with no sign of choice. So we unhesitatingly call them senseless.

Just so we form our decision upon the deepest of all philosophic problems: Is the [C]osmos [the universe] an expression of intelligence rational in its inward nature, or a brute external fact pure and simple? If we find ourselves, in contemplating it, unable to banish the impression that it is a realm of final purposes, that it exists for the sake of something, we place intelligence at the heart of it and have a religion. If, on the contrary, in surveying its irremediable flux, we can think of the present only as so much mere mechanical sprouting from the past, occurring with no reference to the future, we are atheists and materialists.

1.2 JOHN B. WATSON

Psychology as the Behaviorist Views It

From the 1920s through the 1960s the field of psychology was largely dominated by behaviorists, who focus on the objective measurement of behavior. The founder of the school of behaviorism was John B. Watson, whose view of psychology as a "purely objective experimental branch of natural science" had a major influence on early psychologists. Watson's belief that psychology should be the science of overt behavior, modeled after the natural sciences, is expressed in this selection.

Watson (1878–1958) earned his Ph.D. in experimental psychology from the University of Chicago in 1903. He began teaching at the Johns Hopkins University in 1908 and stayed there until he resigned in 1920. Although he left academic psychology after only 12 years of teaching, his influence is still felt in the discipline today.

This selection is from "Psychology as the Behaviorist Views It," published in *Psychological Review* in 1913. This article marked the introduction of the school of behaviorism. In it, Watson discards the subject of consciousness and the method of introspection from psychology and argues for an objective study of the behavior of both people and animals. His goal is to help psychology become more applicable in other areas (such as education, law, and business) as it develops into an experimental natural science.

Key Concept: school of behaviorism

APA Citation: Watson, J. B. (1913). Psychology as the behaviorist views it. *Psychological Review, 20,* 158–177.

*P*sychology as the behaviorist views it is a purely objective experimental branch of natural science. Its theoretical goal is the prediction and control of behavior. Introspection forms no essential part of its methods, nor is the scientific value of its data dependent upon the readiness with which they lend themselves to interpretation in terms of consciousness. The behaviorist, in his efforts to get a unitary scheme of animal response, recognizes no dividing line between man and brute. The behavior of man, with all of its refinement and complexity, forms only a part of the behaviorist's total scheme of investigation. . . .

The time seems to have come when psychology must discard all reference to consciousness; when it need no longer delude itself into thinking that it is making mental states the object of observation. We have become so enmeshed in speculative questions concerning the elements of mind, the nature of conscious content (for example, imageless thought, attitudes,... etc.) that I, as an experimental student, feel that something is wrong with our premises and the types of problems which develop from them. There is no longer any guarantee that we all mean the same thing when we use the terms now current in psychology. Take the case of sensation. A sensation is defined in terms of its attributes. One psychologist will state with readiness that the attributes of a visual sensation are *quality, extension, duration,* and *intensity.* Another will add *clearness.* Still another that of *order.* I doubt if any one psychologist can draw up a set of statements describing what he means by sensation which will be agreed to by three other psychologists of different training. Turn for a moment to the question of the number of isolable sensations. Is there an extremely large number of color sensations—or only four, red, green, yellow and blue? Again, yellow, while psychologically simple, can be obtained by superimposing red and green spectral rays upon the same diffusing surface! If, on the other hand, we say that every just noticeable difference in the spectrum is a simple sensation, and that every just noticeable increase in the white value of a given color gives simple sensations, we are forced to admit that the number is so large and the conditions for obtaining them so complex that the concept of sensation is unusable, either for the purpose of analysis or that of synthesis. Titchener, who has fought the most valiant fight in this country for a psychology based upon introspection, feels that these differences of opinion as to the number of sensations and their attributes; as to whether there are relations (in the sense of elements) and on the many others which seem to be fundamental in every attempt at analysis, are perfectly natural in the present undeveloped state of psychology. While it is admitted that every growing science is full of unanswered questions, surely only those who are wedded to the system as we now have it, who have fought and suffered for it, can confidently believe that there will ever be any greater uniformity than there is now in the answers we have to such questions. I firmly believe that two hundred years from now, unless the introspective method is discarded, psychology will still be divided on the question as to whether auditory sensations have the quality of 'extension,' whether intensity is an attribute which can be applied to color, whether there is a difference in 'texture' between image and sensation and upon many hundreds of others of like character....

I was greatly surprised some time ago when I opened Pillsbury's book and saw psychology defined as the 'science of behavior.' A still more recent text states that psychology is the 'science of mental behavior.' When I saw these promising statements I thought, now surely we will have texts based upon different lines. After a few pages the science of behavior is dropped and one finds the conventional treatment of sensation, perception, imagery, etc., along with certain shifts in emphasis and additional facts which serve to give the author's personal imprint....

This leads me to the point where I should like to make the argument constructive. I believe we can write a psychology, define it as Pillsbury, and never go back upon our definition: never use the terms consciousness, mental states, mind, content, introspectively verifiable, imagery, and the like.... It can be done in terms of stimulus and response, in terms of habit formation, habit integrations and the like. Furthermore, I believe that it is really worthwhile to make this attempt now.

The psychology which I should attempt to build up would take as a starting point, first, the observable fact that organisms, man and animal alike, do adjust themselves to their environment by means of hereditary and habit equipments. These adjustments may be very adequate or they may be so inadequate that the organism barely maintains its existence; secondly, that certain stimuli lead the organisms to make the responses. In a system of psychology completely worked out, given the response the stimuli can be predicted; given the stimuli the response can be predicted. Such a set of statements is crass and raw in the extreme, as all such generalizations must be. Yet they are hardly more raw and less realizable than the ones which appear in the psychology texts of the day. I possibly might illustrate my point better by choosing an everyday problem which anyone is likely to meet in the course of his work. Some time ago I was called upon to make a study of certain species of birds. Until I went to Tortugas I had never seen these birds alive. When I reached there I found the animals doing certain things: some of the acts seemed to work peculiarly well in such an environment, while others seemed to be unsuited to their type of life. I first studied the responses of the group as a whole and later those of individuals. In order to understand more thoroughly the relation between what was habit and what was hereditary in these responses, I took the young birds and reared them. In this way I was able to study the order of appearance of hereditary adjustments and their complexity, and later the beginnings of habit formation. My efforts in determining the stimuli which called forth such adjustments were crude indeed. Consequently my attempts to control behavior and to produce responses at will did not meet with much success. Their food and water, sex and other social relations, light and temperature conditions were all beyond control in a field study. I did find it possible to control their reactions in a measure by using the nest and egg (or young) as stimuli. It is not necessary in this paper to develop further how such a study should be carried out and how work of this kind must be supplemented by carefully controlled laboratory experiments.... In the main, my desire in all such work is to gain an accurate knowledge of adjustments and the stimuli calling them forth. My final reason for this is to learn general and particular methods by which I may control behavior.... If psychology would follow the plan I suggest, the educator, the physician, the jurist and the business man could utilize our data in a practical way, as soon as we are able, experimentally, to obtain them. Those who have occasion to apply psychological principles practically would find no need to complain as they do at the present time. Ask any physician or jurist today whether scientific psychology plays a practical part in his daily routine and you will hear him deny that the psychology of the laboratories finds a place in his scheme of work. I think the criticism is extremely just. One of the earliest conditions which made me dissatisfied with psychology was the feeling that there was no realm of application for the principles which were being worked out in content terms.

What gives me hope that the behaviorist's position is a defensible one is the fact that those branches of psychology which have already partially withdrawn from the parent, experimental psychology, and which are consequently less dependent upon introspection are today in a most flourishing condition. Experimental pedagogy, the psychology of drugs, the psychology of advertising, legal psychology, the psychology of tests, and psychopathology are all vigorous growths. These are sometimes wrongly called "practical" or "applied" psychology. Surely there was never a worse misnomer. In the future there may grow up vocational bureaus which really apply psychology. At present these fields are truly scientific and are in search of broad generalizations which will lead to the control of human behavior. For example, we find out by experimentation whether a series of stanzas may be acquired more readily if the whole is learned at once, or whether it is more advantageous to learn each stanza separately and then pass to the succeeding. We do not attempt to apply our findings. The application of this principle is purely voluntary on the part of the teachers. In the psychology of drugs we may show the effect upon behavior of certain doses of caffeine. We may reach the conclusion that caffeine has a good effect upon the speed and accuracy of work. But these are general principles. We leave it to the individual as to whether the results of our tests shall be applied or not. Again, in legal testimony, we test the effects of recency upon the reliability of a witness's report. We test the accuracy of the report with respect to moving objects, stationary objects, color, etc. It depends upon the judicial machinery of the country to decide whether these facts are ever to be applied. For a 'pure' psychologist to say that he is not interested in the questions raised in these divisions of the science because they relate indirectly to the application of psychology shows, in the first place, that he fails to understand the scientific aim in such problems, and secondly, that he is not interested in a psychology which concerns itself with human life. The only fault I have to find with these disciplines is that much of their material is stated in terms of introspection, whereas a statement of terms of objective results would be far more valuable....

In concluding, I suppose I must confess to a deep bias on these questions. I have devoted nearly twelve years to experimentation on animals. It is natural that such a one should drift into a theoretical position which is in harmony with his experimental work. Possibly I have put up a straw man and have been fighting that.... Certainly the position I advocate is weak enough at present and can be attacked from many standpoints. Yet when all this is admitted I still feel that the considerations which I have urged should have a wide influence upon the type of psychology which is to be developed in the future. What we need to do is to start work upon psychology, making *behavior*, not *consciousness*, the objective point of our attack. Certainly there are enough problems in the control of behavior to keep us all working many lifetimes without ever allowing us time to think of consciousness.... Once launched in the undertaking, we will find ourselves in a short time as far divorced from an introspective psychology as the psychology of the present time is divorced from faculty psychology.

1.3 MARY WHITON CALKINS

Experimental Psychology at Wellesley College

Most people have learned about the discipline of psychology through taking academic courses in college. Mary Whiton Calkins was a pioneer in the field. She not only taught but also was active in psychological research and leadership in the American Psychological Association.

Calkins (1863–1930) studied under American psychologist and philosopher William James at Harvard University, but it seems that she was refused her Ph.D. simply because she was a woman. She accepted a position at Wellesley College, where she conducted research on memory, perception, personality, emotion, and dreaming. Calkins was elected as the first woman president of the American Psychological Association in 1905 and worked to reconcile the structural and functional schools of psychology.

In the following selection from "Experimental Psychology at Wellesley College," published in 1892 in the *American Journal of Psychology,* Calkins provides a glimpse into her psychology classroom. She carefully describes the details of her experimental psychology class, along with some student experiences and her own insights into the teaching presentations. As you read this selection, imagine what a psychology course was like at the time that Calkins's work was published. Compare your current course experiences with those of students in 1892. How has psychology changed during the past century?

Key Concept: teaching psychology, history

APA Citation: Calkins, M. W. (1892). Experimental psychology at Wellesley College. *American Journal of Psychology, 5,* 464–471.

*A*fter the discussion of the relative merits of experimental as compared with merely introspective psychology, a practical question suggests itself concerning the introduction of experimental psychology into the regular college curriculum. This is a complicated problem of expediency, the question of the equipment of the laboratory, of the relative amount of laboratory work, of the proper direction of students' experiments. Such questions are especially prominent in cases in which psychology is a required subject, and in which our course is a general one and must be adapted to students without especial scientific training or without particular interest in experimental work. In such a course, it is sometimes urged, the introduction of experimental methods burdens the general student with details valuable only to the specialist, substitutes technical minutiae for psychological principle and tends to confuse psychology with the other sciences.

This paper is an attempt to meet with difficulties of this sort by the record of a year's experience with a general course in psychology, making extensive use of experimental methods. In the fall of 1892 a course in "Psychology, including Experimental Psychology," was offered at Wellesley College as one of the alternative senior requirements in psychology. The course was taken by fifty-four students, of whom all but one or two had had no previous training in the subject. All of these had taken a year's course, including laboratory work, in chemistry, and only three had failed to follow a similar course in physics. Most had no training in physiology, and many of them had a more or less pronounced distaste for laboratory work. The aim throughout was to supplement, and in no sense to supersede, introspection; to lead students to observe in detail and to verify facts of their ordinary experience; to familiarize them with the results of modern investigation and with the usual experimental methods, and to introduce them to the important works of psychological literature.

The first month was devoted to a study of cerebral physiology. Ladd's "Elements of Psychology" was used in this early part of the course as a text-book. The class work included recitations, informal lectures and some written work on the part of the students. One of these papers, for example, required an enumeration, accompanying a rough diagram, of the parts of the human brain, as developed from the dorsal and ventral sides respectively of the three "primary bulbs." The study of the brain by text-book, by plates, and especially by models, preceded the dissection by each student of a lamb's brain. The brains had been preserved according to Dr. James's directions.[1] (Wide-mouthed candy jars, fitted with rubbers to prevent evaporation, proved an inexpensive substitute for the regular Whitehall and Taitum jars.) The dissection was under the general direction of the instructor. The students were provided with simple directions and were required to identify the most important parts of the brain. The results of this work were very satisfactory. The students, even those who had dreaded the dissection, were practically unanimous in regard to its value, as clearing up the difficult points in cerebral anatomy. In the class room, during this week, in which the dissection was going on, the principal theories of cerebral localization were discussed.

The next six weeks were spent in experimental study of sensation. About seventy experiments were performed by the students on sensations of contact, of pressure, of temperature, of taste, of hearing and of sight. The experiments, almost without exception, were selected from those suggested by Dr. E. C. Sanford in his "Laboratory Course in Psychology,"[2] but re-arranged with reference to the plan of the lectures and of the class discussion. Papyrographed descriptions of the experiments were distributed to the students and commented on in class before the experiments were undertaken. The instructor kept daily laboratory hours in order to answer questions and to offer assistance. Each student was responsible for the record of her own experiments.

In class, reports were made on the results of experiments, and recitations were conducted on the physiology of the different senses. The bearing of the different experiments on the theory of perception was carefully discussed. Special effort was made to free the word "sensation" from the vague, dualistic meaning which it often carries with it; sensation was treated as essentially "the first thing in the way of consciousness." The three theories of perception, Associationist, Intellectualist and Physiological-psychological, were carefully studied, and in this connection parts of Dr. James's chapters on "The Mind-Stuff Theory," "Sensations" and "Perception" were assigned for reading. Of course, in so elementary a course no new experimental results were gained. All the more important experiments usually performed were repeated. The taste experiments were so unpopular that I should never repeat them in a general class of students who are not specializing in the subject. I should also omit most experiments involving exact measurement. For instance, I should do no more than familiarize the class with the use of the Galton bar and of the perimeter.

Some of the students were genuinely interested in the experiments, carried them further than required and made independent observations; a large number, on the other hand, performed them conscientiously, but without especial enthusiasm; some cordially detested them from beginning to end; but almost all recognized their value as a stimulus to observation and as a basis for psychological theory.

The following questions, asked at an informal, forty-five minute examination, suggest the character of the experimental work:—

I. Describe fully the following experiments. State the theories on which they bear and the conclusions which you draw from them:—

a. The "colored shadows" experiment.

b. Scheiner's experiment.

II. What are the dermal senses?

III. What is the (so-called) joint sense? Describe an experiment proving its existence.

In the study of association, the old distinction between association "by contiguity" and that "by similarity" was replaced by one between "desistent association," in which no part of the earlier object of consciousness persists in consciousness and "persistent association," in which all or part of it persists.[3] Dr. James's quantitative distinctions, corresponding with the terms "total," "partial" and "focalized," were also made. Students were referred to Hobbes, to Hartley, to Bain and to Dr. James, and were required to illustrate, by original examples or by quotation, the different sorts of association. This work proved very interesting and was valuable in co-ordinating psychological with literary study. The experimental work accompanying this study illustrated the value of association in shortening intellectual processes, and consisted simply in comparing the slower reading of one hundred unconnected monosyllables with the reading of one hundred connected words. Reading of passages of one hundred words in different languages was also carefully timed and compared.

A more extended experiment in association was later carried out. Each student wrote a list of thirty words, so associated that each suggested the next. The starting point was the word "book," suggested in writing, but not read until the time of the experiment. Each list was studied by its writer, who marked with a V the names of objects or events which were visualized; indicated with a C those connected with childhood life; classified the association, as desistent or as persistent (of quality or of object); and indicated, in each case, the so-called secondary law of the association (recency, frequency or vividness). Of course each list was written when the subject was alone and undisturbed. . . .

The subject of attention was discussed on the basis of Dr. James's admirable chapter. The experimental work was in divided attention, the performance and accurate timing of two intellectual processes, first separately and then in combination.

A brief study of consciousness in its "identifying" and "discriminating" aspects was followed by a six-weeks' study of space-perception. Lectures were offered on the three chief theories, the Empiricist, and Nativist-Kantian and the Nativist-Sensational. The required reading included references to Berkeley, to Mill, to Spencer, to D.A. Spalding (MacMillan, February, 1873), to Preyer (Appendix C of Vol. II., The Mind of The Child)[4] to James (parts of the Space-Chapter), to Kant (Aesthetic, "Metaphysical Deduction").

The experiments, of which there were more than thirty, illustrated the methods of gaining, or at least of developing, the space-consciousness. The theories of single vision were carefully studied and were illustrated by diagrams and by "Cyclopean eye" experiments. The study of the perception of depth included an adaptation from Hering's experiment, in which the subject, looking through a tube, finds that he can correctly distinguish, within very small distances, whether a shot is dropped before or behind a black string, stretched before a white background. The fact and the laws of convergence were studied with the aid of a Wheatstone stereoscope.

There followed a consideration of illusions of space; and of Unvisual space, including the experiments suggested by Dr. James on so-called tympanum spatial-sensations, and others, with a telegraph-snapper, on the location of sounds. . . .

In the study of memory and of the imagination, the only experiments were a few on "The Mental Span." Students were referred to James, to Burnham, to Lewes, to Ruskin and to Everett. Paramnesia was of course discussed.

Abnormal psychology received, throughout the course, comparatively little attention, because it seemed so evident that a careful study of the facts of normal consciousness must precede any scholarly consideration of the abnormal; because, also, there seemed special need of combating the popular notion which apparently regards psychology as a synonym for hypnotism and telepathy. The abnormal was therefore treated throughout from the point of view of the ordinary consciousness and its phenomena were discussed as exaggerated manifestations of the phases of all consciousness. The subject was naturally introduced by a study of dreams; hypnotism was the only other topic considered.

The study of the emotions and of the will was accompanied by no experimental work. Chapters of Höffding, of James, of Mill, of Spencer and of Darwin formed the required reading; James's theory of the emotions was discussed; a classification of the feelings, adapted from Mercier[5], but rejecting his physiological principle of division, was the starting-point of a somewhat practical discussion.

The last week of the course was occupied with reaction-time experiments, which had been postponed to this time, only through necessary delay in procuring the apparatus; the work should properly have been scattered through the year. There was time for little more than an illustration of method and an approximate verification of the more important results in reactions to sound and in more complicated reactions, involving association, discrimination and choice. Averages of simple reaction-times, with and then without signal, showing a general increase in the time of the latter, were made by several students and included in essays on attention. Students were required to read Jastrow's "Time-Relations of Mental Phenomena."

The study of volition led to several days' discussion of the problems of determinism and indeterminism. This was undertaken with the express remark that the subject is metaphysical and not psychological. The favorable result of this study confirms my opinion of the value of an occasional consideration of so-called metaphysical problems in a general course of psychology, with students who are neither studying philosophy nor specializing in psychology....

In place of a final examination, a psychological essay was required. The subjects assigned were very general and were intended as subjects for study rather than as definite essay-headings. The immediate topic of the paper was to be decided after the study and not before. Such subjects as "Association," "Attention," "Memory," "Imagination," "The Psychology of Language," "The Psychology of Childhood," "The Psychology of Blindness," "Aphasia," "Animal Psychology," were chosen in this way.

NOTES

1. Since published in the Briefer Course in Psychology, pp. 81–90.

2. American Journal of Psychology.

3. Cf. an article in the Philosophical Review, July, 1892.

4. Inquiries into Human Faculty, pp. 191–203.

5. Mind, Vol. IX.

The Fragmentation of Psychology?

How do we define the scope of the discipline of psychology? Since the emergence of psychology from philosophy and biology over 100 years ago, psychologists have been trying to answer this question. In recent years, there has been a trend toward increasing specialization. As president of the American Psychological Society (APS), Gordon H. Bower addressed this issue.

Bower (b. 1932) earned his Ph.D. in experimental psychology in 1959 at Yale University. He then joined the faculty at Stanford University, where he is currently a professor of psychology. He served as president of the APS in 1992.

This selection is from "The Fragmentation of Psychology?" which was published in *American Psychologist* in 1993. In it, Bower discusses the trend toward specialization in psychology. Psychologists study a range of topics, and each area requires specialized training. Bower points out, however, that there are common issues that involve all psychologists, and national organizations such as the American Psychological Association and the American Psychological Society provide opportunities for communication and common action. How do you define psychology? As you study the various subfields, try to focus on the core issues in psychology as a discipline.

Key Concept: the discipline of psychology

APA Citation: Bower, G. H. (1993). The fragmentation of psychology? *American Psychologist, 48,* 905–907.

The topic of this article—the fragmentation of psychology—is one of those perennial chestnuts to which there is no agreed-upon answer at present, nor is one likely in the near future. Probably William James and Titchener argued about this at the first meeting of the American Psychological Association (APA) 100 years ago. The basic difficulty is that psychology itself is an ill-defined field; few of us could agree on what is the proper purview of the discipline of psychology. Similarly, the unity or fragmentation of any intellectual discipline can be assessed from many different perspectives, such as agreement among its devotees regarding the legitimate problems to be investigated or agreement in their philosophical orientation, fundamental concepts, or methods of investigation.

A simple resolution might be to define the field of psychology in operational terms, as simply the collection of professional activities that people who call themselves psychologists engage in. And if we discover that psychologists engage in many different types of activities, then we can conclude that there are many different types of psychologists or fragments of the field.

Now there is no question that people who call themselves psychologists are working in large numbers of vastly different settings doing vastly different things. Some of us are university teachers, laboratory researchers, survey researchers studying social problems or human-factors specialists interfacing people to machines. Some of us study or intervene in large organizations, such as commercial enterprises, communities, or prisons; others counsel school children, help the mentally or physically handicapped, help improve preschool programs, or provide psychotherapy to distressed individuals. Even the laboratory psychologists differ greatly in what they actually study and do.

So, if we classify psychologists by what we do, there is little doubt that the field has been fragmented for years, and its fragmentation is increasing as psychologists become involved in an ever-expanding range of activities. We may ask, what is causing this fragmentation, and does fragmentation portend bad things for the science and profession of psychology?

I think the fragmentation reflects two different trends. One trend has been the development of a diverse range of applications of psychology to many different sorts of problems. Each applied setting has its own breed of specialist, from industrial organizations to the school counselor's office, from mental health clinics to rehabilitation centers, and so on. Psychologists also tend to cluster into topical interest groups, such as those with interests in political or religious behavior, conflict resolution, women's issues, minorities, or cross-cultural studies. These applied and topical interests have spawned the many divisions of APA that attract their adherents to specialized meetings within and beyond the APA convention. So, that is one reason for the fragmentation of psychology.

A second reason is that fragmentation is a perfectly natural outgrowth of the maturing of a science. We are following in exactly the same path as older sciences, such as mathematics, chemistry, and biology. A science grows over time by covering more ground, addressing new but related problems, distinguishing between cases and differentiating among types of things or topics that it formerly lumped together, and obtaining new findings and elaborating new concepts and theories around them. A frequent metaphor for the growth of a science views it as an expanding tree that sends out branches, then more branches on those branches as more phenomena are discovered and as new concepts are developed to explain them. To carry this metaphor to an unflattering extreme, an individual scientist is like a small bug feeding on a succulent leaf at one end of a tiny branch and perhaps talking to the other bugs feeding on the same leaf.

Each branch is a topical specialty. In psychology as in other disciplines, we have many hierarchical levels of specialization. For example, in the study of human abilities, one high-level ability is sensory perception, which divides into different senses of vision, audition, and so forth. Each of these divides further (e.g., vision divides into the perception of color, brightness, motion, objects, depth, and scenes). Furthermore, each of these subspecialties can be examined from different perspectives, in neurophysiological or behavioral terms, or one can study its development from infancy. In this manner, it is only a bit of a stretch for us to understand why someone might become a specialist in comparative development of neurophysiological substrates of color vision in mammals and still be called a psychologist.

This last example also illustrates another division in psychology that we all live with, namely, that psychology really has three distinct subject matters. Roughly speaking, they are behavior and its neurobiological substrates and phenomenological experience. Although psychologists typically specialize in one of these subject matters, we occasionally try to tie together two or more of the areas. Some of the more interesting research attempts to correlate brain events with either behavioral or phenomenological events. For example, Mike Posner and his associates (Posner, Petersen, Fox, & Raichle, 1988) have correlated a higher metabolic rate in a frontal cortical area as measured by position emission tomography (PET scan) with a specific kind of cognitive operation in humans, or electrophysiologists have correlated the P300 bump in the evoked cortical response with the subjective experience of being surprised. In fact, human neuropsychology is a field dedicated to looking for correlations between brain events and psychological functions.

To return to the theme of the fragmentation of psychology, I have noted that it is a consequence of the natural maturation of the science and the expanding range of its applications. But rather than call this *fragmentation*, why not label the process one of *specialization*, which has fewer negative connotations? After all, most people do not think specialization is so bad, especially when they need a doctor who specializes in what ails them.

I do not deny that this increasing specialization creates serious tensions when we must decide what topics and specialties should be covered in training students at both undergraduate and graduate levels. We are all familiar with these vexing questions: "What is the core of psychology? What must be taught, and in what order? How do we certify sufficient expertise by the teachers or by the students who want to become credentialed psychologists?" Many of these are local decisions best left to the training faculty at a given school. Then I think we should permit free market forces to operate, letting students and the society as a whole decide, by voting with their feet, whether they want to pay for that kind of training or hire graduates of that kind of training program. But these issues are highly politicized at present, and it would be foolhardy to try to do justice to them in this brief essay....

However, despite this specialization, I still firmly believe that there are several important functions to be performed by large national umbrella organizations such as APS [American Psychological Society], APA, and the Federation. Such organizations provide many professional services for their members, such as publications, international exchanges, job placement services, and interesting newsletters that maintain a sense of community. The societies also help to set uniform standards for professional ethics and for accreditation of training programs, and they hold national conventions at which members can exchange information and at least try to talk to one another.

National umbrella organizations also provide us with a forum and a platform in which we can come together to reaffirm our common interests and values. As a group, psychologists share a large number of personal and scientific values and beliefs. These include an interest in understanding the mind and behavior, a respect for empirical evidence to decide whatever issues it can, a preference for data over tradition and authorities, and a generally liberal political agenda that includes using our knowledge to reduce suffering and to promote mental health, social equality, personal freedom, and human welfare. We certainly should not be reticent to acknowledge or promote these common values.

But for me personally, one strong reason to support national professional organizations is that, unlike the smaller specialty groups, the umbrella organizations help us to aggregate and focus our advocacy of policy issues that are under consideration by Congress, the administration, regulatory agencies, and federal agencies. One need not be a rocket scientist to realize that the health of our profession, our educational system, and our mental-health delivery system is strongly impacted by the actions of Congress and the administration because they make funding and regulatory decisions that trickle down to affect nearly every one of us, whether we be academics or practitioners.

REFERENCES

Posner, M. I., Petersen, S. E., Fox, P. T., & Raichle, M. E. (1988). Localization of cognitive operations in the human brain. *Science, 240,* 1627–1631.

CHAPTER 2

Psychobiology

2.1 ROGER W. SPERRY

Hemisphere Deconnection and Unity in Conscious Awareness

The fact that the human brain is divided into two cerebral hemispheres has always intrigued scientists. In the 1950s, neurosurgeon Philip Vogel developed the technique of cutting the corpus callosum (the neural bundle connecting the two cerebral hemispheres) to reduce the severity of seizures in epileptic patients. This allowed researchers, particularly Roger W. Sperry, to study the conscious behavior of so-called split-brain patients.

Sperry (1913–1994) received his Ph.D. from the University of Chicago in 1941. He became a professor of psychobiology at the California Institute of Technology in 1954. Sperry initially studied cerebral hemisphere disconnection in cats, then moved on to study humans who underwent split-brain surgery. In 1981, Sperry received a Nobel Prize in physiology and medicine for his research on the brain.

This selection from "Hemisphere Deconnection and Unity in Conscious Awareness," which was published in 1968 in *American Psychologist*, describes some of the research conducted by Sperry and his colleagues. Through his research, Sperry discovered that the two cerebral hemispheres have distinct functions—the left side is involved in reasoning, language, and writing, whereas the right side is involved in nonverbal processes, such as art, music, and creativity. This selection conveys the excitement of discovering how human consciousness functions and the intricacies of the human brain.

Key Concept: split-brain research

APA Citation: Sperry, R. W. (1968). Hemisphere deconnection and unity in conscious awareness. *American Psychologist, 23,* 723–733.

*T*he following article is a result of studies my colleagues and I have been conducting with some neurosurgical patients of Philip J. Vogel of Los Angeles. These patients were all advanced epileptics in whom an extensive midline section of the cerebral commissures had been carried out in an effort to contain severe epileptic convulsions not controlled by medication. In all these people the surgical sections included division of the corpus callosum in its entirety, plus division also of the smaller anterior and hippocampal commissures, plus in some instances the massa intermedia. So far as I know, this is the most radical disconnection of the cerebral hemispheres attempted thus far in human surgery. The full array of sections was carried out in a single operation.

No major collapse of mentality or personality was anticipated as a result of this extreme surgery: earlier clinical observations on surgical section of the corpus callosum in man, as well as the results from dozens of monkeys on which I had carried out this exact same surgery, suggested that the functional deficits might very likely be less damaging than some of the more common forms of cerebral surgery, such as frontal lobotomy, or even some of the unilateral lobotomies performed more routinely for epilepsy.

The first patient on whom this surgery was tried had been having seizures for more than 10 years with generalized convulsions that continued to worsen despite treatment that had included a sojourn in Bethesda at the National Institutes of Health. At the time of the surgery, he had been averaging two major attacks per week, each of which left him debilitated for another day or so. Episodes of *status epilepticus* (recurring seizures that fail to stop and represent a medical emergency with a fairly high mortality risk) had also begun to occur at 2- to 3-month intervals. Since leaving the hospital following his surgery over 5½ years ago, this man has not had, according to last reports, a single generalized convulsion. It has further been possible to reduce the level of medication and to obtain an overall improvement in his behavior and well being (see Bogen & Vogel, 1962).

The second patient, a housewife and mother in her 30s, also has been seizure-free since recovering from her surgery, which was more than 4 years ago (Bogen, Fisher, & Vogel, 1965). Bogen related that even the EEG has regained a normal pattern in this patient. The excellent outcome in the initial, apparently hopeless, last-resort cases led to further application of the surgery to some nine more individuals to date, the majority of whom are too recent for therapeutic evaluation. Although the alleviation of the epilepsy has not held up 100% throughout the series (two patients are still having seizures, although their convulsions are much reduced in severity and frequency and tend to be confined to one side), the results on the whole continue to be predominantly beneficial, and the overall outlook at this time remains promising for selected severe cases.

The therapeutic success, however, and all other medical aspects are matters for our medical colleagues, Philip J. Vogel and Joseph E. Bogen. Our own work has been confined entirely to an examination of the functional outcome, that is, the behavioral, neurological, and psychological effects of this surgical disruption of all direct cross-talk between the hemispheres. Initially we were concerned as to whether we would be able to find in these patients any of the numerous symptoms of hemisphere deconnection that had been demonstrated in the so-called "split-brain" animal studies of the 1950s (Myers, 1961; Sperry, 1967a, 1967b). The outcome in man remained an open question in view of the historic Akelaitis (1944) studies that had set the prevailing doctrine of the 1940s and 1950s. This doctrine maintained that no important functional symptoms are found in man following even complete surgical section of the corpus callosum and anterior commissure, provided that other brain damage is excluded.

These earlier observations on the absence of behavioral symptoms in man have been confirmed in a general way to the extent that it remains fair to say today that the most remarkable effect of sectioning the neocortical commissures is the apparent lack of effect so far as ordinary behavior is concerned. This has been true in our animal studies throughout, and it seems now to be true for man also, with certain qualifications that we will come to later. At the same time, however—and this is in contradiction to the earlier doctrine set by the Akelaitis studies—we know today that with appropriate tests one can indeed demonstrate a large number of behavioral symptoms that correlate directly with the loss of the neocortical commissures in man as well as in animals (Gazzaniga, 1967; Sperry, 1967a, 1967b; Sperry, Gazzaniga, & Bogen, 1968). Taken collectively, these symptoms may be referred to as the syndrome of the neocortical commissures or the syndrome of the forebrain commissures or, less specifically, as the syndrome of hemisphere deconnection.

One of the more general and also more interesting and striking features of this syndrome may be summarized as an apparent doubling in most of the realms of conscious awareness. Instead of the normally unified single stream of consciousness, these patients behave in many ways as if they have two independent streams of conscious awareness, one in each hemisphere, each of which is cut off from and out of contact with the mental experiences of the other. In other words, each hemisphere seems to have its own separate and private sensations; its own perceptions; its own concepts; and its own impulses to act, with related volitional, cognitive, and learning experiences. Following the surgery, each hemisphere also has thereafter its own separate chain of memories that are rendered inaccessible to the recall processes of the other.

This presence of two minds in one body, as it were, is manifested in a large number and variety of test responses which, for the present purposes, I will try to review very briefly and in a somewhat streamlined and simplified form. First, however, let me take time to emphasize that the work reported here has been very much a team project. The surgery was performed by Vogel at the White Memorial Medical Center in Los Angeles. He has been assisted in the

Roger W.
Sperry

surgery and in the medical treatment throughout by Joseph Bogen. Bogen has also been collaborating in our behavioral testing program, along with a number of graduate students and postdoctoral fellows, among whom M. S. Gazzaniga, in particular, worked closely with us during the first several years and managed much of the testing during that period. The patients and their families have been most cooperative, and the whole project gets its primary funding from the National Institute of Mental Health.

Most of the main symptoms seen after hemisphere deconnection can be described for convenience with reference to a single testing setup—shown in Figure 1. Principally, it allows for the lateralized testing of the right and left halves of the visual field, separately or together, and the right and left hands and legs with vision excluded. The tests can be arranged in different combinations and in association with visual, auditory, and other input, with provisions for eliminating unwanted stimuli. In testing vision, the subject with one eye covered centers his gaze on a designated fixation point on the upright translucent screen. The visual stimuli on 35-millimeter transparencies are arranged in a standard projector equipped with a shutter and are then back-projected at $1/10$ of a second or less—too fast for eye movements to get the material into the wrong half of the visual field. Figure 2 is merely a reminder that everything seen to the left of the vertical meridian through either eye is projected to the right hemisphere and vice versa. The midline division along the vertical meridian is found to be quite precise without significant gap or overlap (Sperry, 1968).

When the visual perception of these patients is tested under these conditions the results indicate that these people have not one inner visual world any longer, but rather two separate visual inner worlds, one serving the right half of the field of vision and the other the left half—each, of course, in its respective hemisphere. This doubling in the visual sphere shows up in many ways: For example, after a projected picture of an object has been identified and responded to in one half field, we find that it is recognized again only if it reappears in the same half of the field of vision. If the given visual stimulus reappears in the opposite half of the visual field, the subject responds as if he had no recollection of the previous exposure. In other words, things seen through the right half of the visual field (i.e., through the left hemisphere) are registered in mental experience and remembered quite separately from things seen in the other half of the field. Each half of the field of vision in the commissurotomized patient has its own train of visual images and memories.

This separate existence of two visual inner worlds is further illustrated in reference to speech and writing, the cortical mechanisms for which are centered in the dominant hemisphere. Visual material projected to the right half of the field—left-hemisphere system of the typical right-handed patient—can be described in speech and writing in an essentially normal manner. However, when the same visual material is projected into the left half of the field, and hence to the right hemisphere, the subject consistently insists that he did not see anything or that there was only a flash of light on the left side. The subject acts as if he were blind or agnostic for the left half of the visual field. If, however, instead of asking the subject to tell you what he saw, you instruct him to use his left hand to point to a matching picture or object presented among a collection

FIGURE 1

Apparatus for Studying Lateralization of Visual, Tactual, Lingual,
and Associated Functions in the Surgically Separated Hemispheres

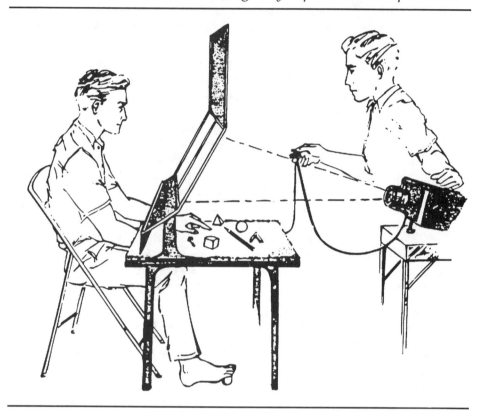

of other pictures or objects, the subject has no trouble as a rule in pointing out consistently the very item that he has just insisted he did not see.

We do not think the subjects are trying to be difficult or to dupe the examiner in such tests. Everything indicates that the hemisphere that is talking to the examiner did in fact not see the left-field stimulus and truly had no experience with, nor recollection of, the given stimulus. The other, the right or nonlingual hemisphere, however, did see the projected stimulus in this situation and is able to remember and recognize the object and can demonstrate this by pointing out selectively the corresponding or matching item. This other hemisphere, like a deaf mute or like some aphasics, cannot talk about the perceived object and, worse still, cannot write about it either.

If two different figures are flashed simultaneously to the right and left visual fields, as for example a "dollar sign" on the left and a "question mark" on the right and the subject is asked to draw what he saw using the left hand out of sight, he regularly reproduces the figure seen on the left half of the field, that is, the dollar sign. If we now ask him what he has just drawn, he tells us without

FIGURE 2

Things Seen to the Left of a Central Fixation Point With Either
Eye Are Projected to the Right Hemisphere and Vice-Versa

Roger W.
Sperry

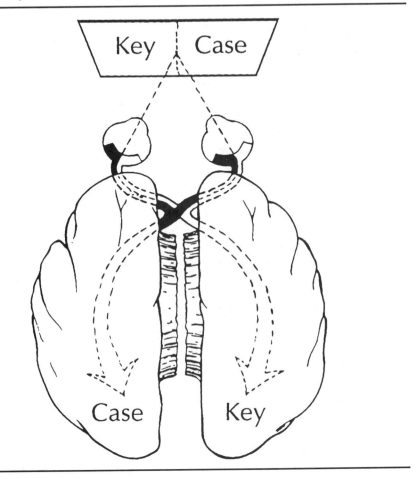

hesitation that the figure he drew was the question mark, or whatever appeared in the right half of the field. In other words, the one hemisphere does not know what the other hemisphere has been doing. The left and the right halves of the visual field seem to be perceived quite separately in each hemisphere with little or no cross-influence.

When words are flashed partly in the left field and partly in the right, the letters on each side of the midline are perceived and responded to separately. In the "key case" example shown in Figure 2 the subject might first reach for and select with the left hand a key from among a collection of objects indicating perception through the minor hemisphere. With the right hand he might then spell out the word "case" or he might speak the word if verbal response is in order. When asked what kind of "case" he was thinking of here, the answer coming from the left hemisphere might be something like "in *case* of fire" or "the *case* of the missing corpse" or "a *case* of beer," etc., depending upon the particular mental set of the left hemisphere at the moment. Any reference to "key case" under these conditions would be purely fortuitous, assuming that visual, auditory, and other cues have been properly controlled.

A similar separation in mental awareness is evident in tests that deal with stereognostic [involving tactile recognition] or other somesthetic [related to bodily sensations] discriminations made by the right and left hands, which are projected separately to the left and right hemispheres, respectively. Objects put in the right hand for identification by touch are readily described or named in speech or writing, whereas, if the same objects are placed in the left hand, the subject can only make wild guesses and may often seem unaware that anything at all is present. As with vision in the left field, however, good perception, comprehension, and memory can be demonstrated for these objects in the left hand when the tests are so designed that the subject can express himself through nonverbal responses. For example, if one of these objects which the subject tells you he cannot feel or does not recognize is taken from the left hand and placed in a grab bag or scrambled among a dozen other test items, the subject is then able to search out and retrieve the initial object even after a delay of several minutes is deliberately interposed. Unlike the normal subject, however, these people are obliged to retrieve such an object with the same hand with which it was initially identified. They fail at cross-retrieval. That is, they cannot recognize with one hand something identified only moments before with the other hand. Again, the second hemisphere does not know what the first hemisphere has been doing.

When the subjects are first asked to use the left hand for these stereognostic tests they commonly complain that they cannot "work with that hand," that the hand "is numb," they they "just can't feel anything or can't do anything with it," or that they "don't get the message from that hand." If the subjects perform a series of successful trials and correctly retrieve a group of objects which they previously stated they could not feel, and if this contradiction is then pointed out to them, we get comments like "Well, I was just guessing," or "Well, I must have done it unconsciously." . . .

Much of the foregoing is summarized schematically in Figure 3. The left hemisphere in the right-handed patients is equipped with the expressive mechanisms for speech and writing and with the main centers for the comprehension and organization of language. This "major" hemisphere can communicate its experiences verbally and in an essentially normal manner. It can communicate, that is, about the visual experiences of the right half of the optic field and about the somesthetic and volitional experiences of the right hand and leg and right half of the body generally. In addition, and not indicated in the figure, the major hemisphere also communicates, of course, about all of the more general, less lateralized cerebral activity that is bilaterally represented and common to both hemispheres. On the other side we have the mute aphasic and agraphic right hemisphere, which cannot express itself verbally, but which through the use of nonverbal responses can show that it is not agnostic; that mental processes are indeed present centered around the left visual field, left hand, left leg, and left half of the body; along with the auditory, vestibular, axial somatic, and all

Roger W. Sperry

FIGURE 3

Schematic Outline of the Functional Lateralization Evident in Behavioral Tests of Patients With Forebrain Commissurotomy

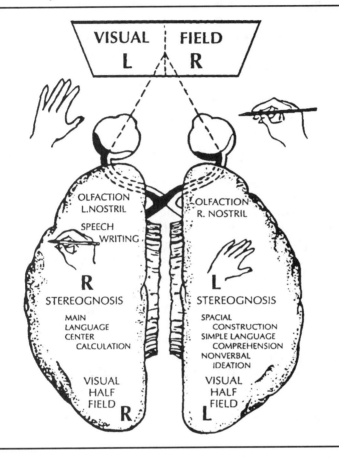

other cerebral activities that are less lateralized and for which the mental experiences of the right and left hemispheres may be characterized as being similar but separate.

It may be noted that nearly all of the symptoms of cross-integrational impairment that I have been describing are easily hidden or compensated under the conditions of ordinary behavior. For example, the visual material has to be flashed at $1/10$ of a second or less to one half of the field in order to prevent compensation by eye movements. The defects in manual stereognosis are not apparent unless vision is excluded; nor is doubling in olfactory perception evident without sequential occlusion of right and left nostril and elimination of visual cues. In many tests the major hemisphere must be prevented from talking to the minor hemisphere and thus giving away the answer through auditory channels. And, similarly, the minor hemisphere must be prevented from giving nonverbal signals of various sorts to the major hemisphere. There is a great diversity of indirect strategies and response signals, implicit as well as overt, by which the informed hemisphere can be used to cue-in the uninformed hemisphere (Levy-Agresti, 1968).

Normal behavior under ordinary conditions is favored also by many other unifying factors. Some of these are very obvious, like the fact that these two separate mental spheres have only one body, so they always get dragged to the same places, meet the same people, and see and do the same things all the time and thus are bound to have a great overlap of common, almost identical, experience. Just the unity of the optic image—and even after chiasm section in animal experiments, the conjugate movements of the eyes—means that both hemispheres automatically center on, focus on, and hence probably attend to, the same items in the visual field all the time. Through sensory feedback a unifying body schema is imposed in each hemisphere with common components that similarly condition in parallel many processes of perception and motor action onto a common base. To get different activities going and different experiences and different memory chains built up in the separated hemispheres of the bisected mammalian brain, as we do in the animal work, requires a considerable amount of experimental planning and effort. . . .

Let me emphasize again in closing that the foregoing represents a somewhat abbreviated and streamlined account of the syndrome of hemisphere deconnection as we understand it at the present time. The more we see of these patients and the more of these patients we see, the more we become impressed with their individual differences, and with the consequent qualifications that must be taken into account. Although the general picture has continued to hold up in the main as described, it is important to note that, with respect to many of the deconnection symptoms mentioned, striking modifications and even outright exceptions can be found among the small group of patients examined to date. Where the accumulating evidence will settle out with respect to the extreme limits of such individual variations and with respect to a possible average "type" syndrome remains to be seen.

REFERENCES

Akelaitis, A. J. A study of gnosis, praxis, and language following section of the corpus callosum and anterior commissure. *Journal of Neurosurgery,* 1944, 1, 94–102.

Bogen, J. E., Fisher, E. D., & Vogel, P. J. Cerebral commissurotomy: A second case report. *Journal of the American Medical Association,* 1965, 194, 1328–1329.

Bogen, J. E., & Vogel, P. J. Cerebral commissurotomy: A case report. *Bulletin of the Los Angeles Neurological Society,* 1962, 27, 169.

Gazzaniga, M. S. The split brain in man. *Scientific American,* 1967, 217, 24–29.

Levy-Agresti, J. Ipsilateral projection systems and minor hemisphere function in man after neocommissurotomy. *Anatomical Record,* 1968, 160, 384.

Myers, R. E. Corpus callosum and visual gnosis. In J. F. Delafresnaye (Ed.), *Brain mechanisms and learning.* Oxford: Blackwell, 1961.

Sperry, R. W. Mental unity following surgical disconnection of the hemispheres. *The Harvey lectures.* Series 62. New York: Academic Press, 1967. (a)

Sperry, R. W. Split-brain approach to learning problems. In G. C. Quarton, T. Melnechuk, & F. O. Schmitt (Eds.), *The neurosciences: A study program.* New York: Rockefeller University Press, 1967. (b)

Sperry, R. W. Apposition of visual half-fields after section of neocortical commissures. *Anatomical Record,* 1968, 160, 498–499.

Sperry, R. W., Gazzaniga, M. S., & Bogen, J. E. Function of neocortical commissures: Syndrome of hemisphere deconnection. In P. J. Vinken & G. W. Bruyn (Eds.), *Handbook of neurology.* Amsterdam: North Holland, 1968, in press.

The Localization of a Simple Type of Learning and Memory

Where in the brain are memories stored? Researchers have been trying for many years to unlock the mystery of where we store our thoughts and experiences. Although early global attempts were largely unsuccessful, more recently researchers have had success with simple types of learning such as classical eyeblink conditioning. Joseph E. Steinmetz has been active in this inquiry.

Steinmetz (b. 1956) received his Ph.D. in biopsychology from Ohio University in 1983. He is currently professor and chair of the psychology department at Indiana University. His research on the anatomical pathways that are used when learning a simple association earned him recognition from the National Academy of Sciences in 1996. Although he has tested humans, most of his research has focused on learning in rabbits.

The following selection, from "The Localization of a Simple Type of Learning and Memory: The Cerebellum and Classical Eyeblink Conditioning," was published in *Current Directions in Psychological Science* in 1998. In it, Steinmetz reveals how the cerebellum, the hindbrain structure involved in motor control and body balance, is a focal point for the various aspects of classical conditioning. He reviews some of the recent exciting research studies that are demonstrating where this type of memory is stored.

Key Concept: brain localization of memory

APA Citation: Steinmetz, J. E. (1998). The location of a simple type of learning and memory: The cerebellum and classical eyeblink conditioning. *Current Directions in Psychological Science, 7,* 72–77.

One of the most intriguing problems in psychology and neuroscience that has been widely studied over the past century is how the vertebrate brain encodes learning and memory. During this time, a number of researchers using a variety of methods have systematically explored locations in the brain where learning and memory may be encoded. These studies have shown that the brain is composed of a variety of learning and memory systems that are involved in encoding the rich variety of classes of learning and memory that vertebrates are capable of exhibiting.

Classical eyeblink conditioning in rabbits is one form of simple associative learning that has been widely studied, and this paradigm has become the model behavioral system of choice for studying many aspects of the neural correlates of simple learning and memory. This simple yet very elegant set of procedures was initially described and characterized by Gormezano and his colleagues (Gormezano, Kehoe, & Marshall-Goodell, 1983). In this paradigm, a tone or light is the conditioned stimulus (CS). The unconditioned stimulus (US) is an airpuff or electric shock near the eyes. Initially, the US causes a vigorous reflexive eyeblink called the unconditioned response (UR). With continued paired presentation of the CS before the US, however, the CS comes to elicit an eyeblink response (the conditioned response, or CR). For eyeblink conditioning to occur, the time between the presentation of the CS and US can range from about 100 ms to about 4 s; the most rapid conditioning occurs in the rabbit when a 250- to 500-ms interval is used.

DISCOVERY OF A CEREBELLAR SUBSTRATE FOR EYEBLINK CONDITIONING

For a number of reasons, this model behavioral paradigm has been adopted by researchers interested in studying the neural substrates of associative learning (Romano & Patterson, 1987). After it became clear that rabbits could learn and retain classically conditioned eyeblink responses after all forebrain tissue was removed, Richard Thompson and his colleagues began a systematic search for brain-stem areas that might be critically involved in encoding this simple form of learning. In the early 1980s, this research group published a series of reports that identified the cerebellum (a hindbrain structure) as a critical and essential component of the brain circuitry involved in encoding classical eyeblink conditioning (e.g., McCormick & Thompson, 1984). Lesions in the interpositus nucleus, one of the deep cerebellar nuclei located beneath cerebellar cortex, abolished an eyeblink CR that had already been learned and prevented acquisition of the CR if the lesion was created before behavioral training. Because of parallel brain circuitry involved in executing the reflexive UR, the interpositus nucleus lesions did not cause a decrement in the UR, an important observation that ruled out the possibility that the interpositus nucleus lesion caused a general performance deficit that affected all eye blinking. Remarkably, lesions of the cerebellar interpositus nucleus appear to produce a nonrecoverable deficit; rabbits trained daily for up to 12 months postlesion show no reacquisition of the learned response (Steinmetz, Logue, & Steinmetz, 1992). Damage to cerebellar cortex appears to cause less devastating effects, but does lead to significant disruptions in how quickly the CR is acquired, the magnitude of the learned response, and when the CR occurs after presentation of the CS.

Studies involving electrophysiological recordings support the findings of the lesion studies (e.g., Berthier & Moore, 1986, 1990). Recording studies typically involve monitoring the electrical activity of neurons using microelectrodes that are lowered into the brain. Recordings from the interpositus nucleus have revealed populations of neurons with action potential discharge rates that signal the arrival of the CS and the US and other populations of neurons that discharge in a manner related to the execution of the CR. The latter group of neurons is very interesting in that they fire prior to the behavioral response and with an amplitude and time course that seem to "model" the behavioral CR (i.e., they appear to be the neurons responsible for execution of the CR). Similarly, Purkinje cell neurons, which are the output neurons of the cerebellar cortex (actually inhibiting neurons in the interpositus nucleus) also show response related to conditioning. Some Purkinje cells discharge when the CS, US, or both are presented, and others either increase their firing rates or decrease their firing rates in a manner that "models" the behavioral CR (i.e., much like interpositus neurons, they fire prior to the behavioral response with an amplitude and time course that seem to model the behavioral CR). In essence, these recording studies provide important additional evidence of the involvement of the cerebellum in classical eyeblink conditioning: Patterns of action potentials from cerebellar neurons appear to reflect the encoding of the CS and US as well as the generation of the learned response.

CONVERGENCE OF CS, US, AND CR PATHWAYS IN THE CEREBELLUM

Figure 1 depicts how my colleagues and I currently conceptualize the basic brain-stem and cerebellar neural circuit involved in encoding the classically conditioned eyeblink response. The CR output pathway from the interpositus nucleus is somewhat simple: Neurons in the interpositus nucleus send axons that make synapses on neurons in the red nucleus (a motor-related structure in the midbrain). The red nucleus neurons then send axons to clusters of motor neurons that are responsible for generating eyeblinks. The neural pathways involved in transmitting the CS and US to the cerebellum have also been delineated. Using recording, lesion, and stimulation methods, we have delineated neural pathways that appear to convey a tone CS and an airpuff US to the cerebellum (see Steinmetz, 1996, for a review). The tone CS is routed from the ear through the cochlear nuclei (a set of neurons that encode auditory stimuli) to lateral regions of a very large group of brain-stem relay neurons known as the basilar pontine nuclei. The auditory-sensitive neurons in the lateral pontine nuclei in turn send axons directly to many areas of cerebellar cortex, as well as to the interpositus nucleus. The airpuff US appears to be routed from the eye to the trigeminal nucleus (one of the cranial nerve nuclei located in the brain stem), which, in turn, sends US information to the inferior olivary complex, a brain-stem structure that processes sensory and motor information. Inferior olive neurons then send axons to well-defined zones in cerebellar cortex and to the interpositus nucleus. The UR is actually mediated through a circuit of neurons located deep in the brain stem. In addition to sending input to the inferior olive, the trigeminal nucleus sends axons to neurons in the reticular formation (within the brain stem), which, in turn, sends axons to cranial nerve nuclei, such as the facial nucleus and the accessory abducens nucleus, that contain clusters of motor neurons responsible for activating muscles involved in the eyeblink.

FIGURE 1

*Schematic Diagram Depicting Key Structures in the
Brain Stem and Cerebellum That Make Up the Basic Essential
Neural Circuit That Encodes Classical Eyeblink Conditioning*

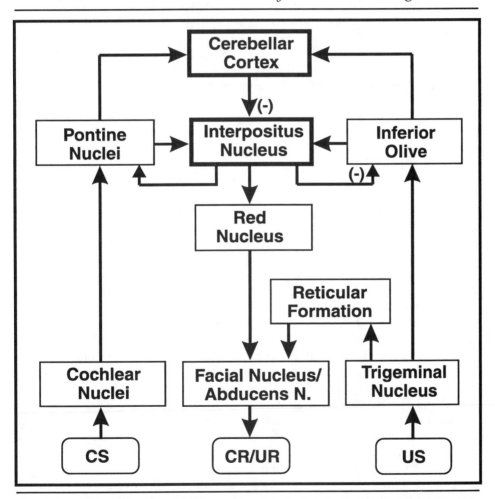

Note: The minus signs indicate inhibitory connections in the circuit. All other connections are excitatory. The bold boxes indicate the two sites where evidence suggests plasticity in this system (convergence) occurs. Abducens N. = abducens nucleus; CR = conditioned response; CS = conditioned stimulus; UR = unconditioned response; US = unconditioned stimulus.

My colleagues and I have hypothesized that cellular changes that are the basis for the learning and memory of classical eyeblink conditioning occur at synapses between neurons in the cerebellar cortex and the interpositus. We have collected anatomical and electrophysiological data that support the idea that these two regions of the cerebellum receive convergent CS and US inputs. Injections of horseradish peroxidase (HRP), an anatomical tracer that identifies (labels) the location of neurons, into the areas of the interpositus nucleus or cerebellar cortex suspected to receive convergent CS and US input retrogradely labels neurons in the lateral pontine nucleus as well as in the dorsal accessory inferior olive (Steinmetz & Sengelaub, 1992). Furthermore, HRP injections into the deep cerebellar nuclei label cortical cells that receive convergent CS and US input. We have also shown that single-pulse electrical stimulation of the lateral pontine nucleus and the inferior olive can induce neuronal activity in the regions of the interpositus nucleus and cerebellar cortex suspected to receive convergent CS and US input (Gould, Sears, & Steinmetz, 1993). In fact, we have been able to activate the same interpositus neuron with pontine stimulation and with olivary stimulation, thus demonstrating that these cells could receive convergent CS and US input, making them candidate neurons in which plasticity processes associated with CS-US pairing may occur.

EVIDENCE FOR NEURONAL PLASTICITY IN THE CEREBELLUM

Although some progress has been made in defining the basic cerebellum and associated brain-stem circuitry thought to be critical for the acquisition and performance of the classically conditioned eyeblink response, these basic data do not provide insight into the basic question as to where precisely in this circuitry the fundamental synaptic plasticity that is responsible for the learning occurs. The data I have cited suggest that the interpositus nucleus and cerebellar cortex are likely locations for this plasticity because they receive converging CS and US inputs that could produce learning-related associative changes. Three lines of evidence more directly indicate that this is indeed the case.

First, my colleagues and I showed that eyeblink conditioning can be obtained without the presentation of external stimuli (Steinmetz, Lavond, & Thompson, 1989). In this study, we implanted electrodes in the lateral pontine nuclei and the inferior olive and trained the animals by delivering electrical stimulation to these structures in lieu of external stimuli. Before training, stimulation of the pontine nuclei as a CS produced no movement, and stimulation of the inferior olive as a US produced a number of discrete movements (depending on electrode location), including discrete eyeblinks. Continued pairing of the pontine stimulation (CS) and olivary stimulation (US) eventually produced conditioned movements. With pairing, the CS came to elicit the movement generated by the US. Because the only structure found efferent to the points of stimulation was the cerebellum, these data argue strongly that critical sites of plasticity underlying the conditioning were in the cerebellum.

Second, David Lavond and his colleagues have used reversible cooling techniques to demonstrate that the essential neuronal plasticity that underlies conditioning occurs in the cerebellum (Clark, Zhang, & Lavond, 1992). In these studies, a miniature cold probe is inserted into the brain near a target structure. When the cold probe is activated, neurons near the probe are cooled and hence rendered inactive. This technique is completely and nearly instantaneously reversible in that the probe can be heated slightly to restore neuronal function. Lavond and his colleagues have shown that after rabbits have been trained, eyeblink CRs disappear when either the interpositus nucleus or the red nucleus (its output target) is cooled. The CRs return immediately when the cooling is reversed. Even more interesting results have been obtained with untrained rabbits. Lavond and his colleagues cooled the interpositus nucleus during several days of acquisition training and then turned the cold probe off for several additional days of training. They reasoned that if critical cellular processes related to conditioning occur in the interpositus nucleus, these processes would be blocked by cooling and the rabbits would show no evidence of learning from previous paired trial presentations when the postcooling training first began, but would show normal rates of conditioning over the course of training when the cooling probe was not active. This is precisely what was observed. Cooling the red nucleus (to which the interpositus nucleus provides input) during acquisition training did not produce the same effect. As expected, cooling the red nucleus blocked expression of CRs during the initial days of training, but CRs were immediately present on the first training session when the cold probe was inactive. Apparently, plasticity processes in the cerebellum, from which the red nucleus receives input, occurred during cooling of the red nucleus.

Third, Krupa, Thompson, and Thompson (1993) used a pharmacological method to demonstrate that cellular processes within cerebellar neurons are responsible for plasticity underlying classical eyeblink conditioning. Initially, they infused muscimol, which temporarily inactivates neurons, into the cerebellum of trained rabbits and showed that muscimol abolished established eyeblink CRs. They then infused muscimol over several days of paired training given to previously untrained rabbits and demonstrated normal CR acquisition rates on subsequent paired training sessions without muscimol injections. These results suggest that muscimol infusion effectively prevented the occurrence of plasticity-related cellular processes in the cerebellum during conditioning and that critical cellular changes that underlie the acquisition and performance of the eyeblink CR take place in the cerebellum.

Together, the CS-US stimulation, brain-cooling, and muscimol studies provide strong evidence that critical changes in neuronal function associated with classical eyeblink conditioning occur in the cerebellum.

REFERENCES

Berthier, N. E., & Moore, J. W. (1986). Cerebellar Purkinje cell activity related to the classically conditioned nictitating membrane response. *Experimental Brain Research, 63,* 341–350.

Berthier, N. E., & Moore, J. W. (1990). Activity of deep cerebellar nuclear cells during classical conditioning of nictitating membrane extension in rabbits. *Experimental Brain Research, 83,* 44–54.

Clark, R. E., Zhang, A. A., & Lavond, D. G. (1992). Reversible lesions of the cerebellar interpositus nucleus during acquisition and retention of a classically conditioned behavior. *Behavioral Neuroscience, 106,* 879–888.

Gormezano, I., Kehoe, E. J., & Marshall-Goodell, B. S. (1983). Twenty years of classical conditioning research with the rabbit. In J. M. Sprague & A. N. Epstein (Eds.), *Progress in physiological psychology* (pp. 197–275). New York: Academic Press.

Gould, T. J., Sears, L. L., & Steinmetz, J. E. (1993). Possible CS and US pathways for rabbit classical eyelid conditioning: Electrophysiological evidence for projections from the pontine nuclei and inferior olive to cerebellar cortex and nuclei. *Behavioral and Neural Biology, 60,* 172–185.

Krupa, D. J., Thompson, J. K., & Thompson, R. F. (1993). Localization of a memory trace in the mammalian brain. *Science, 260,* 989–991.

McCormick, D. A., & Thompson, R. F. (1984). Neuronal responses of the rabbit cerebellum during acquisition and performance of a classically conditioned nictitating membrane-eyelid response. *Journal of Neuroscience, 4,* 2811–2822.

Romano, A. G., & Patterson, M. M. (1987). The rabbit in Pavlovian conditioning. In I. Gormezano, W. F. Prokasy, & R. F. Thompson (Eds.), *Classical conditioning* (3rd ed., pp. 1–36). Hillsdale, NJ: Erlbaum.

Steinmetz, J. E. (1996). The brain substrates of classical eyeblink conditioning in rabbits. In J. R. Bloedel, T. J. Ebner, & S. P. Wise (Eds.), *The acquisition of motor behavior in vertebrates* (pp. 89–114). Cambridge, MA: MIT Press.

Steinmetz, J. E., Lavond, D. G., & Thompson, R. F. (1989). Classical conditioning in rabbit using pontine nucleus stimulation as a conditioned stimulus and inferior olive stimulation as an unconditioned stimulus. *Synapse, 3,* 225–233.

Steinmetz, J. E., Logue, S. F., & Steinmetz, S. S. (1992). Rabbit classically conditioned eyelid responses do not reappear after interpositus nucleus lesion and extensive post-lesion training. *Behavioural Brain Research, 51,* 103–114.

Steinmetz, J. E., & Sengelaub, D. R. (1992). Possible conditioned stimulus pathway for classical eyelid conditioning in rabbits: I. Anatomical evidence for direct projections for the pontine nuclei to the cerebellar interpositus nucleus. *Behavioral and Neural Biology, 57,* 103–115.

2.3 BARRY L. JACOBS

Serotonin, Motor Activity and Depression-Related Disorders

Recently, a great deal of attention has been devoted to the study of how brain chemicals called neurotransmitters can affect people's behavior and moods. Of particular interest are drugs such as Prozac, which alter neuro-transmitters, because they appear to have great abilities to treat psycholog-ical disorders. How does the brain chemical serotonin affect behavior and mood? Psychologist Barry L. Jacobs and his colleagues are trying to find out.

Jacobs is currently a professor of psychology and director of the neu-roscience program at Princeton University in Princeton, New Jersey. His research on serotonin makes him one of the leading authorities in this field.

This selection from "Serotonin, Motor Activity and Depression-Related Disorders," which was published in *American Scientist* in 1994, provides an exciting look into the chemical processes affecting depression. Especially intriguing is the finding that motor activity could be important in treating depression and obsessive-compulsive disorder. The technical details of this selection may be challenging, but it is more important to focus on the impli-cations for better understanding everyday emotion. Does exercise improve your mood? How might an exercise program be developed to help people who feel depressed?

Key Concept: neurotransmitters and behavior

APA Citation: Jacobs, B. L. (1994). Serotonin, motor activity and depression-related disorders. *American Scientist, 82,* 456–463.

Prozac, Zoloft and Paxil are drugs that have been widely celebrated for their effectiveness in the treatment of depression and obsessive-compulsive dis-orders. The popular press has also made much of Prozac's ability to alleviate minor personality disorders such as shyness or lack of popularity. The glam-orous success of these drugs has even inspired some writers to propose that we are at the threshold of a new era reminiscent of Aldous Huxley's *Brave New World,* in which one's day-to-day emotions can be fine-tuned by simply taking a pill. Yet for all the public attention that has been focused on the apparent benefits of Prozac-like drugs, the fundamental players in this story—the cells and the chemicals in the brain modified by these drugs—have been largely ignored.

This is partly a consequence of the complexity of the nervous system and the fact that so little is known about *how* the activity of cells in the brain translates into mood or behavior. We do know that Prozac-like drugs work by altering the function of neurons that release the signaling chemical (neurotransmitter) serotonin. Serotonin has been implicated in a broad range of behavioral disorders involving the sleep cycle, eating, the sex drive and mood. Prozac-like drugs prevent a neuron from taking serotonin back into the cell. Hence Prozac and related drugs are collectively known as selective serotonin reuptake inhibitors, or SSRIs. In principle, blocking the reuptake of serotonin should result in a higher level of activity in any part of the nervous system that uses serotonin as a chemical signal between cells. The long-term effects of these drugs on the function of a serotonin-based network of neurons, however, are simply not known.

My colleagues and I have attempted to understand the role of serotonin in animal physiology and behavior by looking at the activity of the serotonin neurons themselves. For more than 10 years at Princeton University, Casimir Fornal and I have been studying the factors that control the activity of serotonin neurons in the brain. I believe these studies provide the linchpin for understanding depression and obsessive-compulsive disorders and their treatment with therapeutic drugs. Our work provides some unique and unexpected perspectives on these illnesses and will serve, we hope, to open new avenues of clinical research.

SEROTONIN, DRUGS AND DEPRESSION

Communication between neurons is mediated by the release of small packets of chemicals into the tiny gap, the synapse, that separates one neuron from another. The brain uses a surprisingly large number of these chemical neurotransmitters, perhaps as many as 100. However, the preponderance of the work is done by four chemicals that act in a simple and rapid manner: glutamate and aspartate (both of which excite neurons) and gamma-aminobutyric acid (GABA) and glycine (both of which inhibit neurons). Other neurotransmitters, such as serotonin, norepinephrine and dopamine are somewhat different. They can produce excitation *or* inhibition, often act over a longer time scale, and tend to work in concert with one of the four chemical workhorses in the brain. Hence they are also referred to as neuromodulators.

Even though serotonin, norepinephrine and dopamine may be considered to be comparatively minor players in the overall function of the brain, they appear to be major culprits in some of the most common brain disorders: schizophrenia, depression and Parkinson's disease. It is interesting to observe that glutamate, aspartate, GABA and glycine are generally not centrally involved in psychiatric or neurological illnesses. It may be the case that a primary dysfunction of these systems is incompatible with sustaining life.

Serotonin's chemical name is 5-hydroxytryptamine, which derives from the fact that it is synthesized from the amino acid *L*-tryptophan. After a meal, foods are broken down into their constituent amino acids, including tryptophan, and then transported throughout the body by the circulatory system. Once tryptophan is carried into the brain and into certain neurons, it is converted into serotonin by two enzymatic steps.

Serotonin's actions in the synapse are terminated primarily by its being taken back into the neuron that released it. From that point, it is either recycled for reuse as a neurotransmitter or broken down into its metabolic by-products and transported out of the brain. With this basic understanding of serotonin neurotransmission, we can begin to understand the mechanisms of action of antidepressant drugs.

One of the earliest antidepressant drugs, iproniazid, elevates the level of a number of brain chemicals by inhibiting the action of an enzyme, monoamine oxidase, involved in their catabolism. For example, monoamine oxidase inhibitors (MAOIs) block the catabolism of serotonin into its metabolite, 5-hydroxyindole acetic acid (5-HIAA), leading to a buildup of serotonin in the brain. Unfortunately, because monoamine oxidase catabolizes a number of brain chemicals (including norepinephrine and dopamine), there are a number of side-effects associated with these drugs. Some interactive toxicity of MAOIs is also a major drawback for their use in the treatment of depression.

Tricyclic antidepressants (so named because of their three-ringed chemical structure), do not share the interactive toxicity of MAOIs. Tricyclics such as imipramine act to block the reuptake of serotonin from the synapse back into the neuron that released it. In a sense, this floods the synapse with serotonin. These drugs are quite effective in treating depression, but they also induce some unpleasant side-effects, such as constipation, headache and dry mouth. This may be due to the fact that tricyclic antidepressants not only block the reuptake of serotonin, but also exert similar effects on norepinephrine and dopamine.

The obvious benefit of the selective serotonin reuptake inhibitors is that their action is effectively limited to the reuptake of serotonin. This probably accounts for the fewer side-effects experienced by people taking SSRIs. Like other antidepressant drugs, the SSRIs have a therapeutic lag. They typically require 4 to 6 weeks to exert their full effects. Claude DeTontigny and his colleagues at McGill University have suggested that one of the consequences of increasing the levels of serotonin in the brain is a compensatory feedback inhibition that decreases the discharge of brain serotonergic neurons. This results in a "zero sum game" in which there is no net increase in functional serotonin. However, with continuous exposure to serotonin, the receptors mediating this feedback inhibition (the $5\text{-}HT_{1A}$ receptor) become desensitized. It is hypothesized that after several weeks this results in progressively less feedback, increased serotonergic neurotransmission and clinical improvement.

BEHAVIOR OF SEROTONIN NEURONS

Essentially all of the serotonin-based activity in the brain arises from neurons that are located within cell clusters known as the raphe nuclei. These clusters of serotonin neurons are located in the brainstem, the most primitive part of the brain. It is not surprising, then, that serotonin appears to be involved in some fundamental aspects of physiology and behavior, ranging from the control of body temperature, cardiovascular activity and respiration to involvement in such behaviors as aggression, eating and sleeping.

The broad range of physiology and behavior associated with serotonin's actions is at least partly attributable to the widespread distribution of serotonin-containing nerve-fiber terminals that arise from the raphe nuclei. Indeed, the branching of the serotonin network comprises the most expansive neurochemical system in the brain. Serotonin neurons project fibers to virtually all parts of the central nervous system, from the various layers of the cerebral cortex down to the tip of the spinal cord....

Serotonin neurons have a characteristic discharge pattern that distinguishes them from most other cells in the brain. They are relatively regular, exhibiting a slow and steady generation of spikes. Serotonin neurons retain this rhythmic pattern even if they are removed from the brain and isolated in a dish, suggesting that their clocklike regularity is intrinsic to the individual neurons.

One of the first significant discoveries about the behavior of serotonin neurons in the brain was that the rate of these discharges was dramatically altered during different levels of behavioral arousal. When an animal is quiet but awake, the typical serotonin neuron discharges at about 3 spikes per second. As the animal becomes drowsy and enters a phase known as slow-wave sleep, the number of spikes gradually declines. During rapid-eye movement (REM) sleep, which is associated with dreaming in human beings, the serotonin neurons fall completely silent. In anticipation of waking, however, the neuronal activity returns to its basal level of 3 spikes per second. When an animal is aroused or in an active waking state, the discharge rate may increase to 4 or 5 spikes per second....

Interestingly, some serotonin neurons tend to become active just *before* a movement begins. Their activity may also occasionally synchronize with a specific phase of the movement—discharging most, for example, during a particular aspect of the quadrupedal stepping cycle. Moreover, the rate of the spike discharge often increases linearly with increases in the rate or strength of a movement, such as an increase in running speed or the depth of respiration.

One final observation provides a noteworthy clue to the function of serotonin neurons. When an animal is presented with a strong or novel stimulus, such as a sudden loud noise, it often suppresses all ongoing behavior, such as walking or grooming, and turns toward the stimulus. This orienting is essentially a "what is it?" response. In such instances serotonin neurons fall completely silent for several seconds, and then resume their normal activity.

Anatomical evidence supports these observations about the activity of serotonin neurons. For one thing, serotonin neurons preferentially make contacts with neurons that are involved in tonic and gross motor functions, such as those that control the torso and limbs. Reciprocally, serotonin neurons tend not to make connections with neurons that carry out episodic behavior and fine movements, such as those neurons that control the eyes or the fingers.

Our observations of the activity of serotonin neurons during different aspects of an animal's behavior lead us to conclude that the primary function of the brain serotonin system is to prime and facilitate gross motor output in both tonic and repetitive modes. At the same time, the system acts to inhibit sensory-information processing while coordinating autonomic and neuroendocrine functions with the specific demands of the motor activity. When the serotonin system is not active (for example, during an orientation response), the relations are reversed: Motor output is disfacilitated, and sensory-information processing is disinhibited.

BRAIN CELLS AND MENTAL DISORDERS

Although we are far from understanding the precise neural mechanisms involved in the manifestation of any mental illness, a number of studies have linked serotonin to depression. One of the most notable findings is that the major metabolite of serotonin (5-HIAA) appears to be significantly reduced in the cerebrospinal fluid of suicidally depressed patients. Our own studies suggest that serotonin neurons may be centrally involved in the physiological abnormality that underlies depression-related disorders. Recall that serotonin neurons appear to play crucial roles in facilitating tonic motor actions and inhibiting sensory-information processing. If an animal's serotonin neurons are responding abnormally, such that the rate or pattern of their activity is modified, then one might expect that both motor functions and sensory-information processing would be impaired.

Depression is frequently associated with motor retardation and cognitive impairment. If serotonin neurons are not facilitating tonic motor activity, then it should not be surprising that depressed patients feel listless and often appear to require enormous effort merely to raise themselves out of bed. Inappropriate activity during sensory-information processing might also account for the lapses of memory and the general lack of interest in the environment experienced by depressed patients. It might also be worth noting here that the well-known efficacy of REM-sleep deprivation for treating depression is at least partly dependent on serotonin. Since serotonin neurons are usually silent during REM sleep, depriving an animal of REM sleep maintains a generally higher level of activity in the system. Preliminary research in my laboratory suggests that the deprivation of REM sleep also increases the activity of serotonin neurons when the animal is in the awake state.

The activity of serotonin neurons may also be central to the manifestation of obsessive-compulsive disorders. Since our results show that repetitive motor acts increase serotonin neuronal activity, patients with this disorder may be engaging in repetitive rituals such as hand washing or pacing as a means of self-medication. In other words, they have learned to activate their brain serotonin system in order to derive some benefit or rewarding effect, perhaps the reduction of anxiety. Since the compulsive acts tend to be repeated, often to the point of becoming continuous, such activity may provide an almost limitless supply of serotonin to the brain. (The same may also be true for repetitive obsessional thoughts, but this is obviously difficult to test in animals.) Treating obsessive-compulsive disorders with a selective serotonin reuptake inhibitor ultimately accomplishes the same neurochemical endpoint, thus allowing these people to disengage from time-consuming, socially unacceptable and often physically harmful behavior.

Our studies suggest that regular motor activity may be important in the treatment of affective disorders. For example, if there is a deficiency of serotonin in some forms of depression, then an increase in tonic motor activity or some form of repetitive motor task, such as riding a bicycle or jogging, may help to relieve the depression. Indeed, there are various reports that jogging and other forms of exercise have salutary effects for depressed patients. This does not mean that exercise is a panacea for depressive disorders. Since the long-term effects of exercise on brain serotonin levels are not known, the benefits may prove to be transient. On the other hand, exercise may be an important adjunct to drug treatments, and may permit a reduction in the required drug dosage. . . .

CONCLUSION

Our research raises the issue of why the manipulation of a system that is primarily a modulator of motor activity has profound effects on mood. Aside from recognizing that the raphe nuclei are connected to regions of the brain that are known to be involved in the emotions (such as the limbic system), it is worth noting that a common organizational plan underlies the distribution of serotonin cell bodies and fiber terminals in essentially all vertebrate brains. This implies that the system has been conserved through evolution, and suggests that there may be some adaptive significance to linking mood and motor activity.

Consider the following possibility. We know that emotions play a role in allowing an animal to withdraw from an ongoing sequence of activities to consider alternative paths. When something bad (perhaps even life-threatening) transpires, it seems reasonable to suppress motor activity and to contemplate the available options. To put it another way: If something negative has happened in one's world, it might be counterproductive, or even dangerous, to explore and engage the environment. The most adaptive response is to withdraw and ruminate. In this light, emotions act at a higher level of complexity in the service of effective motor behavior. When one's mood is bright and expansive, on the other hand, it may be profitable to explore new options. Wide mood swings may allow an exploration of a broader spectrum of perspectives and thus may be related to the well-documented relationship between mood disorders and creativity in artists, writers and composers.

As a final note, the brain serotonin system may be involved in some non-clinical aspects of human behavior. Why do some people endlessly engage in rhythmic leg bouncing? What is rewarding about chewing gum? What underlies the therapeutic or reinforcing effects of breathing exercises, and the twirling or dancing movements employed by various cults and religious groups? The reader can probably think of other behaviors that increase serotonin release in his or her brain.

Barry L. Jacobs

Environment and Genes: Determinants of Behavior

The importance of nature (genetics) and nurture (environment) on behavioral development has been debated for centuries. Only in the past few decades, however, have psychologists begun to discover the specific mechanisms by which heredity influences cognition and behavior. At the same time, psychologists have found that behavior is also influenced by one's environment and that, in fact, all behavior is the result of the interaction of heredity and the environment. Behavior geneticist Robert Plomin has been studying this interaction.

Plomin (b. 1948) earned his Ph.D. in biological psychology from the University of Texas at Austin in 1974. He worked at the University of Colorado and Pennsylvania State University before accepting his current position at the University of London Psychiatry Research Center. He has been actively involved in behavioral genetic research, and he is coauthor of the textbook *Behavioral Genetics: A Primer,* 3rd ed. (Worth, 1997).

This selection is from "Environment and Genes: Determinants of Behavior," which was published in *American Psychologist* in 1989. In it, Plomin reviews some of the research findings in the field of behavior genetics that came to light during the 1980s. The field of behavior genetics is important because it helps us understand ourselves and those around us. Today, reports are being made regularly on how specific genes influence intelligence, personality, and psychopathology, as well as other bodily processes. As you read this selection, notice Plomin's emphasis on how both heredity and environment influence human behavior.

Key Concept: behavior genetics

APA Citation: Plomin, R. (1989). Environment and genes: Determinants of behavior. *American Psychologist, 44,* 105–111.

*A*BSTRACT: *Recent behavioral genetic research has demonstrated that genetic influence on individual differences in behavioral development is usually significant and often substantial and, paradoxically, also supports the important role of the environment. This article reviews research on the heritability of intellectual factors, personality* *factors, and psychopathology. It discusses the importance of investigating within-family environmental differences in order to understand the environmental origins of individual differences in development.*

Robert Plomin

Increasing acceptance of hereditary influence on individual differences in development represents one of the most remarkable changes in the field of psychology that has occurred during the decade since the 1979 special issue of the *American Psychologist* on children. Even for IQ scores, traditionally one of the most controversial areas, a recent survey of over 1,000 scientists and educators indicates that most now believe that individual differences in IQ scores are at least partially inherited (Snyderman & Rothman, 1987). Recent behavioral genetic research providing the empirical basis for this trend is reviewed in the first half of this article.

The wave of acceptance of genetic influence on behavior is growing into a tidal wave that threatens to engulf the second message of this research: These same data provide the best available evidence for the importance of environmental influence. Variability in complex behaviors of interest to psychologists and to society is due at least as much to environmental influences as it is to genetic influences. Because its methods recognize both environmental and genetic influences on behavior, behavioral genetic research has made some novel advances in understanding the environment....

Although the brevity of this article precludes a discussion of the theory and methods of behavioral genetics, the two major methods are the twin design, in which identical twin resemblance is compared with fraternal twin resemblance, and the adoption design, in which genetically related individuals reared apart and genetically unrelated individuals reared together are studied. These methods are used to assess heritability, a statistic that describes the proportion of observed variance for a behavior that can be ascribed to genetic differences among individuals in a particular population....

Two conceptual issues about the field of behavioral genetics need to be mentioned. First, behavioral genetic theory and methods address the genetic and environmental sources of differences among individuals. Behavioral genetics has little to say about universals of development (e.g., why the human species uses language) or about average differences between groups (e.g., why girls perform better than boys on verbal tests). This critical issue, the cause of much misunderstanding, is discussed at length elsewhere (Plomin, DeFries, & Fulker, 1988). Second, when genetic differences among children are found to relate to differences in their behavior, this is a probabilistic relationship in much the same way as finding associations between environmental factors and children's development.... [G]enetic influences on behavior are multifactorial —that is, they involve many genes, each with small effects—as well as environmental influences. In other words, genetic influences on the complex behaviors of interest to psychologists do not fit the deterministic model of a single-gene effect—like Mendel's pea-plant characteristics or like some genetic diseases such as sickle-cell anemia—which operates independently of other genes or of environmental influences....

HIGHLIGHTS OF RECENT
BEHAVIORAL GENETIC RESEARCH

This section provides a brief overview of recent human behavioral genetic research indicating that behavior can no longer be considered innocent of genetic influence until proven guilty. The litany includes intellectual factors, including IQ, specific cognitive abilities, academic achievement, reading disability . . . ; personality factors, including extraversion and neuroticism, temperament in childhood, and attitudes and beliefs; and psychopathology, including schizophrenia, affective disorders, delinquent and criminal behavior, and alcoholism.

Intellectual Factors

IQ. More behavioral genetic data have been obtained for IQ than for any other trait. A summary of dozens of studies prior to 1980 includes nearly 100,000 twins and biological and adoptive relatives and makes it difficult to escape the conclusion that heredity importantly influences individual differences in IQ scores (Bouchard & McGue, 1981). For example, genetically related individuals adopted apart show significant resemblance, and identical twins are substantially more similar than fraternal twins. An interesting twist is that, for reasons as yet unknown, studies in the 1970s yielded lower estimates of heritability (about 50%) than older studies (about 70%; Plomin & DeFries, 1980; cf. Loehlin, Willerman, & Horn, 1988).

Recent studies include two ongoing studies of twins reared apart that will triple the number of identical twins reared apart who have been studied for IQ and will also, for the first time, add hundreds of pairs of the equally important group of fraternal twins reared apart. Preliminary reports from these two studies indicate that their results are in line with the rest of the behavioral genetics literature in implicating substantial genetic influence on IQ scores (Bouchard, 1984; Pedersen, McClearn, Plomin, & Friberg, 1985). . . .

Specific cognitive abilities. Although there is some evidence that verbal and spatial abilities show greater genetic influence than do perceptual speed tests and memory tests, the general message is that diverse cognitive tests show significant and often substantial (almost as much as for IQ) genetic influence throughout the life span (Plomin, 1988). In 10 twin studies, tests of creativity show less genetic influence than any other dimension within the cognitive domain, especially when IQ is controlled (R. C. Nichols, 1978).

Research on specific cognitive abilities during the past decade includes a study of over 6,000 individuals in nearly 2,000 families, three twin studies in childhood and one in adulthood, and several parent–offspring adoption studies in addition to the two studies of twins reared apart mentioned in relation to IQ (Plomin, 1986).

Academic achievement. Although no new behavioral genetic research on school-relevant behavior has been reported during the past decade, genetic influence is pervasive here as well. Twin studies of academic-achievement test scores show substantial genetic influence, about the same as for specific cognitive abilities. Even report-card grades and years of schooling show substantial genetic influence. Vocational interests are also substantially influenced by genetic factors, as shown in twin and adoption studies. (For references, see Plomin, 1986.)

Reading disability. Reading disability shows considerable familial resemblance (DeFries, Vogler, & LaBuda, 1985). One recent twin study found evidence for a genetic basis for this familial resemblance (DeFries, Fulker, & LaBuda, 1987); another twin study found genetic influence on spelling disability but not on other aspects of reading disability (Stevenson, Graham, Fredman, & McLoughlin, 1987). A single-gene effect has been proposed for spelling disability (Smith, Kimberling, Pennington, & Lubs, 1983), although subsequent analyses have not confirmed the linkage (Kimberling, Fain, Ing, Smith, & Pennington, 1985; McGuffin, 1987)....

Personality Factors

Extraversion and neuroticism. One focus of recent research on personality involves two "super factors" of personality: extraversion and neuroticism. A review of research involving over 25,000 pairs of twins yielded heritability estimates of about 50% for these two traits (Henderson, 1982). This review also pointed out that extraversion and other personality traits often show evidence for nonadditive genetic variance. Nonadditive effects of genes involve unique combinations of genes that contribute to the similarity of identical twins but not to the resemblance of first-degree relatives. These conclusions are supported by a recent large-scale twin study in Australia (N. G. Martin & Jardine, 1986) and by two studies of twins reared apart (Pedersen, Plomin, McClearn, & Friberg, 1988; Tellegen et al., 1988). The presence of nonadditive genetic variance may be responsible for the lower estimates of heritability from adoption studies of first-degree relatives (Loehlin, Willerman, & Horn, 1982, 1985; Scarr, Webber, Weinberg, & Wittig, 1981).

Emotionality, activity, and sociability (EAS). Extraversion and neuroticism are global traits that encompass many dimensions of personality. The core of extraversion, however, is sociability, and the key component of neuroticism is emotionality. From infancy to adulthood, these two traits and activity level have been proposed as the most heritable components of personality, a theory referred to with the acronym EAS (Buss & Plomin, 1984). A review of behavioral genetic data for these three traits in infancy, childhood, adolescence, and adulthood lends support to the EAS theory (Plomin, 1986). However, note that many personality traits display genetic influence, and it is difficult to prove that some traits are more heritable than others, perhaps because of the pervasive genetic influence of extraversion and neuroticism (Loehlin, 1982)....

Attitudes and beliefs. Surprisingly, some attitudes and beliefs show almost as much genetic influence as do other behavioral traits. One focus of recent interest is traditionalism, the tendency to follow rules and authority and to endorse high moral standards and strict discipline. For example, a large twin study estimated that half of the variance on this measure is due to genetic influence (N. G. Martin et al., 1986), and a report of twins reared apart has also found substantial genetic influence for traditionalism (Tellegen et al., 1988). Religiosity and certain political beliefs, however, show no genetic influence.

Psychopathology

Behavioral genetic research on psychopathology in children and adults is especially active (Loehlin et al., 1988; Vandenberg, Singer, & Pauls, 1986). This section provides a brief overview of recent research in schizophrenia, affective disorders, delinquent and criminal behavior, alcoholism, and other psychopathology.

Schizophrenia. In 14 older studies involving over 18,000 first-degree relatives of schizophrenics, the risk for first-degree relatives was about 8%, eight times greater than the risk for individuals chosen randomly from the population (Gottesman & Shields, 1982). Recent family studies continue to yield similar results.

Twin studies suggest that this familial resemblance is due to heredity. The most recent twin study involved all male twins who were veterans of World War II (Kendler & Robinette, 1983). Twin concordances were 30.9% for 164 pairs of identical twins and 6.5% for 268 pairs of fraternal twins. Adoption studies of schizophrenia support the twin findings of genetic influence on schizophrenia. . . .

Affective disorders. Although twin results for affective disorders suggest even greater genetic influence than for schizophrenia, adoption studies indicate less genetic influence (Loehlin et al., 1988). In one recent adoption study, affective disorders were diagnosed in only 5.2% of biological relatives of affectively-ill adoptees, although this risk is greater than the risk of 2.3% found in the biological relatives of control adoptees (Wender et al., 1986). The biological relatives of affected adoptees also showed greater rates of alcoholism (5.4% vs. 2.0%) and attempted or actual suicide (7.3% vs. 1.5%). . . .

Delinquent and criminal behavior. The spotlight on controversies concerning genetic influence on IQ has switched to criminal behavior with the publication of a recent book (Wilson & Herrnstein, 1985) claiming that biology affects such behaviors. Six twin studies of juvenile delinquency yielded 87% concordance for identical twins and 72% concordance for fraternal twins, suggesting slight genetic influence and substantial environmental sources of resemblance (Gottesman, Carey, & Hanson, 1983). A recent quantitative study of delinquent acts indicated greater genetic influence than did earlier studies that attempted to diagnose delinquency (Rowe, 1983b).

It has been suggested that juvenile delinquents who go on to become adult criminals may have a genetic liability (Wilson & Herrnstein, 1985). Eight older twin studies of adult criminality yielded identical and fraternal twin concordances of 69% and 33%, respectively. Adoption studies are consistent with the hypothesis of some genetic influence on adult criminality, although the evidence is not as striking as in the twin studies (Mednick, Gabrielli, & Hutchings, 1984).

Alcoholism.   Alcoholism runs in families. Alcoholism in a first-degree relative is by far the single best predictor of alcoholism (Mednick, Moffitt, & Stack, 1987). About 25% of the male relatives of alcoholics are themselves alcoholics, as compared with fewer than 5% of the males in the general population. Although twin studies of normal drinkers show substantial genetic influence (for example, Pedersen, Friberg, Floderus-Myrhed, McClearn, & Plomin, 1984), no twin studies have focused on alcoholism per se. A Swedish adoption study provides the best evidence for genetic influence on alcoholism, at least in males (Bohman, Cloninger, Sigvardsson, & von Knorring, 1987; cf. Peele, 1986). Twenty-two percent of the adopted-away sons of biological fathers who abused alcohol were alcoholic, suggesting substantial genetic influence.

Other psychopathology.   Although most research on psychopathology has focused on psychoses, criminality, and alcoholism, attention has begun to turn to other disorders. Areas of recent research include a family study of anxiety neurosis sometimes known as panic disorder, twin and family studies of anorexia nervosa, and family and adoption studies of somatization disorder that involves multiple and chronic physical complaints of unknown origin (Loehlin et al., 1988).

Summary

The first message of behavioral genetic research is that genetic influence on individual differences in behavioral development is usually significant and often substantial. Genetic influence is so ubiquitous and pervasive in behavior that a shift in emphasis is warranted: Ask not what is heritable, ask what is not heritable.

The second message is just as important: These same data provide the best available evidence of the importance of the environment. The data reviewed in this section suggest pandemic genetic influence, but they also indicate that nongenetic factors are responsible for more than half of the variance for most complex behaviors. For example, identical twins show concordance of less than 40% for schizophrenia. Because identical twins are genetically identical, most of the reason one person is diagnosed as schizophrenic and another is not has to do with environmental rather than genetic reasons. The phrase "behavioral genetics" is in a sense a misnomer because it is as much the study of nurture as nature. In addition to documenting the importance of environmental variation, it provides a novel perspective for viewing environmental influences, especially the family environment, in the context of heredity....

The move away from a rigid adherence to environmental explanations of behavioral development to a more balanced perspective that recognizes genetic as well as environmental sources of individual differences must be viewed as healthy for the social and behavioral sciences. The danger now, however, is that the swing from environmentalism will go too far. During the 1970s, I found I had to speak gingerly about genetic influence, gently suggesting heredity might be important in behavior. Now, however, I more often have to say, "Yes, genetic influences are significant and substantial, but environmental influences are just as important." This seems to be happening most clearly in the field of psychopathology, where evidence of significant genetic influence has led to a search for single genes and simple neurochemical triggers at the expense of research on its psychosocial origins. It would be wonderful if some simple, and presumably inexpensive, biochemical cure could be found for schizophrenia. However, this happy outcome seems highly unlikely given that schizophrenia is as much influenced by environmental factors as it is by heredity.

Furthermore, as mentioned earlier, genetic effects on behavior are polygenic and probabilistic, not single gene and deterministic. The characteristics in the pea plant that Mendel studied and a few diseases such as Huntington's disease and sickle-cell anemia are due to single genes that have their effects regardless of the environment or the genetic background of the individual. The complexity of behaviors studied by psychologists makes it unlikely that such a deterministic model and the reductionistic approach that it suggests will pay off. There is as yet no firm evidence for a single-gene effect that accounts for a detectable amount of variation for any complex behavior. . . .

As the pendulum swings from environmentalism, it is important that the pendulum be caught midswing before its momentum carries it to biological determinism. Behavioral genetic research clearly demonstrates that both nature and nurture are important in human development.

REFERENCES

Bohman, M., Cloninger, R., Sigvardsson, S., & von Knorring, A. L. (1987). The genetics of alcoholisms and related disorders. *Journal of Psychiatric Research, 21,* 447–452.

Bouchard, T. J. (1984). Twins reared together and apart: What they tell us about human diversity. In S. W. Fox (Ed.), *Individuality and determinism* (pp. 147–178). New York: Plenum Press.

Bouchard, T. J., Jr., & McGue, M. (1981). Familial studies of intelligence: A review. *Science, 212,* 1055–1059.

Buss, A. H., & Plomin, R. (1984). *Temperament: Early developing personality traits.* Hillsdale, NJ: Erlbaum.

DeFries, J. C., Fulker, D. W., & LaBuda, M. C. (1987). Evidence for a genetic etiology in reading disability in twins. *Nature, 329,* 537–539.

DeFries, J. C., Vogler, G. P., & LaBuda, M. C. (1985). Colorado Family Reading Study: An overview. In J. L. Fuller & E. C. Simmel (Eds.), *Behavior genetics: Principles and applications II.* (pp.357–368). Hillsdale, NJ: Erlbaum.

Donis-Keller, H., Green, P., Helms, C., Cartinhour, S., & Weiffenbach, B. (1987). A human gene map. *Cell, 51,* 319–337.

Egeland, J. A., Gerhard, D. S., Pauls, D. L., Sussex, J. N., & Kidd, K. K. (1987). Bipolar affective disorders linked to DNA markers on chromosome 11. *Nature, 325,* 783–787.

Gottesman, I. I., Carey, G., & Hanson, D. R. (1983). Pearls and perils in epigenetic psychopathology. In S. B. Guze, E. J. Earls, & J. E. Barrett (Eds.), *Childhood psychopathology and development* (pp. 287–300). New York: Raven Press.

Gottesman, I. I., & Shield, J. (1982). *Schizophrenia: The epigenetic puzzle.* Cambridge, England: Cambridge University Press.

Gusella, J. F., Wexler, N. S., Conneally, P. M., Naylor, S. L., Anderson, M. A., Tanzi, R. E., Watkins, P. C., & Ottina, K. (1983). A polymorphic DNA marker genetically linked to Huntington's disease. *Nature, 306,* 234–238.

Henderson, N. D. (1982). Human behavior genetics. *Annual Review of Psychology, 33,* 403–440.

Kendler, K. S., & Robinette, C. D. (1983). Schizophrenia in the National Academy of Sciences–National Research Council twin registry: A 16-year update. *American Journal of Psychiatry, 140,* 1551–1563.

Kimberling, W. J., Fain, P. R., Ing, P. S., Smith, S. D., & Pennington, B. F. (1985). Linkage analysis of reading disability with chromosome 15. *Behavior Genetics, 15,* 597–598.

Loehlin, J. C. (1982). Are personality traits differentially heritable? *Behavior Genetics, 12,* 417–428.

Loehlin, J. C., Willerman, L., & Horn, J. M. (1982). Personality resemblances between unwed mothers and their adopted-away offspring. *Journal of Personality and Social Psychology, 42,* 1089–1099.

Loehlin, J. C., Willerman, L., & Horn, J. M. (1985). Personality resemblance in adoptive families when the children are late adolescents and adults. *Journal of Personality and Social Psychology, 48,* 376–392.

Loehlin, J. C., Willerman, L., & Horn, J. M. (1988). Human behavior genetics, *Annual Review of Psychology, 38,* 101–133.

Martin, J. B. (1987). Molecular genetics: Applications to the clinical neurosciences. *Science, 238,* 765–772.

Martin, N. G., Eaves, L. J., Heath, A. C., Jardine, R., Feingold, L. M., & Eysenck, H. J. (1986). Transmission of social attitudes. *Proceedings of the National Academy of Sciences, USA, 83,* 4364–4368.

Martin, N. G., & Jardine, R. (1986). Eysenck's contributions to behaviour genetics. In S. Modgil & C. Modgil (Eds.), *Hans Eysenck: Consensus and controversy* (pp. 13–27). Philadelphia: Falmer.

McGuffin, P. (1987). The new genetics and childhood psychiatric disorder. *Journal of Child Psychology and Psychiatry, 28,* 215–222.

Mednick, S. A., Gabrielli, W. F., Jr., & Hutchings, B. (1984). Genetic influences in criminal convictions: Evidence from an adoption cohort. *Science, 224,* 891–894.

Mednick, S. A., Moffitt, T. E., & Stack, S. (1987). *The causes of crime: New biological approaches.* New York: Cambridge University Press.

Nichols, R. C. (1978). Twin studies of ability, personality, and interests. *Homo, 29,* 158–173.

Pedersen, N. L., Friberg, L., Floderus-Myrhed, B., McClearn, G. E., & Plomin, R. (1984). Swedish early separated twins: Identification and characterization. *Acta Geneticae Medicae et Gemellologiae, 33,* 243–250.

Pedersen, N. L., McClearn, G. E., Plomin, R., & Friberg, L. (1985). Separated fraternal twins: Resemblance for cognitive abilities. *Behavior Genetics, 15,* 407–419.

Pedersen, N. L., Plomin, R., McClearn, G. E., & Friberg, L. (1988). Neuroticism, extraversion, and related traits in adult twins reared apart and reared together. *Journal of Personality and Social Psychology, 55,* 950–957.

Peele, S. (1986). The implications and limitations of genetic models of alcoholism and other addictions. *Journal of Studies on Alcohol, 47,* 63–73.

Plomin, R. (1986). *Development, genetics, and psychology.* Hillsdale, NJ: Erlbaum.

Plomin, R. (1988). The nature and nurture of cognitive abilities. In R. J. Sternberg (Ed.), *Advances in the psychology of human intelligence* (Vol. 4, pp. 1–33). Hillsdale, NJ: Erlbaum.

Plomin, R., & DeFries, J. C. (1980). Genetics and intelligence: Recent data. *Intelligence, 4,* 15–24.

Plomin, R., DeFries, J. C., & Fulker D. W. (1988). *Nature and nurture during infancy and early childhood.* New York: Cambridge University Press.

Roew, D. C. (1983b). Biometrical genetic models of self-reported delinquent behavior: Twin study. *Behavior Genetics, 13,* 473–489.

Scarr, S., Webber, P. I., Weinberg, R. A., & Wittig, M. A. (1981). Personality resemblance among adolescents and their parents in biologically related and adoptive families. *Journal of Personality and Social Psychology, 40,* 885–898.

Smith, S. D., Kimberling, W. J., Pennington, B. F., & Lubs, H. A. (1983). Specific reading disability: Identification of an inherited form through linkage analysis. *Science, 219,* 1345–1347.

Snyderman, M., & Rothman, S. (1987). Survey of expert opinion on intelligence and aptitude testing. *American Psychologist, 42,* 137–144.

Stevenson, J., Graham, P., Fredman, G., & McLoughlin, V. (1987). A twin study of genetic influences on reading and spelling ability and disability. *Journal of Child Psychology and Psychiatry, 28,* 229–247.

Tellegen, A., Lykken, D. T., Bouchard, T. J., Wilcox, K., Segal, N., & Rich, S. (1988). Personality similarity in twins reared apart and together. *Journal of Social and Personality Psychology, 54,* 1031–1039.

Vandenberg, S. G., Singer, S. M., & Pauls, D. L. (1986). *The heredity of behavior disorders in adults and children.* New York: Plenum.

Wender, P. H., Kety, S. S., Rosenthal, D., Schulsinger, F., Ortmann, J., & Lunde, I. (1986). Psychiatric disorders in the biological and adoptive families of adopted individuals with affective disorders. *Archives of General Psychiatry, 43,* 923–929.

Wilson, J. Q., & Herrnstein, R. J. (1985). *Crime and human nature.* New York: Simon & Schuster.

Wyman, A. R., & White, R. L. (1980). A highly polymorphic locus in human DNA. *Proceedings of the National Academy of Sciences, 77,* 6754–6758.

Preparation of this article was supported in part by grants from the National Science Foundation (BNS-8643938) and the National Institute of Aging (AG-04563).

CHAPTER 3 Development

3.1 JEAN PIAGET

The Stages of the Intellectual Development of the Child

Psychologists have traditionally had difficulty studying cognitive development in children because young children cannot effectively communicate their thoughts to others. Swiss psychologist Jean Piaget, however, became interested in cognitive development in infants and children, and he spent nearly 60 years investigating the differences between the thought processes of children and those of adults.

Piaget (1896–1980) earned his Ph.D. in zoology from the University of Neuchâtel, Switzerland, in 1918. His educational training helped him in his studies on children's cognitive development because he learned how to make careful observations of noncommunicative organisms solving problems. He theorized that when children are unsuccessful at solving particular problems, they develop more complex mental structures to help them in the future. Piaget was the founder and director of the International Center of Genetic Epistemology in Geneva and a professor of psychology at the University of Geneva.

The selection that follows is from "The Stages of the Intellectual Development of the Child," which was published in *Bulletin of the Menninger Clinic* in 1962. Here Piaget describes the four periods of cognitive development through which people progress. These periods trace the development of intelligence from simple reflexes to complex reasoning. As you read this selection, note the ages at which Piaget suggests each stage begins. Consider the implications for understanding how infants and children think. Why is it important to realize that children think differently from how adults do?

Key Concept: cognitive development

APA Citation: Piaget, J. (1962). The stages of the intellectual development of the child. *Bulletin of the Menninger Clinic, 26,* 120–128.

A consideration of the stages of the development of intelligence should be preceded by asking the question, What is intelligence? Unfortunately, we find ourselves confronted by a great number of definitions. For [Swiss psychologist Edouard] Claparède, intelligence is an adaptation to new situations. When a situation is new, when there are no reflexes, when there are no habits to rely on, then the subject is obliged to search for something new. That is to say, Claparède defines intelligence as groping, as feeling one's way, trial-and-error behavior. We find this trial-and-error behavior in all levels of intelligence, even at the superior level, in the form of hypothesis testing. As far as I am concerned, this definition is too vague, because trial and error occurs in the formation of habits, and also in the earliest established reflexes: when a newborn baby learns to suck.

Karl Bühler defines intelligence as an act of immediate comprehension; that is to say, an insight. Bühler's definition is also very precise, but it seems to me too narrow. I know that when a mathematician solves a problem, he ends by having an insight, but up to that moment he feels, or gropes for, his way; and to say that the trial-and-error behavior is not intelligent and that intelligence starts only when he finds the solution to the problem, seems a very narrow definition. I would, therefore, propose to define intelligence not by a static criterion, as in previous definitions, but by the direction that intelligence follows in its evolution, and then I would define intelligence as a form of equilibration, or forms of equilibration, toward which all cognitive functions lead.

But I must first define equilibration. Equilibration in my vocabulary is not an exact and automatic balance, as it would be in Gestalt theory; I define equilibration principally as a compensation for an external disturbance.

When there is an external disturbance, the subject succeeds in compensating for this by an activity. The maximum equilibration is thus the maximum of the activity, and not a state of rest. It is a mobile equilibration, and not an immobile one. So equilibration is defined as compensation; compensation is the annulling of a transformation by an inverse transformation. The compensation which intervenes in equilibration implies the fundamental idea of reversibility, and this reversibility is precisely what characterizes the operations of the intelligence. An operation is an internalized action, but it is also a reversible action. But an operation is never isolated; it is always subordinated to other operations; it is part of a more inclusive structure. Consequently, we define intelligence in terms of operations, coordination of operations.

Take, for example, an operation like addition: Addition is a material action, the action of reuniting. On the other hand, it is a reversible action, because addition may be compensated by subtraction. Yet addition leads to a structure of a whole. In the case of numbers, it will be the structure that the mathematicians call a "group." In the case of addition of classes which intervene in the logical structure it will be a more simple structure that we will call a grouping, and so on.

Consequently, the study of the stages of intelligence is first a study of the formation of operational structures. I shall define every stage by a structure of a whole, with the possibility of its integration into succeeding stages, just as it was prepared by preceding stages. Thus, I shall distinguish four great stages, or four great periods, in the development of intelligence: first, the sensori-motor period before the appearance of language; second, the period from about two to seven years of age, the preoperational period which precedes real operations; third, the period from seven to 12 years of age, a period of concrete operations (which refers to concrete objects); and finally after 12 years of age, the period of formal operations, or positional operations.

SENSORI-MOTOR STAGE

Before language develops, there is behavior that we can call intelligent. For example, when a baby of 12 months or more wants an object which is too far from him, but which rests on a carpet or blanket, and he pulls it to get to the object, this behavior is an act of intelligence. The child uses an intermediary, a means to get to his goal. Also, getting to an object by means of pulling a string when the object is tied to the string, or when the child uses a stick to get the object, are acts of intelligence. They demonstrate in the sensori-motor period a certain number of stages, which go from simple reflexes, from the formation of the first habits, up to the coordination of means and goals.

Remarkable in this sensori-motor stage of intelligence is that there are already structures. Sensori-motor intelligence rests mainly on actions, on movements and perceptions without language, but these actions are coordinated in a relatively stable way. They are coordinated under what we may call schemata of action. These schemata can be generalized in actions and are applicable to new situations. For example, pulling a carpet to bring an object within reach constitutes a schema which can be generalized to other situations when another object rests on a support. In other words, a schema supposes an incorporation of new situations into the previous schemata, a sort of continuous assimilation of new objects or new situations to the actions already schematized. For example, I presented to one of my children an object completely new to him—a box of cigarettes, which is not a usual toy for a baby. The child took the object, looked at it, put it in his mouth, shook it, then took it with one hand and hit it with the other hand, then rubbed it on the edge of the crib, then shook it again, and gave the impression of trying to see if there were noise. This behavior is a way of exploring the object, of trying to understand it by assimilating it to schemata already known. The child behaves in this situation as he will later in Binet's famous vocabulary test, when he defines by usage, saying, for instance, that a spoon is for eating, and so on.

But in the presence of a new object, even without knowing how to talk, the child knows how to assimilate, to incorporate this new object into each of his already developed schemata which function as practical concepts. Here is a structuring of intelligence. Most important in this structuring is the base, the point of departure of all subsequent operational constructions. At the sensori-motor level, the child constructs the schema of the permanent object.

The knowledge of the permanent object starts at this point. The child is not convinced at the beginning that when an object disappears from view, he can find it again. One can verify by tests that object permanence is not yet developed at this stage. But there is there the beginning of a subsequent fundamental idea which starts being constructed at the sensori-motor level. This is also true of the construction of the ideas of space, of time, of causality. What is being done at the sensori-motor level concerning all the foregoing ideas will constitute the substructure of the subsequent, fully achieved ideas of permanent objects, of space, of time, of causality. . . .

PRE-OPERATIONAL STAGE

From one and one-half to two years of age, a fundamental transformation in the evolution of intelligence takes place in the appearance of symbolic functions. Every action of intelligence consists in manipulating significations (or meanings) and whenever (or wherever) there is significations, there are on the one hand the "significants" and on the other the "significates." This is true in the sensori-motor level, but the only significants that intervene there are perceptual signs or signals (as in conditioning) which are undifferentiated in regard to the significate; for example, a perceptual cue, like distance, which will be a cue for the size of the distant object, or the apparent size of an object, which will be the cue for the distance of the object. There, perhaps, both indices are different aspects of the same reality, but they are not yet differentiated significants. At the age of one and one-half to two years a new class of significants arises, and these significants are differentiated in regard to their significates. These differentiations can be called symbolic function. The appearance of symbols in a children's game is an example of the appearance of new significants. At the sensori-motor level the games are nothing but exercises; now they become symbolic play, a play of fiction; these games consist in representing something by means of something else. Another example is the beginning of delayed imitation, an imitation that takes place not in the presence of the original object but in its absence, and which consequently constitutes a kind of symbolization or mental image.

At the same time that symbols appear, the child acquires language; that is to say, there is the acquisition of another phase of differentiated significants, verbal signals, or collective signals. This symbolic function then brings great flexibility into the field of intelligence. Intelligence up to this point refers to the immediate space which surrounds the child and to the present perceptual situation; thanks to language, and to the symbolic functions, it becomes possible to invoke objects which are not present perceptually, to reconstruct the past, or to make projects, plans for the future, to think of objects not present but very distant in space—in short, to span spatio-temporal distances much greater than before.

But this new stage, the stage of representation of thought which is superimposed on the sensori-motor stage, is not a simple extension of what was referred to at the previous level. Before being able to prolong, one must in fact reconstruct, because behavior in words is a different thing from representing something in thought. When a child knows how to move around in his house or garden by following the different successive cues around him, it does not mean that he is capable of representing or reproducing the total configuration of his house or his garden. To be able to represent, to reproduce something, one must be capable of reconstructing this group of displacements, but at a new level, that of the representation of the thought.

I recently made an amusing test with Nel Szeminska. We took children of four to five years of age who went to school by themselves and came back home by themselves, and asked them if they could trace the way to school and back for us, not in design, which would be too difficult, but like a construction game, with concrete objects. We found that they were not capable of representation; there was a kind of motor-memory, but it was not yet a representation of a whole—the group of displacements had not yet been reconstructed on the plan of the representation of thought. In other words, the operations were not yet formed. There are representations which are internalized actions, but actions still centered on the body itself, on the activity itself. These representations do not allow the objective combinations, the decentrated combinations that the operations would. The actions are centered on the body. I used to call this egocentrism; but it is better thought of as lack of reversibility of action.

At this level, the most certain sign of the absence of operations which appear at the next stage is the absence of the knowledge of conservation. In fact, an operation refers to the transformation of reality. The transformation is not of the whole, however; something constant is always untransformed. If you pour a liquid from one glass to another there is transformation; the liquid changes form, but its liquid property stays constant. So at the pre-operational level, it is significant from the point of view of the operations of intelligence that the child has not yet a knowledge of conservation. For example, in the case of liquid, when the child pours it from one bottle to the other, he thinks that the quantity of the liquid has changed. When the level of the liquid changes, the child thinks the quantity has changed—there is more or less in the second glass than in the first. And if you ask the child where the larger quantity came from, he does not answer this question. What is important for the child is that perceptually it is not the same thing any more. We find this absence of conservation in all object properties, in the length, surface, quantity, and weight of things....

STAGE OF CONCRETE OPERATIONS

The first operations of the manipulation of objects, the concrete operations, deal with logical classes and with logical relations, or the number. But these operations do not deal yet with propositions, or hypotheses, which do not appear until the last stage.

Let me exemplify these concrete operations: the simplest operation is concerned with classifying objects according to their similarity and their difference. This is accomplished by including the subclasses within larger and more general classes, a process that implies inclusion. This classification, which seems very simple at first, is not acquired until around seven to eight years of age. Before that, at the pre-operational level, we do not find logical inclusion. For example, if you show a child at the pre-operational level a bouquet of flowers of which one half is daisies and the other half other flowers and you ask him if in this bouquet there are more flowers or more daisies, you are confronted with this answer, which seems extraordinary until it is analyzed: The child cannot tell you whether there are more flowers than daisies; either he reasons on the basis of the whole or of the part. He cannot understand that the part is complementary to the rest, and he says there are more daisies than flowers, or as many daisies as flowers, without understanding this inclusion of the subclass, the daisies, in the class of flowers. It is only around seven to eight years of age that a child is capable of solving a problem of inclusion.

Another system of operation that appears around seven to eight years of age is the operation of serializing; that is, to arrange objects according to their size, or their progressive weight. It is also a structure of the whole, like the classification which rests on concrete operations, since it consists of manipulating concrete objects. At this level there is also the construction of numbers, which is, too, a synthesis of classification and seriation. In numbers, as in classes, we have inclusion, and also a serial order, as in serializing. These elementary operations constitute structures of wholes. There is no class without classification; there is no symmetric relation without serialization; there is not a number independent of the series of numbers. But the structures of these wholes are simple structures, groupings in the case of classes and relations, which are already groups in the case of numbers, but very elementary structures compared to subsequent structures.

STAGE OF FORMAL OPERATIONS

The last stage of development of intelligence is the stage of formal operations or propositional operations. At about eleven to twelve years of age we see great progress; the child becomes capable of reasoning not only on the basis of objects, but also on the basis of hypotheses, or of propositions.

An example which neatly shows the difference between reasoning on the basis of propositions and reasoning on the basis of concrete objects comes from Burt's tests. Burt asked children of different ages to compare the colors of the hair of three girls: Edith is fairer than Susan, Edith is darker than Lilly; who is the darkest of the three? In this question there is seriation, not of concrete objects, but of verbal statements which supposes a more complicated mental manipulation. This problem is rarely solved before the age of 12.

Here a new class of operations appears which is superimposed on the operations of logical class and number, and these operations are the propositional operations. Here, compared to the previous stage, are fundamental changes. It is not simply that these operations refer to language, and then to operations with concrete objects, but that these operations have much richer structures.

The first novelty is a combinative structure; like mathematical structures, it is a structure of a system which is superimposed on the structure of simple classifications or seriations which are not themselves systems, because they do not involve a combinative system. A combinative system permits the grouping in flexible combinations of each element of the system with any other element of that system. The logic of propositions supposes such a combinative system. If children of different ages are shown a number of colored disks and asked to combine each color with each other two by two, or three by three, we find these combinative operations are not accessible to the child at the stage of concrete operations. The child is capable of some combination, but not of all the possible combinations. After the age of 12, the child can find a method to make all the possible combinations. At the same time he acquires both the logic of mathematics and the logic of propositions, which also supposes a method of combining.

A second novelty in the operations of propositions is the appearance of a structure which constitutes a group of four transformations. Hitherto there were two reversibilities: reversibility by inversion, which consists of annulling, or canceling; and reversibility which we call reciprocity, leading not to cancellation, but to another combination. Reciprocity is what we find in the field of a relation. If A equals B, by reciprocity B equals A. If A is smaller than B, by reciprocity B is larger than A. At the level of propositional operations a new system envelops these two forms of reversibility. Here the structure combines inversion and reversibility in one single but larger and more complicated structure. It allows the acquisition of a series of fundamental operational schemata for the development of intelligence, which schemata are not possible before the constitution of this structure.

It is around the age of 12 that the child, for example, starts to understand in mathematics the knowledge of proportions, and becomes capable of reasoning by using two systems of reference at the same time. For example, if you advance the position of a board and a car moving in opposite directions, in order to understand the movement of the board in relation to the movement of the car and to other movement, you need a system of four transformations. The same is true in regard to proportions, to problems in mathematics or physics, or to other logical problems.

The four principal stages of the development of intelligence of the child progress from one stage to the other by the construction of new operational structures, and these structures constitute the fundamental instrument of the intelligence of the adult.

Infant–Mother Attachment

How babies form attachments to their parents is of interest to a variety of people, from parents to educators to psychologists. Especially intriguing is the notion that there are different patterns of attachment behavior shown by infants. A major contribution to our knowledge in this area has been provided by psychologist Mary D. Salter Ainsworth.

Ainsworth was born in 1913 in Glendale, Ohio, and spent most of her childhood in Toronto. She earned her Ph.D. in personality psychology in 1939 from the University of Toronto. She taught at Johns Hopkins University from 1956 to 1975, when she became a professor of psychology at the University of Virginia. She retired at Virginia in 1984, and remained there until her death in March 1999. Among her many publications in the area of development and attachment is her 1967 book, *Infancy in Uganda: Infant Care and the Growth of Love* (Johns Hopkins University Press).

This selection is from "Infant–Mother Attachment," which was published in *American Psychologist* in 1979. In it, Ainsworth describes her classic research on the development of attachment. Her "strange situation" is used to test the behavior patterns of infants, and it has shown at least three distinguishable attachment patterns. Ainsworth argues that the infant's crying is a key to determining how the infant–mother interaction will develop. As you read this selection, speculate about the long-term development of attachment patterns. How will the secure, anxious, and avoidant babies relate to other people when they become adults?

Key Concept: infant attachment

APA Citation: Ainsworth, M. D. S. (1979). Infant—mother attachment. *American Psychologist, 34,* 932–937.

Bowlby's (1969) ethological–evolutionary attachment theory implies that it is an essential part of the ground plan of the human species—as well as that of many other species—for an infant to become attached to a mother figure. This figure need not be the natural mother but can be anyone who plays the role of principal caregiver. This ground plan is fulfilled, except under extraordinary circumstances when the baby experiences too little interaction with any one caregiver to support the formation of an attachment. The literature on maternal deprivation describes some of these circumstances, but it cannot be reviewed here, except to note that research has not yet specified an acceptable minimum amount of interaction required for attachment formation.

Mary D. Salter
Ainsworth

However, there have been substantial recent advances in the areas of individual differences in the way attachment behavior becomes organized, differential experiences associated with the various attachment patterns, and the value of such patterns in forecasting subsequent development. These advances have been much aided by a standardized laboratory situation that was devised to supplement a naturalistic, longitudinal investigation of the development of infant–mother attachment in the first year of life. This *strange situation*, as we entitled it, has proved to be an excellent basis for the assessment of such attachment in 1-year-olds (Ainsworth, Blehar, Waters, & Wall, 1978).

The assessment procedure consists of classification according to the pattern of behavior shown in the strange situation, particularly in the episodes of reunion after separation. Eight patterns were identified, but I shall deal here only with the three main groups into which they fell—Groups A, B, and C. To summarize, Group B babies use their mothers as a secure base from which to explore in the preseparation episodes; their attachment behavior is greatly intensified by the separation episodes so that exploration diminishes and distress is likely; and in the reunion episodes they seek contact with, proximity to, or at least interaction with their mothers. Group C babies tend to show some signs of anxiety even in the preseparation episodes; they are intensely distressed by separation; and in the reunion episodes they are ambivalent with the mother, seeking close contact with her and yet resisting contact or interaction. Group A babies, in sharp contrast, rarely cry in the separation episodes and, in the reunion episodes, avoid the mother, either mingling proximity-seeking and avoidant behaviors or ignoring her altogether.

COMPARISON OF STRANGE-SITUATION BEHAVIOR AND BEHAVIOR ELSEWHERE

Groups A, B, and C in our longitudinal sample were compared in regard to their behavior at home during the first year. Stayton and Ainsworth (1973) had identified a security–anxiety dimension in a factor analysis of fourth-quarter infant behavior. Group B infants were identified as securely attached because they significantly more often displayed behaviors characteristic of the secure pole of this dimension, whereas both of the other groups were identified as anxious because their behaviors were characteristic of the anxious pole. A second dimension was clearly related to close bodily contact, and this was important in distinguishing Group A babies from those in the other two groups, in that Group A babies behaved less positively to being held and yet more negatively to being put down. The groups were also distinguished by two behaviors not included in the factor analysis—cooperativeness and anger. Group B babies were more cooperative and less angry than either A or C babies; Group A babies were even more angry than those in Group C. Clearly, something went awry in the physical-contact interaction Group A babies had with their mothers, and as I explain below, I believe it is this that makes them especially prone to anger.

Ainsworth et al. (1978) reviewed findings of other investigators who had compared A–B–C groups of 1-year-olds in terms of their behavior elsewhere. Their findings regarding socioemotional behavior support the summary just cited, and in addition three investigations using cognitive measures found an advantage in favor of the securely attached.

COMPARISON OF INFANT STRANGE-SITUATION BEHAVIOR WITH MATERNAL HOME BEHAVIOR

Mothers of the securely attached (Group B) babies were, throughout the first year, more sensitively responsive to infant signals than were the mothers of the two anxiously attached groups, in terms of a variety of measures spanning all of the most common contexts for mother–infant interaction (Ainsworth et al., 1978). Such responsiveness, I suggest, enables an infant to form expectations, primitive at first, that moderate his or her responses to events, both internal and environmental. Gradually, such an infant constructs an inner representation—or "working model" (Bowlby, 1969)—of his or her mother as generally accessible and responsive to him or her. Therein lies his or her security. In contrast, babies whose mothers have disregarded their signals, or have responded to them belatedly or in a grossly inappropriate fashion, have no basis for believing the mother to be accessible and responsive; consequently they are anxious, not knowing what to expect of her.

In regard to interaction in close bodily contact, the most striking finding is that the mothers of avoidant (Group A) babies all evinced a deep-seated aversion to it, whereas none of the other mothers did. In addition they were more rejecting, more often angry, and yet more restricted in the expression of affect than were Group B or C mothers. Main (e.g., in press) and Ainsworth et al. (1978) have presented a theoretical account of the dynamics of interaction of avoidant babies and their rejecting mothers. This emphasizes the acute approach–avoidance conflict experienced by these infants when their attachment behavior is activated at high intensity—a conflict stemming from painful rebuff consequent upon seeking close bodily contact. Avoidance is viewed as a defensive maneuver, lessening the anxiety and anger experienced in the conflict situation and enabling the baby nevertheless to remain within a tolerable range of proximity to the mother.

Findings and interpretations such as these raise the issue of direction of effects. To what extent is the pattern of attachment of a baby attributable to the mother's behavior throughout the first year, and to what extent is it attributable to built-in differences in potential and temperament? I have considered this problem elsewhere (Ainsworth, 1979) and have concluded that in our sample of normal babies there is a strong case to be made for differences in attachment quality being attributable to maternal behavior. Two studies, however (Connell, 1976; Waters, Vaughn, & Egeland, in press), have suggested that Group C babies may as newborns be constitutionally "difficult." Particularly if the mother's personality or life situation makes it hard for her to be sensitively responsive to infant cues, such a baby seems indeed likely to form an attachment relationship of anxious quality.

Mary D. Salter
Ainsworth

Contexts of Mother–Infant Interaction

Of the various contexts in which mother–infant interaction commonly takes place, the face-to-face situation has been the focus of most recent research. By many (e.g., Walters & Parke, 1965), interaction mediated by distance receptors and behaviors has been judged especially important in the establishment of human relationships. Microanalytic studies, based on frame-by-frame analysis of film records, show clearly that maternal sensitivity to infant behavioral cues is essential for successful pacing of face-to-face interaction (e.g., Brazelton, Koslowski, & Main, 1974; Stern, 1974). Telling evidence of the role of vision, both in the infant's development of attachment to the mother and in the mother's responsiveness to the infant, comes from Fraiberg's (1977) longitudinal study of blind infants.

So persuasive have been the studies of interaction involving distance receptors that interaction involving close bodily contact has been largely ignored. The evolutionary perspective of attachment theory attributes focal importance to bodily contact. Other primate species rely on the maintenance of close mother–infant contact as crucial for infant survival. Societies of hunter–gatherers, living much as the earliest humans did, are conspicuous for very much more mother–infant contact than are western societies (e.g., Konner, 1976). Blurton Jones (1972) presented evidence suggesting that humans evolved as a species in which infants are carried by the mother and are fed at frequent intervals, rather than as a species in which infants are left for long periods, are cached in a safe place, and are fed but infrequently. Bowlby (1969) pointed out that when attachment behavior is intensely activated it is close bodily contact that is specifically required. Indeed, Bell and Ainsworth (1972) found that even with the white, middle-class mothers of their sample, the most frequent and the most effective response to an infant's crying throughout the first year was to pick up the baby. A recent analysis of our longitudinal findings (Blehar, Ainsworth, & Main, Note 1) suggests that bodily contact is at least as important a context of interaction as face-to-face is, perhaps especially in the first few months of life. Within the limits represented by our sample, however, we found that it was *how* the mother holds her baby rather than *how much* she holds him or her that affects the way in which attachment develops.

In recent years the feeding situation has been neglected as a context for mother–infant interaction, except insofar as it is viewed as a setting for purely social, face-to-face interaction. Earlier, mother's gratification or frustration of infant interest to both psychoanalytically oriented and social-learning research, on the assumption that a mother's gratification or frustration of infant instinctual drives, or her role as a secondary reinforcer, determined the nature of the baby's tie to her. Such research yielded no evidence that methods of feeding significantly affected the course of infant development, although these negative findings seem almost certainly to reflect methodological deficiencies (Caldwell, 1964). In contrast, we have found that sensitive maternal responsiveness to infant signals relevant to feeding is closely related to the security or anxiety of attachment that eventually develops (Ainsworth & Bell, 1969). Indeed, this analysis seemed to redefine the meaning of "demand" feeding—letting infant behavioral cues determine not only when feeding is begun but also when it is terminated, how the pacing of feeding proceeds, and how new foods are introduced.

Our findings do not permit us to attribute overriding importance to any one context of mother–infant interaction. Whether the context is feeding, close bodily contact, face-to-face interaction, or indeed the situation defined by the infant's crying, mother–infant interaction provides the baby with opportunity to build up expectations of the mother and, eventually, a working model of her as more or less accessible and responsive. Indeed, our findings suggest that a mother who is sensitively responsive to signals in one context tends also to be responsive to signals in other contexts....

Using the Mother as a Secure Base from Which to Explore

Attachment theory conceives of the behavioral system serving attachment as only one of several important systems, each with its own activators, terminators, predictable outcomes, and functions. During the prolonged period of human infancy, when the protective function of attachment is especially important, its interplay with exploratory behavior is noteworthy. The function of exploration is learning about the environment—which is particularly important in a species possessing much potential for adaptation to a wide range of environments. Attachment and exploration support each other. When attachment behavior is intensely activated, a baby tends to seek proximity/contact rather than exploring; when attachment behavior is at low intensity a baby is free to respond to the pull of novelty. The presence of an attachment figure, particularly one who is believed to be accessible and responsive, leaves the baby open to stimulation that may activate exploration.

Nevertheless, it is often believed that somehow attachment may interfere with the development of independence. Our studies provide no support for such a belief. For example, Blehar et al. (Note 1) found that babies who respond positively to close bodily contact with their mothers also tend to respond positively to being put down again and to move off into independent exploratory play. Fostering the growth of secure attachment facilitates rather than hampers the growth of healthy self-reliance (Bowlby, 1973).

Response to Separation from Attachment Figures

Schaffer (1971) suggested that the crucial criterion for whether a baby has become attached to a specific figure is that he or she does not consider this figure interchangeable with any other figure. Thus, for an infant to protest the mother's departure or continued absence is a dependable criterion for attachment (Schaffer & Callender, 1959). This does not imply that protest is an invariable response to separation from an attachment figure under all circumstances; the context of the separation influences the likelihood and intensity of protest. Thus there is ample evidence, which cannot be cited here, that protest is unlikely to occur, at least initially, in the case of voluntary separations, when the infant willingly leaves the mother in order to explore elsewhere. Protest is less likely to occur if the baby is left with another attachment figure than if he or she is left with an unfamiliar person or alone. Being left in an unfamiliar environment is more distressing than comparable separations in the familiar environment of the home—in which many infants are able to build up expectations that reassure them of mother's accessibility and responsiveness even though she may be absent. Changes attributable to developmental processes affect separation protest in complex ways. Further research will undoubtedly be able to account for these shifts in terms of progressive cognitive achievements. . . .

Other Attachment Figures

Many have interpreted Bowlby's attachment theory as claiming that an infant can become attached to only one person—the mother. This is a mistaken interpretation. There are, however, three implications of attachment theory relevent to the issue of "multiple" attachments. First, as reported by Ainsworth (1967) and Schaffer and Emerson (1964), infants are highly selective in their choices of attachment figures from among the various persons familiar to them. No infant has been observed to have many attachment figures. Second, not all social relationships may be identified as attachments. Harlow (1971) distinguished between the infant–mother and peer–peer affectional systems, although under certain circumstances peers may become attachment figures in the absence of anyone more appropriate (see, e.g., Freud & Dann, 1951; Harlow, 1963). Third, the fact that a baby may have several attachment figures does not imply that they are all equally important. Bowlby (1969) suggested that they are not—that there is a principal attachment figure, usually the principal caregiver, and one or more secondary figures. Thus a hierarchy is implied. A baby may both enjoy and derive security from all of his or her attachment figures but, under certain circumstances (e.g., illness, fatigue, stress), is likely to show a clear preference among them.

In recent years there has been a surge of interest in the father as an attachment figure, as reported elsewhere in this issue. Relatively lacking is research into attachments to caregivers other than parents. Do babies become attached to their regular baby-sitters or to caregivers in day-care centers? Studies by Fleener (1973), Farran and Ramey (1977), and Ricciuti (1974) have suggested that they may but that the preference is nevertheless for the mother figure. Fox (1977) compared the mother and the *metapelet* as providers of security to kibbutz-reared infants in a strange situation, but surely much more research is needed into the behavior of infants and young children toward caregivers as attachment figures in the substitute-care environment.

Consequences of Attachment

... In comparison with anxiously attached infants, those who are securely attached as 1-year-olds are later more cooperative with and affectively more positive as well as less aggressive and/or avoidant toward their mothers and other less familiar adults. Later on, they emerge as more competent and more sympathetic in interaction with peers. In free-play situations they have longer bouts of exploration and display more intense exploratory interest, and in problem-solving situations they are more enthusiastic, more persistent, and better able to elicit and accept their mothers' help. They are more curious, more self-directed, more ego-resilient—and they usually tend to achieve better scores on both developmental tests and measures of language development. Some studies also reported differences between the two groups of anxiously attached infants, with the avoidant ones (Group A) continuing to be more aggressive, noncompliant, and avoidant, and the ambivalent ones (Group C) emerging as more easily frustrated, less persistent, and generally less competent.

Conclusion

It is clear that the nature of an infant's attachment to his or her mother as a 1-year-old is related both to earlier interaction with the mother and to various aspects of later development. The implication is that the way in which the infant organizes his or her behavior toward the mother affects the way in which he or she organizes behavior toward other aspects of the environment, both animate and inanimate. This organization provides a core of continuity in development despite changes that come with developmental acquisitions, both cognitive and socioemotional.

NOTES

1. Blehar, M. C., Ainsworth, M. D. S., & Main, M. *Mother–infant interaction relevant to close bodily contact.* Monograph in preparation, 1979.

REFERENCES

Ainsworth, M. D. S. *Infancy in Uganda: Infant care and the growth of love.* Baltimore, Md.: Johns Hopkins Press, 1967.

Ainsworth, M. D. S. Attachment as related to mother–infant interaction. In J. S. Rosenblatt, R. A. Hinde, C. Beer, & M. Busnel (Eds.), *Advances in the study of behavior* (Vol. 9). New York: Academic Press, 1979.

Ainsworth, M. D. S., & Bell, S. M. Some contemporary patterns of mother–infant interaction in the feeding situation. In A. Ambrose (Ed.), *Stimulation in early infancy*. London: Academic Press, 1969.

Ainsworth, M. D. S., Blehar, M. C., Waters, E., & Wall, S. *Patterns of attachment: A psychological study of the strange situation*. Hillsdale, N.J.: Erlbaum, 1978.

Bell, S. M., & Ainsworth, M. D. S. Infant crying and maternal responsiveness. *Child Development*, 1972, *43*, 1171–1190.

Blurton Jones, N. G. Comparative aspects of mother–child contact. In N. G. Blurton Jones (Ed.), *Ethological studies of child behavior*. London: Cambridge University Press, 1972.

Bowlby, J. *Attachment and loss: Vol. 1. Attachment*. New York: Basic Books, 1969.

Bowlby, J. *Attachment and loss: Vol. 2. Separation: Anxiety and anger*. New York: Basic Books, 1973.

Brazelton, T. B., Koslowski, B., & Main, M. The origins of reciprocity: The early mother–infant interaction. In M. Lewis & L. A. Rosenblum (Eds.), *The effect of the infant on its caregiver*. New York: Wiley, 1974.

Caldwell, B. M. The effects of infant care. In M. L. Hoffman & L. W. Hoffman (Eds.), *Review of child development research* (Vol. 1). New York: Russell Sage Foundation, 1964.

Connell, D. B. *Individual differences in attachment: An investigation into stability, implications, and relationships to the structure of early language development*. Unpublished doctoral dissertation, Syracuse University, 1976.

Farran, D. C., & Ramey, C. T. Infant day care and attachment behavior toward mother and teachers. *Child Development*, 1977, *48*, 1112–1116.

Fleener, D. E. Experimental production of infant-maternal attachment behaviors. *Proceedings of the 81st Annual Convention of the American Psychological Association*, 1973, *8*, 57–58. (Summary)

Fox, N. Attachment of kibbutz infants to mother. *Child Development*, 1977, *48*, 1228–1239.

Fraiberg, S. *Insights from the blind*. New York: Basic Books, 1977.

Freud, A., & Dann, S. An experiment in group upbringing. *Psychoanalytic Study of the Child*, 1951, *6*, 127–168.

Harlow, H. F. The maternal affectional system. In B. M. Foss (Ed.), *Determinants of infant behaviour* (Vol. 2) New York: Wiley, 1963.

Harlow, H. F. *Learning to love*. San Francisco: Albion, 1971.

Konner, M. J. Maternal care, infant behavior, and development among the !Kung. In R. B. Lee & I. DeVore (Eds.), *Kalahari hunter–gatherers*. Cambridge, Mass.: Harvard University Press, 1976.

Main, M. Avoidance in the service of proximity. In K. Immelmann, G. Barlow, M. Main, & L. Petrinovich (Eds.), *Behavioral development: The Bielefeld Interdisciplinary Project*. New York: Cambridge University Press, in press.

Ricciuti, H. N. Fear and the development of social attachments in the first year of life. In M. Lewis & L. A. Rosenblum (Eds.), *The origins of fear*. New York: Wiley, 1974.

Schaffer, H. R. *The growth of sociability*. London: Penguin Books, 1971.

Schaffer, H. R., & Callender, W. M. Psychological effects of hospitalization in infancy. *Pediatrics*, 1959, *25*, 528–539.

Schaffer, H. R., & Emerson, P. E. The development of social attachments in infancy. *Monographs of the Society for Research in Child Development*, 1964, *3* (Serial No. 94).

Stayton, D. J., & Ainsworth, M. D. S. Individual differences in infant responses to brief, everyday separations as related to other infant and maternal behaviors. *Developmental Psychology,* 1973, *9,* 226–235.

Stern, D. N. Mother and infant at play: The dyadic interaction involving facial, vocal, and gaze behaviors. In M. Lewis & L. A. Rosenblum (Eds.), *The effect of the infant on its caregiver.* New York: Wiley, 1974.

Walters, R. H., & Parke, R. D. The role of the distance receptors in the development of social responsiveness. In L. P. Lipsitt & C. C. Spiker (Eds.), *Advances in child development and behavior.* New York: Academic Press, 1965.

Waters, E., Vaughn, B. E., & Egeland, B. R. Individual differences in infant–mother attachment relationships at age one: Antecedents in neonatal behavior in an urban economically disadvantaged sample. *Child Development,* in press.

3.3 LAWRENCE KOHLBERG

The Child as a Moral Philosopher

The development of the awareness of ethical behavior, or moral development, is an important part of a child's socialization. Psychologists are therefore interested in how an individual acquires moral reasoning. One important theory, based on three levels of moral thinking, was proposed by Lawrence Kohlberg.

Kohlberg (1927–1987) spent a considerable part of his career studying moral development. He is particularly well known for his 1969 book *Stages in the Development of Moral Thought and Action.*

This selection from "The Child as a Moral Philosopher," which was published in 1968 in *Psychology Today*, gives a very readable account of Kohlberg's theory of moral development. In addition to outlining his theory, Kohlberg describes the results of some cross-cultural research that confirm the generality of his data. Note that the original data were collected only on boys. As you read this selection, consider whether the results are applicable to both sexes or only to males.

Key Concept: moral development

APA Citation: Kohlberg, L. (1968). The child as a moral philosopher. *Psychology Today, 2,* 24–30.

*H*ow can one study morality? Current trends in the fields of ethics, linguistics, anthropology and cognitive psychology have suggested a new approach which seems to avoid the morass of semantical confusions, value-bias and cultural relativity in which the psychoanalytic and semantic approaches to morality have foundered. New scholarship in all these fields is now focusing upon structures, forms and relationships that seem to be common to all societies and all languages rather than upon the features that make particular languages or cultures different.

For 12 years, my colleagues and I studied the same group of 75 boys, following their development at three-year intervals from early adolescence through young manhood. At the start of the study, the boys were aged 10 to 16. We have now followed them through to ages 22 to 28. In addition, I have explored moral development in other cultures—Great Britain, Canada, Taiwan, Mexico and Turkey.

Inspired by Jean Piaget's pioneering effort to apply a structural approach to moral development, I have gradually elaborated over the years of my study a typological scheme describing general structures and forms of moral thought which can be defined independently of the specific content of particular moral decisions or actions.

The typology contains three distinct levels of moral thinking, and within each of these levels distinguishes two related stages. These levels and stages may be considered separate moral philosophies, distinct views of the socio-moral world.

We can speak of the child as having his own morality or series of moralities. Adults seldom listen to children's moralizing. If a child throws back a few adult cliches and behaves himself, most parents—and many anthropologists and psychologists as well—think that the child has adopted or internalized the appropriate parental standards.

Actually, as soon as we talk with children about morality, we find that they have many ways of making judgments which are not "internalized" from the outside, and which do not come in any direct and obvious way from parents, teachers or even peers.

MORAL LEVELS

The *preconventional* level is the first of three levels of moral thinking; the second level is *conventional*, and the third *postconventional* or autonomous. While the preconventional child is often "well-behaved" and is responsive to cultural labels of good and bad, he interprets these labels in terms of their physical consequences (punishment, reward, exchange of favors) or in terms of the physical power of those who enunciate the rules and labels of good and bad.

This level is usually occupied by children aged four to 10, a fact long known to sensitive observers of children. The capacity of "properly behaved" children of this age to engage in cruel behavior when there are holes in the power structure is sometimes noted as tragic (*Lord of the Flies, High Wind in Jamaica*), sometimes as comic (Lucy in *Peanuts*).

The second or *conventional* level also can be described as conformist, but that is perhaps too smug a term. Maintaining the expectations and rules of the individual's family, group or nation is perceived as valuable in its own right. There is a concern not only with *conforming* to the individual's social order but in *maintaining*, supporting and justifying this order.

The *postconventional* level is characterized by a major thrust toward autonomous moral principles which have validity and application apart from authority of the groups or persons who hold them and apart from the individual's identification with those persons or groups.

MORAL STAGES

Within each of these three levels there are two discernible stages. At the preconventional level we have:

Stage 1: Orientation toward punishment and unquestioning deference to superior power. The physical consequences of action regardless of their human meaning or value determine its goodness or badness.

Stage 2: Right action consists of that which instrumentally satisfies one's own needs and occasionally the needs of others. Human relations are viewed in terms like those of the marketplace. Elements of fairness, of reciprocity and equal sharing are present, but they are always interpreted in a physical, pragmatic way. Reciprocity is a matter of "you scratch my back and I'll scratch yours" not of loyalty, gratitude or justice.

And at the conventional level we have:

Stage 3: Good-boy–good-girl orientation. Good behavior is that which pleases or helps others and is approved by them. There is much conformity to stereotypical images of what is majority or "natural" behavior. Behavior is often judged by intention—"he means well" becomes important for the first time, and is overused, as by Charlie Brown in *Peanuts*. One seeks approval by being "nice."

Stage 4: Orientation toward authority, fixed rules and the maintenance of the social order. Right behavior consists of doing one's duty, showing respect for authority and maintaining the given social order for its own sake. One earns respect by performing dutifully.

At the postconventional level, we have:

Stage 5: A social-contract orientation, generally with legalistic and utilitarian overtones. Right action tends to be defined in terms of general rights and in terms of standards which have been critically examined and agreed upon by the whole society. There is a clear awareness of the relativism of personal values and opinions and a corresponding emphasis upon procedural rules for reaching consensus. Aside from what is constitutionally and democratically agreed upon, right or wrong is a matter of personal "values" and "opinion." The result is an emphasis upon the "legal point of view," but with an emphasis upon the possibility of *changing* law in terms of rational considerations of social utility, rather than freezing it in the terms of Stage 4 "law and order." Outside the legal realm, free agreement and contract are the binding elements of obligation. This is the "official" morality of American government, and finds its ground in the thought of the writers of the Constitution.

Stage 6: Orientation toward the decisions of conscience and toward self-chosen *ethical principles* appealing to logical comprehensiveness, universality and consistency. These principles are abstract and ethical (the Golden Rule, the categorical imperative); they are not concrete moral rules like the Ten Commandments. Instead, they are universal principles of *justice,* of the *reciprocity* and *equality* of human rights, and of respect for the dignity of human beings as *individual persons....*

MORAL REASONS

In our research, we have found definite and universal levels of development in moral thought. In our study of 75 American boys from early adolescence on, these youths were presented hypothetical moral dilemmas, all deliberately philosophical, some of them found in medieval works of casuistry.

On the basis of their reasoning about these dilemmas at a given age, each boy's stage of thought could be determined for each of 25 basic moral concepts or aspects. One such aspect, for instance, is "Motive Given for Rule Obedience or Moral Action." In this instance, the six stages look like this:

1. Obey rules to avoid punishment.
2. Conform to obtain rewards, have favors returned, and so on.
3. Conform to avoid disapproval, dislike by others.
4. Conform to avoid censure by legitimate authorities and resultant guilt.
5. Conform to maintain the respect of the impartial spectator judging in terms of community welfare.
6. Conform to avoid self-condemnation.

In another of these 25 moral aspects, the value of human life, the six stages can be defined thus:

1. The value of a human life is confused with the value of physical objects and is based on the social status or physical attributes of its possessor.
2. The value of a human life is seen as instrumental to the satisfaction of the needs of its possessor or of other persons.
3. The value of a human life is based on the empathy and affection of family members and others toward its possessor.
4. Life is conceived as sacred in terms of its place in a categorical moral or religious order of rights and duties.
5. Life is valued both in terms of its relation to community welfare and in terms of life being a universal human right.
6. Belief in the sacredness of human life as representing a universal human value of respect for the individual.

I have called this scheme a typology. This is because about 50 per cent of most people's thinking will be at a single stage, regardless of the moral dilemma involved. We call our types *stages* because they seem to represent an *invariant developmental sequence.* "True" stages come one at a time and always in the same order.

All movement is forward in sequence, and does not skip steps. Children may move through these stages at varying speeds, of course, and may be found half in and half out of a particular stage. An individual may stop at any given stage and at any age, but if he continues to move, he must move in accord with these steps. Moral reasoning of the conventional or Stage 3–4 kind never occurs before the preconventional Stage-1 and Stage-2 thought has taken place. No adult in Stage 4 has gone through Stage 6, but all Stage-6 adults have gone at least through 4.

While the evidence is not complete, my study strongly suggests that moral change fits the stage pattern just described. (The major uncertainty is whether all Stage 6s go through Stage 5 or whether these are two alternate mature orientations.) . . .

ACROSS CULTURES

When I first decided to explore moral development in other cultures, I was told by anthropologist friends that I would have to throw away my culture-bound moral concepts and stories and start from scratch learning a whole new set of values for each new culture. My first try consisted of a brace of villages, one Atayal (Malaysian aboriginal) and the other Taiwanese.

My guide was a young Chinese ethnographer who had written an account of the moral and religious patterns of the Atayal and Taiwanese villages. Taiwanese boys in the 10–13 age group were asked about a story involving theft of food. A man's wife is starving to death but the store owner won't give the man any food unless he can pay, which he can't. Should he break in and steal some food? Why? Many of the boys said, "He should steal the food for his wife because if she dies he'll have to pay for her funeral and that costs a lot."

My guide was amused by these responses, but I was relieved: they were of course "classic" Stage-2 responses. In the Atayal village, funerals weren't such a big thing, so the Stage-2 boys would say, "He should steal the food because he needs his wife to cook for him."

This means that we need to consult our anthropologists to know what content a Stage-2 child will include in his instrumental exchange calculations, or what a Stage-4 adult will identify as the proper social order. But one certainly doesn't have to start from scratch. What made my guide laugh was the difference in form between the children's Stage-2 thought and his own, a difference definable independently of particular cultures. . . .

In summary, the nature of our sequence is not significantly affected by widely varying social, cultural or religious conditions. The only thing that is affected is the *rate* at which individuals progress through this sequence.

Why should there be such a universal invariant sequence of development? In answering this question, we need first to analyze these developing social concepts in terms of their internal logical structure. At each stage, the same basic moral concept or aspect is defined, but at each higher stage this definition is more differentiated, more integrated and more general or universal. When one's concept of human life moves from Stage 1 to Stage 2 the value of life becomes more differentiated from the value of property, more integrated (the value of life enters an organizational hierarchy where it is "higher" than property so that one steals property in order to save life) and more universalized (the life of any sentient being is valuable regardless of status or property). The same advance is true at each stage in the hierarchy. Each step of development then is a better cognitive organization than the one before it, one which takes account of everything present in the previous stage, but making new distinctions and organizing them into a more comprehensive or more equilibrated structure. The fact that this is the case has been demonstrated by a series of studies indicating that children and adolescents comprehend all stages up to their own, but not more than one stage beyond their own. And importantly, *they prefer this next stage.*

We have conducted experimental moral discussion classes which show that the child at an earlier stage of development tends to move forward when confronted by the views of a child one stage further along. In an argument between a Stage-3 and Stage-4 child, the child in the third stage tends to move toward or into Stage 4, while the Stage-4 child understands but does not accept the arguments of the Stage-3 child.

Moral thought, then, seems to behave like all other kinds of thought. Progress through the moral levels and stages is characterized by increasing differentiation and increasing integration, and hence is the same kind of progress that scientific theory represents. Like acceptable scientific theory—or like *any* theory or structure of knowledge—moral thought may be considered partially to generate its own data as it goes along, or at least to expand so as to contain in a balanced, self-consistent way a wider and wider experiential field. The raw data in the case of our ethical philosophies may be considered as conflicts between roles, or values, or as the social order in which men live.

3.4 ELEANOR E. MACCOBY

Gender and Relationships: A Developmental Account

Psychologists have shown increasing interest in gender differences during the past two decades. Much of the research that has been conducted has focused on individual differences, such as cognitive abilities, mathematical problem-solving skills, emotional expression, and verbal skills. Leading developmental psychologist Eleanor E. Maccoby has argued that focusing on individual differences obscures important dimensions of gender differences in social relationships.

Maccoby (b. 1917) earned her Ph.D. in experimental psychology from the University of Michigan in 1950. She worked in the Laboratory of Human Development at Harvard University until 1958 and then moved to Stanford University, where she is currently a professor emeritus. Among her many publications are the classic book *The Psychology of Sex Differences* (Stanford University Press, 1974), coauthored by Carol Jacklin and the recent book *The Two Sexes: Growing Up Apart, Coming Together* (Belknap Press of Harvard University Press, 1998).

This selection is from "Gender and Relationships: A Developmental Account," which was published in *American Psychologist* in 1990. In it, Maccoby argues that behavioral sex differences are minimal when children are tested individually but that they appear in social situations. One important finding is that children prefer same-sex play partners and often segregate themselves in social settings. Note how the distinctive interactive styles that develop in same-sex groups are carried over into mixed-sex group interactions. How can a better understanding of these gender differences help in everyday social interactions?

Key Concept: gender and social relationships

APA Citation: Maccoby, E. E. (1990). Gender and relationships: A developmental account. *American Psychologist, 45,* 513–520.

*H*istorically, the way we psychologists think about the psychology of gender has grown out of our thinking about individual differences. We are accustomed to assessing a wide variety of attributes and skills and giving scores to individuals based on their standing relative to other individuals in a sample population. On most psychological attributes, we see wide variation among individuals, and a major focus of research has been the effort to identify correlates or sources of this variation. Commonly, what we have done is to classify individuals by some antecedent variable, such as age or some aspect of their environment, to determine how much of the variance among individuals in their performance on a given task can be accounted for by this so-called *antecedent* or *independent* variable. Despite the fact that hermaphrodites exist, almost every individual is either clearly male or clearly female. What could be more natural for psychologists than to ask how much variance among individuals is accounted for by this beautifully binary factor?

Fifteen years ago, Carol Jacklin and I put out a book summarizing the work on sex differences that had come out of the individual differences perspective (Maccoby & Jacklin, 1974). We felt at that time that the yield was thin. That is, there were very few attributes on which the average values for the two sexes differed consistently. Furthermore, even when consistent differences were found, the amount of variance accounted for by sex was small, relative to the amount of variation within each sex. Our conclusions fitted in quite well with the feminist zeitgeist of the times, when most feminists were taking a minimalist position, urging that the two sexes were basically alike and that any differences were either illusions in the eye of the beholder or reversible outcomes of social shaping. Our conclusions were challenged as having both overstated the case for sex differences (Tieger, 1980) and for having understated it (Block, 1976).

In the last 15 years, work on sex differences has become more methodologically sophisticated, with greater use of meta analyses to reveal not only the direction of sex differences but quantitative estimates of their magnitude. In my judgment, the conclusions are still quite similar to those Jacklin and I arrived at in 1974: There are still some replicable sex differences, of moderate magnitude, in performance on tests of mathematical and spatial abilities, although sex differences in verbal abilities have faded. Other aspects of intellectual performance continue to show gender equality. When it comes to attributes in the personality-social domain, results are particularly sparse and inconsistent. Studies continue to find that men are more often agents of aggression than are women (Eagly, 1987; Huston, 1985; Maccoby & Jacklin, 1980). Eagly (1983, 1987) reported in addition that women are more easily influenced than men and that men are more altruistic in the sense that they are more likely to offer help to others. In general, however, personality traits measured as characteristics of individuals do not appear to differ systematically by sex (Huston, 1985). This no doubt reflects in part the fact that male and female persons really are much alike, and their lives are governed mainly by the attributes that all persons in a given culture have in common. Nevertheless, I believe that the null findings coming out of comparisons of male and female individuals on personality measures are partly illusory. That is, they are an artifact of our historical reliance on an individual differences perspective. Social behavior, as many have pointed out, is never a function of the individual alone. It is a function of the interaction between two or more persons. Individuals behave differently with different partners. There are certain important ways in which gender is implicated in social behavior—ways that may be obscured or missed altogether when behavior is summed across all categories of social partners.

An illustration is found in a study of social interaction between previously unacquainted pairs of young children (mean age, 33 months; Jacklin & Maccoby, 1978). In some pairs, the children had same-sex play partners; in others, the pair was made up of a boy and a girl. Observers recorded the social behavior of each child on a time-sampling basis. Each child received a score for total social behavior directed toward the partner. This score included both positive and negative behaviors (e .g., offering a toy and grabbing a toy; hugging and pushing; vocally greeting, inviting, protesting, or prohibiting). There was no overall sex difference in the amount of social behavior when this was evaluated without regard to sex of partner. But there was a powerful interaction between sex of the subject and that of the partner: Children of each sex had much higher levels of social behavior when playing with a same-sex partner than when playing with a child of the other sex. This result is consistent with the findings of Wasserman and Stern (1978) that when asked to approach another child, children as young as age three stopped farther away when the other child was of the opposite sex, indicating awareness of gender similarity or difference, and wariness toward the other sex.

The number of time intervals during which a child was simply standing passively watching the partner play with the toys was also scored. There was no overall sex difference in the frequency of this behavior, but the behavior of girls was greatly affected by the sex of the partner. With other girls, passive behavior seldom occurred; indeed, in girl-girl pairs it occurred less often than it did in boy-boy pairs. However when paired with boys, girls frequently stood on the sidelines and let the boys monopolize the toys. Clearly, the little girls in this study were not more passive than the little boys in any overall, trait-like sense. Passivity in these girls could be understood only in relation to the characteristics of their interactive partners. It was a characteristic of girls in cross-sex dyads. This conclusion may not seem especially novel because for many years we have known that social behavior is situationally specific. However, the point here is that interactive behavior is not just situationally specific, but that it depends on the gender category membership of the participants. We can account for a good deal more of the behavior if we know the gender mix of dyads, and this probably holds true for larger groups as well.

An implication of our results was that if children at this early age found same-sex play partners more compatible, they ought to prefer same-sex partners when they entered group settings that included children of both sexes. There were already many indications in the literature that children do have same-sex playmate preferences, but there clearly was a need for more systematic attention to the degree of sex segregation that prevails in naturally occurring children's groups at different ages. As part of a longitudinal study of children from birth to age six, Jacklin and I did time-sampled behavioral observation of approximately 100 children on their preschool playgrounds, and again two years later when the children were playing during school recess periods (Maccoby & Jacklin, 1987). Same-sex playmate preference was clearly apparent in preschool when the children were approximately 4½. At this age, the children were spending nearly 3 times as much time with same-sex play partners as with children of the other sex. By age 6½, the preference had grown much stronger. At this time, the children were spending 11 times as much time with same-sex as with opposite-sex partners.

Elsewhere we have reviewed the literature on playmate choices (Maccoby, 1988; Maccoby & Jacklin, 1987), and here I will simply summarize what I believe the existing body of research shows:

1. Gender segregation is a widespread phenomenon. It is found in all the cultural settings in which children are in social groups large enough to permit choice.
2. The sex difference in the gender of preferred playmates is large in absolute magnitude, compared to sex differences found when children are observed or tested in nonsocial situations.
3. In a few instances, attempts have been made to break down children's preferences for interacting with other same-sex children. It has been found that the preferences are difficult to change.
4. Children choose same-sex playmates spontaneously in situations in which they are not under pressure from adults to do so. In modern co-educational schools, segregation is more marked in situations that have not been structured by adults than in those that have (e.g., Eisenhart & Holland, 1983). Segregation is situationally specific, and the two sexes can interact comfortably under certain conditions, for example, in an absorbing joint task, when structures and roles are set up by adults, or in nonpublic settings (Thorne, 1986).
5. Gender segregation is not closely linked to involvement in sex-typed activities. Preschool children spend a great deal of their time engaged in activities that are gender neutral, and segregation prevails in these activities as well as when they are playing with dolls or trucks.
6. Tendencies to prefer same-sex playmates can be seen among three-year-olds and at even earlier ages under some conditions. But the preferences increase in strength between preschool and school and are maintained at a high level between the ages of 6 and at least age 11.
7. The research base is thin, but so far it appears that a child's tendency to prefer same-sex playmates has little to do with that child's standing on measures of individual differences. In particular, it appears to be unrelated to measures of masculinity or femininity and also to measures of gender schematicity (Powlishta, 1989).

Why do we see such pronounced attraction to same-sex peers and avoidance of other-sex peers in childhood? [E]vidence point[s] to two factors that seem to be important in the preschool years (Maccoby, 1988). The first is the rough-and-tumble play style characteristic of boys and their orientation toward issues of competition and dominance. These aspects of male–male interaction appear to be somewhat aversive to most girls. At least, girls are made wary by male play styles. The second factor of importance is that girls find it difficult to influence boys. Some important work by Serbin and colleagues (Serbin, Sprafkin, Elman, & Doyle, 1984) indicates that between the ages of 3½ and 5½, children greatly increase the frequency of their attempts to influence their play partners. This indicates that children are learning to integrate their activities with those of others so as to be able to carry out coordinated activities. Serbin and colleagues found that the increase in influence attempts by girls was almost entirely an increase in making polite suggestions to others, whereas among boys the increase took the form of more use of direct demands. Furthermore, during this formative two-year period just before school entry, boys were becoming less and less responsive to polite suggestions, so that the style being progressively adopted by girls was progressively less effective with boys. Girls' influence style was effective with each other and was well adapted to interaction with teachers and other adults.

These asymmetries in influence patterns were presaged in our study with 33-month-old children: We found then that boys were unresponsive to the vocal prohibitions of female partners (in that they did not withdraw), although they would respond when a vocal prohibition was issued by a male partner. Girls were responsive to one another and to a male partner's prohibitions. Fagot (1985) also reported that boys are "reinforced" by the reactions of male peers— in the sense that they modify their behavior following a male peer's reaction— but that their behavior appears not to be affected by a female's response.

My hypothesis is that girls find it aversive to try to interact with someone who is unresponsive and that they begin to avoid such partners. Students of power and bargaining have long been aware of the importance of reciprocity in human relations. Pruitt (1976) said, "Influence and power are omnipresent in human affairs. Indeed, groups cannot possibly function unless their members can influence one another" (p. 343). From this standpoint, it becomes clear why boys and girls have difficulty forming groups that include children of both sexes.

Why do little boys not accept influence from little girls? Psychologists almost automatically look to the nuclear family for the origins of behavior patterns seen in young children. It is plausible that boys may have been more reinforced for power assertive behavior by their parents, and girls more for politeness, although the evidence for such differential socialization pressure has proved difficult to come by. However, it is less easy to imagine how or why parents should reinforce boys for being unresponsive to *girls*. Perhaps it is a matter of observational learning: Children may have observed that between their two parents, their fathers are more influential than their mothers. I am skeptical about such an explanation. In the first place, mothers exercise a good deal of managerial authority within the households in which children live, and it is common for fathers to defer to their judgment in matters concerning the children. Or, parents form a coalition, and in the eyes of the children they become a joint authority, so that it makes little difference to them whether it is a mother or a father who is wielding authority at any given time. Furthermore, the asymmetry in children's cross-sex influence with their peers appears to have its origins at quite an early age—earlier, I would suggest, than children have a very clear idea about the connection between their own sex and that of the same-sex parent. In other words, it seems quite unlikely that little boys ignore girls' influence attempts because little girls remind them of their mothers. I think we simply do not know why girls' influence styles are ineffective with boys, but the fact that they are has important implications for a variety of social behaviors, not just for segregation.

Here are some examples from recent studies. Powlishta (1987) observed preschool-aged boy–girl pairs competing for a scarce resource. The children were brought to a playroom in the nursery school and were given an opportunity to watch cartoons through a movie-viewer that could only be accessed by one child at a time. Powlishta found that when the two children were alone together in the playroom, the boys got more than their share of access to the movie-viewer. When there was an adult present, however, this was no longer the case. The adult's presence appeared to inhibit the boys' more power-assertive techniques and resulted in girls having at least equal access.

This study points to a reason why girls may not only avoid playing with boys but may also stay nearer to a teacher or other adult. Following up on this possibility, Greeno (1989) brought four-child groups of kindergarten and first-grade children into a large playroom equipped with attractive toys. Some of the quartets were all-boy groups, some all-girl groups, and some were made up of two boys and two girls. A female adult sat at one end of the room, and halfway through the play session, moved to a seat at the other end of the room. The question posed for this study was: Would girls move closer to the teacher when boys were present than when they were not? Would the sex composition of a play group make any difference to the locations taken up by the boys? The results were that in all-girl groups, girls actually took up locations *farther* from the adult than did boys in all-boy groups. When two boys were present, however, the two girls were significantly closer to the adult than were the boys, who tended to remain at intermediate distances. When the adult changed position halfway through the session, boys' locations did not change, and this was true whether there were girls present or not. Girls in all-girl groups tended to move in the opposite direction when the adult moved, maintaining distance between themselves and the adult; when boys were present, however, the girls tended to move *with* the adult, staying relatively close. It is worth noting, incidentally, that in all the mixed-sex groups except one, segregation was extreme; both boys and girls behaved as though there was only one playmate available to them, rather than three.

There are some fairly far-reaching implications of this study. Previous observational studies in preschools had indicated that girls are often found in locations closer to the teacher than are boys. These studies have been done in mixed-sex nursery school groups. Girls' proximity seeking toward adults has often been interpreted as a reflection of some general affiliative trait in girls and perhaps as a reflection of some aspect of early socialization that has bound them more closely to caregivers. We see in the Greeno study that proximity seeking toward adults was *not* a general trait in girls. It was a function of the gender composition of the group of other children present as potential interaction partners. The behavior of girls implied that they found the presence of boys to be less aversive when an adult was nearby. It was as though they realized that the rough, power-assertive behavior of boys was likely to be moderated in the presence of adults, and indeed, there is evidence that they were right.

We have been exploring some aspects of girls' avoidance of interaction with boys. Less is known about why boys avoid interaction with girls, but the fact is that they do. In fact, their cross-sex avoidance appears to be even stronger. Thus, during middle childhood both boys and girls spend considerable portions of their social play time in groups of their own sex. This might not matter much for future relationships were it not for the fact that fairly distinctive styles of interaction develop in all-boy and all-girl groups. Thus, the segregated play groups constitute powerful socialization environments in which children acquire distinctive interaction skills that are adapted to same-sex partners. Sex-typed modes of interaction become consolidated, and I wish to argue that the distinctive patterns developed by the two sexes at this time have implications for the same-sex and cross-sex relationships that individuals form as they enter adolescence and adulthood.

It behooves us, then, to examine in somewhat more detail the nature of the interactive milieus that prevail in all-boy and all-girl groups. Elsewhere I have reviewed some of the findings of studies in which these two kinds of groups have been observed (Maccoby, 1988). Here I will briefly summarize what we know.

The two sexes engage in fairly different kinds of activities and games (Huston, 1985). Boys play in somewhat larger groups, on the average, and their play is rougher (Humphreys & Smith, 1987) and takes up more space. Boys more often play in the streets and other public places; girls more often congregate in private homes or yards. Girls tend to form close, intimate friendships with one or two other girls, and these friendships are marked by the sharing of confidences (Kraft & Vraa, 1975). Boys' friendships, on the other hand, are more oriented around mutual interests in activities (Erwin, 1985). The breakup of girls' friendships is usually attended by more intense emotional reactions than is the case for boys.

For our present purposes, the most interesting thing about all-boy and all-girl groups is the divergence in the interactive styles that develop in them. In male groups, there is more concern with issues of dominance. Several psycholinguists have recorded the verbal exchanges that occur in these groups, and Maltz and Borker (1983) summarized the findings of several studies as follows: Boys in their groups are more likely than girls in all-girl groups to interrupt one another; use commands, threats, or boasts of authority; refuse to comply with another child's demand; give information; heckle a speaker; tell jokes or suspenseful stories; top someone else's story; or call another child names. Girls in all-groups, on the other hand, are more likely than boys to express agreement with what another speaker has just said, pause to give another girl a chance to speak, or when starting a speaking turn, acknowledge a point previously made by another speaker. This account indicates that among boys, speech serves largely egoistic functions and is used to establish and protect an individual's turf. Among girls, conversation is a more socially binding process.

In the past five years, analysts of discourse have done additional work on the kinds of interactive processes that are seen among girls, as compared with those among boys. The summary offered by Maltz and Borker has been both supported and extended. Sachs (1987) reported that girls soften their directives to partners, apparently attempting to keep them involved in a process of planning a play sequence, while boys are more likely simply to tell their partners what to do. Leaper (1989) observed children aged five and seven and found that verbal exchanges among girls more often take the form of what he called "collaborative speech acts" that involve positive reciprocity, whereas among boys, speech acts are more controlling and include more negative reciprocity. Miller and colleagues (Miller, Danaher, & Forbes, 1986) found that there was more conflict in boys' groups, and given that conflict had occurred, girls were more likely to use "conflict mitigating strategies," whereas boys more often used threats and physical force. Sheldon (1989) reported that when girls talk, they seem to have a double agenda: to be "nice" and sustain social relationships, while at the same time working to achieve their own individual ends. For boys, the agenda is more often the single one of self-assertion. Sheldon (1989) has noted that in interactions among themselves, girls are *not* unassertive. Rather, girls do successfully pursue their own ends, but they do so while toning down coercion and dominance, trying to bring about agreement, and restoring or maintaining group functioning. It should be noted that boys' confrontational style does not necessarily impede effective group functioning, as evidenced by boys' ability to cooperate with teammates for sports. A second point is that although researchers' own gender has been found to influence to some degree the kinds of questions posed and the answers obtained, the summary provided here includes the work of both male and female researchers, and their findings are consistent with one another.

As children move into adolescence and adulthood, what happens to the interactive styles that they developed in their largely segregated childhood groups? A first point to note is that despite the powerful attraction to members of the opposite sex in adolescence, gender segregation by no means disappears. Young people continue to spend a good portion of their social time with same-sex partners. In adulthood, there is extensive gender segregation in workplaces (Reskin, 1984), and in some societies and some social-class or ethnic groups, leisure time also is largely spent with same-sex others even after marriage. The literature on the nature of the interactions that occur among same-sex partners in adolescence and adulthood is quite extensive and cannot be reviewed here. Suffice it to say in summary that there is now considerable evidence that the interactive patterns found in sex-homogeneous dyads or groups in adolescence and adulthood are very similar to those that prevailed in the gender-segregated groups of childhood (e.g., Aries, 1976; Carli, 1989; Cowan, Drinkard, & MacGavin, 1984; Savin-Williams, 1979).

How can we summarize what it is that boys and girls, or men and women, are doing in their respective groups that distinguishes these groups from one another? There have been a number of efforts to find the major dimensions that best describe variations in interactive styles. Falbo and Peplau (1980) have factor analyzed a battery of measures and have identified two dimensions: one called direct versus indirect, the other unilateral versus bilateral. Hauser et al. (1987) have distinguished what they called *enabling* interactive styles from *constricting* or *restrictive* ones, and I believe this distinction fits the styles of the two sexes especially well. A restrictive style is one that tends to derail the interaction —to inhibit the partner or cause the partner to withdraw, thus shortening the interaction or bringing it to an end. Examples are threatening a partner, directly contradicting or interrupting, topping the partner's story, boasting, or engaging in other forms of self-display. Enabling or facilitative styles are those, such as acknowledging another's comment or expressing agreement, that support whatever the partner is doing and tend to keep the interaction going. I want to suggest that it is because women and girls use more enabling styles that they are able to form more intimate and more integrated relationships. Also I think it likely that it is the male concern for turf and dominance—that is, with not showing weakness to other men and boys—that underlies their restrictive interaction style and their lack of self-disclosure.

Eleanor E. Maccoby

REFERENCES

Aries, E. (1976). Interaction patterns and themes of male, female, and mixed groups. *Small Group Behavior, 7,* 7–18.

Block J. H. (1976). Debatable conclusions about sex differences. *Contemporary Psychology, 21,* 517–522.

Carli, L. L. (1989). Gender differences in interaction style and influence. *Journal of Personality and Social Psychology, 56,* 565–576.

Cowan, C., Drinkard, J., & MacGavin, L. (1984). The effects of target, age and gender on use of power strategies. *Journal of Personality and Social Psychology, 47,* 1391–1398.

Eagly, A. H. (1983). Gender and social influence. *American Psychologist, 38,* 971–981.

Eagly, A. H. (1987). *Sex differences in social behavior: A social role interpretation.* Hillsdale, NJ: Erlbaum.

Eisenhart, M. A., & Holland, D. C. (1983). Learning gender from peers: The role of peer group in the cultural transmission of gender. *Human Organization, 42,* 321–332.

Erwin. P. (1985). Similarity of attitudes and constructs in children's friendships. *Journal of Experimental Child Psychology, 40,* 470–485.

Fagot, B. I. (1985). Beyond the reinforcement principle: Another step toward understanding sex roles. *Developmental Psychology, 21,* 1097–1104.

Falbo, T., & Peplau, L. A. (1980). Power strategies in intimate relationships. *Journal of Personality and Social Psychology, 38,* 618–628.

Greeno, C. G. (1989). *Gender differences in children's proximity to adults.* Unpublished doctoral dissertation, Stanford University, Stanford, CA.

Hauser, S. T., Powers, S. I., Weiss-Perry, B., Follansbee, D. J., Rajapark, D., & Greene, W. M. (1987). *The constraining and enabling coding system manual.* Unpublished manuscript.

Humphreys, A. P., & Smith, P. K. (1987). Rough and tumble friendship and dominance in school children: Evidence for continuity and change with age in middle childhood. *Child Development, 58,* 201–212.

Huston, A. C. (1985). The development of sex-typing: Themes from recent research. *Developmental Review, 5,* 1–17.

Jacklin, C. N., & Maccoby, E. E. (1978). Social behavior at 33 months in same-sex and mixed-sex dyads. *Child Development, 49,* 557–569.

Kraft, L. W., & Vraa, C. W. (1975). Sex composition of groups and pattern of self-disclosure by high school females. *Psychological Reports, 37,* 733–734.

Leaper, C. (1989). *The sequencing of power and involvement in boys' and girls' talk.* Unpublished manuscript (under review), University of California, Santa Cruz.

Maccoby, E. E. (1988). Gender as a social category. *Developmental Psychology, 26,* 755–765.

Maccoby, E. E., & Jacklin, C. N. (1974). *The psychology of sex differences.* Stanford, CA: Stanford University Press.

Maccoby, E. E., & Jacklin, C. N. (1980). Sex differences in aggression: A rejoinder and reprise. *Child Development, 51,* 964–980.

Maccoby, E. E., & Jacklin, C. N. (1987). Gender segregation in childhood. In H. W. Reese (Ed.), *Advances in child development and behavior* (Vol. 20, pp. 239–288). New York: Academic Press.

Maltz, D. N., & Borker, R. A. (1983). A cultural approach to male-female miscommunication. In John A. Gumperz (Ed.), *Language and social identity* (pp. 195–216). New York: Cambridge University Press.

Miller, P., Danaher, D., & Forbes. D. (1986). Sex-related strategies for coping with interpersonal conflict in children aged five and seven. *Developmental Psychology, 22* 543–548.

Powlishta, K. K. (1987, April). *The social context of cross-sex interactions.* Paper presented at biennial meeting of the Society for Research in Child Development, Baltimore, MD.

Powlishta, K. K. (1989). *Salience of group membership: The case of gender.* Unpublished doctoral dissertation, Stanford University, Stanford, CA.

Pruitt, D. G. (1976). Power and bargaining. In B. Seidenberg & A. Snadowsky (Eds.), *Social psychology: An introduction* (pp. 343–375). New York: Free Press.

Reskin, B. F. (Ed.). (1984). *Sex segregation in the workplace: Trends, explanations and remedies.* Washington, DC: National Academy Press.

Sachs, J. (1987). Preschool boys' and girls' language use in pretend play. In S. U. Phillips, S. Steele, & C. Tanz (Eds.), *Language, gender and sex in comparative perspective* (pp. 178–188). Cambridge, England: Cambridge University Press.

Savin-Williams, R. C. (1979). Dominance hierarchies in groups of early adolescents. *Child Development, 50,* 923–935.

Serbin, L. A., Sprafkin, C., Elman, M., & Doyle, A. (1984). The early development of sex differentiated patterns of social influence. *Canadian Journal of Social Science, 14,* 350–363.

Sheldon, A. (1989, April). *Conflict talk: Sociolinguistic challenges to self-assertion and how young girls meet them.* Paper presented at the biennial meeting of the Society for Research in Child Development, Kansas City.

Thorne, B. (1986). Girls and boys together, but mostly apart. In W. W. Hartup & L. Rubin (Eds.), *Relationships and development* (pp. 167–184). Hillsdale, NJ: Erlbaum.

Tieger, T. (1980). On the biological basis of sex differences in aggression. *Child Development, 51,* 943–963.

Wasserman, G. A., & Stern, D. N. (1978). An early manifestation of differential behavior toward children of the same and opposite sex. *Journal of Genetic Psychology, 133,* 129–137.

PART TWO

Perceptual Processes

On the Internet . . .

Sites appropriate to Part Two

The *Joy of Visual Perception,* a Web book by Peter Kaiser of York University is presented on this site.

    http://www.yorku.ca/eye/

A series of visual illusions created by Dr. David Landrigan, University of Massachusetts–Lowell.

    http://dragon.uml.edu/psych/illusion.html

Sources on the Internet for the scientific study of consciousness are listed on this site.

    http://www.phil.vt.edu/ASSC/resources.html

The Sleep Home Pages are maintained by WebSciences, Brain Information Service.

    http://bisleep.medsch.ucla.edu

SleepNet provides resources and information on sleep disorders.

    http://www.sleepnet.com

CHAPTER 4 Sensation and Perception

4.1 ELEANOR J. GIBSON AND RICHARD D. WALK

The "Visual Cliff"

Vision is an important sense for humans, and psychologists believe that knowledge of how visual perception develops in infants can help us understand its role in a child's adjustment. Psychologists have also shown interest in depth perception (the ability to perceive distance to an object) because it can shed light on the importance of heredity and environment in human development. Experimental psychologists Eleanor J. Gibson and Richard D. Walk developed the "visual cliff" described in this selection to study depth perception in human infants and young animals.

Gibson (b. 1910) earned her Ph.D. in experimental psychology from Yale University in 1938. She taught at Smith College until 1949 and then went to Cornell University, where she is currently a professor emeritus. Walk (b. 1920) received his Ph.D. in experimental psychology from Harvard University in 1951. He taught psychology at George Washington University until his retirement in 1991.

This selection is from "The 'Visual Cliff,'" which was published in *Scientific American* in 1960. The "visual cliff" that Gibson and Walk devised allowed them to test depth perception in infants as soon as they could crawl. As you read this selection, consider the degree to which heredity and experience might determine depth perception. Also, why do you think the experimenters tested animals in addition to humans?

Key Concept: the "visual cliff" and depth perception

APA Citation: Gibson, E. J., & Walk, R. D. (1960). The "visual cliff." *Scientific American, 202,* 67–71.

87

*H*uman infants at the creeping and toddling stage are notoriously prone to falls from more or less high places. They must be kept from going over the brink by side panels on their cribs, gates on stairways and the vigilance of adults. As their muscular coordination matures they begin to avoid such accidents on their own. Common sense might suggest that the child learns to recognize falling-off places by experience—that is, by falling and hurting himself. But is experience really the teacher? Or is the ability to perceive and avoid a brink part of the child's original endowment?

Answers to these questions will throw light on the genesis of space perception in general. Height perception is a special case of distance perception: information in the light reaching the eye provides stimuli that can be utilized for the discrimination both of depth and or receding distance on the level. At what stage of development can an animal respond effectively to these stimuli? Does the onset of such response vary with animals of different species and habitats?

At Cornell University we have been investigating these problems by means of a simple experimental setup that we call a visual cliff. The cliff is a simulated one and hence makes it possible not only to control the optical and other stimuli (auditory and tactual, for instance) but also to protect the experimental subjects. It consists of a board laid across a large sheet of heavy glass which is supported a foot or more above the floor. On one side of the board a sheet of patterned material is placed flush against the undersurface of the glass, giving the glass the appearance as well as the substance of solidity. On the other side a sheet of the same material is laid upon the floor; this side of the board thus becomes the visual cliff.

We tested 36 infants ranging in age from six months to 14 months on the visual cliff. Each child was placed upon the center board, and his mother called him to her from the cliff side and the shallow side successively. All of the 27 infants who moved off the board crawled out on the shallow side at least once; only three of them crept off the brink onto the glass suspended above the pattern on the floor. Many of the infants crawled away from the mother when she called to them from the cliff side; others cried when she stood there, because they could not come to her without crossing an apparent chasm. The experiment thus demonstrated that most human infants can discriminate depth as soon as they can crawl.

The behavior of the children in this situation gave clear evidence of their dependence on vision. Often they would peer down through the glass on the deep side and then back away. Others would pat the glass with their hands, yet despite this tactual assurance of solidity would refuse to cross. It was equally clear that their perception of depth had matured more rapidly than had their locomotor abilities. Many supported themselves on the glass over the deep side as they maneuvered awkwardly on the board; some even backed out onto the glass as they started toward the mother on the shallow side. Were it not for the glass some of the children would have fallen off the board. Evidently infants should not be left close to a brink, no matter how well they may discriminate depth.

Eleanor J. Gibson and Richard D. Walk

This experiment does not prove that the human infant's perception and avoidance of the cliff are innate. Such an interpretation is supported, however, by the experiments with nonhuman infants. On the visual cliff we have observed the behavior of chicks, turtles, rats, lambs, kids, pigs, kittens and dogs. These animals showed various reactions, each of which proved to be characteristic of their species. In each case the reaction is plainly related to the role of vision in the survival of the species, and the varied patterns of behavior suggest something about the role of vision in evolution.

In the chick, for example, depth perception manifests itself with special rapidity. At an age of less than 24 hours the chick can be tested on the visual cliff. It never makes a "mistake" and always hops off the board on the shallow side. Without doubt this finding is related to the fact that the chick, unlike many other young birds, must scratch for itself a few hours after it is hatched.

Kids and lambs, like chicks, can be tested on the visual cliff as soon as they can stand. The response of these animals is equally predictable. No goat or lamb ever stepped onto the glass of the deep side, even at one day of age. When one of these animals was placed upon the glass on the deep side, it displayed characteristic stereotyped behavior. It would refuse to put its feet down and would back up into a posture of defense, its front legs rigid and its hind legs limp. In this state of immobility it could be pushed forward across the glass until its head and field of vision crossed the edge of the surrounding solid surface, whereupon it would relax and spring forward upon the surface.

At the Cornell Behavior Farm a group of experimenters has carried these experiments with kids and goats a step further. They fixed the patterned material to a sheet of plywood and were thus able to adjust the "depth" of the deep side. With the pattern held immediately beneath the glass, the animal would move about the glass freely. With the optical floor dropped more than a foot below the glass, the animal would immediately freeze into its defense posture. Despite repeated experience of the tactual solidity of the glass, the animals never learned to function without optical support. Their sense of security or danger continued to depend upon the visual cues that give them their perception of depth.

The rat, in contrast, does not depend predominantly upon visual cues. Its nocturnal habits lead it to seek food largely by smell, when moving about in the dark, it responds to tactual cues from the stiff whiskers (vibrissae) on its snout. Hooded rats tested on the visual cliff show little preference for the shallow side so long as they can feel the glass with their vibrissae. Placed upon the glass over the deep side, they move about normally. But when we raise the center board several inches, so that the glass is out of reach of their whiskers, they evince good visual depth-discrimination: 95 to 100 per cent of them descend on the shallow side.

Cats, like rats, are nocturnal animals, sensitive to tactual cues from their vibrissae. But the cat, as a predator, must rely more strongly on its sight. Kittens proved to have excellent depth-discrimination. At four weeks—about the earliest age that a kitten can move about with any facility—they invariably choose the shallow side of the cliff. On the glass over the deep side, they either freeze or circle aimlessly backward until they reach the center board.

The animals that showed the poorest performance in our series were the turtles. The late Robert M. Yerkes of Harvard University found in 1904 that aquatic turtles have somewhat poorer depth-discrimination than land turtles. On the visual cliff one might expect an aquatic turtle to respond to the reflections from the glass as it might to water and so prefer the deep side. They showed no such preference: 76 per cent of the aquatic turtles crawled off the board on the shallow side. The relatively large minority that choose the deep side suggests either that this turtle has poorer depth-discrimination than other animals, or that its natural habitat gives it less occasion to "fear" a fall.

All of these observations square with what is known about the life history and ecological niche of each of the animals tested. The survival of a species requires that its members develop discrimination of depth by the time they take up independent locomotion, whether at one day (the chick and the goat), three to four weeks (the rat and the cat) or six to 10 months (the human infant). That such a vital capacity does not depend on possibly fatal accidents of learning in the lives of individuals is consistent with evolutionary theory.

To make sure that no hidden bias was concealed in the design of the visual cliff we conducted a number of control experiments. In one of them we eliminated reflections from the glass by lighting the patterned surfaces from below the glass (to accomplish this we dropped the pattern below the glass on both sides, but more on one side than on the other). The animals—hooded rats—still consistently chose the shallow side. As a test of the role of the patterned surface we replaced it on either side of the centerboard with a homogeneous gray surface. Confronted with this choice, the rats showed no preference for either the shallow or the deep side. We also eliminated the optical difference between the two sides of the board by placing the patterned surface directly against the undersurface of the glass on each side. The rats then descended without preference to either side. When we lowered the pattern 10 inches below the glass on each side, they stayed on the board.

We set out next to determine which of two visual cues plays the decisive role in depth perception. To an eye above the center board the optical pattern on the two sides differs in at least two important respects. On the deep side distance decreases the size and spacing of the pattern elements projected on the retina. "Motion parallax," on the other hand, causes the pattern elements on the shallow side to move more rapidly across the field of vision when the animal moves its head, just as nearby objects seen from a moving car appear to pass by more quickly than distant ones. To eliminate the potential distance cue provided by pattern density we increased the size and spacing of the pattern elements on the deep side in proportion to its distance from the eye. With only the cue of motion parallax to guide them, adult rats still preferred the shallow side, though not so strongly as in the standard experiment. Infant rats chose the shallow side nearly 100 per cent of the time under both conditions, as did day-old chicks. Evidently both species can discriminate depth by differential motion alone, with no aid from texture density and probably little help from other cues. The perception of distance by binocular parallax, which doubtless plays an important part in human behavior, would not seem to have a significant role, for example, in the depth perception of chicks and rats.

Eleanor J. Gibson and Richard D. Walk

To eliminate the cue of motion parallax we placed the patterned material directly against the glass on either side of the board but used smaller and more densely spaced pattern-elements on the cliff side. Both young and adult hooded rats preferred the side with the larger pattern, which evidently "signified" a nearer surface. Day-old chicks, however, showed no preference for the larger pattern. It may be that learning plays some part in the preference exhibited by the rats, since the young rats were tested at a somewhat older age than the chicks. This supposition is supported by the results of our experiments with animals reared in the dark.

The effects of early experience and of such deprivations as dark-rearing represent important clues to the relative roles of maturation and learning in animal behavior. The first experiments along this line were performed by K. S. Lashley and James T. Russell at the University of Chicago in 1934. They tested light-reared and dark-reared rats on a "jumping stand" from which they induced animals to leap toward a platform placed at varying distances. Upon finding that both groups of animals jumped with a force closely correlated with distance, they concluded that depth perception in rats is innate. Other investigators have pointed out, however, that the dark-reared rats required a certain amount of "pretraining" in the light before they could be made to jump. Since the visual-cliff technique requires no pretraining, we employed it to test groups of light-reared and dark-reared hooded rats. At the age of 90 days both groups showed the same preference for the shallow side of the apparatus, confirming Lashley's and Russell's conclusion.

Recalling our findings in the young rat, we then took up the question of whether the dark-reared rats relied upon motion parallax or upon contrast in texture density to discriminate depth. When the animals were confronted with the visual cliff, cued only by motion parallax, they preferred the shallow side, as had the light-reared animals. When the choice was cued by pattern density, however, they departed from the pattern of the normal animals and showed no significant preference. The behavior of dark-reared rats thus resembles that of the day-old chicks, which also lack visual experience. It seems likely, therefore, that of the two cues only motion parallax is an innate cue for depth discrimination. Responses to differential pattern-density may be learned later.

One cannot automatically extrapolate these results to other species. But experiments with dark-reared kittens indicate that in these animals, too, depth perception matures independently of trial and error learning. In the kitten, however, light is necessary for normal visual maturation. Kittens reared in the dark to the age of 27 days at first crawled or fell off the center board equally often on the deep and shallow sides. Placed upon the glass over the deep side, they did not back in a circle like normal kittens but showed the same behavior that they had exhibited on the shallow side. Other investigators have observed equivalent behavior in dark-reared kittens; they bump into obstacles, lack normal eye movement and appear to "stare" straight ahead. These difficulties pass after a few days in the light. We accordingly tested the kittens every day. By the end of the week they were performing in every respect like normal kittens. They showed the same unanimous preference for the shallow side. Placed upon the glass over the deep side, they balked and circled backward to a visually secure surface. Repeated descents to the deep side, and placement upon the glass during their "blind" period, had not taught them that the deep side was "safe." Instead they avoided it more and more consistently. The initial blindness of dark-reared kittens makes them ideal subjects for studying the maturation of depth perception. With further study it should be possible to determine which cues they respond to first and what kinds of visual experience accelerate or retard the process of maturation.

From our first few years of work with the visual cliff we are ready to venture the rather broad conclusion that a seeing animal will be able to discriminate depth when its locomotion is adequate, even when locomotion begins at birth. But many experiments remain to be done, especially on the role of different cues and on the effects of different kinds of early visual experience.

4.2 DAVID H. HUBEL

Exploration of the Primary Visual Cortex, 1955–78

Unraveling the complexities of the brain has proven to be a slow process. A giant leap in our understanding of the brain's role in visual perception occurred with the research of David H. Hubel and Torsten N. Wiesel, who mapped the visual cortex of the brain. They received the Nobel Prize in medicine for their efforts in 1981.

Hubel was born in 1926 in Windsor, Ontario, Canada. He attended McGill College as an undergraduate and then earned an M.D. from McGill Medical School. He worked at Johns Hopkins Hospital before joining Harvard Medical School in 1958, where he has remained. Among his writings is his book *Eye, Brain, and Vision* (Freeman, 1995).

The selection that follows is from "Exploration of the Primary Visual Cortex, 1955–78," which was published in *Nature* in 1982. In it, Hubel provides a fascinating glimpse of the development of a research program. He shows how a complex area was studied one step at a time. By measuring the electrical activity of individual neurons in the visual cortex of a cat, it was found that each cell responded individually to lines of varying orientations.

Key Concept: visual cortex

APA Citation: Hubel, D. H. (1982). Exploration of the primary visual cortex, 1955–78. *Nature, 299,* 515–524.

*I*n the early spring of 1958 I drove over to Baltimore from Washington DC, and in a cafeteria at Johns Hopkins Hospital met Stephen Kuffler and Torsten Wiesel for a discussion that was more momentous for Torsten's and my future than either of us could have possibly imagined.

I had been at Walter Reed Army Institute of Research for 3 years, in the Neuropsychiatry Section headed by David Rioch, working under the supervision of M. G. F. Fuortes. I began at Walter Reed by developing a tungsten microelectrode and a technique for using it to record from cats with permanently implanted electrodes, and I had been comparing the firing of cells in the visual pathways of sleeping and waking animals.

It was time for a change in my research tactics. In sleeping cats, only diffuse light could reach the retina through the closed eyelids. Whether the cat

93

was asleep or awake, diffuse light failed to stimulate the cells in the striate cortex. In waking animals I had succeeded in activating many cells with moving spots on a screen, and had found that some cells were very selective in that they responded to movement when a spot moved in one direction across the screen (for example, from left to right) but not when it moved in the opposite direction[1]. There were many cells that I could not influence at all. Obviously there was a gold mine in the visual cortex, but methods were needed that would permit recording of single cells for many hours, and with the eyes immobilized, if the mine were ever to begin producing.

I had planned to do a postdoctoral fellowship at Johns Hopkins Medical School with Vernon Mountcastle, but the timing was awkward for him because he was remodelling his laboratories. One day Kuffler called and asked if I would like to work in his laboratory at the Wilmer Institute of Ophthalmology at the Johns Hopkins Hospital with Torsten Wiesel, until the remodelling was completed. That was expected to take about a year. I did not have to be persuaded; some rigorous training in vision was just what I needed, and though Kuffler himself was no longer working in vision the tradition had been maintained in his laboratory. Torsten and I had visited each other's laboratories and it was clear that we had common interests and similar outlooks. Kuffler suggested that I come over to discuss plans, and that was what led to the meeting in the cafeteria.

It was not hard to decide what to do. Kuffler had described two types of retinal ganglion cells which he called 'ON-centre' and 'OFF-centre'. The receptive field of each type was made up of two mutually antagonistic regions, a centre and a surround, one excitatory and the other inhibitory. In 1957, Barlow, FitzHugh and Kuffler had gone on to show that, as a consequence, retinal ganglion cells are less sensitive to diffuse light than to a spot just filling the receptive-field centre[2]. It took me some time to realize what this meant: that the way a cell responds to any visual scene will change very little when, for example, the sun goes behind a cloud and the light reflected from black and white objects decreases by a large factor. The cell virtually ignores this change, and our subjective assessment of the objects as black or white is likewise practically unaffected. Kuffler's centre–surround receptive fields thus began to explain why the appearance of objects depends so little on the intensity of the light source. Some years later Edwin Land showed that the appearance of a scene is similarly relatively independent of the exact wavelength composition of the light source. The physiological basis of this colour independence has yet to be worked out.

The strategy (to return to our cafeteria) seemed obvious. Torsten and I would simply extend Stephen Kuffler's work to the brain; we would record from geniculate cells and cortical cells, map receptive fields with small spots, and look for any further processing of the visual information.

My reception in Kuffler's office the first day was memorable. I was nervous and out of breath. Steve, at his desk, rotated around in his chair and said "Hi David! Take off your coat, hang up your hat, do up your fly". His manner was informal! But it took me a month, given my Canadian upbringing, to force myself to call him Steve. For the first three months no paycheck arrived, and finally I screwed up the courage to go in and tell him. He laughed and laughed, and then said, "I forgot!"

Torsten and I did not waste much time. Within a week of my coming to Hopkins (to a dark and dingy inner windowless room at the Wilmer Institute basement, deemed ideal for visual studies) we did our first experiment. For the time being we finessed the geniculate (at Walter Reed I had convinced myself that the cells were centre–surround) and began right away with cortex. The going was rough. We had only the equipment for retinal stimulation and recording that had been designed a few years before by Talbot and Kuffler[3]. A piece of apparatus resembling a small cyclotron held the anaesthetized and paralysed cat with its head facing almost directly upward. A modified ophthalmoscope projected a background light and a spot stimulus onto the retina. The experimenter could look in, see the retina with its optic disk, area centralis, and blood vessels, and observe the background light and the stimulus spots. Small spots of light were produced by sliding 2 × 5 cm metal rectangles containing various sizes of holes into a slot in the apparatus, just as one puts a slide into a slide projector. To obtain a black spot on a light background one used a piece of glass like a microscope slide, onto which a black dot had been glued. All this was ideal for stimulating the retina and recording directly from retinal ganglion cells, since one could see the electrode tip and know where to stimulate, but for cortical recording it was horrible. Finding a receptive field on the retina was difficult, and we could never remember what part of the retina we had stimulated. After a month or so we decided to have the cat face a projection screen, as I had at Walter Reed and as Talbot and Marshall had in 1941[4]. Having no other head holder, we continued for a while to use the ophthalmoscope's head holder, which posed a problem since the cat was facing directly up. To solve this we brought in some bed sheets which we slung between the pipes and cobwebs that graced the ceiling of the Wilmer basement, giving the setup the aura of a circus tent. On the sheets we projected our spots and slits. One day Mountcastle walked in on this scene, and was horror struck at the spectacle. The method was certainly inconvenient since we had to stare at the ceiling for the entire experiment. Then I remembered having seen in Mountcastle's laboratory a Horsley-Clarke head holder that was not only no longer being used but also had the name of the Wilmer Institute engraved on it. It was no other than the instrument that Talbot had designed for visual work when he and Marshall mapped out visual areas I and II in the cat in 1941[4]. For years Vernon had used it in his somatosensory work, but he had recently obtained a fancier one. Torsten and I decided to reclaim the Wilmer instrument, not without some trepidation. To give ourselves confidence we both put on lab coats, for the first and last times in our lives, and looking very professional walked over to Physiology. Though Mountcastle was his usual friendly and generous self, I suspect he was loath to part with this treasure, but the inscription on the stainless steel was not to be denied and we walked off with it triumphantly. It is still in use (now at Harvard; we literally stole it from the Wilmer), and has probably the longest history of uninterrupted service of any Horsley-Clarke in the world.

A short while before this adventure we had gone to a lecture by Vernon (this was a few years after the discovery of cortical columns)[5] in which he had amazed us by reporting on the results of recording from some 900 somatosensory cortical cells, for those days an astronomic number. We knew we could never catch up, so we catapulted ourselves to respectability by calling our first cell No. 3000 and numbering subsequent ones from there. When Vernon visited our circus tent we were in the middle of a three-unit recording, cells number 3007, 3008 and 3009. We made sure that we mentioned their identification numbers. All three cells had the same receptive-field orientation, but neither Vernon nor we realized, then, what that implied.

Our first real discovery came about as a surprise. We had been doing experiments for about a month. We were still using the Talbot-Kuffler ophthalmoscope and were not getting very far; the cells simply would not respond to our spots and annuli. One day we made an especially stable recording. [We had adapted my technique for recording, which used long-term implantations and the Davies closed chamber[6], to the short-term experiments, and no vibrations short of an earthquake were likely to dislodge things.] The cell in question lasted 9 hours, and by the end we had a very different feeling about what the cortex might be doing. For 3 to 4 hours we got absolutely nowhere. Then gradually we began to elicit some vague and inconsistent responses by stimulating somewhere in the midperiphery of the retina. We were inserting the glass slide with its black spot into the slot of the ophthalmoscope when suddenly over the audiomonitor the cell went off like a machine gun. After some fussing and fiddling we found out what was happening. The response had nothing to do with the black dot. As the glass slide was inserted its edge was casting onto the retina a faint but sharp shadow, a straight dark line on a light background. That was what the cell wanted, and it wanted it, moreover, in just one narrow range of orientations.

This was unheard of. It is hard, now, to think back and realize just how free we were from any idea of what cortical cells might be doing in an animal's daily life. That the retinas mapped onto the visual cortex in a systematic way was, of course, well known, but it was far from clear what this apparently unimaginative remapping was good for. It seemed inconceivable that the information would enter the cortex and leave it unmodified, especially when Kuffler's work in the retina had made it so clear that interesting transformations took place there between input and output. One heard the word 'analysis' used to describe what the cortex might be doing, but what one was to understand by that vague term was never spelled out. In the somatosensory cortex, the only other cortical area being closely scrutinized, Mountcastle had found that the cells had properties not dramatically different from those of neurones at earlier stages. . . .

It took us months to convince ourselves that we were not at the mercy of some optical artefact, such as anyone can produce by squinting their eyes and making vertical rays emanate from street lights. We did not want to make fools of ourselves quite so early in our careers. But recording in sequence in the same penetration several cells, with several different optimal orientations would, I think, have convinced anyone. By January we were ready to take the cells we thought we could understand (we later called them 'simple cells') and write them up. Then, as always, what guided and sustained us was the attitude of Kuffler, who never lectured or preached but simply reacted with buoyant enthusiasm whenever he thought we had found something interesting, and acted vague and noncommittal when he found something dull.

During the years 1959–62, first at the Wilmer Institute and then at Harvard Medical School, we were mainly concerned with comparing responses of cells in the lateral geniculate body and primary visual cortex of the cat. In the lateral geniculate we quickly confirmed my Walter Reed finding that the receptive fields are like those of retinal ganglion cells in having an antagonistic concentric centre–surround organization. But now we could directly compare the responses of a geniculate cell with those of a fibre from an afferent retinal ganglion cell, and we found that in geniculate cells the power of the receptive-field surround to cancel the input from the centre was increased. This finding was subsequently confirmed and extended in a beautiful set of experiments by Cleland *et al.* [7], and for many years it remained the only known function of the lateral geniculate body.

In the cat striate cortex it soon became evident that the cells were more complex than geniculate cells, and came in several degrees of complexity[8]. One set of cells could be described by techniques similar to those used in the retina by Kuffler; we called these 'simple'[9,10]. Their receptive fields, like the fields of retinal ganglion cells and of lateral geniculate cells, were subdivided into antagonistic regions, illumination of any one of which tended to increase or decrease the rate of firing. But simple cells differed from retinal ganglion cells and lateral geniculate cells in the striking departure of their receptive fields from circular symmetry; instead of a single circular boundary between centre and surround, the antagonistic subdivisions were separated by parallel straight lines whose orientation (vertical, horizontal or oblique) soon emerged as a fundamental property. The optimal stimulus—a slit, dark bar or edge—was easily predictable from the geometry of the receptive field, so that a stationary line stimulus worked optimally when its boundaries coincided with the boundaries of the subdivisions, and displacing the line to a new position parallel to the old one generally resulted in a sharp decline in the response. Perhaps most remarkable was the precision of the spatial distribution of excitatory and inhibitory effects: not only did diffuse light produce no response (as though the excitatory and inhibitory effects were mutually cancelling with the precision of an acid–base titration), but any line oriented 90° to the optimal was also without effect, regardless of its position along the field, suggesting that the subpopulations of receptors so stimulated also had precisely mutually cancelling effects.

In the cat, simple cells are mostly found in layer 4, which is the site of termination of the bulk of the afferents from the lateral geniculate body. The exact connections that lead to orientation specificity are still unknown, but it is easy to think of plausible circuits. For example, the behaviour of one of the commonest kinds of simple cells may be explained by supposing that the cell receives convergent excitatory input from a set of geniculate cells whose ON-centres are distributed in overlapping fashion over a straight line. In the monkey, the cells of layer 4C (where most geniculate fibres terminate) all seem to be concentric centre–surround, and the simple layers immediately superficial to 4C. No one knows why this extra stage of centre–surround cells is intercalated in the monkey's visual pathway.

The next set of cells we called 'complex' because their properties cannot be derived in a single logical step from those of lateral geniculate cells (or, in the monkey, from the concentric cells of layer 4C). For the complex cell (compared with the simple cell), the position of an optimally oriented line need not be so carefully specified: the line works anywhere in the receptive field, evoking about the same response wherever it is placed. This can most easily be explained by supposing that the complex cell receives inputs from many simple cells, all of whose receptive fields have the same orientation but differ slightly in position. Sharpness of tuning for orientation varies from cell to cell, but the optimal orientation of a typical complex cell in layer 2 or 3 in the monkey can be easily determined to the nearest 5–10°, with no more stimulating equipment than a slide projector and a screen.

FIGURE 1

Complex Cell Showing Response to a Moving Horizontal Bar.

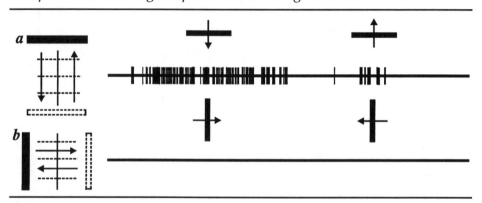

a, Downward movement was superior to upward;
b, there was no response to a moving vertical bar.

For a complex cell, a properly oriented line produces especially powerful responses when it is swept across the receptive field (Fig. 1). The discharge is generally well sustained as long as the line keeps moving, but falls off quickly if the stimulus is stationary. About half of the complex cells fire much better to one direction of movement than to the opposite direction, a quality called 'directional selectivity', which probably cannot be explained by any simple projection of simple cells onto complex cells, but seems to require inhibitory connections with time delays of the sort proposed for rabbit retinal ganglion cells by Barlow and Levick[11].

Many cat or monkey cells, perhaps 10 to 20% in area 17, respond best to a line (a slit, an edge, or a dark bar) of limited length; when the line is prolonged in one direction or both, the response falls off. This is called 'end stopping'. In some cells the response to a very long line fails completely[12]. We originally called these cells 'hypercomplex' because we looked on them as next in an ordered hierarchical series, after the simple and the complex. We saw hypercomplex cells first in areas 18 and 19 of the cat, and only later in area 17. Dreher subsequently found cells, in all other ways resembling simple cells, that showed a similar fall-off in response as the length of the stimulus exceeded some optimum[13]. It seems awkward to call these cells hypercomplex: they are probably better termed 'simple end-stopped', in contrast to 'complex end-stopped'.

Complex cells come in a wide variety of subtypes. Typical cells of layers 2 and 3 have relatively small receptive fields and low spontaneous activity, and in the monkey may be not only highly orientation-selective but also fussy about wavelength, perhaps responding to red lines but not white. They may or may not be end-stopped. Cells in layers 5 and 6 have larger fields. Those in layer 5 have high spontaneous activity, and many respond just as well to a very short moving line as to a long one. Many cells in layer 6 respond best to very long lines[14]. These differences are doubtless related to the important fact, first shown with physiological techniques by Toyama *et al.*[15] and confirmed and extended by anatomical techniques, that different layers project to different destinations —the upper layers mainly to other cortical regions; layer 5 to the superior colliculus, pons and pulvinar; and layer 6 back to the lateral geniculate body and to the claustrum.

In the past 10 or 15 years the subject of cortical receptive-field types has become rather a jungle, partly because the terms simple and complex are used differently by different people and partly because the categories themselves are not cleanly separated. Our original idea was to emphasize the tendency towards increased complexity as one moves centrally along the visual path and the possibility of accounting for a cell's behavior in terms of its inputs. The circuit diagrams we proposed were just a few examples from a number of plausible possibilities. Even today the actual circuit by which orientation specificity is derived from centre–surround cells is unknown, and indeed the techniques necessary for solving this may still not be available. One can nevertheless say that cells of different complexities whose receptive fields are in the same part of the visual field and which have the same optimal orientation are likely to be interconnected, whereas cells with different optimal orientations are far less likely to be interconnected. In the monkey, a major difficulty with the hierarchical scheme outlined here is the relative scarcity of simple cells, compared with the huge numbers of cells with concentric fields in layer 4C or with the large number of complex cells above and below layer 4. The fact that the simple cells have been found mainly in layer 4B also agrees badly with Jennifer Lund's finding that layer 4C β projects not to layer 4B but to layer 3. One has to consider the possibility that in the monkey the simple-cell step may be skipped, perhaps by summing the inputs from cells in layer 4 on dendrites of complex cells. In such a scheme each main dendritic branch of a complex cell would perform the function of a simple cell. All such speculation only emphasizes our ignorance of the exact way in which the properties of complex cells are built up.

Knowing how cortical cells respond to some visual stimuli and ignore others allows us to predict how a cell will react to any given visual scene. Most cortical cells respond poorly to diffuse light, so that when I gaze at a white object, say an egg, on a dark background I know that those cells in my area 17 whose receptive fields fall entirely within the boundaries of the object will be unaffected. Only the fields that are cut by the borders of the egg will be influenced, and then only if the local orientation of a border is about the same as the orientation of the receptive field. Slightly changing the position of the egg without changing its orientation will produce a dramatic change in the population of activated simple cells, but a much smaller change in the activated complex cells.

Orientation-specific simple or complex cells are specific for the direction of a short line segment. The cells are thus best not thought of as line detectors: they are no more line detectors than they are curve detectors. If our perception of a certain line or curve depends on simple or complex cells it presumably depends on a whole set of them, and how the information from such sets of cells is assembled at subsequent stages in the path to build up what we call percepts of lines or curves (if indeed anything like that happens at all) is still a complete mystery.

REFERENCES

1. Hubel, D. H. *Am. J. Ophthal.* **46,** 110 (1958).
2. Barlow, H. B., FitzHugh, R. & Kuffler, S. W. *J. Physiol., Lond.* **137,** 327 (1957).
3. Talbot, S. A. & Kuffler S. W. *J. Opt. Soc. Am.* **42,** 931 (1952).
4. Talbot, S. A. & Marshall, W. H. *Am. J. Ophthal.* **24,** 1255 (1941).
5. Mountcastle, V. B. *J. Neurophysiol.* **20,** 408 (1957).
6. Davies, P. W. *Science* **124,** 179 (1956).
7. Cleland, B. G., Dubin, M. W. & Levick, W. R. *Nature new Biol.* **231,** 191 (1971).
8. Hubel, D. H. & Wiesel T. N. *J. Physiol., Lond.* **160,** 106 (1962).
9. Hubel, D. H. & Wiesel, T. N. *21st Int. Congr. Physiol.,* Buenos Aires (1959).
10. Hubel, D. H. & Wiesel, T. N. *J. Physiol., Lond.* **148,** 574 (1959).
11. Barlow, H. B. & Levick, W. R. *J. Physiol., Lond.* **178,** 477 (1965).
12. Hubel, D. H. & Wiesel, T. N. *J. Neurophysiol.* **28,** 229 (1965).
13. Dreher, B. *Invest, Ophthal.* **11,** 355 (1972).
14. Gilbert, C. D. *J. Physiol., Lond.* **268,** 391 (1977).
15. Toyama, T., Matsunami, K. & Ohno, T. *Brain Res.* **14,** 513 (1969).

CHAPTER 5 Consciousness

5.1 ERNEST R. HILGARD

Weapon Against Pain: Hypnosis Is No Mirage

Hypnosis has fascinated and frustrated psychologists for over 100 years. Many people have voiced skepticism over the purported uses of hypnosis, such as to reduce pain. One of the most complete scientific investigations of hypnosis has been conducted by Ernest R. Hilgard.

Hilgard (b. 1904) earned a degree in chemical engineering at Yale University and studied at Yale Divinity School before deciding on a career in psychology. He earned his Ph.D. in experimental psychology from Yale University in 1930. He taught at Yale University before taking a position at Stanford University, where he has remained since 1933. His many books include *Theories of Learning* (1948), *Introduction to Psychology* (1953), *Personality and Hypnosis* (1970), and *Psychology in America* (1987).

This selection is from "Weapon Against Pain: Hypnosis Is No Mirage," which was published in *Psychology Today* in 1974. It is a very readable account of some of the vast research that explores the properties of this altered state of consciousness. As you read the selection, think about the possible uses of hypnosis in medical procedures, relaxation, and perhaps as a memory aid. Why do you think hypnosis has been widely criticized? What other applications for hypnosis can you think of?

Key Concept: hypnosis

APA Citation: Hilgard, E. R. (1974). Weapon against pain: Hypnosis is no mirage. *Psychology Today, 8,* 121–128.

*H*ypnosis works. Laboratory research to date allows us to say that with confidence, even as the clinical applications of hypnosis proliferate. From the pain-filled rooms of cancer patients to antismoking clinics, from dental surgeries to maternity wards, hypnosis is gaining ever wider acceptance as a weapon against pain. While there are many unanswered questions about how hypnosis works and whom it will work for; enough evidence is in to support it fully as a therapeutic tool.

Hypnosis has come a long way from the parlor magic of Franz Anton Mesmer and his theory of animal magnetism. But in part because of those lurid beginnings, and in part because of its association with charlatans, bad movies, and entertainers, hypnosis still is suspect in some quarters. Many psychologists argue that the hypnotic trance is a mirage. It would be unfortunate if this skeptical view were to gain such popularity that the benefits of hypnosis are denied to the numbers of those who could be helped. Consider, for example, the experience of women who give birth while in hypnotic trance. Obstetrician R. V. August delivered babies of 1,000 women from 1957 to 1960. Of the 850 women who gave birth under hypnosis, only 36 required chemical anesthesia in addition. And five of the women who relied solely on hypnoanesthesia delivered their babies by Caesarian section.

PHANTOM-LIMB PAIN   C. H. Harding reported successful treatment of migraine and vascular headaches with hypnotic suggestion. Of 90 patients he treated with four to seven sessions of hypnotic induction, 38 percent reported complete relief for periods of up to eight years. Thirty-two percent rated their relief as substantial. Only 11 of the 90 cases reported no relief from hypnotic treatment.

Hypnosis has also been used in the treatment of phantom-limb pain. About 57 percent of all amputees suffer from this peculiar affliction, which feels different from pain in the stump of the limb and is often extremely difficult to relieve. About 33 percent of these cases respond favorably to hypnotic suggestion. C. Cedercreutz and E. Uusitalo of Finland treated 37 cases of phantom-limb pain with hypnotic suggestion. Twenty patients lost all of their pain and another 10 improved so much that medication was no longer needed. Follow-up studies conducted from one to eight years after treatment revealed that eight patients were still totally pain-free and 10 others still showed some relief. The researchers concluded that, for phantom-limb pain, hypnosis is far better than other available treatments.

While hypnosis is used successfully in clinical settings, the skeptics argue that there is no true reduction in pain. Theodore Sarbin and his colleagues believe that a person adopts the role that is appropriate to his situation. When hypnotized, he plays the role of a hypnotized person, behaving as he believes a hypnotized person should. Similarly, Sarbin believes that reports by patients of pain relief indicate only a desire to please the therapist, to perform as he expects. The patient becomes so absorbed by the role, Sarbin believes, that in extreme cases it can lead to phenomena such as voodoo death.

HAND IMMOBILITY   Martin Orne, a psychologist at the University of Pennsylvania, found some truth in Sarbin's notion. He demonstrated hypnosis before two groups of students. Half of the students saw hypnotized subjects whose dominant hand was immobile; this fact was pointed out to the class as characteristic of the hypnotic state. The remaining students witnessed similar demonstrations except that the subject's hand did not become immobile. After the demonstration, members of each group were hypnotized; the hypnotist, however, did not know which demonstration a given student had witnessed. As expected, the students who had observed the model with hand immobility showed that characteristic while the other students did not.

These results are consistent with other studies that show the power of the experimental situation over the behavior of the subject. The efforts of the subject to please the experimenter, even when his demands are unreasonable, are so strong that Orne refers to the "demand characteristics" of the experimental situation. Critics of hypnosis feel that hypnotized subjects may simply be responding to the implied demands of the hypnotist. Response to demands does not lead Orne to reject hypnosis; his point is that the experimental evidence must be viewed critically. Nobody denies that hypnosis includes responses to suggestions, obvious or implicit.

One way to identify hypnosis as something unique would be to produce physiological evidence for the existence of the hypnotic state. It is difficult to prove whether or not a hypnotized person differs physiologically from one who is awake. Those who have been hypnotized report feeling quite different, and we know that at the deepest levels of hypnosis, a person may lose any further responsiveness to hypnotic suggestions. The EEG [electroencephalogram] patterns of hypnotized subjects are no different from those of their normal waking state, but they do differ from the patterns associated with sleep. We know that highly hypnotizable subjects produce more alpha waves in the normal waking state than do poor hypnotic subjects. In our laboratory we found a moderately strong correlation between the amount of alpha activity in a person's waking state and his susceptibility to hypnosis, but this correlation has to do with the potential for hypnotic response and not with the hypnotic state itself.

RIGHT AND LEFT LOOKERS

Other work suggests that a correlation exists between hypnotic suggestibility and hemispheric activity. When asked a question such as, "How many letters are in the word 'Washington'?" a person will typically look to the left or the right. About 75 percent of these eye movements will be to one side. Left-eye movements have been found to suggest that the brain's right hemisphere is dominant, while right-eye movements are associated with left-hemisphere dominance. Paul Bakan gave a test of hypnotic suggestibility to 46 undergraduate students and had them tested for eye movement. He found that left-lookers produced the highest hypnotic suggestibility scores, while the lowest scores came from right-lookers; his work, originally done in our laboratory, has been confirmed and extended here by Raquel and Ruben Gur.

Psychoactive drugs can also affect hypnotic suggestibility. Bernard Sjoberg found that LSD and mescaline increase suggestibility and that this effect lasts beyond the normal effects of the drug. We also know that hypnotic suggestibility is a regular function of age; it reaches a peak between eight and 11 years and then declines gradually. But none of the evidence concerning the physiological correlates of hypnosis proves conclusively that the hypnotic trance has distinctive physiological signs, such as the brain waves and rapid-eye movements associated with dreaming. A better question is whether or not hypnosis produces consequences that are real. We know, for example, that under hypnotic suggestion some people will do things they would otherwise not do. They will erase imaginary words from a blank blackboard, see and hear things that are not there, and *not* see and hear things that are there.

FREEZING WATER   To find out how real hypnotic effects are, much of the laboratory research has studied the hypnotic reduction of pain. It is possible to get objective measures of the degree of pain and to compare these with subjective reports of pain intensity. If people under hypnotic suggestion endure greater amounts of pain, and if they say they feel less pain than during the waking state, then hypnosis would seem to be genuine.

One technique for inducing pain in the laboratory is to immerse the volunteer's hand and forearm in freezing water. The subject rates the intensity of the pain he feels when awake, and after the hypnotic suggestion that his hand and arm are insensitive. We then compare the two ratings to determine if hypnotic suggestion reduces pain.

In one of our first experiments, we gave 54 volunteers a test of hypnotic suggestibility and then gave them the hypnotic suggestion that they would not feel pain. The subjects then rated the pain they felt during the ice-water test. Pain reduction was clearly related to hypnotic susceptibility. Of the highly hypnotizable subjects, 67 percent showed a 33 percent reduction in pain, while only 13 percent of the least hypnotizable subjects showed as much relief. At the same time, only seven percent of the highly suggestible volunteers showed 10 percent or less reduction in pain, while 56 percent of the subjects low in suggestibility showed this small amount of relief.

Our results were confirmed several years later by Michael Evans and Gordon Paul in another laboratory. They also found that ice-water pain could be reduced by hypnotic suggestion and that the amount of reduction increased with a person's susceptibility to hypnosis.

Evans and Paul conducted their experiment with college women. Each volunteer immersed her hand in the icy water for one minute. Then she rated the pain she had felt on a seven-point scale, ranging from pleasant to very painful. Later, each subject received one of four treatment procedures. One fourth of the volunteers were hypnotized and given the suggestion that they would not feel pain. Another group was hypnotized but not given the antipain suggestion. A third group was taught self-relaxation and given the suggestion that they would not feel pain. The last group learned self-relaxation but received no suggestion that their ability to feel pain would diminish. After she received one of the four sets of instructions, each woman again immersed her hand in the frigid water and rated the pain she felt. Evans and Paul compared this second rating with the first. Those who received the analgesic suggestion showed a greater reduction in pain than those who did not, but it made no difference whether the suggestion had been given under hypnosis or during the waking state, under self-relaxation.

Other studies of this sort have produced similar results, leading critics of hypnosis to decide that the results of suggested pain reduction are genuine, but that a prior induction of hypnosis is not necessary, and that therefore the concept of hypnosis is superfluous. However, these studies involve random selections of students, which make conclusions regarding the legitimacy of hypnosis of dubious value....

CAREFUL FOCUS   Hypnotic induction seems to facilitate the use of imagination. During hypnosis, one woman pretended she was inside the *Venus de Milo* statue. Since she had no arms, she could feel no pain during the ice-water experiment. Another subject pretended he was somewhere else; since he was not in the experimental situation, he could not be hurt. Others imagine that they have been given an injection of an anesthetic; numbness spreads through their arms as the imaginary anesthetic dissipates.

It is not clear why imagination should be helpful in reducing pain. Hypnosis is often described as a state of heightened awareness in which attention is focused intensely on the suggestions of the hypnotist. Perhaps hypnotized subjects are able to focus attention so carefully on some imagined stimulus, such as those the hypnotist suggests, that competing stimuli are physiologically inhibited. All of us have had the experience of becoming so engrossed in a book, a conversation or some other activity that we did not hear our name being called. It is not just that we deny hearing our name; we actually do not hear it. This may not be so different from the experience of the hypnotic subject.

There is overwhelming evidence that some people get relief from pain by hypnotic suggestion; they are not merely withholding reports of suffering to please the hypnotist. The hundreds of patients who have received relief from pain through hypnotic suggestion do not need convincing. And those who may be helped in the future should not be denied the benefits of hypnosis simply because we do not yet understand precisely what hypnosis is or why it works. For now, it is enough to know that it does.

The Dream as a Wish-Fulfilment

If you sleep eight hours per night, you spend approximately two of those hours dreaming. People have always been fascinated with dreams, and many have proposed theories to explain the functions and meaning of dreams. The most popular and well known dream theory was proposed by Sigmund Freud in 1900. Freud believed that dreams were the road to the elusive unconscious mind. His theory of dreams as wish fulfillments, which is examined in this selection, has sparked a great deal of controversy over the years.

Freud (1856–1939), a neurologist, received his M.D. in 1881 from Vienna University. He spent most of his life in Vienna, Austria, practicing medicine and studying mental disorders through clinical observation. As the father of psychoanalysis, Freud significantly influenced many areas of psychology, including personality, development, and clinical psychology.

In Freud's book *The Interpretation of Dreams* (1900), he presents his theory of the meaning of dreams. This selection is from chapter 3, "The Dream as a Wish-Fulfilment," of that book, and it illustrates one of the main points of Freud's dream theory. This selection allows you to see how Freud conceptualized dream interpretation as well as psychoanalysis. As you read this selection, think about how you interpret your own dreams.

Key Concept: Freud's theory of dreaming

APA Citation: Freud, S. (1900). *The interpretation of dreams.* New York: Random House. (c1950 Random House Trans by A. A. Brill)

When, after passing through a narrow defile, one suddenly reaches a height beyond which the ways part and a rich prospect lies outspread in different directions, it is well to stop for a moment and consider whither one shall turn next. We are in somewhat the same position after we have mastered this first interpretation of a dream. We find ourselves standing in the light of a sudden discovery. The dream is not comparable to the irregular sounds of a musical instrument, which, instead of being played by the hand of a musician, is struck by some external force; the dream is not meaningless, not absurd, does not pre-suppose that one part of our store of ideas is dormant while another part begins to awake. It is a perfectly valid psychic phenomenon, actually a wish-fulfilment; it may be enrolled in the continuity of the intelligible psychic activities of the waking state; it is built up by a highly complicated intellectual activity. But at the very moment when we are about to rejoice in this discovery a host of prob-lems besets us. If the dream, as this theory defines it, represents a fulfilled wish, what is the cause of the striking and unfamiliar manner in which this fulfilment is expressed? What transformation has occurred in our dream-thoughts before the manifest dream, as we remember it on waking, shapes itself out of them? How has this transformation taken place? Whence comes the material that is worked up into the dream? What causes many of the peculiarities which are to be observed in our dream-thoughts; for example, how is it that they are able to contradict one another? ... Is the dream capable of teaching us something new concerning our internal psychic processes, and can its content correct opinions which we have held during the day? I suggest that for the present all these problems be laid aside, and that a single path be pursued. We have found that the dream represents a wish as fulfilled. Our next purpose should be to ascer-tain whether this is a general characteristic of dreams, or whether it is only the accidental content of [a] particular dream ... ; for even if we conclude that every dream has a meaning and psychic value, we must nevertheless allow for the possibility that this meaning may not be the same in every dream. The first dream ... [may be] the fulfilment of a wish; another may turn out to be the realization of an apprehension; a third may have a reflection as its content; a fourth may simply reproduce a reminiscence. Are there, then, dreams other than wish-dreams; or are there none but wish-dreams?

It is easy to show that the wish-fulfilment in dreams is often undisguised and easy to recognize, so that one may wonder why the language of dreams has not long since been understood. There is, for example, a dream which I can evoke as often as I please, experimentally, as it were. If, in the evening, I eat anchovies, olives, or other strongly salted foods, I am thirsty at night, and therefore I wake. The waking, however, is preceded by a dream, which has always the same con-tent, namely, that I am drinking. I am drinking long draughts of water; it tastes as delicious as only a cool drink can taste when one's throat is parched; and then I wake, and find that I have an actual desire to drink. The cause of this dream is thirst, which I perceive when I wake. From this sensation arises the wish to drink, and the dream shows me this wish as fulfilled. It hereby serves a func-tion, the nature of which I soon surmise. I sleep well, and am not accustomed to being waked by a bodily need. If I succeed in appeasing my thirst by means of the dream that I am drinking, I need not wake up in order to satisfy that thirst. It is thus a *dream of convenience*. The dream takes the place of action, as elsewhere in life. Unfortunately, the need of water to quench the thirst cannot be satisfied by a dream, as can my thirst for revenge upon [some adversary], but the inten-tion is the same. Not long ago I had the same dream in a somewhat modified form. On this occasion I felt thirsty before going to bed, and emptied the glass of water which stood on the little chest beside my bed. Some hours later, during the night, my thirst returned, with the consequent discomfort. In order to obtain water, I should have had to get up and fetch the glass which stood on my wife's bed-table. I thus quite appropriately dreamt that my wife was giving me a drink from a vase; this vase was an Etruscan cinerary urn, which I had brought home from Italy, and had since given away. But the water in it tasted so salty (apparently on account of the ashes) that I was forced to wake. It may be observed how conveniently the dream is capable of arranging matters. Since the fulfilment of a wish is its only purpose, it may be perfectly egoistic. Love of comfort is really not compatible with consideration for others. The introduction of the cinerary urn is probably once again the fulfilment of a wish; I regret that I no longer possess this vase; it, like the glass of water at my wife's side, is inaccessible to me. The cinerary urn is appropriate also in connection with the sensation of an increasingly salty taste, which I know will compel me to wake.

Such convenience-dreams came very frequently to me in my youth. Accustomed as I had always been to working until late at night, early waking was always a matter of difficulty. I used then to dream that I was out of bed and standing at the washstand. After a while I could no longer shut out the knowledge that I was not yet up; but in the meantime I had continued to sleep. The same sort of lethargy-dream was dreamed by a young colleague of mine, who appears to share my propensity for sleep. With him it assumed a particularly amusing form. The landlady with whom he was lodging in the neighbourhood of the hospital had strict orders to wake him every morning at a given hour, but she found it by no means easy to carry out his orders. One morning sleep was especially sweet to him. The woman called into his room: "Herr Pepi, get up; you've got to go to the hospital." Whereupon the sleeper dreamt of a room in the hospital, of a bed in which he was lying, and of a chart pinned over his head, which read as follows: "Pepi M., medical student, 22 years of age." He told himself in the dream: "If I am already at the hospital, I don't have to go there," turned over, and slept on. He had thus frankly admitted to himself his motive for dreaming.

Here is yet another dream of which the stimulus was active during sleep: One of my women patients, who had been obliged to undergo an unsuccessful operation on the jaw, was instructed by her physicians to wear by day and night a cooling apparatus on the affected cheek; but she was in the habit of throwing it off as soon as she had fallen asleep. One day I was asked to reprove her from doing so; she had again thrown the apparatus on the floor. The patient defended herself as follows: "This time I really couldn't help it; it was the result of a dream which I had during the night. In the dream I was in a box at the opera, and was taking a lively interest in the performance. But Herr Karl Meyer was lying in the sanatorium and complaining pitifully on account of pains in his jaw. I said to myself, 'Since I haven't the pains, I don't need the apparatus either'; that's why I threw it away." The dream of this poor sufferer reminds me of an expression which comes to our lips when we are in a disagreeable situation: "Well, I can imagine more amusing things!" The dream presents these "more amusing things!" Herr Karl Meyer, to whom the dreamer attributed her pains, was the most casual acquaintance of whom she could think.

It is quite as simple a matter to discover the wish-fulfilment in several other dreams which I have collected from healthy persons. A friend who was acquainted with my theory of dreams, and had explained it to his wife, said to me one day: "My wife asked me to tell you that she dreamt yesterday that she was having her menses. You will know what that means." Of course I know: if the young wife dreams that she is having her menses, the menses have stopped. I can well imagine that she would have liked to enjoy her freedom a little longer, before the discomforts of maternity began. It was a clever way of giving notice of her first pregnancy. Another friend writes that his wife had dreamt not long ago that she noticed milk-stains on the front of her blouse. This also is an indication of pregnancy, but not of the first one; the young mother hoped she would have more nourishment for the second child than she had for the first.

A young woman who for weeks had been cut off from all society because she was nursing a child who was suffering from an infectious disease dreamt, after the child had recovered, of a company of people in which Alphonse Daudet, Paul Bourget, Marcel Prévost and others were present; they were all very pleasant to her and amused her enormously. In her dream these different authors had the features which their portraits give them. M. Prévost, with whose portrait she is not familiar, looked like the man who had disinfected the sickroom the day before, the first outsider to enter it for a long time. Obviously the dream is to be translated thus: "It is about time now for something more entertaining than this eternal nursing."

Perhaps this collection will suffice to prove that frequently, and under the most complex conditions, dreams may be noted which can be understood only as wish-fulfilments, and which present their content without concealment. In most cases these are short and simple dreams, and they stand in pleasant contrast to the confused and overloaded dream-compositions which have almost exclusively attracted the attention of the writers on the subject. But it will repay us if we give some time to the examination of these simple dreams. The simplest dreams of all are, I suppose, to be expected in the case of children whose psychic activities are certainly less complicated than those of adults. Child psychology, in my opinion, is destined to render the same services to the psychology of adults as a study of the structure or development of the lower animals renders to the investigation of the structure of the higher orders of animals. Hitherto but few deliberate efforts have been made to make use of the psychology of the child for such a purpose.

The dreams of little children are often simple fulfilments of wishes, and for this reason are, as compared with the dreams of adults, by no means interesting. They present no problem to be solved, but they are invaluable as affording proof that the dream, in its inmost essence, is the fulfilment of a wish. I have been able to collect several examples of such dreams from the material furnished by my own children.

For two dreams, one that of a daughter of mine, at that time eight and a half years of age, and the other that of a boy of five and a quarter, I am indebted to an excursion to Hallstatt, in the summer of 1896. I must first explain that we were living that summer on a hill near Aussee, from which, when the weather was fine, we enjoyed a splendid view of the Dachstein. With a telescope we could easily distinguish the Simony hut. The children often tried to see it through the telescope—I do not know with what success. Before the excursion I had told the children that Hallstatt lay at the foot of the Dachstein. They looked forward to the outing with the greatest delight. From Hallstatt we entered the valley of Eschern, which enchanted the children with its constantly changing scenery. One of them, however, the boy of five, gradually became discontented. As often as a mountain came into view, he would ask: "Is that the Dachstein?" whereupon I had to reply: "No, only a foot-hill." After this question had been repeated several times he fell quite silent, and did not wish to accompany us up the steps leading to the waterfall. I thought he was tired. But the next morning he came to me, perfectly happy, and said: "Last night I dreamt that we went to the Simony hut." I understood him now; he had expected, when I spoke of the Dachstein, that on our excursion to Hallstatt he would climb the mountain, and would see at close quarters the hut which had been so often mentioned when the telescope was used. When he learned that he was expected to content himself with foot-hills and a waterfall he was disappointed, and became discontented. But the dream compensated him for all this. I tried to learn some details of the dream; they were scanty. "You go up steps for six hours," as he had been told.

On this excursion the girl of eight and a half had likewise cherished wishes which had to be satisfied by a dream. We had taken with us to Hallstatt our neighbour's twelve-year-old boy; quite a polished little gentleman, who, it seemed to me, had already won the little woman's sympathies. Next morning she related the following dream: "Just think, I dreamt that Emil was one of the family, that he said 'papa' and 'mamma' to you, and slept at our house, in the big room, like one of the boys. Then mamma came into the room and threw a handful of big bars of chocolate, wrapped in blue and green paper, under our beds." The girl's brothers, who evidently had not inherited an understanding of dream-interpretation, declared . . . : "That dream is nonsense." The girl defended at least one part of the dream, and from the standpoint of the theory of the neuroses it is interesting to learn which part it was that she defended: "That Emil was one of the family was nonsense, but that part about the bars of chocolate wasn't." It was just this latter part that was obscure to me, until my wife furnished the explanation. On the way home from the railway-station the children had stopped in front of a slot-machine, and had wanted exactly such bars of chocolate, wrapped in paper with a metallic lustre, such as the machine, in their experience, provided. But the mother thought, and rightly so, that the day had brought them enough wish-fulfilments, and therefore left this wish to be satisfied in the dream. This little scene had escaped me. That portion of the dream which had been condemned by my daughter I understood without any difficulty. I myself had heard the well-behaved little guest enjoining the children, as they were walking ahead of us, to wait until 'papa' or 'mamma' had come up. For the little girl the dream turned this temporary relationship into a permanent adoption. Her affection could not as yet conceive of any other way of enjoying her friend's company permanently than the adoption pictured in her dream, which was suggested by her brothers. Why the bars of chocolate were thrown under the bed could not, of course, be explained without questioning the child.

From a friend I have learned of a dream very much like that of my little boy. It was dreamed by a little girl of eight. Her father, accompanied by several children, had started on a walk to Dornbach, with the intention of visiting the

Rohrer hut, but had turned back, as it was growing late, promising the children to take them some other time. On the way back they passed a signpost which pointed to the Hameau. The children now asked him to take them to the Hameau, but once more, and for the same reason, they had to be content with the promise that they should go there some other day. Next morning the little girl went to her father and told him, with a satisfied air: "Papa, I dreamed last night that you were with us at the Rohrer hut, and on the Hameau." Thus, in the dream her impatience had anticipated the fulfilment of the promise made by her father.

Another dream, with which the picturesque beauty of the Aussee inspired my daughter, at that time three and a quarter years of age, is equally straightforward. The little girl had crossed the lake for the first time, and the trip has passed too quickly for her. She did not want to leave the boat at the landing, and cried bitterly. The next morning she told us: "Last night I was sailing on the lake." Let us hope that the duration of this dream-voyage was more satisfactory to her.

My eldest boy, at that time eight years of age, was already dreaming of the realization of his fancies. He had ridden in a chariot with Achilles, with Diomedes as charioteer. On the previous day he had shown a lively interest in a book on the myths of Greece which had been given to his elder sister.

If it can be admitted that the talking of children in their sleep belongs to the sphere of dreams, I can relate the following as one of the earliest dreams in my collection: My youngest daughter, at that time nineteen months old, vomited one morning, and was therefore kept without food all day. During the night she was heard to call excitedly in her sleep: "Anna F(r)eud, *st'awbewy, wild st'awbewy, om'lette, pap!*" She used her name in this way in order to express the act of appropriation; the menu presumably included everything that would seem to her a desirable meal; the fact that two varieties of strawberry appeared in it was a demonstration against the sanitary regulations of the household, and was based on the circumstance, which she had by no means overlooked, that the nurse had ascribed her indisposition to an over-plentiful consumption of strawberries; so in her dream she avenged herself for this opinion which met with her disapproval.

When we call childhood happy because it does not yet know sexual desire, we must not forget what a fruitful source of disappointment and renunciation, and therefore of dream-stimulation, the other great vital impulse may be for the child. Here is a second example. My nephew, twenty-two months of age, had been instructed to congratulate me on my birthday, and to give me a present of a small basket of cherries, which at that time of the year were scarce, being hardly in season. He seemed to find the task a difficult one, for he repeated again and again: "Cherries in it," and could not be induced to let the little basket go out of his hands. But he knew how to indemnify himself. He had, until then, been in the habit of telling his mother every morning that he had dreamt of the "white soldier," an officer of the guard in a white cloak, whom he had once admired in the street. On the day after the sacrifice on my birthday he woke up joyfully with the announcement, which could have referred only to a dream: *"He[r] man eaten all the cherries!"*

What animals dream of I do not know. A proverb for which I am indebted to one of my pupils professes to tell us, for it asks the question: "What does the goose dream of?" and answers: "Of maize." The whole theory that the dream is the fulfilment of a wish is contained in these two sentences.

We now perceive that we should have reached our theory of the hidden meaning of dreams by the shortest route had we merely consulted the vernacular. Proverbial wisdom, it is true, often speaks contemptuously enough of dreams—it apparently seeks to justify the scientists when it says that "dreams are bubbles"; but in colloquial language the dream is predominantly the gracious fulfiller of wishes. "I should never have imagined that in my wildest dreams," we exclaim in delight if we find that the reality surpasses our expectations.

PART THREE

Learning and Cognitive Processes

On the Internet . . .

Sites appropriate to Part Three

This site contains information on classical conditioning and is maintained by Margaret Anderson of Cortland College.

```
http://syncorva.cortland.edu/~andersmd/
    ccond/cc.html
```

This Theory Into Practice site provides links to descriptions of the major theories of learning.

```
http://www.gwu.edu/~tip/theories.html
```

This Alzheimer's Home Page site provides information on Alzheimer's disease.

```
http://www.macalester.edu/~psych/whathap/
    UBNRP/alzheimer/alzhome.html
```

Language Learning and The World Wide Web is Virginia Commonwealth University's foreign language learning site.

```
http://www.ncsa.uiuc.edu/SDG/IT94/
    Proceedings/Arts/godwin-jones/
    godwin.html
```

CHAPTER 6 Learning

6.1 I. P. PAVLOV

Conditioned Reflexes: An Investigation of the Physiological Activity of the Cerebral Cortex

Learning has been a topic of great interest to psychologists during most of psychology's history. Indeed, it could be argued that learning is involved in everything we do. One of the most significant research programs was conducted not by a psychologist but rather a medical physiologist living in Russia.

I. P. Pavlov (1849–1936) earned a medical degree from the Imperial Medicosurgical Academy in 1879 and studied physiology in Germany before accepting a position as professor of pharmacology at the St. Petersburg Institute of Experimental Medicine in 1890. Pavlov won a Nobel Prize in 1904 for his research on the physiology of digestion in dogs.

The selection that follows is from chapter 1 of Pavlov's book *Conditioned Reflexes: An Investigation of the Physiological Activity of the Cerebral Cortex,* originally published in 1927 by Oxford University Press. Pavlov designed the laboratory where he studied conditioned reflexes in dogs. He presents the basic terminology of classical conditioning and discusses some of the factors that influence learning. Pavlov uses a lecture format and includes demonstrations of the actual research experiments.

Key Concept: classical conditioning

APA Citation: Pavlov, I. P. (1927). *Conditioned reflexes: An investigation of the physiological activity of the cerebral cortex.* London: Oxford University Press.

To come to the general technique of the [salivary secretion] experiments, it is important to remember that our research deals with the highly specialized activity of the cerebral cortex, a signalizing apparatus of tremendous complexity and of most exquisite sensitivity, through which the animal is influenced by countless stimuli from the outside world. Every one of these stimuli produces a certain effect upon the animal, and all of them taken together may clash and interfere with, or else reinforce, one another. Unless we are careful to take special precautions the success of the whole investigation may be jeopardized, and we should get hopelessly lost as soon as we began to seek for cause and effect among so many and various influences, so intertwined and entangled as to form a veritable chaos. It was evident that the experimental conditions had to be simplified, and that this simplification must consist in eliminating as far as possible any stimuli outside our control which might fall upon the animal, admitting only such stimuli as could be entirely controlled by the experimenter. It was thought at the beginning of our research that it would be sufficient simply to isolate the experimenter in the research chamber with the dog on its stand, and to refuse admission to anyone else during the course of an experiment. But this precaution was found to be wholly inadequate, since the experimenter, however still he might try to be, was himself a constant source of a large number of stimuli. His slightest movements—blinking of the eyelids or movement of the eyes, posture, respiration and so on—all acted as stimuli which, falling upon the dog, were sufficient to vitiate the experiments by making exact interpretation of the results extremely difficult. In order to exclude this undue influence on the part of the experimenter as far as possible, he had to be stationed outside the room in which the dog was placed, and even this precaution proved unsuccessful in laboratories not specially designed for the study of these particular reflexes. The environment of the animal, even when shut up by itself in a room, is perpetually changing. Footfalls of a passer-by, chance conversations in neighbouring rooms, slamming of a door or vibration from a passing van, street-cries, even shadows cast through the windows into the room, any of these casual uncontrolled stimuli falling upon the receptors of the dog set up a disturbance in the cerebral hemispheres and vitiate the experiments. To get over all these disturbing factors a special laboratory was built at the Institute of Experimental Medicine in Petrograd, the funds being provided by a keen and public-spirited Moscow business man. The primary task was the protection of the dogs from uncontrolled extraneous stimuli, and this was effected by surrounding the building with an isolating trench and employing other special structural devices. Inside the building all the research rooms (four to each floor) were isolated from one another by a cross-shaped corridor; the top and ground floors, where these rooms were situated, were separated by an intermediate floor. Each research room was carefully partitioned by the use of sound-proof materials into two compartments—one for the animal, the other for the experimenter. For stimulating the animal, and for registering the corresponding reflex response, electrical methods or pneumatic transmission were used. By means of these arrangements it was possible to get something of that stability of environmental conditions so essential to the carrying out of a successful experiment....

The foregoing remarks give an idea of our general aim and of the technical side of our methods. I propose to introduce you to the first and most elementary principles of the subject matter of our research by means of a few demonstrations:

DEMONSTRATION.— The dog used in the following experiment has been operated upon [so that the opening of the salivary duct is transplanted to the outside skin in order to more easily measure secretory activity of the gland]. It can be seen that so long as no special stimulus is applied the salivary glands remain quite inactive. But when the sounds from a beating metronome are allowed to fall upon the ear, a salivary secretion begins after 9 seconds, and in the course of 45 seconds eleven drops have been secreted. The activity of the salivary gland has thus been called into play by impulses of sound—a stimulus quite alien to food. This activity of the salivary gland cannot be regarded as anything else than a component of the alimentary reflex. Besides the secretory, the motor component of the food reflex is also very apparent in experiments of this kind. In this very experiment the dog turns in the direction from which it has been customary to present the food and begins to lick its lips vigorously.

This experiment is an example of a central nervous activity depending on the integrity of the hemispheres. A decerebrate dog would never have responded by salivary secretion to any stimulus of the kind. It is obvious also that the underlying principle of this activity is signalization. The sound of the metronome is the signal for food, and the animal reacts to the signal in the same way as if it were food; no distinction can be observed between the effects produced on the animal by the sounds of the beating metronome and showing it real food.

DEMONSTRATION.— Food is shown to the animal. The salivary secretion begins after 5 seconds, and six drops are collected in the course of 15 seconds. The effect is the same as that observed with the sounds of the metronome. It is again a case of signalization, and is due to the activity of the hemispheres.

That the effect of sight and smell of food is not due to an inborn reflex, but to a reflex which has been acquired in the course of the animal's own individual existence, was shown by experiments carried out by Dr. Zitovich in the laboratory of the late Prof. Vartanov. Dr. Zitovich took several young puppies away from their mother and fed them for a considerable time only on milk. When the puppies were a few months old he established fistulae of their salivary ducts, and was thus able to measure accurately the secretory activity of the glands. He now showed these puppies some solid food—bread or meat—but no secretion of saliva was evoked. It is evident, therefore, that the sight of food does not in itself act as a direct stimulus to salivary secretion. Only after the puppies have been allowed to eat bread and meat on several occasions does the sight or smell of these foodstuffs evoke the secretion.

The following experiment serves to illustrate the activity of the salivary gland as an inborn reflex in contrast to signalization:

DEMONSTRATION.— Food is suddenly introduced into the dog's mouth; secretion begins in 1 to 2 seconds. The secretion is brought about by the physical and chemical properties of the food itself acting upon receptors in the mucous membrane of the mouth and tongue. It is purely reflex.

This comparatively simple experiment explains how a decerebrate dog can die of starvation in the midst of plenty, for it will only start eating if food chances to come into contact with its mouth or tongue. Moreover, the elementary nature of the inborn reflexes, with their limitations and inadequacy, are clearly brought out in these experiments, and we are now able to appreciate the fundamental importance of those stimuli which have the character of *signals*.

Our next step will be to consider the question of the nature of signalization and of its mechanism from a purely physiological point of view.... [A] reflex is an inevitable reaction of the organism to an external stimulus, brought about along a definite path in the nervous system. Now it is quite evident that in signalization all the properties of a reflex are present. In the first place an external stimulus is required. This was given in our first experiment by the sounds of a metronome. These sounds falling on the auditory receptor of the dog caused the propagation of an impulse along the auditory nerve. In the brain the impulse was transmitted to the secretory nerves of the salivary glands, and passed thence to the glands, exciting them to active secretion. It is true that in the experiment with the metronome an interval of several seconds elapsed between the beginning of the stimulus and the beginning of the salivary secretion, whereas the time interval for the inborn reflex secretion was only 1 to 2 seconds. The longer latent period was, however, due to some special conditions of the experiment, as will come out more clearly as we proceed. But generally speaking the reaction to signals under natural conditions is as speedy as are the inborn reflexes....

In our general survey we characterized a reflex as a necessary reaction following upon a strictly definite stimulus under strictly defined conditions. Such a definition holds perfectly true also for signalization; the only difference is that the type of the effective reaction to signals depends upon a greater number of conditions. But this does not make signalization differ fundamentally from the better known reflexes in any respect, since in the latter, variations in character or force, inhibition and absence of reflexes, can also be traced to some definite change in the conditions of the experiment.

Thorough investigation of the subject shows that accident plays no part whatever in the signalizing activity of the hemispheres, and all experiments proceed strictly according to plan. In the special laboratory I have described, the animal can frequently be kept under rigid experimental observation for 1 to 2 hours without a single drop of saliva being secreted independently of stimuli

applied by the observer, although in the ordinary type of physiological laboratory experiments are very often distorted by the interference of extraneous and
uncontrolled stimuli.

All these conditions leave no grounds for regarding the phenomena which
we have termed "signalization" as being anything else than reflex. There is,
however, another aspect of the question which at a first glance seems to point
to an essential difference between the better known reflexes and signalization.
Food, through its chemical and physical properties, evokes the salivary reflex in
every dog right from birth, whereas this new type claimed as reflex—"the signal reflex"—is built up gradually in the course of the animal's own individual
existence. But can this be considered as a fundamental point of difference, and
can it hold as a valid argument against employing the term "reflex" for this new
group of phenomena? It is certainly a sufficient argument for making a definite
distinction between the two types of reflex and for considering the signal reflex
in a group distinct from the inborn reflex. But this does not invalidate in any
way our right logically to term both "reflex," since the point of distinction does
not concern the character of the response on the part of the organism, but only
the mode of formation of the reflex mechanism. We may take the telephonic
installation as an illustration. Communication can be effected in two ways. My
residence may be connected directly with the laboratory by a private line, and
I may call up the laboratory whenever it pleases me to do so; or on the other
hand, a connection may have to be made through the central exchange. But the
result in both cases is the same. The only point of distinction between the methods is that the private line provides a permanent and readily available cable,
while the other line necessitates a preliminary central connection being established. In the one case the communicating wire is always complete, in the other
case a small addition must be made to the wire at the central exchange. We have
a similar state of affairs in reflex action. The path of the inborn reflex is already
completed at birth; but the path of the signalizing reflex has still to be completed
in the higher nervous centres. We are thus brought to consider the mode of formation of new reflex mechanisms. A new reflex is formed inevitably under a
given set of physiological conditions, and with the greatest ease, so that there
is no need to take the subjective states of the dog into consideration. With a
complete understanding of all the factors involved, the new signalizing reflexes
are under the absolute control of the experimenter; they proceed according to
as rigid laws as do any other physiological processes, and must be regarded as
being in every sense a part of the physiological activity of living beings. I have
termed this new group of reflexes conditioned reflexes to distinguish them from
the inborn or unconditioned reflexes. The term "conditioned" is becoming more
and more generally employed, and I think its use is fully justified in that, compared with the inborn reflexes, these new reflexes actually do depend on very
many conditions, both in their formation and in the maintenance of their physiological activity. Of course the terms "conditioned" and "unconditioned" could
be replaced by others of arguably equal merit. Thus, for example, we might
retain the term "inborn reflexes," and call the new type "acquired reflexes";
or call the former "species reflexes" since they are characteristic of the species,
and the latter "individual reflexes" since they vary from animal to animal in a
species, and even in the same animal at different times and under different con-

ditions. Or again we might call the former "conduction reflexes" and the latter "connection reflexes."

There should be no theoretical objection to the hypothesis of the formation of new physiological paths and new connections within the cerebral hemispheres. Since the especial function of the central nervous system is to establish most complicated and delicate correspondences between the organism and its environment we may not unnaturally expect to find there, on the analogy of the methods used by the technician in everyday experience, a highly developed connector system superimposed on a conductor system. The physiologist certainly should not object to this conception seeing that he has been used to employing the German conception of "Bahnung," which means a laying down of fresh physiological paths in the centres. Conditioned reflexes are phenomena of common and widespread occurrence: their establishment is an integral function in everyday life. We recognize them in ourselves and in other people or animals under such names as "education," "habits," and "training;" and all of these are really nothing more than the results of an establishment of new nervous connections during the post-natal existence of the organism. They are, in actual fact, links connecting definite extraneous stimuli with their definite responsive reactions. I believe that the recognition and the study of the conditioned reflex will throw open the door to a true physiological investigation probably of all the highest nervous activities of the cerebral hemispheres, and the purpose of the present lectures is to give some account of what we have already accomplished in this direction.

We come now to consider the precise conditions under which new conditioned reflexes or new connections of nervous paths are established. The fundamental requisite is that any external stimulus which is to become the signal in a conditioned reflex must overlap in point of time with the action of an unconditioned stimulus. In the experiment which I chose as my example the unconditioned stimulus was food. Now if the intake of food by the animal takes place simultaneously with the action of a neutral stimulus which has been hitherto in no way related to food, the neutral stimulus readily acquires the property of eliciting the same reaction in the animal as would food itself. This was the case with the dog employed in our experiment with the metronome. On several occasions this animal had been stimulated by the sound of the metronome and immediately presented with food—*i.e.* a stimulus which was neutral of itself had been superimposed upon the action of the inborn alimentary reflex. We observed that, after several repetitions of the combined stimulation, the sounds from the metronome had acquired the property of stimulating salivary secretion and of evoking the motor reactions characteristic of the alimentary reflex. The first demonstration was nothing but an example of such a conditioned stimulus in action. Precisely the same occurs with the mild defence reflex to rejectable substances. Introduction into the dog's mouth of a little of an acid solution brings about a quite definite responsive reaction. The animal sets about getting rid of the acid, shaking its head violently, opening its mouth and making movements with its tongue. At the same time it produces a copious salivary secretion. The same reaction will infallibly be obtained from any stimulus which has previously been applied a sufficient number of times while acid was being introduced into the dog's mouth. Hence a first and most essential requisite for the formation of a new conditioned reflex lies in a coincidence in time of the action of any previously neutral stimulus with some definite unconditioned stimulus. Further, it is not enough that there should be overlapping between the two stimuli; it is also and equally necessary that the conditioned stimulus should begin to operate before the unconditioned stimulus comes into action.

If this order is reversed, the unconditioned stimulus being applied first and the neutral stimulus second, the conditioned reflex cannot be established at all. Dr. Krestovnikov performed these experiments with many different modifications and controls, but the effect was always the same. The following are some of his results:

In one case 427 applications were made in succession of the odour of vanillin together with the introduction of acid into the dog's mouth, but the acid was always made to precede the vanillin by some 5 to 10 seconds. Vanillin failed to acquire the properties of a conditioned stimulus. However, in the succeeding experiment, in which the order of stimuli was reversed, the odour, this time of amyl acetate, became an effective conditioned stimulus after only 20 combinations. With another dog the loud buzzing of an electric bell set going 5 to 10 seconds after administration of food failed to establish a conditioned alimentary reflex even after 374 combinations, whereas the regular rotation of an object in front of the eyes of the animal, the rotation beginning before the administration of food, acquired the properties of a conditioned stimulus after only 5 combinations. The electric buzzer set going before the administration of food established a conditioned alimentary reflex after only a single combination.

Dr. Krestovnikov's experiments were carried out on five dogs, and the result was always negative when the neutral stimulus was applied, whether 10 seconds, 5 seconds or only a single second after the beginning of the unconditioned stimulus. During all these experiments not only the secretory reflex but also the motor reaction of the animal was carefully observed, and these observations always corroborated one another. We thus see that the first set of conditions required for the formation of a new conditioned reflex encompasses the time relation between the presentation of the unconditioned stimulus and the presentation of that agent which has to acquire the properties of a conditioned stimulus.

As regards the condition of the hemispheres themselves, an alert state of the nervous system is absolutely essential for the formation of a new conditioned reflex. If the dog is mostly drowsy during the experiments, the establishment of a conditioned reflex becomes a long and tedious process, and in extreme cases is impossible to accomplish. The hemispheres must, however, be free from any other nervous activity, and therefore in building up a new conditioned reflex it is important to avoid foreign stimuli which, falling upon the animal, would cause other reactions of their own. If this is not attended to, the establishment of a conditioned reflex is very difficult, if not impossible. Thus, for example, if the dog has been so fastened up that anything causes severe irritation, it does not matter how many times the combination of stimuli is repeated, we shall not be able to obtain a conditioned reflex. A somewhat similar case was described [elsewhere]—that of the dog which exhibited the *freedom reflex* in an exaggerated degree. It can also be stated as a rule that the establishment of the first conditioned reflex in an animal is usually more difficult than the establishment of succeeding ones. It is obvious that this must be so, when we consider that even in the most favourable circumstances the experimental conditions themselves will be sure to provoke numerous different reflexes—*i.e.* will give rise to one or other disturbing activity of the hemispheres. But this statement must be qualified by remarking that in cases where the cause of these uncontrolled reflexes is not found out, so that we are not able to get rid of them, the hemispheres themselves will help us. For if the environment of the animal during the experiment does not contain any powerful disturbing elements, then practically always the extraneous reflexes will with time gradually and spontaneously weaken in strength.

The third factor determining the facility with which new conditioned reflexes can be established is the health of the animal. A good state of health will ensure the normal functioning of the cerebral hemispheres, and we shall not have to bother with the effects of any internal pathological stimuli.

The fourth, and last, group of conditions has to do with the properties of the stimulus which is to become conditioned, and also with the properties of the unconditioned stimulus which is selected. Conditioned reflexes are quite readily formed to stimuli to which the animal is more or less indifferent at the outset, though strictly speaking no stimulus within the animal's range of perception exists to which it would be absolutely indifferent. In a normal animal the slightest alteration in the environment—even the very slightest sound or faintest odour, or the smallest change in intensity of illumination—immediately evokes the reflex which I refer... to... as the investigatory reflex—"What is it?"—manifested by a very definite motor reaction. However, if these neutral stimuli keep recurring, they spontaneously and rapidly weaken in their effect upon the hemispheres, thus bringing about bit by bit the removal of this obstacle to the establishment of a conditioned reflex. But if the extraneous stimuli are strong or unusual, the formation of a conditioned reflex will be difficult, and in extreme cases impossible.

6.2 JOHN B. WATSON AND ROSALIE RAYNER

Conditioned Emotional Reactions

The desire of early researchers to apply the techniques of classical and operant conditioning—two forms of behavioral learning involving stimulus association and reinforcement—to understand practical problems led to John B. Watson's well-known Little Albert experiment, which is discussed in this selection. This classic experiment of how Albert learned to fear a white rat—and other furry or rat-like stimuli—has been a favorite of students and instructors alike.

Watson (1878–1958), the founder of the school of behaviorism, received his Ph.D. from the University of Chicago in 1903, where he taught for five years before moving to the Johns Hopkins University. Rosalie Rayner (d. 1935) was an assistant in the psychology laboratory during the Little Albert experiment. Eventually, Rayner and Watson were married.

This selection is from "Conditioned Emotional Reactions," which was published in *Journal of Experimental Psychology* in 1920. Although the Little Albert experiment was originally intended as a pilot study and had some methodological flaws, it serves as a classic example of how conditioning can modify behavior. Watson and Rayner describe explicitly the procedures they used and the results they obtained. Unfortunately, Albert's mother removed him from the hospital after the experiment was conducted; hence, the experimenters could not develop a technique to remove the conditioned fear reaction from him. As you read this selection, try to remember how you learned to fear certain events as you were growing up.

Key Concept: conditioned emotional reactions in infants

APA Citation: Watson, J. B., & Rayner, R. (1920). Conditioned emotional reactions. *Journal of Experimental Psychology, 3,* 1–14.

*I*n recent literature various speculations have been entered into concerning the possibility of conditioning various types of emotional response, but direct experimental evidence in support of such a view has been lacking. If the theory advanced by Watson and Morgan to the effect that in infancy the original emotional reaction patterns are few, consisting so far as observed of fear, rage and love, then there must be some simple method by means of which the range of stimuli which can call out these emotions and their compounds is greatly increased. Otherwise, complexity in adult response could not be accounted for. These authors without adequate experimental evidence advanced the view that this range was increased by means of conditioned reflex factors. It was suggested there that the early home life of the child furnishes a laboratory situation for establishing conditioned emotional responses. The present authors have recently put the whole matter to an experimental test.

Experimental work has been done so far on only one child, Albert B. This infant was reared almost from birth in a hospital environment; his mother was a wet nurse in the Harriet Lane Home for Invalid Children. Albert's life was normal: he was healthy from birth and one of the best developed youngsters ever brought to the hospital, weighing twenty-one pounds at nine months of age. He was on the whole stolid and unemotional. His stability was one of the principal reasons for using him as a subject in this test. We felt that we could do him relatively little harm by carrying out such experiments as those outlined below.

At approximately nine months of age we ran him through the emotional tests that have become a part of our regular routine in determining whether fear reactions can be called out by other stimuli than sharp noises and the sudden removal of support.... In brief, the infant was confronted suddenly and for the first time successively with a white rat, a rabbit, a dog, a monkey, with masks with and without hair, cotton wool, burning newspapers, etc. A permanent record of Albert's reactions to these objects and situations has been preserved in a motion picture study. Manipulation was the most usual reaction called out. *At no time did this infant ever show fear in any situation.* These experimental records were confirmed by the casual observations of the mother and hospital attendants. No one had ever seen him in a state of fear and rage. The infant practically never cried.

Up to approximately nine months of age we had not tested him with loud sounds. The test to determine whether a fear reaction could be called out by a loud sound was made when he was eight months, twenty-six days of age. The sound was that made by striking a hammer upon a suspended steel bar four feet in length and three-fourths of an inch in diameter. The laboratory notes are as follows:

> One of the two experimenters caused the child to turn its head and fixate her moving hand; the other, stationed back of the child, struck the steel bar a sharp blow. The child started violently, his breathing was checked and the arms were raised in a characteristic manner. On the second stimulation the same thing occurred, and in addition the lips began to pucker and tremble. On the third stimulation the child broke into a sudden crying fit. This is the first time an emotional situation in the laboratory has produced any fear or even crying in Albert.

We had expected just these results on account of our work with other infants brought up under similar conditions. It is worth while to call attention to the fact that removal of support (dropping and jerking the blanket upon which the infant was lying) was tried exhaustively upon this infant on the same occasion. It was not effective in producing the fear response. This stimulus is effective in younger children. At what age such stimuli lose their potency in producing fear is not known. Nor is it known whether less placid children ever lose their fear of them. This probably depends upon the training the child gets. It is well known that children eagerly run to be tossed into the air and caught. On the other hand it is equally well known that in the adult fear responses are called out quite clearly by the sudden removal of support, if the individual is walking across a bridge, walking out upon a beam, etc. There is a wide field of study here which is aside from our present point.

The sound stimulus, thus, at nine months of age, gives us the means of testing several important factors. I. Can we condition fear of an animal, *e.g.*, a white rat, by visually presenting it and simultaneously striking a steel bar? II. If such a conditioned emotional response can be established, will there be a transfer to other animals or other objects? . . .

I. The establishment of conditioned emotional responses. At first there was considerable hesitation upon our part in making the attempt to set up fear reactions experimentally. A certain responsibility attaches to such a procedure. We decided finally to make the attempt, comforting ourselves by the reflection that such attachments would arise anyway as soon as the child left the sheltered environment of the nursery for the rough and tumble of the home. We did not begin this work until Albert was eleven months, three days of age. Before attempting to set up a conditioned response we, as before, put him through all of the regular emotional tests. *Not the slightest sign of a fear response was obtained in any situation.*

The steps taken to condition emotional responses are shown in our laboratory notes.

11 Months 3 Days

1. White rat suddenly taken from the basket and presented to Albert. He began to reach for rat with left hand. Just as his hand touched the animal the bar was struck immediately behind his head. The infant jumped violently and fell forward, burying his face in the mattress. He did not cry, however.
2. Just as the right hand touched the rat the bar was again struck. Again the infant jumped violently, fell forward and began to whimper.

In order not to disturb the child too seriously no further tests were given for one week.

11 Months 10 Days

1. Rat presented suddenly without sound. There was steady fixation but no tendency at first to reach for it. The rat was then placed nearer,

whereupon tentative reaching movements began with the right hand. When the rat nosed the infant's left hand, the hand was immediately withdrawn. He started to reach for the head of the animal with the forefinger of the left hand, but withdrew it suddenly before contact. It is thus seen that the two joint stimulations given the previous week were not without effect. He was tested with his blocks immediately afterwards to see if they shared in the process of conditioning. He began immediately to pick them up, dropping them, pounding them, etc. In the remainder of the tests the blocks were given frequently to quiet him and to test his general emotional state. They were always removed from sight when the process of conditioning was under way.

2. Joint stimulation with rat and sound. Started, then fell over immediately to right side. No crying.
3. Joint stimulation. Fell to right side and rested upon hands, with head turned away from rat. No crying.
4. Joint stimulation. Same reaction.
5. Rat suddenly presented alone. Puckered face, whimpered and withdrew body sharply to the left.
6. Joint stimulation. Fell over immediately to right side and began to whimper.
7. Joint stimulation. Started violently and cried, but did not fall over.
8. Rat alone. *The instant the rat was shown the baby began to cry. Almost instantly he turned sharply to the left, fell over on left side, raised himself on all fours and began to crawl away so rapidly that he was caught with difficulty before reaching the edge of the table.*

This was as convincing a case of a completely conditioned fear response as could have been theoretically pictured. In all seven joint stimulations were given to bring about the complete reaction. It is not unlikely had the sound been of greater intensity or of a more complex clang character that the number of joint stimulations might have been materially reduced. Experiments designed to define the nature of the sounds that will serve best as emotional stimuli are under way.

II. When a conditioned emotional response has been established for one object, is there a transfer? Five days later Albert was again brought back into the laboratory and tested as follows:

11 Months 15 Days

1. Tested first with blocks. He reached readily for them, playing with them as usual. This shows that there has been no general transfer to the room, table, blocks, etc.
2. Rat alone. Whimpered immediately, withdrew right hand and turned head and trunk away.
3. Blocks again offered. Played readily with them, smiling and gurgling.

4. Rat alone. Leaned over to the left side as far away from the rat as possible, then fell over, getting up on all fours and scurrying away as rapidly as possible.

5. Blocks again offered. Reached immediately for them, smiling and laughing as before. The above preliminary test shows that the conditioned response to the rat had carried over completely for the five days in which no tests were given. The question as to whether or not there is a transfer was next taken up.

6. Rabbit alone. The rabbit was suddenly placed on the mattress in front of him. The reaction was pronounced. Negative responses began at once. He leaned as far away from the animal as possible, whimpered, then burst into tears. When the rabbit was placed in contact with him he buried his face in the mattress, then got up on all fours and crawled away, crying as he went. This was a most convincing test.

7. The blocks were next given him, after an interval. He played with them as before. It was observed by four people that he played far more energetically with them than ever before. The blocks were raised high over his head and slammed down with a great deal of force.

8. Dog alone. The dog did not produce as violent a reaction as the rabbit. The moment fixation occurred the child shrank back and as the animal came nearer he attempted to get on all fours but did not cry at first. As soon as the dog passed out of his range of vision he became quiet. The dog was then made to approach the infant's head (he was lying down at the moment). Albert straightened up immediately, fell over to the opposite side and turned his head away. He then began to cry.

9. The blocks were again presented. He began immediately to play with them.

10. Fur coat (seal). Withdrew immediately to the left side and began to fret. Coat put close to him on the left side, he turned immediately, began to cry and tried to crawl away on all fours.

11. Cotton wool. The wool was presented in a paper package. At the end the cotton was not covered by the paper. It was placed first on his feet. He kicked it away but did not touch it with his hands. When his hand was laid on the wool he immediately withdrew it but did not show the shock that the animals or fur coat produced in him. He then began to play with the paper, avoiding contact with the wool itself. He finally, under the impulse of the manipulative instinct, lost some of his negativism to the wool.

12. Just in play W. put his head down to see if Albert would play with his hair. Albert was completely negative. Two other observers did the same thing. He began immediately to play with their hair. W. then brought the Santa Claus mask and presented it to Albert. He was again pronouncedly negative....

From the above results it would seem that emotional transfers do take place. Furthermore it would seem that the number of transfers resulting from an experimentally produced conditioned emotional reaction may be very large. In our observations we had no means of testing the complete number of transfers which may have resulted....

INCIDENTAL OBSERVATIONS

(a) Thumb sucking as a compensatory device for blocking fear and noxious stimuli. During the course of these experiments,... it was noticed that whenever Albert was on the verge of tears or emotionally upset generally he would continually thrust his thumb into his mouth. The moment the hand reached the mouth he became impervious to the stimuli producing fear. Again and again while the motion pictures were being made at the end of the thirty-day rest period, we had to remove the thumb from his mouth before the conditioned response could be obtained. This method of blocking noxious and emotional stimuli (fear and rage) through erogenous stimulation seems to persist from birth onward....

(b) Equal primacy of fear, love and possibly rage. While in general the results of our experiment offer no particular points of conflict with Freudian concepts, one fact out of harmony with them should be emphasized. According to proper Freudians sex (or in our terminology, love) is the principal emotion in which conditioned responses arise which later limit and distort personality. We wish to take sharp issue with this view on the basis of the experimental evidence we have gathered. Fear is as primal a factor as love in influencing personality. Fear does not gather its potency in any derived manner from love. It belongs to the original and inherited nature of man. Probably the same may be true of rage although at present we are not so sure of this....

It is probable that many of the phobias in psychopathology are true conditioned emotional reactions either of the direct or the transferred type. One may possibly have to believe that such persistence of early conditioned responses will be found only in persons who are constitutionally inferior. Our argument is meant to be constructive. Emotional disturbances in adults cannot be traced back to sex alone. They must be retraced along at least three collateral lines—to conditioned and transferred responses set up in infancy and early youth in all three of the fundamental human emotions.

Shaping and Maintaining Operant Behavior

Reinforcement—an event that increases the probability that the behavior preceding it will be repeated—can have a profound effect on behavior, and we typically do things that lead to reinforcement. Much of what scientists originally discovered about the effects of reinforcement on animals has been applied to human behavior. The study of how reinforcement changes behavior is known as operant conditioning.

B. F. Skinner (1904–1990) was a pioneer in the study of operant conditioning. Skinner earned a B.A. in English from Hamilton College in 1926, but he decided he did not have anything important to say, so he went back to school and earned a Ph.D. in psychology from Harvard University in 1931. Indeed, he did have much to say, and he wrote numerous books, including *The Behavior of Organisms* (1938) and the fictional *Walden Two* (1948), in which Skinner describes a utopian society run in accordance with operant principles. In *Beyond Freedom and Dignity* (Alfred A. Knopf, 1971), he explains why it is important to understand how we control behavior in our day-to-day lives.

This selection is from chapter 6, "Shaping and Maintaining Operant Behavior," of Skinner's *Science and Human Behavior* (Free Press, 1953). Although Skinner's favorite subject for study was the pigeon, as illustrated in this selection, he believed that the laws of behavior apply to all organisms. Note how Skinner neatly applies the results of his animal research to human beings, as well as how clearly he defines the four intermittent schedules of reinforcement.

Key Concept: operant conditioning

APA Citation: Skinner, B. F. (1953). *Science and human behavior.* New York: Macmillan.

THE CONTINUITY OF BEHAVIOR

Operant conditioning [a process in which reinforcement changes the frequency of a behavior] shapes behavior as a sculptor shapes a lump of clay. Although at some point the sculptor seems to have produced an entirely novel object, we can always follow the process back to the original undifferentiated lump, and we can make the successive stages by which we return to this condition as small as we wish. At no point does anything emerge which is very different from what preceded it. The final product seems to have a special unity or integrity of design, but we cannot find a point at which this suddenly appears. In the same sense, an operant [behavior generated by reinforcement consequences] is not something which appears full grown in the behavior of the organism. It is the result of a continuous shaping process.

The pigeon experiment demonstrates this clearly. "Raising the head" is not a discrete unit of behavior. It does not come, so to speak, in a separate package. We reinforce only slightly exceptional values of the behavior observed while the pigeon is standing or moving about. We succeed in shifting the whole range of heights at which the head is held, but there is nothing which can be accurately described as a new "response." A response such as turning the latch in a problem box appears to be a more discrete unit, but only because the continuity with other behavior is more difficult to observe. In the pigeon, the response of pecking at a spot on the wall of the experimental box seems to differ from stretching the neck because no other behavior of the pigeon resembles it. If in reinforcing such a response we simply wait for it to occur—and we may have to wait many hours or days or weeks—the whole unit appears to emerge in its final form and to be strengthened as such. There may be no appreciable behavior which we could describe as "almost pecking the spot."

The continuous connection between such an operant and the general behavior of the bird can nevertheless easily be demonstrated. It is the basis of a practical procedure for setting up a complex response. To get the pigeon to peck the spot as quickly as possible we proceed as follows: We first give the bird food when it turns slightly in the direction of the spot from any part of the cage. This increases the frequency of such behavior. We then withhold reinforcement until a slight movement is made toward the spot. This again alters the general distribution of behavior without producing a new unit. We continue by reinforcing positions successively closer to the spot, then by reinforcing only when the head is moved slightly forward, and finally only when the beak actually makes contact with the spot. We may reach this final response in a remarkably short time. A hungry bird, well adapted to the situation and to the food tray, can usually be brought to respond in this way in two or three minutes.

The original probability of the response in its final form is very low; in some cases it may even be zero. In this way we can build complicated operants which would never appear in the repertoire of the organism otherwise. By reinforcing a series of successive approximations, we bring a rare response to a very high probability in a short time. This is an effective procedure because it recognizes and utilizes the continuous nature of a complex act. The total act of turning toward the spot from any point in the box, walking toward it, raising the head, and striking the spot may seem to be a functionally coherent unit of behavior; but it is constructed by a continual process of differential reinforcement from undifferentiated behavior, just as the sculptor shapes his figure from a lump of clay. When we wait for a single complete instance, we reinforce a similar sequence but far less effectively because the earlier steps are not optimally strengthened.

This account is inaccurate in one respect. We may detect a discontinuity between bringing the head close to the spot and pecking. The pecking movement usually emerges as an obviously preformed unit. There are two possible explanations. A mature pigeon will already have developed a well-defined pecking response which may emerge upon the present occasion. The history of this response might show a similar continuity if we could follow it. It is possible, however, that there is a genetic discontinuity, and that in a bird such as the pigeon the pecking response has a special strength and a special coherence as a form of species behavior. Vomiting and sneezing are human responses which probably have a similar genetic unity. Continuity with other behavior must be sought in the evolutionary process. But these genetic units are rare, at least in the vertebrates. The behavior with which we are usually concerned, from either a theoretical or practical point of view, is continuously modified from a basic material which is largely undifferentiated.

Through the reinforcement of slightly exceptional instances of his behavior, a child learns to raise himself, to stand, to walk, to grasp objects, and to move them about. Later on, through the same process, he learns to talk, to sing, to dance, to play games—in short, to exhibit the enormous repertoire characteristic of the normal adult. When we survey behavior in these later stages, we find it convenient to distinguish between various operants which differ from each other in topography and produce different consequences. In this way behavior is broken into parts to facilitate analysis. These parts are the units which we count and whose frequencies play an important role in arriving at laws of behavior. They are the "acts" into which, in the vocabulary of the layman, behavior is divided. But if we are to account for many of its quantitative properties, the ultimately continuous nature of behavior must not be forgotten....

THE MAINTENANCE OF BEHAVIOR

One reason the term "learning" is not equivalent to "operant conditioning" is that traditionally it has been confined to the process of learning *how to do something*. In trial-and-error learning, for example, the organism learns how to get out of a box or how to find its way through a maze. It is easy to see why the acquisition of behavior should be emphasized. Early devices for the study of learning did not reveal the basic process directly. The effect of operant reinforcement is most conspicuous when there is a gross change in behavior. Such a chance occurs when an organism learns how to make a response which it did not or could not make before. A more sensitive measure, however, enables us to deal with cases in which the acquisition of behavior is of minor importance.

Operant conditioning continues to be effective even when there is no further change which can be spoken of as acquisition or even as improvement in skill. Behavior continues to have consequences and these continue to be important. If consequences are not forthcoming, extinction occurs. When we come to consider the behavior of the organism in all the complexity of its everyday life, we need to be constantly alert to the prevailing reinforcements, which maintain its behavior. We may, indeed, have little interest in how that behavior was first acquired. Our concern is only with its present probability of occurrence, which can be understood only through an examination of current contingencies of reinforcement. This is an aspect of reinforcement which is scarcely ever dealt with in classical treatments of learning.

INTERMITTENT REINFORCEMENT

In general, behavior which acts upon the immediate physical environment is consistently reinforced. We orient ourselves toward objects and approach, reach for, and seize them with a stable repertoire of responses which have uniform consequences arising from the optical and mechanical properties of nature. It is possible, of course, to disturb the uniformity. In a "house of mirrors" in an amusement park, or in a room designed to supply misleading cues to the vertical, well-established responses may fail to have their usual effects. But the fact that such conditions are so unusual as to have commercial value testifies to the stability of the everyday world.

A large part of behavior, however, is reinforced only intermittently. A given consequence may depend upon a series of events which are not easily predicted. We do not always win at cards or dice, because the contingencies are so remotely determined that we call them "chance." We do not always find good ice or snow when we go skating or skiing. Contingencies which require the participation of people are especially likely to be uncertain. We do not always get a good meal in a particular restaurant because cooks are not always predictable. We do not always get an answer when we telephone a friend because the friend is not always at home. We do not always get a pen by reaching into our pocket because we have not always put it there. The reinforcements characteristic of industry and education are almost always intermittent because it is not feasible to control behavior by reinforcing every response.

As might be expected, behavior which is reinforced only intermittently often shows an intermediate frequency of occurrence, but laboratory studies of various schedules have revealed some surprising complexities. Usually such behavior is remarkably stable and shows great resistance to extinction.* An experiment has already been mentioned in which more than 10,000 responses appeared in the extinction curve of a pigeon which had been reinforced on a special schedule. Nothing of the sort is ever obtained after continuous reinforcement. Since this is a technique for "getting more responses out of an organism" in return for a given number of reinforcements, it is widely used. Wages are paid in special ways and betting and gambling devices are designed to "pay off" on special schedules because of the relatively large return on the reinforcement in such a case. Approval, affection, and other personal favors are frequently intermittent, not only because the person supplying the reinforcement may behave in different ways at different times, but precisely because he may have found that such a schedule yields a more stable, persistent, and profitable return.

---

* [Extinction is a decline in behavior frequency due to the withholding of reinforcement.—Ed.]

It is important to distinguish between schedules which are arranged by a system outside the organism and those which are controlled by the behavior itself. An example of the first is a schedule of reinforcement which is determined by a clock—as when we reinforce a pigeon every five minutes, allowing all intervening responses to go unreinforced. An example of the second is a schedule in which a response is reinforced after a certain number of responses have been emitted—as when we reinforce every fiftieth response the pigeon makes. The cases are similar in the sense that we reinforce intermittently in both, but subtle differences in the contingencies lead to very different results, often of great practical significance.

Interval Reinforcement

If we reinforce behavior at regular intervals, an organism such as a rat or pigeon will adjust with a nearly constant rate of responding, determined by the frequency of reinforcement. If we reinforce it every minute, the animal responds rapidly; if every five minutes, much more slowly. A similar effect upon probability of response is characteristic of human behavior. How often we call a given number on the telephone will depend, other things being equal, upon how often we get an answer. If two agencies supply the same service, we are more likely to call the one which answers more often. We are less likely to see friends or acquaintances with whom we only occasionally have a good time, and we are less likely to write to a correspondent who seldom answers. The experimental results are precise enough to suggest that in general the organism gives back a certain number of responses for each response reinforced. We shall see, however, that the results of schedules of reinforcement are not always reducible to a simple equating of input with output.

Since behavior which appears under interval reinforcement is especially stable, it is useful in studying other variables and conditions. The size or amount of each reinforcement affects the rate—more responses appearing in return for a larger reinforcement. Different kinds of reinforcers also yield different rates, and these may be used to rank reinforcers in the order of their effectiveness. The rate varies with the immediacy of the reinforcement: a slight delay between response and the receipt of the reinforcer means a lower over-all rate. Other variables which have been studied under interval reinforcement will be discussed in later chapters. They include the degree of deprivation and the presence or absence of certain emotional circumstances.

Optimal schedules of reinforcement are often of great practical importance. They are often discussed in connection with other variables which affect the rate. Reinforcing a man with fifty dollars at one time may not be so effective as reinforcing him with five dollars at ten different times during the same period. This is especially the case with primitive people where conditioned reinforcers have not been established to bridge the temporal span between a response and its ultimate consequence. There are also many subtle interactions between schedules of reinforcement and levels of motivation, immediacy of reinforcement, and so on.

If behavior continues to be reinforced at fixed intervals, another process intervenes. Since responses are never reinforced just after reinforcement, a change... eventually takes place in which the rate of responding is low for a short time after each reinforcement. The rate rises again when an interval of time has elapsed which the organism presumably cannot distinguish from the interval at which it is reinforced. These changes in rate are not characteristic of the effect of wages in industry, which would otherwise appear to be an example of a fixed-interval schedule. The discrepancy is explained by the fact that other reinforcing systems are used to maintain a given level of work.... Docking a man for time absent guarantees his presence each day by establishing a time-card entry as a conditioned reinforcer. The aversive reinforcement supplied by a supervisor or boss is, however, the principal supplement to a fixed-interval wage.

A low probability of response just after reinforcement is eliminated with what is called *variable-interval* reinforcement. Instead of reinforcing a response every five minutes, for example, we reinforce every five minutes *on the average,* where the intervening interval may be as short as a few seconds or as long as, say, ten minutes. Reinforcement occasionally occurs just after the organism has been reinforced, and the organism therefore continues to respond at that time. Its performance under such a schedule is remarkably stable and uniform. Pigeons reinforced with food with a variable interval averaging five minutes between reinforcements have been observed to respond for as long as fifteen hours at a rate of from two to three responses per second without pausing longer than fifteen or twenty seconds during the whole period. It is usually very difficult to extinguish a response after such a schedule. Many sorts of social or personal reinforcement are supplied on what is essentially a variable-interval basis, and extraordinarily persistent behavior is sometimes set up.

Ratio Reinforcement

An entirely different result is obtained when the schedule of reinforcement depends upon the behavior of the organism itself—when, for example, we reinforce every fiftieth response. This is reinforcement at a "fixed ratio"— the ratio of reinforced to unreinforced responses. It is a common schedule in education, where the student is reinforced for completing a project or a paper or some other specific amount of work. It is essentially the basis of professional pay and of selling on commission. In industry it is known as piecework pay. It is a system of reinforcement which naturally recommends itself to employers because the cost of the labor required to produce a given result can be calculated in advance.

Fixed-ratio reinforcement generates a very high rate of response provided the ratio is not too high. This should follow from the input-output relation alone. Any slight increase in rate increases the frequency of reinforcement with the result that the rate should rise still further. If no other factor intervened, the rate should reach the highest possible value. A limiting factor, which makes itself felt in industry, is simple fatigue. The high rate of responding and the long hours of work generated by this schedule can be dangerous to health. This is the main reason why piecework pay is usually strenuously opposed by organized labor.

Another objection to this type of schedule is based upon the possibility that as the rate rises, the reinforcing agency will move to a larger ratio. In the laboratory, after first reinforcing every tenth response and then every fiftieth, we may find it possible to reinforce only every hundredth, although we could not have used this ratio in the beginning. In industry, the employee whose productivity has increased as the result of a piecework schedule may receive so large a weekly wage that the employer feels justified in increasing the number of units of work required for a given unit of pay.

Under ratios of reinforcement which can be sustained, the behavior eventually shows a very low probability just after reinforcement, as it does in the case of fixed-interval reinforcement. The effect is marked under high fixed ratios because the organism always has "a long way to go" before the next reinforcement. Wherever a piecework schedule is used—in industry, education, salesmanship, or the professions—low morale or low interest is most often observed just after a unit of work has been completed. When responding begins, the situation is improved by each response and the more the organism responds, the better the chances of reinforcement become. The result is a smooth gradient of acceleration as the organism responds more and more rapidly. The condition eventually prevailing under high fixed-ratio reinforcement is not an efficient over-all mode of responding. It makes relatively poor use of the available time, and the higher rates of responding may be especially fatiguing.

The laboratory study of ratio reinforcement has shown that for a given organism and a given measure of reinforcement there is a limiting ratio beyond which behavior cannot be sustained. The result of exceeding this ratio is an extreme degree of extinction of the sort which we call abulia. Long periods of inactivity begin to appear between separate ratio runs. This is not physical fatigue, as we may easily show by shifting to another schedule. It is often called "mental" fatigue, but this designation adds nothing to the observed fact that beyond a certain high ratio of reinforcement the organism simply has no behavior available. In both the laboratory study of ratio reinforcement and its practical application in everyday life, the first signs of strain imposed by too high a ratio are seen in these breaks. Before a pigeon stops altogether—in complete "abulia" —it will often not respond for a long time after reinforcement. In the same way, the student who has finished a term paper, perhaps in a burst of speed at the end of the gradient, finds it difficult to start work on a new assignment.

Exhaustion can occur under ratio reinforcement because there is no self-regulating mechanism. In interval reinforcement, on the other hand, any tendency toward extinction is opposed by the fact that when the rate declines, the next reinforcement is received in return for fewer responses. The variable-interval schedule is also self-protecting: an organism will stabilize its behavior at a given rate under any length of interval.

We get rid of the pauses after reinforcement on a fixed-ratio schedule by adopting essentially the same practice as in variable-interval reinforcement: we simply vary the ratios over a considerable range around some mean value. Successive responses may be reinforced or many hundreds of unreinforced responses may intervene. The probability of reinforcement at any moment remains essentially constant and the organism adjusts by holding to a constant rate. This "variable-ratio reinforcement" is much more powerful than a fixed-ratio schedule with the same mean number of responses. A pigeon may respond as rapidly as five times per second and maintain this rate for many hours.

The efficacy of such schedules in generating high rates has long been known to the proprietors of gambling establishments. Slot machines, roulette wheels, dice cages, horse races, and so on pay off on a schedule of variable-ratio reinforcement. Each device has its own auxiliary reinforcements, but the schedule is the important characteristic. Winning depends upon placing a bet and in the long run upon the number of bets placed, but no particular payoff can be predicted. The ratio is varied by any one of several "random" systems. The pathological gambler exemplifies the result. Like the pigeon with its five responses per second for many hours, he is the victim of an unpredictable contingency of reinforcement. The long-term net gain or loss is almost irrelevant in accounting for the effectiveness of this schedule.

CHAPTER 7 Memory

7.1 R. M. SHIFFRIN AND R. C. ATKINSON

Storage and Retrieval Processes in Long-Term Memory

People have always been fascinated with how human memory works. For the past three decades, the dominant model of human memory has been the three-memory store theory described by R. M. Shiffrin and R. C. Atkinson. According to this theory, information is processed in the sensory register, short-term store, and long-term store.

Shiffrin received his Ph.D. from Stanford University in 1968. He served as a Guggenheim Fellow prior to accepting his current position as professor of psychology and director of the cognitive science program at Indiana University.

Atkinson (b. 1929) earned his Ph.D. in 1955 from Indiana University. He served as professor of psychology at Stanford University from 1956 until 1975, when he became director of the National Science Foundation. He is currently with the University of California at Oakland.

The selection that follows, from "Storage and Retrieval Processes in Long-Term Memory," was published in *Psychological Review* in 1969. The authors suggest that memory is transferred from the sensory register to the short-term store and then to the long-term store, where it is permanently housed. They theorize that if one is unable to retrieve a memory, it is because other information is interfering with it. As you read this selection, think of applications for improving your memory based on this model.

Key Concept: model of memory

APA Citation: Shiffrin, R. M., & Atkinson, R. C. (1969). Storage and retrieval processes in long-term memory. *Psychological Review, 76,* 179–193.

We begin by describing the overall conception of the memory system. The system follows that described in Atkinson and Shiffrin (1965, 1968a), and is similar to those proposed by Feigenbaum (1966) and Norman (1968). The major components of the system are diagrammed in Figure 1: the sensory register, the short-term store (STS) and the long-term store (LTS). The solid arrows in the diagram represent directions in which information is transferred from one part of the system to another. Note that transfer is not meant to imply the removal of information from one store and the placing of it in the next; rather, transfer is an operation in which information in one store is "copied" into the next without affecting its status in the original store. It should be emphasized that our hypotheses about the various memory stores do not require any assumptions regarding the physiological locus of these stores; the system is equally consistent with the view that the stores are separate physiological structures as with the view that the short-term store is simply a temporary activation of information permanently stored in the long-term store. The control processes listed in Figure 1 are a sample of those which the subject (*S*) can call into play at his discretion, depending upon such factors as the task and the instructions. Control processes govern informational flow, rehearsal, memory search, output of responses, and so forth.

The sensory register is a very short-lived memory store which temporarily holds incoming sensory information while it is being initially processed and transferred to the short-term store. In the visual modality, for example, information will decay from the sensory register in a period of several hundred milliseconds (Sperling, 1960). Information in the short-term store, if not attended to by *S*, will decay and be lost in a period of about 30 seconds or less, but control processes such as rehearsal can maintain information in STS for as long as *S* desires (the buffer process in Figure 1 is one highly organized rehearsal scheme). While information resides in STS, portions of it are transferred to LTS. The long-term store is assumed to be a permanent repository of information; we realize that factors such as traumatic brain damage, lesions, and deterioration with extreme age must lead to memory loss, but such effects should be negligible in the types of experiments considered in this paper. Thus it is hypothesized that information, once stored in LTS, is never thereafter destroyed or eliminated. Nevertheless, the ability to retrieve information from LTS varies considerably with time and interfering material.

The short-term store serves a number of useful functions. On the one hand it decouples the memory system from the external environment and relieves the system from the responsibility of moment-to-moment attention to environmental changes. On the other hand, STS provides a working memory in which

FIGURE 1

A Flow Chart of the Memory System.

R. M. Shiffrin
and R. C.
Atkinson

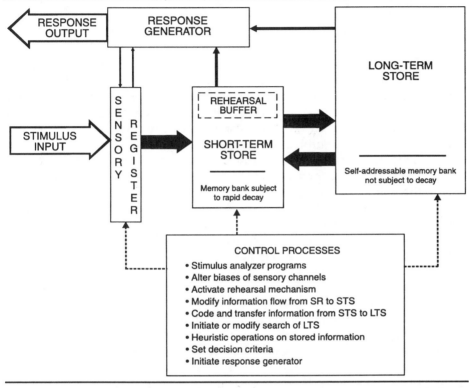

(Solid lines indicate paths of information transfer. Dashed lines indicate connections which permit comparison of information arrays residing in different parts of the system; they also indicate paths along which control signals may be sent which activate information transfer, rehearsal mechanisms, etc.)

manipulations of information may take place on a temporary basis. Because STS is a memory store in which information can be maintained if desired, it is often used as the primary memory device in certain types of tasks; in these tasks the information presented for retention is maintained in STS until the moment of test and then emitted. Tasks in which STS is utilized for this purpose, and the mechanisms and control processes that may come into play, have been examined extensively in Atkinson and Shiffrin (1968a). In this report we are primarily interested in STS as a temporary store in which information is manipulated for the purposes of storage and retrieval from LTS, rather than as a store in which information is maintained until test. In the remainder of this paper, discussion is limited to that component of memory performance which involves LTS retrieval, and the components arising from STS and the sensory register will not be considered.

LONG-TERM STORE

In describing the structure of LTS, an analogy with computer memories is helpful. The usual computer memory is "location addressable"; if the system is given a certain location it will return with the contents of that location. When given the contents of a word (a "word" refers to a single computer memory location), such a system must be programmed to examine each location in turn in order to find the possible locations of these contents in the memory. It seems untenable that an exhaustive serial search is made of all of LTS whenever retrieval is desired. An alternative type of memory may be termed "content-addressable"; if the system is given the contents of a word it will return with the locations in memory containing those contents. One way in which such a memory may be constructed utilizes a parallel search through all memory locations; the system then returns with the locations of all matches. If this view is adopted, however, an additional process is needed to select the desired location from among the many returned by the parallel search. Thus, if we feed the system the word "red," it would not be useful for the system to return with all references or locations of "red"; there are simply too many and the original retrieval problem would not be significantly reduced in scale. There is, however, an alternative method for forming a content-addressable memory; in this method, the contents to be located themselves contain the information necessary to specify the storage location(s). This can occur if the information is originally stored in locations specified by some master plan dependent upon the contents of the information. Such a system will be termed "self-addressing." A self-addressing memory may be compared with a library shelving system which is based upon the contents of the books. For example, a book on "caulking methods used for 12th century Egyptian rivercraft" will be placed in a specific library location (in the Egyptian room, etc.). If a user desires this book it may be located by following the same shelving plan used to store it in the first place. We propose that LTS is to a large degree just such a self-addressable memory. An ensemble of information presented to the memory system will define a number of memory areas in which that information is likely to be stored; the memory search will therefore have certain natural starting points. The system is assumed to be only partially self-addressing in that the degree to which the storage locations are specified will vary from one ensemble to the next and one moment to the next, in much the way as proposed in stimulus sampling theory (Estes, 1959). Thus it may be necessary to embark upon a memory search within the specified locations, a search which may proceed serially from one location to the next. This conception of LTS leads to a number of predictions. For example, a recognition test of memory will not proceed via exhaustive scanning of all stored codes, nor will a recognition test eliminate in all cases the necessity for an LTS search. If information is presented and S must indicate whether this information has been presented previously, then the likely storage location(s) is queried. To the degree that the information has highly salient characteristics which precisely identify the storage location, the extent of the LTS search will be reduced. Thus, for items with highly salient characteristics, S should be able to identify quickly and accurately whether the item was presented previously, and the identification might not require a memory search which interrogates more than a single storage location. The less well-specified the storage location, the greater the memory search needed to make an accurate recognition response. . . .

The term "location" is used in relation to the organizational schema; an LTS location is defined by the place in the organizational structure occupied by an information ensemble. The location will be defined in terms of the modality of the information (e.g., visual versus auditory), the level of analysis, (e.g., spelling versus syntactic structure), and all other dimensions of organization that may be relevant. Two locations will be said to be "close" if the information in them tends to be retrieved together. In particular, we shall refer to a *code*, or an *image*, as an ensemble of information that is closely related and very likely to be retrieved together. We do not wish to imply that there is some unitary atom of storage called a code or an image. The information making up a code in one task may be considered to be several codes in a different task. For example, an entire sentence may be considered a code if we are comparing the meaning of that sentence with others; however, the same sentence might be considered to be made up of a series of codes if we are comparing it with sentences of the same meaning but different grammatical form. Nevertheless, for most tasks the concept of a code or image as representing a cohesive array of information in a single storage location proves useful. . . .

141

*R. M. Shiffrin
and R. C.
Atkinson*

STORAGE AND RETRIEVAL

Since LTS is self-addressing, storage and retrieval have many features in common, one process mirroring the other. Storage is assumed to consist of three primary mechanisms: *transfer, placement,* and *image-production.* The transfer mechanism includes those control processes by which S decides what to store, when to store, and how to store information in LTS. The placement mechanism determines the locations in which the ensemble of information under consideration will be stored. To a large degree, the components of the ensemble itself will determine the location of storage. That is, in the action of encoding the desired information for storage, S may supplement the information currently in STS with pertinent information retrieved from LTS; the resultant ensemble in STS determines the storage location. The image-production mechanism determines what proportion of the current ensemble of information in STS will be placed in the designated LTS location(s). The proportion stored should be a function of the duration of the period that the ensemble is maintained in STS. Retrieval, like storage, is assumed to consist of three primary mechanisms: *search, recovery,* and *response generation.* The search process is a recursive loop in which locations or images are successively selected for examination. As each image is examined, the recovery process determines how much information will be recovered from the image and placed in STS. The response generation process then examines the recovered information and decides whether to continue the search or terminate and emit a response. If the search does not terminate, the selection of the next location or image for examination may depend upon information already uncovered during the search.

Although storage and retrieval are treated separately in this paper, we do not wish to imply that these processes are separated in time, one following the other. Rather, long-term storage is continually occurring for the information residing in short-term store. In addition, retrieval is continually occurring during storage attempts by S; for example, S may try to store a paired-associate by searching LTS for prominent associations to the stimulus, associations which could then be used as mediators. . . .

APPLICATIONS OF THE SYSTEM

Forgetting

Decrements in performance occur in the system as a result of the input of additional information to LTS. These decrements result from three related mechanisms. First is a mechanical effect; information sufficient to respond correctly at one point in time may prove inadequate after additional information has been added. For example, a paired-associate GAX-4 may be stored as G**-4, and this code will be sufficient for correct responding (if recovered) when GAX is tested. Suppose, however, that GEK-3 is now presented and stored as G**-3. When either of these stimuli is tested later, both codes may be retrieved from LTS and therefore S will have to guess whether the correct response is 3 or 4.

The second cause of forgetting arises from a breakdown in the directed component of the search mechanism. That is, correct retrieval requires that the same memory area be searched at test as was used for storage during study. This may not occur, however, if only a portion of the input information is used to direct storage during study, for a different portion might be utilized to locate the storage area during retrieval. This process could be viewed within the framework of stimulus sampling theory (Estes, 1959) if the stimulus elements are taken to represent dimensions of organization. For clarity, let us denote the image which encodes the correct response for the current test as a "c code," and denote the other codes as "i codes." Thus the i codes are irrelevant codes which should lead to intrusion errors, whereas the c code, if examined, should lead to a correct response. Then the directed component of search can be characterized by the probability that the c code is in the examination subset, called p_c. In experiments in which clues are available to denote the organizational dimensions to be searched, p_c may be close to 1.0. In other situations, such as continuous tasks with randomly chosen stimuli and responses, p_c will be lower and dependent upon such factors as the amount of information in the c code and its age (where "age" denotes the position of the code on the temporal dimension). Although the breakdown in the directed component can provide a reasonable degree of forgetting, we shall focus primarily upon the third mechanism of forgetting: the increasing size of the examination subset.

When searching the examination subset, there are a number of possible results. The c code may be examined and give rise to a correct response, one of the i codes may be examined and produce an intrusion response, or none of the codes may give rise to a response and the search terminates. If the search through the examination subset is at least partially random, then the following conclusions may be reached. When the size of the subset is increased (i.e., the number of i codes is increased), then the probability of giving an intrusion will increase, the average time until the c code is examined will increase, and the probability of giving a correct response will decrease. When we say that the order of search is *partially* random, we mean to imply that the order in which codes in the examination subset are selected for consideration may depend upon both the amount of information in the code and the age of the code. Clearly, as the amount of information in a code tends toward zero, or as the age of a code increases, the probability of examining that code early in the search should decrease....

Interference

Various interference phenomena are readily predicted by the system. Although in general the order of search through the examination subset will depend upon the age and amount of information in the codes, suppose for simplicity that the search order is entirely random. Then both nonspecific proactive and retroactive interference effects are predicted, and in a sense are predicted to be equal. That is, extra i codes in the examination subset added either temporally before or after the c code will cause the correct retrieval probability to drop; in the case of a random search the probability decrease will be the same whether caused by an i code preceding or following the c code. The drop occurs because the extra codes increase the amount of time required to find the c code. Therefore, if the size of the examination subset is increased, it is more likely that either response time will run out or an intrusion response will occur. Obviously the greater the degree to which the search is ordered temporally backwards from the most recent item, the less the proactive, and the greater the retroactive interference effect. Thus if codes are examined strictly in temporal order, the average amount of time until the c code is examined will be independent of the number of codes which are older than the c code and hence no proactive effect will be expected. One of the best places to examine nonspecific proactive and retroactive interference effects is in the study of free-verbal recall as a function of list length (Murdock, 1962). In this task a list of words is read to S, who attempts to recall as many of them as possible following their presentation. The data are usually graphed as a serial-position curve which gives the probability of correct recall as a function of the presentation position (and hence as a function of the number of preceding and succeeding items in the list). As the list length is varied, the number of preceding and succeeding items is systematically varied and it is possible to apply the theory to the resultant data. The application of the theory is made particularly easy in this case because S is trying to recall all of the list, and hence the examination subset can be assumed to consist of all codes that have been stored. In fact, a model derived from the theory has been applied to free-verbal recall data as a function of list length and has proved remarkably successful (Atkinson & Shiffrin, 1965, 1968a). The model assumes that performance decreases with list length because more codes are missed in the memory search at longer list lengths. This model also predicts that some of the missed codes should be retrieved if a second recall test is given following the first. Just such an effect was found by Tulving (1967), and its magnitude is predicted accurately by the model. Three successive recall tests were given following a single list presentation and only 50% of the items recalled were recalled on all three tests, even though the actual number recalled remained constant over the three tests.

Item-specific interference is also readily predicted via the search mechanism. Item interference refers to that condition arising when a stimulus originally paired with one response is later paired with a second, different response. In this case two different codes with the same stimulus may be placed in LTS. Thus, the amount of proactive or retroactive interference will depend upon the number of times the wrong code is examined and accepted prior to the correct code. In particular, the degree of temporal ordering in the search will affect the relative amounts of proactive and retroactive effects. That is, the greater the degree that the search is ordered temporally backwards from the most recent item, the less proactive and the greater retroactive effect is predicted. The reasoning is similar to that in the previous paragraph for nonspecific effects. This rather simple view of interference is complicated by at least two factors. First, if S is aware that he will eventually be tested for both responses, he may link them in nearby codes, or in a single code, and thereby reduce interference effects (Dallet & D'Andrea, 1965). Second, when the first response is changed, S may tag the first code with the information that the response is now wrong. If the first code is later recovered during search, then this information will enable him to inhibit an intrusion and continue the search; an effect like this was found by Shiffrin (1968)....

Intrusions

Another useful feature of the model is its natural prediction of intrusions, and of variations in intrusion rates over differing conditions. In a paired-associate task, an intrusion occurs when the response contained in an *i* code is recovered and emitted. Actually, the intrusion process has not yet been specified clearly, since both the probability of being in the examination subset and the probability of accepting the recovered response will be smaller for an *i* code than a *c* code containing an equal amount of information. It may be assumed that the likelihood of an *i* code being in the examination subset will be a function of its similarity to the test stimulus, since storage is carried out primarily on the basis of stimulus information. The probability of accepting an *i* code as being correct will similarly depend upon the generalization from the test stimulus to the stimulus information encoded in the *i* code. Given that the *i* code is examined and accepted, however, the probability that a response will be recovered and emitted should depend directly upon the response information encoded, just as for a *c* code....

Another phenomenon predicted by the theory is that of second-guessing, where second-guessing refers to the giving of a second response after S has been told that his first response is incorrect. A variety of assumptions can be made about this process, the simplest of which postulates that S continues his search of the examination subset from the point where the intrusion occurred. This assumption predicts that the level of second-guessing will be above chance, an effect found by Binford and Gettys (1965). If the search is temporally ordered to any degree, then strong predictions can be made concerning the second-guessing rate depending upon whether the response given in error was paired in the sequence with a stimulus occurring before or after the tested stimulus (assuming that the task utilizes a set of unique responses). In fact, examination of this effect is one method of determining the temporal characteristics of the search.

Latency of Responses

Another variable which may be predicted from the theory in a straightforward way is the latency of responses. The basic assumption requires latency to be a monotonic increasing function of the number of images examined before a response is emitted. Among the implications of this assumption are the following. Latencies of correct responses should increase with increases in the number of intervening items. This prediction holds whenever there is some temporal component to the search, or whenever the number of items preceding the tested item is large. If the reasonable assumption is made that codes containing more information are examined earlier in the search, then a decrease in correct response latency is expected as the number of reinforcements increase, since the item will gain stored information over reinforcements and therefore tend to be examined earlier in the search. This effect has been found by Rumelhart (1967) and Shiffrin (1968) in a continuous paired-associate task. In general, any manipulation designed to vary the number of codes examined, whether by instructions, by organization of the presented material, or by other means should affect the response latencies in a specifiable way.

Recognition and Recall

In terms of the present system the search proceeds in a similar manner whether recognition or recall is the mode of test; the difference lies in the size of the examination subset in the two cases. Once information is recovered from LTS, however, the decision process involved in response generation may be somewhat different for recognition and recall. In a paired-associate design, the search will begin with an attempted recognition of the stimulus, with the decision whether to continue the search dependent upon a positive stimulus recognition (Martin, 1967). Hypotheses which ascribe different retrieval mechanisms for recognition and recall are not necessary. In both recognition and recall the presented stimulus will be sorted into an LTS area, and a search initiated there. In the case of recognition, this search can be quite limited, perhaps consisting of an examination of a single image. In the case of recall, the stimulus may be recognized with little search needed, but the necessity for recovering the response may entail a larger search, although "larger" might imply only examination of two to five additional items (Shiffrin, 1968).

REFERENCES

ATKINSON, R. C., & SHIFFRIN, R. M. Mathematical models for memory and learning. Technical Report 79, Institute for Mathematical Studies in the Social Sciences, Stanford University, 1965. (Republished: D. P. Kimble (Ed.), *Proceedings of the third conference on learning, remembering and forgetting.* New York: New York Academy of Science, in press.)

ATKINSON, R. C., & SHIFFRIN, R. M. Human memory: A proposed system and its control processes. In K. W. Spence & J. T. Spence (Eds.), *The psychology of learning and motivation: Advances in research and theory*, Vol. 2. New York: Academic Press, 1968. (a)

BINFORD, J. R., & GETTYS, C. Nonstationarity in paired-associate learning as indicated by a second guess procedure. *Journal of Mathematical Psychology*, 1965, **2**, 190–195.

DALLET, K. M., & D'ANDREA, L. Mediation instructions versus unlearning instructions in the A-B, A-C paradigm. *Journal of Experimental Psychology*, 1965, **69**, 460–466.

ESTES, W. K. The statistical approach to learning theory. In S. Koch (Ed.), *Psychology: A study of a science.* Vol. 2. New York: McGraw-Hill, 1959.

FEIGENBAUM, E. A. Information processing and memory. In *Proceedings of the fifth Berkeley symposium on mathematical statistics and probability, 1966.* Vol. IV. Berkeley: University of California Press, 1966.

MARTIN, E. Stimulus recognition in aural paired-associate learning. *Journal of Verbal Learning and Verbal Behavior, 1967*, **6**, 272–276.

MURDOCK, B. B., JR. The serial position effect of free recall. *Journal of Experimental Psychology*, 1962, **64**, 482–488.

NORMAN, D. A. Toward a theory of memory and attention. *Psychological Review*, 1968, **75**, 522–536.

RUMELHART, D. E. The effects of interpresentation intervals in a continuous paired-associate task. Technical Report 116, Institute for Mathematical Studies in the Social Sciences, Stanford University, 1967.

SHIFFRIN, R. M. Search and retrieval processes in long-term memory. Technical Report 137, Institute for Mathematical Studies in the Social Sciences, Stanford University, 1968.

SPERLING, G. The information available in brief visual presentations. *Psychological Monographs*, 1960, **74**(11, Whole No. 498).

TULVING, E. The effects of presentation and recall of material in free-recall learning. *Journal of Verbal Learning and Verbal Behavior*, 1967, **6**, 175–184.

7.2 ENDEL TULVING

What Is Episodic Memory?

Ultimately, what we learn must enter our long-term memory, which appears to have an unlimited capacity and is relatively permanent. In the past two decades, psychologists have debated the structure of long-term memory with respect to the number of memory systems that exist. One theory comes from psychologist Endel Tulving, who supports a classification scheme that consists of three memory systems: procedural, semantic, and episodic.

Tulving (b. 1927) received his B.A. from the University of Toronto in 1953 and his Ph.D. in experimental psychology from Harvard University in 1957. He taught at Yale University before going to the University of Toronto in 1974, where he is currently professor emeritus of psychology. He also serves as Tanenbaum Chair in Cognitive Neuroscience at Rotman Research Institute of Baycrest Centre in Toronto, Ontario, Canada. Tulving, a leader in the area of long-term memory, has many publications, including *Elements of Episodic Memory* (Oxford University Press, 1983).

This selection is from "What Is Episodic Memory?" which was published in the American Psychological Society's journal *Current Directions in Psychological Science* in 1993. In it, Tulving clarifies the distinction between episodic and semantic memory and discusses the characteristics of each. He points out that episodic memory is unique in that it requires the person to be aware of the past event that is remembered (he uses the term *autonoetic awareness*). As you read this selection, try to think of situations in which you have experienced episodic memory as distinct from semantic memory.

Key Concept: long-term memory

APA Citation: Tulving, E. (1993). What is episodic memory? *Current Directions in Psychological Science, 2*, 67–70.

*F*ew problems in science are as difficult as those of working out the precise relation between two complex concepts that are deceptively similar. The relation between episodic and semantic memory belongs in this category. Intuition and rational thought reveal many similarities between these two kinds of memory and tempt us to think of the two as one. Yet, closer scrutiny reveals a number of fundamental differences. In this article, I discuss one such difference, namely, the nature of conscious awareness that characterizes retrieval of episodic and semantic information. . . .

EPISODIC AND SEMANTIC MEMORY SYSTEMS

In a nutshell, the theory [of episodic memory] holds that episodic and semantic memory are two of the five major human memory systems for which reasonably adequate evidence is now available. The other three systems are procedural, perceptual representation, and short-term memory.[1] Although each system serves particular functions that other systems cannot serve (the so-called criterion of functional incompatibility[2]), several systems usually interact in the performance of tasks in everyday life as well as in the memory laboratory.

Semantic memory registers and stores knowledge about the world in the broadest sense and makes it available for retrieval. If a person knows something that is in principle describable in the propositional form, that something belongs to the domain of semantic memory. Semantic memory enables individuals to represent and mentally operate on situations, objects, and relations in the world that are not present to the senses: The owner of a semantic memory system can think about things that are not here now.

Episodic memory enables a person to remember personally experienced events as such. That is, it makes it possible for a person to be consciously aware of an earlier experience in a certain situation at a certain time. Thus, the information of episodic memory could be said to concern the self's experiences in subjective space and time. In contrast, the information of semantic memory processes concerns objects and their relations in the world at large. The owner of an episodic memory system is not only capable of remembering the temporal organization of otherwise unrelated events, but is also capable of mental time travel: Such a person can transport at will into the personal past, as well as into the future, a feat not possible for other kinds of memory.

The relation between episodic and semantic memory is hierarchical: Episodic memory has evolved out of, but many of its operations have remained dependent on, semantic memory. A corollary is that semantic memory can operate (store and retrieve information) independently of episodic memory, but not vice versa. Episodic memory is not necessary for encoding and storing of information into semantic memory, although it may modulate such encoding and storage. Semantic memory develops earlier in childhood than episodic memory: Children are capable of learning facts of the world before they remember their own past experiences. Finally, whereas medial temporal lobe and diencephalic structures, among others, play a critical role in semantic memory, frontal lobe structures seem to be involved in subserving episodic memory.[3]

CONSCIOUS AWARENESS IN REMEMBERING

One idea that was not clearly articulated in the *Elements of Episodic Memory* concerned the nature of conscious awareness that accompanies the act of retrieval of information from the two systems. At that time, there was little objective evidence relevant to that problem. Some progress on this front has now been made, and I summarize some of it here.

The working hypothesis is that episodic and semantic memory differ fundamentally with respect to the nature of conscious awareness that accompanies retrieval of information. The act of remembering a personally experienced event, that is, consciously recollecting it, is characterized by a distinctive, unique awareness of reexperiencing here and now something that happened before, at another time and in another place. The awareness and its feeling-tone are intimately familiar to every normal human being. One seldom mistakes remembering for any other kind of experience—perceiving, imagining, dreaming, daydreaming, or just thinking about things one knows about the world.

I refer to the kind of conscious awareness that characterizes remembering one's past as *autonoetic* awareness, contrasting it with *noetic* awareness, which characterizes retrieval of information from semantic memory, and *anoetic* awareness, which accompanies expression of procedural knowledge.[4] ...

"REMEMBER" AND "KNOW" JUDGMENTS

If amnesics can learn new facts and subsequently know them, in the absence of any autonoetic recollection of the sources of the facts, is it possible that normal people, too, know facts without remembering where or how they acquired them? Of course, it happens all the time. Every person knows hundreds and thousands of facts, without remembering the circumstances of their acquisition. This *source amnesia* that characterizes the learning in hypnotized people and amnesics, as well as older people, is well known to all of us. The phenomenon is simply more extreme in some of these special cases than in normal adults.

Gardiner and his collaborators have reported a number of studies on remembering versus knowing newly learned information in normal people.[5] The interesting feature of these studies is that the information in question is something that is usually associated with episodic memory, namely, occurrence of familiar words in a to-be-remembered list tested by recognition. In a typical experiment, subjects see a list of unrelated words, presented one at a time, on a single study trial, and then take a two-step test. In the test, they are shown both studied and nonstudied words and are asked to make a judgment about each word's presence in or absence from the study list and to indicate the basis of each positive recognition judgment.

Subjects are instructed that there are two ways in which they can tell that a word was in the study list: They either "remember" the event of the word's presentation in the study list or simply "know" on some basis that the item had appeared in the list, without remembering its occurrence.

In one experiment, for example, subjects studied a list of words under the conditions of either full or divided attention and were then tested as described. Division of attention reduced the proportion of "remembered" words (.50 vs. .38) but did not affect the proportion of words "known" to have been in the list (.21 vs. .20). Other experiments have examined the effect of other variables, such as levels of processing, generating versus reading the word at study, retention interval, word frequency, and age of subjects. These too have produced dissociations between the "remember" and "know" components of recognition memory. Yet other studies—done on brain-damaged subjects, or using psychoactive drugs, or recording event-related potentials—have begun to identify some of the neural correlates of "remember" and "know" judgments.[6]

There are other approaches to the study of awareness of source of information,[7] and correspondingly different ways of interpreting these experiments and their results. I prefer the hypothesis that "remember" judgments, based on autonoetic awareness, reflect the operation of the episodic system, whereas "know" judgments, based on noetic awareness, reflect the operation of the semantic system. Thus, subjects have two sources of information concerning the membership of words in a study list—episodic and semantic memory. When they retrieve this information from semantic memory, they appear to suffer source amnesia: They do not remember the particular event of encountering the word. In amnesic patients . . . , the source amnesia is more extensive, covering not just encounters with individual words, but personal encounters of all kinds.

CONCLUSION

Episodic memory is a neurocognitive memory system that enables people to remember past happenings. The *remembering* in this proposition is not a generic term designating all kinds of retrieval of stored information, but rather a specific concept that designates retrieval from episodic memory. For a rememberer to remember something means that he or she is autonoetically aware of a past happening in which he or she has participated. For an experimenter or theorist to study episodic memory means to study autonoetic awareness of past experiences, separately from noetic retrieval of the semantic contents of the remembered episodes.

NOTES

1. E. Tulving, Concepts of human memory, in *Memory; Organization and Locus of Change,* L. R. Squire, N. M. Weinberger, G. Lynch, and J. L. McGaugh, Eds. (Oxford University Press, New York, 1991).

2. D. F. Sherry and D. L. Schacter, The evolution of multiple memory systems, *Psychological Review, 94,* 439–454 (1987).

3. E. Tulving, Memory: Performance, knowledge, and experience, *European Journal of Cognitive Psychology, 1,* 3–26 (1989); A. P. Shimamura, J. J. Janowsky, and L. R. Squire, Memory for the temporal order of events in patients with frontal lobe lesions and amnesic patients, *Neuropsychologia, 28,* 803–813 (1990).

4. E. Tulving, Varieties of consciousness and levels of awareness in memory, in *Attention: Selection, Awareness and Control: A Tribute to Donald Broadbent,* A. Baddeley and L. Weiskrantz, Eds. (Oxford University Press, London, in press).

5. J. M. Gardiner and R. I. Java, Recognizing and remembering, in *Theories of Memory*, A. Collins, M. Conway, S. Gathercole, and P. Morris, Eds. (Erlbaum, Hillsdale, NJ, in press).

6. H. V. Curran, J. M. Gardiner, R. I. Java, and D. Allen, Effects of lorazepam upon recollective experience in recognition memory, *Psychopharmacology*, 110, 374–378 (1993); M. E. Smith, Neurophysiological manifestations of recollective experience during recognition memory judgments, *Journal of Cognitive Neuroscience*, 5, 1–13 (1993); T. A. Blaxton, *The role of temporal lobes in remembering visuospatial materials: Remembering and knowing*, manuscript submitted for publication (1993).

7. G. Mandler, P. Graf, and D. Kraft, Activation and elaboration effects in recognition and word priming, *The Quarterly Journal of Experimental Psychology*, 38A, 645–662 (1986); L. L. Jacoby, A process dissociation framework: Separating automatic from intentional uses of memory, *Journal of Memory and Language*, 30, 513–541 (1991); M. K. Johnson and W. Hirst, MEM: Memory subsystems as processes, in *Theories of Memory*, A. Collins, M. Conway, S. Gathercole, and P. Morris, Eds. (Erlbaum, Hillsdale, NJ, in press).

Leading Questions and the Eyewitness Report

Most people want to believe that they have perfect memories. Psychologists have discovered, however, that memory is subject to a wide variety of distortions. Elizabeth F. Loftus, for example, has studied how asking certain questions of eyewitnesses to an event affects their later recall of the incident.

Loftus (b. 1944) earned her Ph.D. in psychology from Stanford University in 1970. She is currently a professor of psychology and an adjunct professor of law at the University of Washington. Loftus is one of the leading legal consultants in the United States in the area of eyewitness testimony in trials. She has written several books, including *Eyewitness Testimony* (Harvard University Press, 1979), and, with Katherine Ketcham, *The Myth of Repressed Memory* (St. Martin's Press, 1994).

This selection from "Leading Questions and the Eyewitness Report," which was published in *Cognitive Psychology* in 1972, clearly demonstrates how easy it is to modify eyewitness memory. This selection consists of several different but related experiments, and for each one, the methods, the results, and a discussion section are provided. The chi-square (X^2) and the t-test are statistical tests used to determine significance (differences between conditions). A probability (p) less than .05 is significant. As you read this selection, consider the implications that Loftus's research has for everyday situations.

Key Concept: eyewitness memory

APA Citation: Loftus, E. F. (1975). Leading questions and the eyewitness report. *Cognitive Psychology, 7,* 560–572.

A total of 490 subjects, in four experiments, saw films of complex, fast-moving events, such as automobile accidents or classroom disruptions. The purpose of these experiments was to investigate how the wording of questions asked immediately after an event may influence responses to questions asked considerably later. It is shown that when the initial question contains either either true presuppositions (e.g., it postulates the existence of an object that did exist in the scene) or false presuppositions (e.g., postulates the existence of an object that did not exist), the likelihood is increased that *subjects will later report having seen the presupposed object. The results suggest that questions asked immediately after an event can introduce new—not necessarily correct —information, which is then added to the memorial representation of the event, thereby causing its reconstruction or alteration.*

Although current theories of memory are derived largely from experiments involving lists of words or sentences, many memories occurring in everyday life involve complex, largely visual, and often fast-moving events. Of course, we are rarely required to provide precise recall of such experiences—though as we age, we often volunteer them—but on occasion such recall is demanded, as when we have witnessed a crime or an accident. Our theories should be able to encompass such socially important forms of memory. It is clearly of concern to the law, to police and insurance investigators, and to others to know something about the completeness, accuracy, and malleability of such memories.

When one has witnessed an important event, one is sometimes asked a series of questions about it. Do these questions, if asked immediately after the event, influence the memory of it that then develops? This paper first summarizes research suggesting that the wording of such initial questions can have a substantial effect on the answers given, and then reports four new studies showing that the wording of these initial questions can also influence the answers to different questions asked at some later time. The discussion of these findings develops the thesis that questions asked about an event shortly after it occurs may distort the witness' memory for that event.

ANSWERS DEPEND ON THE WORDING OF QUESTIONS

An example of how the wording of a question can affect a person's answer to it has been reported by Harris (1973). His subjects were told that "the experiment was a study in the accuracy of guessing measurements, and that they should make as intelligent a numerical guess as possible to each question" (p. 399). They were then asked either of two questions such as, "How tall was the basketball player?", or, "How short was the basketball player?" Presumably the former form of the question presupposes nothing about the height of the player, whereas the latter form involves a presupposition that the player is short. On the average, subjects guessed about 79 and 69 in. (190 and 175 mm), respectively. Similar results appeared with other pairs of questions. For example, "How long was the movie?", led to an average estimate of 130 min, whereas, "How short was the movie?" led to 100 min. While it was not Harris' central concern, his study clearly demonstrates that the wording of a question may affect the answer.

Past Personal Experiences

In one study (Loftus, unpublished), 40 people were interviewed about their headaches and about headache products under the belief that they were participating in market research on these products. Two of the questions were crucial to the experiment. One asked about products other than that currently being used, in one of two wordings:

(1a) In terms of the total number of products, how many other products have you tried? 1? 2? 3?

(1b) In terms of the total number of products, how many other products have you tried? 1? 5? 10?

The 1/2/3 subjects claimed to have tried an average of 3.3 other products, whereas the 1/5/10 subjects claimed an average of 5.2; $t(38) = 3.14$, $s = .61$, $p < .01$.

The second key question asked about frequency of headaches in one of two ways:

(2a) Do you get headaches frequently, and, if so, how often?

(2b) Do you get headaches occasionally, and, if so, how often?

The "frequently" subjects reported an average of 2.2 headaches/wk, whereas the "occasionally" group reported only 0.7/wk; $t(38) = 3.19$, $s = .47$, $p < .01$.

Recently Witnessed Events

Two examples from the published literature also indicate that the wording of a question put to a person about a recently-witnessed event can affect a person's answer to that question. In one study (Loftus, 1974; Loftus & Zanni, 1975), 100 students viewed a short file segment depicting a multiple-car accident. Immediately afterward, they filled out a 22-item questionnaire which contained six critical questions. Three of these asked about items that had appeared in the film whereas the other three asked about items not present in the film. For half the subjects, all the critical questions began with the words, "Did you see a..." as in, "Did you see a broken headlight?" For the remaining half, the critical questions began with the words, "Did you see the..." as in, "Did you see the broken headlight?"

Thus, the questions differed only in the form of the article, *the* or *a*. One uses "the" when one assumes the object referred to exists and may be familiar to the listener. An investigator who asks, "Did you see the broken headlight?" essentially says, "There was a broken headlight. Did you happen to see it?" His assumption may influence a witness' report. By contrast, the article "a" does not necessarily convey the implication of existence.

The results showed that witnesses who were asked "the" questions were more likely to report having seen something, whether or not it had really appeared in the film, than those who were asked "a" questions. Even this very subtle change in wording influences a witness' report.

In another study (Loftus & Palmer, 1974), subjects saw films of automobile accidents and then answered questions about the accidents. The wording of a question was shown to affect a numerical estimate. In particular, the question, "About how fast were the cars going when they smashed into each other?" consistently elicited a higher estimate of speed than when "smashed" was replaced by "collided," "bumped," "contacted," or "hit."

We may conclude that in a variety of situations the wording of a question about an event can influence the answer that is given. This effect has been observed when a person reports about his own experiences, about events he has recently witnessed, and when answering a general question (e.g., "How short was the movie?") not based on any specific witnessed incident.

Elizabeth F. Loftus

QUESTION WORDING AND ANSWERS TO SUBSEQUENT QUESTIONS

Our concern in this paper is not on the effect of the wording of a question on its answer, but rather on the answers to other questions asked some time afterward. We will interpret the evidence to be presented as suggesting a memorial phenomenon of some importance.

In the present experiments, a key [set of] initial questions contains a *presupposition*, which is simply a condition that must hold in order for the question to be contextually appropriate. For example, the question, "How fast was the car going when it ran the stop sign?" presupposes that there was a stop sign. If a stop sign actually did exist, then in answering this question a subject might review, strengthen, or make more available certain memory representations corresponding to the stop sign. This being the case, the initial question might be expected to influence the answer to a subsequent question about the stop sign, such as the question, "Did you see the stop sign?" A simple extension of the argument of Clark and Haviland (in press) can be made here: When confronted with the initial question, "How fast was the car going when it ran the stop sign?", the subject might treat the presupposed information as if it were an address, a pointer, or an instruction specifying where information related to that presupposition may be found (as well as where new information is to be integrated into the previous knowledge). In the process the presupposed information may be strengthened.

What if the presupposition is false? In that case it will not correspond to any existing representation, and the subject may treat it as new information and enter it into his memory. Subsequently, the new "false" information may appear in verbal reports solicited from the subject.

To explore these ideas, subjects viewed films of complex, fast-moving events. Viewing of the film was followed by initial questions which contained presuppositions that were either true (Experiment 1) or false (Experiments 2–4). In Experiment 1, the initial questions either did or did not mention an object that was in fact present in the film. A subsequent question, asked a few minutes later, inquired as to whether the subject has seen the existing object. In Experiments 2–4, the initial questions were again asked immediately after the film, whereas the subsequent questions were asked after a lapse of 1 wk.

EXPERIMENT 1

Method

One hundred and fifty University of Washington students, in groups of various sizes, were shown a film of a multiple-car accident in which one car, after failing to stop at a stop sign, makes a right-hand turn into the main stream of traffic. In an attempt to avoid a collision, the cars in the oncoming traffic stop suddenly and a five-car, bumper-to-bumper collision results. The film lasts less than 1 min, and the accident occurs within a 4-sec period.

At the end of the film, a 10-item questionnaire was administered. A diagram of the situation labeled the car that ran the stop sign as "A," and the cars involved in the collision as "B" through "F." The first question asked about the speed of Car A in one of two ways:

(1) How fast was Car A going when it ran the stop sign?

(2) How fast was Car A going when it turned right? Seventy-five subjects received the "stop sign" question and 75 received the "turned right" question. The last question was identical for all subjects: "Did you see a stop sign for Car A?" Subjects responded by circling "yes" or "no" on their questionnaires.

Results and Discussion

Fifty-three percent of the subjects in the "stop sign" group responded "yes" to the question, "Did you see a stop sign for Car A?", whereas only 35% in the "turn right" group claimed to have seen the stop sign; $x^2(1) = 4.98, p < .05$. The wording of a presupposition into a question about an event, asked immediately after that event has taken place, can influence the answer to a subsequent question concerning the presupposition itself, asked a very short time later, in the direction of conforming with the supplied information.

There are at least two possible explanations of this effect. The first is that when a subject answers the initial stop sign question, he somehow reviews, or strengthens, or in some sense makes more available certain memory representations corresponding to the stop sign. Later, when asked, "Did you see a stop sign...?", he responds on the basis of the strengthened memorial representation.

A second possibility may be called the "construction hypothesis." In answering the initial stop sign question, the subject may "visualize" or "reconstruct" in his mind that portion of the incident needed to answer the question, and so, if he accepts the presupposition, he introduces a stop sign into his visualization whether or not it was in memory. When interrogated later about the existence of the stop sign, he responds on the basis of his earlier supplementation of the actual incident. In other words, the subject may "see" the stop sign that he has himself constructed. This would not tend to happen when the initial question refers only to the right turn.

The construction hypothesis has an important consequence. If a piece of true information supplied to the subject after the accident augments his memory, then, in a similar way, it should be possible to introduce into memory something that was not in fact in the scene, by supplying a piece of false information. For example, Loftus and Palmer (1974, Expt. 2) showed subjects a film of an automobile accident and followed it by questions about events that occurred in the film. Some subjects were asked "About how fast were the cars going when they smashed into each other?", whereas others were asked the same question with "hit" substituted for "smashed." On a retest 1 wk later, those questioned with "smashed" were more likely than those questioned with "hit" to agree that they had seen broken glass in the scene, even though none was present in the film. In the present framework, we assume that the initial representation of the accident the subject has witnessed is modified toward greater severity when the experimenter uses the term "smashed" because the question supplies a piece of new information, namely, that the cars did indeed *smash* into each other. On hearing the "smashed" question, some subjects may reconstruct the accident, integrating the new information into the existing representation. If so, the result is a representation of an accident in memory that is more severe than, in fact, it actually was. In particular, the more severe accident is more likely to include broken glass.

The presupposition that the cars smashed into each other may be additional information, but it can hardly be said to be false information. It is important to determine whether it is also true that false presuppositions can affect a witness' answer to a later question about that presupposition. Such a finding would imply that a false presupposition can be accepted by a witness, that the hypothesis of a strengthening of an existing memorial representation is untenable (since there should be no representation corresponding to nonexistent objects), and that the construction hypothesis discussed above is supported. Experiment 2 was designed to check this idea.

EXPERIMENT 2

Method

Forty undergraduate students at the University of Washington, again in groups of various sizes, were shown a 3-min videotape taken from the film *Diary of a Student Revolution*. The sequence depicted the disruption of a class by eight demonstrators; the confrontation, which was relatively noisy, resulted in the demonstrators leaving the classroom.

At the end of the videotape, the subjects received one of two questionnaires containing one key and nineteen filler questions. Half of the subjects were asked, "Was the leader of the four demonstrators who entered the classroom a male?", whereas the other half were asked, "Was the leader of the twelve demonstrators who entered the classroom a male?" The subjects responded by circling "yes" or "no."

One week later, all subjects returned and, without reviewing the videotape, answered a series of 20 new questions about the disruption. The subjects were urged to answer the questions from memory and not to make inference.

The critical question here was, "How many demonstrators did you see entering the classroom?"

Results and Discussion

Subjects who had previously been asked the "12" question reported having seen an average 8.85 people 1 wk earlier, whereas those asked the "4" question recalled 6.40 people, $t(38) = 2.50$, s $= .98$ $p < .01$. The actual number was, it will be recalled, eight. One possibility is that some fraction of the subjects remembered the number 12 or the number 4 from the prior questionnaire and were responding to the later question with that number, whereas the remainder had the correct number. An analysis of the actual responses given reveals that 10% of the people who had been interrogated with "12" actually responded "12," and that 10% of those interrogated with "4" actually responded with "4." A recalculation of the means, excluding those subjects in the "12" condition who responded "12" and those in the "4" condition who responded "4," still resulted in a significant difference between the two conditions (8.50 versus 6.67), $t(34) = 1.70$, $p < .05$. This analysis demonstrates that recall of the specific number given in the initial questionnaire is not an adequate alternative explanation of the present results.

The result shows that a question containing a false numerical presupposition can, on the average, affect a witness' answer to a subsequent question about that quantitative fact. The next experiment was designed to test whether the same is true for the existence of objects when the false presupposition concerns one that did not actually exist.

EXPERIMENT 3

Method

One hundred and fifty students at the University of Washington, in groups of various sizes, viewed a brief videotape of an automobile accident and then answered ten questions about the accident. The critical one concerned the speed of a white sports car. Half of the subjects were asked, "How fast was the white sports car going when it passed the barn while traveling along the country road?", and half were asked, "How fast was the white sports car going while traveling along the country road?" In fact, no barn appeared in the scene.

All of the subjects returned 1 wk later and, without reviewing the videotape, answered ten new questions about the accident. The final one was, "Did you see a barn?" The subjects responded by circling "yes" or "no" on their questionnaires.

Results and Discussion

Of the subjects earlier exposed to the question containing the false presupposition of a barn, 17.3% responded "yes" when later asked, "Did you see a barn?", whereas only 2.7% of the remaining subjects claimed to have seen it; $x^2(1) = 8.96$, $p < .01$. An initial question containing a false presupposition can, it appears, influence a witness' later tendency to report the presence of the nonexistent object corresponding to the presupposition.

The last experiment not only extends this finding beyond the single example, but asks whether or not the effect is wholly due to the word "barn" having occurred or not occurred in the earlier session. Suppose an initial question merely asks about, instead of presupposing, a nonexistent object; for example, "Did you see a barn?," when no barn existed. Presumably subjects will mostly respond negatively to such questions. But, what if that same question is asked again some time later? It is possible that a subject will reflect to himself, "I remember something about a barn, so I guess I must have seen one." If this were the case, then merely asking about a nonexistent object could increase the tendency to report the existence of that object at some later time, thereby accounting for the results of Expt III.

EXPERIMENT 4

Method

One hundred and fifty subjects from the University of Washington, run in groups of various sizes, viewed a 3-min 8 mm film clip taken from inside of an automobile which eventually collides with a baby carriage being pushed by a man. Following presentation of the film, each subject received one of three types of booklets corresponding to the experimental conditions. One hundred subjects received booklets containing five key and 40 filler questions. In the "direct" version, the key questions asked, in a fairly direct manner, about items that were not present in the film. One example was, "Did you see a school bus in the film?" In the "False presupposition" version, the key questions contained false presuppositions referring to an item that did not occur in the film. The corresponding example was, "Did you see the children getting on the school bus?" The third group of 50 subjects received only the 40 filler questions and no key questions. The goal of using so many filler items was to minimize the possibility that subjects would notice the false presuppositions.

All subjects returned 1 wk later and, without reviewing the film clip, answered 20 new questions about the incident. Five of these questions were critical: They were direct questions that had been asked a wk earlier in identical form, of only one of the three groups of subjects. The subjects responded to all questions by circling "yes" or "no" on their questionnaires.

Results and Discussion

... Overall, of those who had been exposed to questions including a false presupposition, 29.2% said "yes" to the key nonexistent items; of those who had been exposed to the direct questions, 15.6% said "yes" and of those in the control group, 8.4% said "yes."

For each question individually, the type of prior experience significantly influenced the percentage of "yes" responses, with all chi-square values having $p < .05$. Additional chi-square tests were performed to test for the significance of the differences between the pairs of groups. For each of the five questions, the differences were all significant between the control group and the group exposed to false presuppositions, all chi-square values having $p < .025$. Summing over all five questions, a highly significant chi-square resulted, $x^2(5) = 40.79$, $p < 001$. Similarly, over all five questions, the difference between the group exposed to direct questions and the group exposed to false presuppositions was significant, $x^2(5) = 14.73$, $p < .025$. The difference between the control group and the group exposed to direct questions failed to reach significance, $x^2(5) = 9.24$, $p > .05$.

REFERENCES

Clark, H. H., & Haviland, S. E. Psychological processes as linguistic explanation. In D. Cohen (Ed.), *The nature of explanation in linguistics.* Milwaukee: University of Wisconsin Press, in press.

Harris, R. J. Answering questions containing marked and unmarked adjectives and adverbs. *Journal of Experimental Psychology*, 1973, 97, 399–401.

Loftus, E. F. Reconstructing memory. The incredible eyewitness. *Psychology Today*, 1974, 8, 116–119.

Loftus, E. F., & Palmer, J. C. Reconstruction of automobile destruction: An example of the interaction between language and memory. *Journal of Verbal Learning and Verbal Behavior*, 1974, 13, 585–589.

Loftus, E. F., & Zanni, G. Eyewitness testimony: The influence of the wording of a question. *Bulletin of the Psychonomic Society*, 1975, 5, 86–88.

CHAPTER 8 Intelligence and Language

8.1 ROBERT J. STERNBERG AND TODD I. LUBART

Creativity: Its Nature and Assessment

Research in creativity has often emphasized divergent thinking, where the creative individual comes up with novel solutions to common problems. A different approach to creativity was recently proposed by Robert J. Sternberg and his coresearcher Todd I. Lubart. They developed the investment theory of creativity, which suggests that creative people are able to generate undervalued ideas to advance knowledge in an area.

Sternberg attended Yale University before entering Stanford University for graduate studies, where he received a Ph.D. in psychology in 1975. He then returned to Yale University, where he is currently a professor. He published *Beyond IQ: A Triarchic Theory of Human Intelligence* (Cambridge University Press) in 1985 and *Successful Intelligence* (Simon & Schuster) in 1996. Lubart worked under Sternberg at Yale University, where he received his Ph.D. in cognitive psychology in 1994. Currently Lubart is a professor at the University of René Descartes in Paris, France. Sternberg and Lubart coauthored *Defying the Crowd* (Free Press, 1995).

The following selection from "Creativity: Its Nature and Assessment" was published in *School Psychology International* in 1992. Sternberg and Lubart suggest that the investment approach to creativity includes intelligence, knowledge, thinking style, personality, motivation, and environmental context. They argue that it is necessary to take a broader approach to creativity. As you read this selection, consider how you might test for creativity incorporating all of the resources described.

Key Concept: creativity

APA Citation: Sternberg, R. J., & Lubart, T. I. (1992). Creativity: Its nature and assessment. *School Psychology International, 13,* 243–253.

*S*chool psychologists wishing to measure the intelligence of a pupil at any level of schooling have available to them a staggering number and variety of assessment instruments. It is merely a matter of choosing which one the psychologist prefers. But the school psychologist who wishes to measure the creativity of a pupil has very few options. Indeed, there is only one widely used test, the Torrance Tests of Creative Thinking (TTCT) (Torrance, 1974, 1979, 1984). To what extent do these tests measure creativity, however, and if they measure it only to a limited extent, what other kinds of measures might be available?

THE PSYCHOMETRIC APPROACH

The Torrance Tests are part of the psychometric tradition that is associated with Torrance (1979), Guilford (1956) and others. Much of the psychometric measurement, including the Torrance tests, is based upon Guilford's (1956) structure-of-intellect (SOI) model. According to Guilford, creativity involves fluency, flexibility and originality in the divergent thinking facet of the cube representing his SOI model. In this tradition, one asks children to perform relatively simple verbal and figural fluency tasks, and assesses creativity on the basis of these tasks.

What are the kinds of tasks used? Consider some samples of subtests from the Torrance battery: *Asking Questions*: the examinee writes out all the questions he or she can think of, based on a drawing of a scene. *Guessing Causes*: the examinee lists as many possible causes as he or she can for an action shown in a picture. *Product Improvement*: the examinee lists ways to change a toy monkey so children will have more fun playing with it. *Unusual Uses of Tin Cans*: the examinee lists interesting and unusual uses of tin cans. *Picture Completion*: the examinee is shown unfinished line drawings that he or she is asked to complete. *Circles*: the examinee is instructed to expand each of two pages of blank circles into drawings and then to title them.

The subtests are then scored for constructs such as fluency (total number of relevant responses), flexibility (number of different categories into which responses fall), originality (unusualness of responses) and elaboration (amount of detail in the response). The exact way in which these response categories is used differs from one subtest to another.

Do the TTCT, and similar tasks that have been used at one time or another, actually measure creativity? More fundamentally, how would one know whether these tasks measure creativity? One way is to correlate performance on the TTCT with various kinds of creative performances. How these tasks come out of such external validation depends in large part on whom one asks. Certainly, there have been some significant correlations with creative performance (Torrance, 1988). Of course, most intellectual tests would show some correlation with creative performance within a wide enough range of intellect, and we then run into the problem of how high is high enough to be considered acceptable. We will not try to deal with this question here, because we wish to propose a different criterion for evaluating the success of the Torrance tests, or any other ones.

This different criterion is theory based. To what extent does the test of creativity, whether the Torrance or some other, pick up the aspects of creativity specified by a given theory of creativity? On this view, how good the test is will depend upon its fit to the theory against which it is compared. If one compares the Torrance test against Guilford's theory of divergent thinking, the test will [fare] rather well, we believe. Indeed, it is upon their theory that the test is based. But here we wish to concentrate upon a different theory, one we believe deals with aspects of creativity left untouched by Guilford's theory. This theory is our own investment theory of creativity (Sternberg and Lubart, 1991). This theory is one of several economically-based theories that combine ideas from economics with those from psychology (see also Rubenson and Runco, in press; Walberg, 1988).

THE INVESTMENT APPROACH

According to the investment approach to creative work, when making any kind of investment, including creative investment, people should 'buy low and sell high'. In other words, the greatest creative contributions can generally be made in areas or with ideas that at a given time are undervalued. Perhaps people in general have not yet realized the importance of certain ideas, and hence there is a potential for making significant advances. The more in favor an idea is, the less potential there is for it to appreciate in value, because the idea is already valued.

A theory of creativity needs to account for how people can generate or recognize undervalued ideas. It also needs to specify who will actually pursue these undervalued ideas rather than join the crowd and make contributions that, while of some value, are unlikely to turn around our existing ways of thinking. Such a theory will enable us and our children to invest in a creative future.

Our view is that creativity in children—and in adults—involves six resources: intelligence, knowledge, thinking style, personality, motivation and environmental context. Consider each of these resources in turn.

Intelligence

Major creative innovations often involve seeing an old problem in a new way. For example, Albert Einstein redefined the field of physics by proposing the theory of relativity; Jean Piaget redefined the field of cognitive development by conceiving of the child as scientist. The children we work with are obviously not going to have creative ideas at these levels. But they may redefine problems in their own way, as when they come up with a solution to a problem that we do not think of, or when they take an assignment they are given and produce a product from a point of view that sets them apart from all their peers. The by now overused example of the student who, asked to write a paper on 'spring fever', turned in a blank page, illustrates problem redefinition of a creative sort. One of my own students, asked to devise a test of intelligence, had a related idea, and proposed as her test of intelligence the question, 'What do you believe intelligence is, and how would you measure it?' In other words, she wished to assess children's intelligence not only by their ability to answer questions, but by the kinds of questions they decided to ask, certainly an important part of intelligence (and creativity; see Arlin, 1975; Getzels and Csikszentmihalyi, 1976).

The ability to see problems in ways others do not see them is critical to creativity, and thus constitutes a first aspect of creativity that we would wish to measure.

Knowledge

In order to make creative contributions to a field of knowledge, one must, of course, have knowledge of that field. Without such knowledge, one risks rediscovering what is already known. Without knowledge of the field, it is also difficult for an individual to assess the problems in the field and to judge which problems are important. Indeed, during the past decade or so, an important emphasis in psychology has been on the importance of knowledge to expertise.

Schools can scarcely be faulted for making insufficient efforts to impart knowledge. Indeed, that seems to be their main function. Yet we have a reservation about the extent to which the knowledge they impart is likely to lead to creativity. First, there is a difference between knowledge per se and usable knowledge. Much of what students learn is inert—they cannot use it because they do not know how to use it or for what to use it.

We also need to be concerned about the tradeoff that can develop between knowledge and flexibility. We have suggested that increased expertise in terms of knowledge in a given domain often comes at the expense of flexibility in that domain (Sternberg and Frensch, 1989). We can become so automatic about the way we do certain things that we lose sight of the possibility of other ways. We can become entrenched and have trouble going beyond our very comfortable perspective on things. Because creativity requires one to view things flexibly, there is a danger that, with increasing knowledge, one will lose creativity by losing the ability to think flexibly about the domain in which one works. We need to recognize that sometimes students see things that we do not see—they may have insights we have not had. Thus, if we wish to measure creativity, we need to care not just about what students know, but how flexibly they can use what they know.

*Robert J.
Sternberg and
Todd I. Lubart*

Thinking styles are ways in which people choose to use or exploit their intelligence as well as their knowledge. Thus intellectual styles concern not abilities, but how these abilities and the knowledge acquired through them are used in day-to-day interactions with the environment.

Elsewhere, one of the authors has presented details of a theory of thinking styles based on a notion of mental self-government (Sternberg, 1988). The basic idea is that people need to govern themselves mentally and that styles provide them with ways to do so. The ways in which people govern themselves are internal mirrors of the kinds of government we see in the external world.

Creative people are likely to be those with a 'legislative' style. A legislative individual is someone who enjoys formulating problems and creating new systems of rules and new ways of seeing things. Such a person is in contrast to an individual with an executive style: someone who likes implementing systems, rules and tasks of others. Both differ from an individual with a judicial style: someone who enjoys evaluating people, things and rules. Thus the creative person not only has the ability to see things in new ways but likes to do so. The creative person is also likely to have a global—not just local—perspective on problems. Seeing the forest despite all the trees is the mark of a creative endeavor.

Personality

Creative people seem to share certain personality attributes. Although one can probably be creative in the short term without these attributes, long-term creativity requires most of them. The attributes are tolerance of ambiguity, willingness to surmount obstacles and persevere, willingness to grow, willingness to take risks, and the courage of one's convictions.

First, consider tolerance of ambiguity and its role in creativity. In most creative endeavors, there is a period of time during which an individual is groping —trying to figure out what the pieces of the puzzle are, how to put them together or how to relate them to what is already known. During this period, an individual is likely to feel some anxiety—possibly even alarm—because the pieces are not forming themselves into a creative solution to the problem being confronted. Creative individuals need to be able to tolerate such ambiguity and to wait for the pieces to fall into place. In many schools, most of the assignments students are given are due the next day or within a short period of time, so that students never have the opportunity to develop the tolerance of ambiguity that is such an important part of the creative process.

Second, consider willingness to surmount obstacles and persevere. Almost every major thinker has surmounted obstacles at one time or another, and the willingness not to be derailed is a crucial element of success. Confronting obstacles is almost a certainty in creative endeavor because most such endeavors threaten some kind of established and entrenched interest. Unless one can learn to face adversity and conquer it, one is unlikely to make a creative contribution to one's field. Schools can be good proving grounds for learning to surmount obstacles, because we face so many of them while we are in school (whether as students or as teachers). But students sometimes leave school with the feeling that society is more likely to get in the way of creativity than support it. To the extent that the students learn to fight for their creative beliefs, they will be on the path to developing their own creativity. And let it be said that the same applies for school teachers, administrators and psychologists as well!

Third, consider willingness to grow. When a person has a creative idea and others accept it, that person may be highly rewarded for the idea. It then becomes difficult to move on to still other ideas. The rewards for staying with the first idea are often great, and it feels comfortable to stick with that idea. At the same time, the person who has a creative idea often acquires a deep-seated fear that his or her next idea will not be as good as the last one. But creativity over prolonged periods of time requires that one move beyond one's old ideas, and go on to new ones, however uncomfortable they may make one feel!

Fourth, consider willingness to take risks. A general principle of investment is that, on average, greater return entails greater risk. For the most part, schools are environments that are not conducive to risk-taking. On the contrary, students are as often as not punished for taking risks. Taking a course in a new area or in an area of weakness is likely to lead to a low grade, which in turn may dim a student's future prospects. But to be creative, the student needs to learn to take risks, or to do exactly what the school environment may discourage.

Finally, consider the courage of one's convictions and belief in oneself. There are times in the lives of almost all creative people when they begin to doubt their ideas—and themselves. Their work may not be achieving the recognition it once achieved, or they may not have succeeded in getting recognition in the first place. At these times, it is difficult to maintain a belief in one's ideas or in oneself. At such times, one needs to draw upon deep-seated personal resources and to believe in oneself, even when others do not.

Motivation

There is now good evidence to suggest that motivation plays an important role in creative endeavors. The kind of motivation that is most essential to creative work is intrinsic, task-focused motivation. In other words, the person is motivated to perform a task for its own sake, rather than for some external reward, and the motivation is focused upon the task rather than on the outcomes that may derive from it (see Amabile, 1983). There is little doubt as to the way in which most schools motivate students today: namely, through grades. Grades are the ultimate criterion of one's success in school, and, if one's grades are not good, love of one's work is unlikely to be viewed as much of a compensation. Therefore, many students chart a path in school that is just sufficient to get them an A. Students who once may have performed well for love of an intellectual challenge may come to perform well only to get their next A. Whatever intrinsic motivation children may have had at the start is likely to be drummed out of them by a system that rewards extrinsically rather than intrinsically (Lepper et al., 1973).

Creativity cannot be viewed outside an environmental context. What would be viewed as creative in one context might be viewed as trivial in another. The role of context is relevant to the creative enterprise in at least three different ways. First, a context needs to help foster creativity by sparking new, high-quality ideas. Second, the context needs to help foster creativity by rewarding these ideas when they are produced. Finally, the context needs to be one that values the kinds of creative ideas one has. There is no ultimate criterion as to what constitutes a creative idea. The very same idea that in one environment might be viewed as a stunningly creative contribution in another environment might be viewed as absurd or 'far-out'. Thus one needs to find an environment that rewards the kinds of contributions one has to make....

Robert J.
Sternberg and
Todd I. Lubart

CONCLUSION

We believe that a complete view of creativity requires a theory that considers creativity that is more significant than that required for typical tests of creativity such as the TTCT. Moreover, we believe that a broader theory of creativity is required, one that considers non-cognitive as well as cognitive variables, and the role of the environment as well as that of the individual. The investment theory seems to capture at least some of the major aspects of creativity as it actually applies in school and out. We therefore offer it as a basis for the assessment of creativity that goes beyond somewhat sterile divergent thinking tasks.

REFERENCES

Amabile, T.M. (1983) *The Social Psychology of Creativity*. New York: Springer-Verlag.

Arlin, P.K. (1975) 'Cognitive Development in Adulthood: A Fifth Stage?', *Developmental Psychology* 11: 602–6.

Getzels, J. and Csikszentmihalyi, M. (1976) *The Creative Vision: A Longitudinal Study of Problem-finding in Art*. New York: Wiley-Interscience.

Guilford, J.P. (1956) 'Structure of Intellect', *Psychological Bulletin* 53: 267–93.

Lepper, M., Greene, D. and Nisbett, R. (1973) 'Undermining Children's Intrinsic Interest with Extrinsic Rewards: A Test of the "Overjustification" Hypothesis', *Journal of Personality and Social Psychology* 28: 129–37.

Rubenson, D.L. and Runco, M.A. (in press) 'The Psychoeconomic Approach to Creativity', *New Ideas in Psychology*.

Sternberg, R.J. (1988) 'Mental Self-government: A Theory of Intellectual Styles and Their Development', *Human Development* 34: 1–31.

Sternberg, R.J. and Frensch, P. A. (1989) 'A Balance-level Theory of Intelligent Thinking', *Zeitschrift für Pädagogische Psychologie* 3: 79–96.

Sternberg, R.J. and Lubart, T.I. (1991) 'An Investment Theory of Creativity and its Development', *Human Development* 34: 1–31.

Torrance, E.P. (1974) *The Torrance Tests of Creative Thinking: Technical-norms Manual.* Lexington, MA: Personnel Press.

Torrance, E.P. (1979) *The Search for Satori and Creativity.* Buffalo, NY: Bearly.

Torrance, E.P. (1984) 'Sound and Image Productions of Elementary School Pupils as Predictors of the Creative Achievements of Young Adults', *Creative Child and Adult Quarterly* 7: 8–14.

Torrance, E.P. (1988) 'Creativity as Manifest in Testing', in R.J. Sternberg (ed.), *The Nature of Creativity*, pp. 43–75. New York: Cambridge University Press.

Walberg, H.J. (1988) 'Creativity and Talent as Learning', in R.J. Sternberg (ed.), *The Nature of Creativity*, pp. 340–61. New York: Cambridge University Press.

8.2 ROBERT ROSENTHAL AND LENORE JACOBSON

Teachers' Expectancies: Determinants of Pupils' IQ Gains

Psychological research is sometimes difficult to correctly interpret, in part because people can unintentionally bring bias into the research setting. Without being aware of it, our expectations can alter our perceptions and behavior. The pioneering work of Robert Rosenthal and Lenore Jacobson helped psychologists become more aware of the potential for bias in research studies.

Rosenthal earned his Ph.D. in psychology in 1956 from the University of California, Los Angeles. He is a professor of psychology at Harvard University. Jacobson was with the South San Francisco Unified School District at the time of their research. Rosenthal and Jacobson coauthored a book on expectancy effect entitled, *Pygmalion in the Classroom: Teacher Expectations and Pupils' Intellectual Development* (Holt, Rinehart & Winston, 1968).

This selection, from "Teachers' Expectancies: Determinants of Pupils' I.Q. Gains," was published in *Psychological Reports* in 1966. It demonstrated how teacher expectancy (in this study, expectancy that certain students would "intellectually bloom" during a school year) had a significant effect on student behavior (the randomly selected students increased their IQ scores). As you read this selection, think about your elementary school years. Did you do best in classes in which your teachers expected high performance? How does expectancy play a role in our everyday lives? How could research studies be designed to minimize the effects of expectancy?

Key Concept: bias in psychological research

APA Citation: Rosenthal, R., & Jacobson, L. (1968). Teachers' expectancies: Determinants of pupils' I.Q. gains. *Psychological Reports, 19,* 115–118.

Experiments have shown that in behavioral research employing human or animal *S*s, *E*'s expectancy can be a significant determinant of *S*'s response (Rosenthal, 1964, in press). In studies employing animals, for example, *E*s led to believe that their rat Ss has been bred for superior learning ability obtained performance superior to that obtained by Es led to believe that their rats had been bred for inferior learning ability (Rosenthal & Fode, 1963; Rosenthal & Lawson, 1964). The present study was designed to extend the generality of this finding from Es to teachers and from animal Ss to school children.

Flanagan (1960) has developed a nonverbal intelligence test (*Tests of General Ability* or *TOGA*) which is not explicitly dependent on such school-learned skills as reading, writing, and arithmetic. The test is composed of two types of items, "verbal" and "reasoning." The "verbal" items measure the child's level of information, vocabulary, and concepts. The "reasoning" items measure the child's concept formation ability by employing abstract line drawings. Flanagan's purpose in developing the TOGA was "to provide a relatively fair measure of intelligence for all individuals, even those who have had atypical opportunities to learn" (1960, p. 6).

Flanagan's test was administered to all children in an elementary school, disguised as a test designed to predict academic "blooming" or intellectual gain. Within each of the six grades in the school were three classrooms, one each of children performing at above average, average, and below average levels of scholastic achievement. In each of the 18 classes an average of 20% of the children were assigned to the experimental condition. The names of these children were given to each teacher who was told that their scores on the "test for intellectual blooming" indicated that they would show unusual intellectual gains during the academic year. Actually, the children had been assigned to the experimental condition by means of a table of random numbers. The experimental treatment for these children, then, consisted of nothing more than being identified to their teachers as children who would show unusual intellectual gains.

Eight months after the experimental conditions were instituted all children were retested with the same IQ test and a change score was computed for each child. Table 1 shows the mean gain in IQ points among experimental and control Ss in each of the six grades. For the school as a whole those children from whom the teachers had been led to expect greater intellectual gain showed a significantly greater gain in IQ score than did the control children ($p = .02$, one-tail). Inspection of Table 1 shows that the effects of teachers' expectancies were not uniform across the six grade levels. The lower the grade level, the greater was the effect ($rho = -.94$, $p = .02$, two-tail). It was in the first and second grades that the effects were most dramatic. The largest gain among the three first grade classrooms occurred for experimental Ss who gained 24.8 IQ points *in excess* of the gain (+16.2) shown by the controls. The largest gain among the three second grade classrooms was obtained by experimental Ss who gained 18.2 IQ points in excess of the gain (+4.3) shown by the controls. . . .

There are a number of possible explanations of the finding that teachers' expectancy effects operated primarily at the lower grade levels, including: (a) Younger children have less well-established reputations so that the creation of expectations about their performance would be more credible. (b) Younger children may be more susceptible to the unintended social influence exerted by the expectation of their teacher. (c) Younger children may be more recent arrivals in the school's neighborhood and may differ from the older children

TABLE 1

Mean Gains in IQ

Grade	Controls		Experimentals		Diff.	t	p†
	M	σ	M	σ			
1	12.0	16.6	27.4	12.5	15.4	2.97	.002
2	7.0	10.0	16.5	18.6	9.5	2.28	.02
3	5.0	11.9	5.0	9.3	0.0		
4	2.2	13.4	5.6	11.0	3.4		
5	17.5	13.1	17.4	17.8	−0.1		
6	10.7	10.0	10.0	6.5	−0.7		
Weighted M	8.4*	13.5	12.2**	15.0	3.8	2.15	.02

*Mean number of children per grade = 42.5
**Mean number of children per grade = 10.8
†p one-tailed.

in characteristics other than age. (d) Teachers of lower grades may differ from teachers of higher grades on a variety of dimensions which are correlated with the effectiveness of the unintentional communication of expectancies.

The most important question which remains is that which asks how a teacher's expectation becomes translated into behavior in such a way as to elicit the expected pupil behavior. Prior research on the unintentional communication of expectancies in experimentally more carefully controlled interactions suggests that this question will not be easily unanswered (Rosenthal, in press).

But, regardless of the mechanism involved, there are important substantive and methodological implications of these findings.... For now, one example, in question form, will do: How much of the improvement in intellectual performance attributed to the contemporary educational programs is due to the content and methods of the programs and how much is due to the favorable expectancies of the teachers and administrators involved? Experimental designs to answer such questions are available (Rosenthal, in press) and in view of the psychological, social and economic importance of these programs the use of such designs seems strongly indicated.

REFERENCES

FLANAGAN, J. C. *Tests of general ability: technical report.* Chicago, Ill.: Science Research Associates, 1960.

ROSENTHAL, R. The effect of the experimenter on the results of psychological research. In B. A. Maher (Ed.), *Progress in experimental personality research.* Vol. I. New York: Academic Press, 1964. Pp. 79–114.

ROSENTHAL, R. *Experimenter effects in behavioral research.* New York: Appleton-Century-Crofts, in press.

ROSENTHAL, R. & FODE, K. L. The effect of experimenter bias on the performance of the albino rat. *Behavioral Science,* 1963, 8, 183–189.

ROSENTHAL, R. & LAWSON, R. A longitudinal study of the effects of experimenter bias on the operant learning of laboratory rats. *Journal of Psychiatric Research,* 1964, 2, 61–72.

8.3 JANET F. WERKER AND RENÉE N. DESJARDINS

Listening to Speech in the First Year of Life: Experiential Influences on Phoneme Perception

The use of language is one of the defining characteristics of being human. Somehow during the first years of life, we learn to understand language and to use it to communicate with other people. Janet F. Werker and Renée N. Desjardins are two psychologists on the cutting edge of research designed to understand how infants learn to listen to speech.

Werker earned her Ph.D. in developmental psychology from the University of British Columbia in 1982. She taught at Dalhousie University until 1986, when she returned to the University of British Columbia, and she is currently professor of psychology there. Desjardins earned her Ph.D. in 1997 from the University of British Columbia. She currently has a post-doc position at McMaster University in Hamilton, Ontario.

This selection is from "Listening to Speech in the First Year of Life: Experiential Influences on Phoneme Perception," which was published in *Current Directions in Psychological Science* in 1995. In it, Werker and Desjardins review research indicating that during the first year of life the infant moves from universal to language-specific phoneme recognition. Note the progression of the research, which is designed to determine when the ability to discriminate nonnative phonemes occurs. The researchers started with adolescents and gradually tested younger and younger children until they isolated the change in 6- to 12-month old infants. As you read this selection, consider the implications of the research for parental communication with infants.

Key Concept: language development

APA Citation: Werker, J. F., & Desjardins, R. N. (1995). Listening to speech in the 1st year of life: Experiential influences on phoneme perception. *Current Directions in Psychological Science, 4,* 76–81.

*T*he use of language to share thoughts, ideas, and feelings is a uniquely human characteristic. And to learn a language is one of the biggest challenges of infancy and early childhood. In order to be successful at this momentous task, the child must break down the speech stream, which consists of highly encoded and overlapping information, into smaller units such as clauses, phrases, and words. A yet smaller unit is the phoneme. Two words may differ by only one phoneme (e.g., *bat* vs. *pat*), yet this difference is enough to convey different meanings. Thus, a critical part of the language acquisition process is the ability to distinguish individual syllables on the basis of minimal differences in phonemes. In this review, we discuss the kinds of initial abilities infants bring to the task of phoneme perception, how these sensitivities are influenced by experience in a particular linguistic community, and whether events that occur during the prelinguistic period help prepare the child for the important task of language acquisition.

MAPPING THE CHANGES IN PHONEME PERCEPTION

Sensitive experimental techniques that were developed in the early 1970s allowed testing very young infants' speech perception abilities. These techniques revealed that infants can not only discriminate minimally distinctive phonemes, but can also distinguish phonemes from all the world's languages—including phonemes not used in their language-learning environment. In contrast, research with adults, using different techniques, had led scientists to believe that adults cannot readily discriminate all phonemic distinctions that are not used in their native language. Because adults typically perform better than infants at virtually any task given to them, this counterintuitive pattern of results was most intriguing. Our work was designed to explore the age at which experience first begins to influence phonemic perception and the mechanisms that might be responsible for this change.[1]

To explore the counterintuitive suggestion that infants discriminate non-native phonemes better than adults, we first compared the two groups directly. In order to do this, we needed a procedure that would be adaptable to both infants and adults. The procedure we chose is a category change procedure. In this task, the subject monitors a continuous background of syllables from one phonemic category (e.g., /ba/) and presses a button to signal when the stimuli change to a contrasting phonemic category (e.g., /da/). Correct button-presses are reinforced with the presentation of a flashing light (as feedback for older children and adults) or an electronically activated animal (as a reward for younger children). Incorrect button-presses are not reinforced, and misses are not signaled.

In the infant version of this procedure, called the conditioned head turn task, the infant sits on the parent's lap facing an experimental assistant who maintains the infant's interest by showing toys. The infant is conditioned to turn his or her head toward the sound source when he or she detects a change in

Janet F. Werker
and Renée N.
Desjardins

the phonemic category. Correct head turns are reinforced with the illumination and activation of clapping and drumming toy animals inside a Plexiglas box. In addition, the experimental assistant claps and gives praise and encouragement. As is the case with children and adults, incorrect responses are not reinforced. In our laboratory, the criterion for successful discrimination is set at 9 out of 10 correct consecutive responses within a series of 25 trials, approximately half of which are control trials in which no change occurs.

In the first series of experiments, we compared infants and adults on their ability to discriminate two distinctions that are phonemic (i.e., can differentiate words) in Hindi but not in English and one that is phonemic in both Hindi and English. The Hindi-only contrasts were chosen to vary in their potential difficulty. The first contrast, /Ta/–/ta/, involves two phonemes that both sound like *t* to a native English speaker. The difference between them involves where the tongue is placed. For /Ta/, the tongue is curled back and the tip of the underside hits the roof of the mouth. This is called a retroflex consonant. For /ta/, the tip of the tongue is placed against the front teeth. This is called a dental consonant. An English speaker makes a /t/ by placing the tongue against the alveolar ridge directly behind the front teeth. This alveolar consonant is articulated at a place in between the dental and retroflex consonants.

The second contrast was a Hindi voicing contrast that also involves two phonemes that sound like *t* to an English speaker. In this case, the difference involves the timing and shape of the opening of the vocal cords. Hindi /t^h/ and /d^h/ involve a slightly different combination of timing and shape than is used in production of English phonemes. For linguistic and acoustic reasons, this voicing contrast is potentially easier to discriminate than the retroflex-dental contrast.

Subjects were also tested on the contrast between /ba/ and /da/, which is used in both Hindi and English. This contrast served as a control to ensure that the subjects understood (and, in the case of the infants, were willing to perform) the task.

In the first study done collaboratively with Richard Tees, John Gilbert, and Keith Humphrey, English-learning infants aged 6 to 8 months were compared with both English-speaking adults and Hindi-speaking adults. Virtually all subjects in all groups could discriminate the /ba/–/da/ contrast, and the English-learning infants and the Hindi-speaking adults could easily discriminate both Hindi contrasts. However, the English-speaking adults had difficulty discriminating the Hindi contrasts, and showed particular trouble with the difficult retroflex-dental distinction. A short training procedure (25 trials) was effective in raising the proportion of English-speaking adults who could discriminate the Hindi voicing contrast, but this amount of training did not improve adult performance on the retroflex-dental distinction.

This experiment confirmed what many researchers had expected. Testing using comparable procedures verified that infants discriminate nonnative phoneme contrasts better than adults. But we had no idea as to the age in development when the performance decrement occurs. An influential view at the time was Lenneberg's hypothesis that there is a "critical period" for language acquisition up to the onset of puberty. Extrapolating from this hypothesis led us to test children on the verge of adolescence, as well as two younger age groups.

To our surprise, the results indicated that English-speaking children 12, 8, and even 4 years old perform as poorly as English-speaking adults on the Hindi contrasts not used in English. This effect was evident even though the 4-year-old children could easily discriminate the English contrast, and even though Hindi-learning children of age 4 discriminated both Hindi contrasts successfully when tested with the same procedure.

These results showing that language experience affects phoneme perception by age 4 led to additional tests of children between 6 months and 4 years old. A series of pilot tests led to a focus on the 1st year of life.

Infants between 6 and 12 months of age were tested on the difficult retroflex-dental contrast taken from Hindi, as well as on a new contrast taken from a Native Canadian language, Nthlakampx (one of the Interior Salish languages). The new contrast, glottalized velar /k'/ versus glottalized uvular /q'/, involves a difference in the position of the tongue in the back part of the vocal tract. English listeners hear these two sounds as "funny" *k*s. We found that although English-learning infants aged 6 to 8 months can discriminate both of these contrasts with ease, infants of 10 to 12 months, like English-speaking adults, fail to discriminate the difference in either non-English contrast. The same pattern of results was replicated in a study in which the same infants were tested at 6 to 8, 8 to 10, and 10 to 12 months of age. Thus, it appeared that the change occurs between 6 and 12 months of age. . . .

In a final manipulation, we tested a small number of 11- to 12-month-old infants who were being exposed to either Hindi or Nthlakampx in the home. Infants in each language group discriminated the contrast from their native language with ease, confirming that the change between 6 and 12 months reflects language-specific experience and is not just an age-related decrement in performance on difficult contrasts.

In a subsequent study, we tested English-learning infants using synthetically produced stimuli that varied in equal steps along a continuum from bilabial /ba/ to dental /da/ to retroflex /Da/. We found that English-learning infants aged 6 to 8 months can group stimuli according to the English boundary between labial and dental stimuli, and according to the Hindi boundary between retroflex and dental, but not according to an arbitrary boundary location that does not correspond to any known phonemic category. English-learning infants aged 10 to 12 months can group only according to the bilabial-dental boundary. These results confirm that the sensitivities shown by young infants prior to language-specific tuning are not arbitrary, but rather conform to potential phonemic categories. Also, with these synthetic stimuli, we replicated our finding that language-general perception shifts to language-specific perception between 6 and 12 months of age.

SUMMARY

During the 1st year of life, long before uttering his or her first words, an infant makes remarkable progress toward mastering the sound structure of the native language. The biases and proclivities that allow the neonate to detect regularities in the speech stream are, by 1 year of age, exquisitely tuned to the properties of the native language. Our work documents the infant's movement from universal to language-specific phoneme perception. What we have described, however, represents only a part of the infant's remarkable journey toward becoming a native listener. The challenge for future work is to determine what makes the movement from language-general to language-specific perception possible, and how sensitivity to the various properties of the native language is linked to the functional task of language acquisition.

Janet F. Werker and Renée N. Desjardins

NOTES

1. For a review of the studies discussed in this introduction, see J. F. Werker, Becoming a native listener, *American Scientist, 77*, 54–59 (1989).

PART FOUR

Motivation and Emotion

On the Internet . . .

Sites appropriate to Part Four

The Center for Evolutionary Psychology site at the University of California, Santa Barbara, provides information on evolutionary psychology.

    http://www.psych.ucsb.edu/research/cep/

The Perceptual Science Laboratory at the University of California, Santa Cruz, has put together this facial analysis page, which provides information and resources on researchers such as Paul Ekman.

    http://mambo.ucsc.edu/psl.fanl.html

The Emotion Home Page provides information and resources on research in emotion.

    http://emotion.salk.edu/emotion.html

1001 Ways to Be Romantic® from World of Romance™ by Gregory J. P. Godek.

    http://www.1001waystoberomantic.com/
      home.html

CHAPTER 9 Motivation

9.1 ABRAHAM H. MASLOW

A Theory of Human Motivation

Motivation, a core concept in psychology, has been studied from a wide variety of perspectives. One intriguing perspective is the humanistic theory, which proposes that there is a hierarchy of human needs that, when satisfied, leads to self-actualization, or the realization of one's potential.

Abraham H. Maslow (1908–1970), who first proposed the humanistic theory of motivation, earned his Ph.D. in experimental psychology from the University of Wisconsin in 1934. He taught at Brooklyn College and Brandeis University before going to the Laughlin Foundation in Menlo Park, California, in 1969. A leading proponent of the humanistic approach in psychology, Maslow wrote a number of books, including *Toward a Psychology of Being,* 2d ed. (Van Nostrand Reinhold, 1968) and *Motivation and Personality* (1954).

This selection is from "A Theory of Human Motivation," which was published in *Psychological Review* in 1943. In it, Maslow presents his original thinking in developing his "positive" humanistic theory. He perceives human needs as composing a hierarchy, with self-actualization—becoming what one is capable of becoming—as the ultimate need. Maslow writes in a straightforward style, but he deals with issues that are complex and that, in many ways, form the essence of being human. As you read this selection, consider what motivates you in your everyday life.

Key Concept: humanistic theory of motivation

APA Citation: Maslow, A. H. (1943). A theory of human motivation. *Psychological Review, 50,* 370–396.

*I*t is far easier to perceive and to criticize the aspects in motivation theory than to remedy them. Mostly this is because of the very serious lack of sound data in this area. I conceive this lack of sound facts to be due primarily to the absence of a valid theory of motivation. The present theory then must be considered to be a suggested program or framework for future research and must stand or fall, not so much on facts available or evidence presented, as upon researches yet to be done, researches suggested perhaps, by the questions raised in this paper.

THE BASIC NEEDS

The 'Physiological' Needs.   The needs that are usually taken as the starting point for motivation theory are the so-called physiological drives. Two recent lines of research make it necessary to revise our customary notions about these needs, first, the development of the concept of homeostasis, and second, the finding that appetites (preferential choices among foods) are a fairly efficient indication of actual needs or lacks in the body.

Homeostasis refers to the body's automatic efforts to maintain a constant, normal state of the blood stream. Cannon[1] has described this process for (1) the water content of the blood, (2) salt content, (3) sugar content, (4) protein content, (5) fat content, (6) calcium content, (7) oxygen content, (8) constant hydrogen-ion level (acid-base balance) and (9) constant temperature of the blood. Obviously this list can be extended to include other minerals, the hormones, vitamins, etc.

Young in a recent article[3] has summarized the work on appetite in its relation to body needs. If the body lacks some chemical, the individual will tend to develop a specific appetite or partial hunger for that food element.

Thus it seems impossible as well as useless to make any list of fundamental physiological needs for they can come to almost any number one might wish, depending on the degree of specificity of description. We can not identify all physiological needs as homeostatic. That sexual desire, sleepiness, sheer activity and maternal behavior in animals, are homeostatic, has not yet been demonstrated. Furthermore, this list would not include the various sensory pleasures (tastes, smells, tickling, stroking) which are probably physiological and which may become the goals of motivated behavior....

It should be pointed out again that any of the physiological needs and the consummatory behavior involved with them serve as channels for all sorts of other needs as well. That is to say, the person who thinks he is hungry may actually be seeking more for comfort, or dependence, than for vitamins or proteins. Conversely, it is possible to satisfy the hunger need in part by other activities such as drinking water or smoking cigarettes. In other words, relatively isolable as these physiological needs are, they are not completely so.

Undoubtedly these physiological needs are the most prepotent of all needs [they exceed all others in power]. What this means specifically is, that in the human being who is missing everything in life in an extreme fashion, it is most likely that the major motivation would be the physiological needs rather than any others. A person who is lacking food, safety, love, and esteem would most probably hunger for food more strongly than for anything else....

Obviously a good way to obscure the 'higher' motivations, and to get a lopsided view of human capacities and human nature, is to make the organism extremely and chronically hungry or thirsty. Anyone who attempts to make an emergency picture into a typical one, and who will measure all of man's goals and desires by his behavior during extreme physiological deprivation is certainly being blind to many things. It is quite true that man lives by bread alone—when there is no bread. But what happens to man's desires when there *is* plenty of bread and when his belly is chronically filled?

At once other (and 'higher') needs emerge and these, rather than physiological hungers, dominate the organism. And when these in turn are satisfied, again new (and still 'higher') needs emerge and so on. This is what we mean by saying that the basic human needs are organized into a hierarchy of relative prepotency.

One main implication of this phrasing is that gratification becomes as important a concept as deprivation in motivation theory, for it releases the organism from the domination of a relatively more physiological need, permitting thereby the emergence of other more social goals. The physiological needs, along with their partial goals, when chronically gratified cease to exist as active determinants or organizers of behavior. They now exist only in a potential fashion in the sense that they may emerge again to dominate the organism if they are thwarted. But a want that is satisfied is no longer a want. The organism is dominated and its behavior organized only by unsatisfied needs. If hunger is satisfied, it becomes unimportant in the current dynamics of the individual....

The Safety Needs. If the physiological needs are relatively well gratified, there then emerges a new set of needs, which we may categorize roughly as the safety needs. All that has been said of the physiological needs is equally true, although in lesser degree, of these desires. The organism may equally well be wholly dominated by them. They may serve as the almost exclusive organizers of behavior, recruiting all the capacities of the organism in their service, and we may then fairly describe the whole organism as a safety-seeking mechanism. Again we may say of the receptors, the effectors, of the intellect and the other capacities that they are primarily safety-seeking tools. Again, as in the hungry man, we find that the dominating goal is a strong determinant not only of his current world-outlook and philosophy but also of his philosophy of the future. Practically everything looks less important than safety, (even sometimes the physiological needs which being satisfied, are now underestimated). A man, in this state, if it is extreme enough and chronic enough, may be characterized as living almost for safety alone.

Although in this paper we are interested primarily in the needs of the adult, we can approach an understanding of his safety needs perhaps more efficiently by observation of infants and children, in whom these needs are much more simple and obvious. One reason for the clearer appearance of the threat or danger reaction in infants, is that they do not inhibit this reaction at all, whereas adults in our society have been taught to inhibit it at all costs. Thus even when adults do feel their safety to be threatened we may not be able to see this on the surface. Infants will react in a total fashion and as if they were endangered, if they are disturbed or dropped suddenly, startled by loud noises, flashing light, or other unusual sensory stimulation, by rough handling, by general loss of support in the mother's arms, or by inadequate support....

From these and similar observations, we may generalize and say that the average child in our society generally prefers a safe, orderly, predictable, organized world, which he can count on, and in which unexpected, unmanageable or other dangerous things do not happen, and in which, in any case, he has all-powerful parents who protect and shield him from harm....

The healthy, normal, fortunate adult in our culture is largely satisfied in his safety needs. The peaceful, smoothly running, 'good' society ordinarily makes its members feel safe enough from wild animals, extremes of temperature, criminals, assault and murder, tyranny, etc. Therefore, in a very real sense, he no longer has any safety needs as active motivators. Just as a sated man no longer feels hungry, a safe man no longer feels endangered. If we wish to see these needs directly and clearly we must turn to neurotic or near-neurotic individuals, and to the economic and social underdogs. In between these extremes, we can perceive the expressions of safety needs only in such phenomena as, for instance, the common preference for a job with tenure and protection, the desire for a savings account, and for insurance of various kinds (medical, dental, unemployment, disability, old age).

Other broader aspects of the attempt to seek safety and stability in the world are seen in the very common preference for familiar rather than unfamiliar things, or for the known rather than the unknown. The tendency to have some religion or world-philosophy that organizes the universe and the men in it into some sort of satisfactorily coherent, meaningful whole is also in part motivated by safety-seeking. Here too we may list science and philosophy in general as partially motivated by the safety needs....

The Love Needs.   If both the physiological and the safety needs are fairly well gratified, then there will emerge the love and affection and belongingness needs, and the whole cycle already described will repeat itself with this new center. Now the person will feel keenly, as never before, the absence of friends, or a sweetheart, or a wife, or children. He will hunger for affectionate relations with people in general, namely, for a place in his group, and he will strive with great intensity to achieve this goal. He will want to attain such a place more than anything else in the world and may even forget that once, when he was hungry, he sneered at love....

One thing that must be stressed at this point is that love is not synonymous with sex. Sex may be studied as a purely physiological need. Ordinarily sexual behavior is multi-determined, that is to say, determined not only by sexual but also by other needs, chief among which are the love and affection needs. Also not to be overlooked is the fact that the love needs involve both giving *and* receiving love.

The Esteem Needs.   All people in our society (with a few pathological exceptions) have a need or desire for a stable, firmly based, (usually) high evaluation of themselves, for self-respect, or self-esteem, and for the esteem of others.

By firmly based self-esteem, we mean that which is soundly based upon real capacity, achievement and respect from others. These needs may be classified into two subsidiary sets. These are, first, the desire for strength, for achievement, for adequacy, for confidence in the face of the world, and for independence and freedom. Secondly, we have what we may call the desire for reputation or prestige (defining it as respect or esteem from other people), recognition, attention, importance or appreciation. . . .

Satisfaction of the self-esteem need leads to feelings of self-confidence, worth, strength, capability and adequacy of being useful and necessary in the world. But thwarting of these needs produces feelings of inferiority, of weakness and of helplessness. These feelings in turn give rise to either basic discouragement or else compensatory or neurotic trends. An appreciation of the necessity of basic self-confidence and an understanding of how helpless people are without it, can be easily gained from a study of severe traumatic neurosis.[2]

The Need for Self-Actualization. Even if all these needs are satisfied, we may still often (if not always) expect that a new discontent and restlessness will soon develop, unless the individual is doing what he is fitted for. A musician must make music, an artist must paint, a poet must write, if he is to be ultimately happy. What a man *can* be, he *must* be. This need we may call self-actualization.

This term, first coined by Kurt Goldstein, is being used in this paper in a much more specific and limited fashion. It refers to the desire for self-fulfillment, namely, to the tendency for him to become actualized in what he is potentially. This tendency might be phrased as the desire to become more and more what one is, to become everything that one is capable of becoming.

The specific form that these needs will take will of course vary greatly from person to person. In one individual it may take the form of the desire to be an ideal mother, in another it may be expressed athletically, and in still another it may be expressed in painting pictures or in inventions. It is not necessarily a creative urge although in people who have any capacities for creation it will take this form.

The clear emergence of these needs rests upon prior satisfaction of the physiological, safety, love and esteem needs. We shall call people who are satisfied in these needs, basically satisfied people, and it is from these that we may expect the fullest (and healthiest) creativeness. Since, in our society, basically satisfied people are the exception, we do not know much about self-actualization, either experimentally or clinically. It remains a challenging problem for research.

The Preconditions for the Basic Need Satisfactions. There are certain conditions which are immediate prerequisites for the basic need satisfactions. Danger to these is reacted to almost as if it were a direct danger to the basic needs themselves. Such conditions as freedom to speak, freedom to do what one wishes so long as no harm is done to others, freedom to express one's self, freedom to investigate and seek for information, freedom to defend one's self, justice, fairness, honesty, orderliness in the group are examples of such preconditions for basic need satisfactions. Thwarting in these freedoms will be reacted to with a threat or emergency response. These conditions are not ends in themselves but they are *almost* so since they are so closely related to the basic needs, which are apparently the only ends in themselves. These conditions are defended because without them the basic satisfactions are quite impossible, or at least, very severely endangered.

If we remember that the cognitive capacities (perceptual, intellectual, learning) are a set of adjustive tools, which have, among other functions, that of satisfaction of our basic needs, then it is clear that any danger to them, any deprivation or blocking of their free use, must also be indirectly threatening to the basic needs themselves. Such a statement is a partial solution of the general problems of curiosity, the search for knowledge, truth and wisdom, and the ever-persistent urge to solve the cosmic mysteries....

The Desires to Know and to Understand.　So far, we have mentioned the cognitive needs only in passing. Acquiring knowledge and systematizing the universe have been considered as, in part, techniques for the achievement of basic safety in the world, or, for the intelligent man, expressions of self-actualization. Also freedom of inquiry and expression have been discussed as preconditions of satisfactions of the basic needs. True though these formulations may be, they do not constitute definitive answers to the question as to the motivation role of curiosity, learning, philosophizing, experimenting, etc. They are, at best, no more than partial answers....

FURTHER CHARACTERISTICS OF THE BASIC NEEDS

The Degree of Fixity of the Hierarchy of Basic Needs.　We have spoken so far as if this hierarchy were a fixed order but actually it is not nearly as rigid as we may have implied. It is true that most of the people with whom we have worked have seemed to have these basic needs in about the order that has been indicated. However, there have been a number of exceptions....

Degrees of Relative Satisfaction.　So far, our theoretical discussion may have given the impression that these five sets of needs are somehow in a step-wise, all-or-none relationship to each other. We have spoken in such terms as the following: "If one need is satisfied, then another emerges." This statement might give the false impression that a need must be satisfied 100 percent before the next need emerges. In actual fact, most members of our society who are normal, are partially satisfied in all their basic needs and partially unsatisfied in all their basic needs at the same time. A more realistic description of the hierarchy would be in terms of decreasing percentages of satisfaction as we go up the hierarchy of prepotency. For instance, if I may assign arbitrary figures for the sake of illustration, it is as if the average citizen is satisfied perhaps 85 percent in his physiological needs, 70 percent in his safety needs, 50 percent in his love needs, 40 percent in his self-esteem needs, and 10 percent in his self-actualization needs.

As for the concept of emergence of a new need after satisfaction of the prepotent need, this emergence is not a sudden saltatory phenomenon but rather a gradual emergence by slow degrees from nothingness. For instance, if prepotent need A is satisfied only 10 percent then need B may not be visible at all. However, as this need A becomes satisfied 25 percent, need B may emerge 5 percent, as need A becomes satisfied 75 percent need B may emerge 90 percent, and so on.

Unconscious Character of Needs.   These needs are neither necessarily conscious nor unconscious. On the whole, however, in the average person, they are more often unconscious rather than conscious. It is not necessary at this point to overhaul the tremendous mass of evidence which indicates the crucial importance of unconscious motivation. It would by now be expected, on a priori grounds alone, that unconscious motivations would on the whole be rather more important than the conscious motivations. What we have called the basic needs are very often largely unconscious although they may, with suitable techniques, and with sophisticated people become conscious.

Cultural Specificity and Generality of Needs.   This classification of basic needs makes some attempt to take account of the relative unity behind the superficial differences in specific desires from one culture to another. Certainly in any particular culture an individual's conscious motivational content will usually be extremely different from the conscious motivational content of an individual in another society. However, it is the common experience of anthropologists that people, even in different societies, are much more alike than we would think from our first contact with them, and that as we know them better we seem to find more and more of this commonness. We then recognize the most startling differences to be superficial rather than basic, *e.g.*, differences in style of hairdress, clothes, tastes in food, etc. Our classification of basic needs is in part an attempt to account for this unity behind the apparent diversity from culture to culture. No claim is made that it is ultimate or universal for all cultures. The claim is made only that it is relatively *more* ultimate, more universal, more basic, than the superficial conscious desires from culture to culture, and makes a somewhat closer approach to common-human characteristics. Basic needs are *more* common-human than superficial desires or behaviors.

Multiple Motivations of Behavior.   These needs must be understood *not* to be *exclusive* or single determiners of certain kinds of behavior. An example may be found in any behavior that seems to be physiologically motivated, such as eating, or sexual play or the like. The clinical psychologists have long since found that any behavior may be a channel through which flow various determinants. Or to say it in another way, most behavior is multi-motivated. Within the sphere of motivational determinants any behavior tends to be determined by several or *all* of the basic needs simultaneously rather than by only one of them. The latter would be more an exception than the former. Eating may be partially for the sake of filling the stomach, and partially for the sake of comfort and amelioration of other needs. One may make love not only for pure sexual release, but also to convince one's self of one's masculinity, or to make a conquest, to feel powerful, or to win more basic affection. As an illustration, I may point out that it would be possible (theoretically if not practically) to analyze a single act of an individual and see in it the expression of his physiological needs, his safety needs, his love needs, his esteem needs and self-actualization. This contrasts sharply with the more naive brand of trait psychology in which one trait or one motive accounts for a certain kind of act, *i.e.*, an aggressive act is traced solely to a trait of aggressiveness....

Goals as Centering Principle in Motivation Theory. It will be observed that the basic principle in our classification has been neither the instigation nor the motivated behavior but rather the functions, effects, purposes, or goals of the behavior. It has been proven sufficiently by various people that this is the most suitable point for centering in any motivation theory.

REFERENCES

1. CANNON, W. B. *Wisdom of the body.* New York: Norton, 1932.
2. KARDINER, A. *The traumatic neuroses of war.* New York: Hoeber, 1941.
3. YOUNG, P. T. The experimental analysis of appetite. *Psychol. Bull.*, 1941, 38, 129–164.

9.2 ALBERT BANDURA

Self-Efficacy: Toward a Unifying Theory of Behavioral Change

It is important to have a good understanding of ourselves, including our attitudes and abilities, asserts Albert Bandura. His concept of self-efficacy focuses on the belief that we can behave in a manner that produces successful outcomes. Bandura states that having the expectation that we can master a task has important implications for our self-concept and our ability to adjust to various situations.

Bandura was born in 1925 in Alberta, Canada. He earned his Ph.D. in clinical psychology from the University of Iowa in 1952. He then accepted a position at Stanford University, where he is currently a professor of psychology. His research interests have focused on social cognitive theory, which assigns an important role to cognitive, vicarious, self-regulating, and self-reflective processes in human functioning. He has written numerous influential books, including *Social Foundations of Thought and Action: A Social Cognitive Theory* (Prentice Hall, 1986) and *Self-Efficacy: The Exercise of Control* (Freeman, 1997).

Bandura's theory of self-efficacy is described in this selection from "Self-Efficacy: Toward a Unifying Theory of Behavioral Change," which was published in *Psychological Review* in 1977. In this classic paper, he describes the factors that influence self-efficacy, including performance accomplishments, vicarious experience, verbal persuasion, and physiological arousal. In one part of the original article not included in this selection, Bandura reports that self-efficacy is important for successful behavioral change in therapy. As you read this selection, think about the variables that promote self-efficacy and how you could develop a program to help others improve their coping skills through enhanced self-understanding.

Key Concept: self-efficacy

APA Citation: Bandura, A. (1977). Self-efficacy: Toward a unifying theory of behavioral change. *Psychological Review, 84,* 191–215.

EFFICACY EXPECTATIONS AS A
MECHANISM OF OPERATION

The present theory is based on the principal assumption that psychological procedures, whatever their form, serve as means of creating and strengthening expectations of personal efficacy. Within this analysis, efficacy expectations are distinguished from response–outcome expectancies. The difference is presented schematically in Figure 1.

An outcome expectancy is defined as a person's estimate that a given behavior will lead to certain outcomes. An efficacy expectation is the conviction that one can successfully execute the behavior required to produce the outcomes. Outcome and efficacy expectations are differentiated, because individuals can believe that a particular course of action will produce certain outcomes, but if they entertain serious doubts about whether they can perform the necessary activities such information does not influence their behavior.

In this conceptual system, expectations of personal mastery affect both initiation and persistence of coping behavior. The strength of people's convictions in their own effectiveness is likely to affect whether they will even try to cope with given situations. At this initial level, perceived self-efficacy influences choice of behavioral settings. People fear and tend to avoid threatening situations they believe exceed their coping skills, whereas they get involved in activities and behave assuredly when they judge themselves capable of handling situations that would otherwise be intimidating.

Not only can perceived self-efficacy have directive influence on choice of activities and settings, but, through expectations of eventual success, it can affect coping efforts once they are initiated. Efficacy expectations determine how much effort people will expend and how long they will persist in the face of obstacles and aversive experiences. The stronger the perceived self-efficacy, the more active the efforts. Those who persist in subjectively threatening activities that are in fact relatively safe will gain corrective experiences that reinforce their sense of efficacy, thereby eventually eliminating their defensive behavior. Those who cease their coping efforts prematurely will retain their self-debilitating expectations and fears for a long time.

The preceding analysis of how perceived self-efficacy influences performance is not meant to imply that expectation is the sole determinant of behavior. Expectations alone will not produce desired performance if the component capabilities are lacking. Moreover, there are many things that people can do with certainty of success that they do not perform because they have no incentives to do so. Given appropriate skills and adequate incentives, however, efficacy expectations are a major determinant of people's choice of activities, how much effort they will expend, and of how long they will sustain effort in dealing with stressful situations.

FIGURE 1

Diagrammatic Representation of the Difference Between
Efficacy Expectations and Outcome Expectations

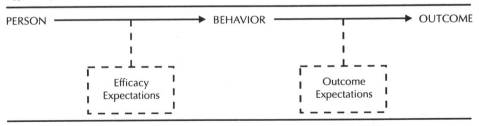

PERSON ⟶ BEHAVIOR ⟶ OUTCOME

Efficacy
Expectations

Outcome
Expectations

DIMENSIONS OF EFFICACY EXPECTATIONS

Empirical tests of the relationship between expectancy and performance of threatening activities have been hampered by inadequacy of the expectancy analysis. In most studies the measures of expectations are mainly concerned with people's hopes for favorable outcomes rather than with their sense of personal mastery. Moreover, expectations are usually assessed globally only at a single point in a change process as though they represent a static, unidimensional factor. Participants in experiments of this type are simply asked to judge how much they expect to benefit from a given procedure. When asked to make such estimates, participants assume, more often than not, that the benefits will be produced by the external ministrations rather than gained through the development of self-efficacy. Such global measures reflect a mixture of, among other things, hope, wishful thinking, belief in the potency of the procedures, and faith in the therapist. It therefore comes as no surprise that outcome expectations of this type have little relation to magnitude of behavioral change (Davison & Wilson, 1973; Lick & Bootzin, 1975).

Efficacy expectations vary on several dimensions that have important performance implications. They differ in *magnitude.* Thus when tasks are ordered in level of difficulty, the efficacy expectations of different individuals may be limited to the simpler tasks, extend to moderately difficult ones, or include even the most taxing performances. Efficacy expectations also differ in *generality.* Some experiences create circumscribed mastery expectations. Others instill a more generalized sense of efficacy that extends well beyond the specific treatment situation. In addition, expectancies vary in *strength.* Weak expectations are easily extinguishable by disconfirming experiences, whereas individuals who possess strong expectations of mastery will persevere in their coping efforts despite disconfirming experiences.

An adequate expectancy analysis, therefore, requires detailed assessment of the magnitude, generality, and strength of efficacy expectations commensurate with the precision with which behavioral processes are measured. Both efficacy expectations and performance should be assessed at significant junctures in the change process to clarify their reciprocal effects on each other. Mastery

191

FIGURE 2

Major Sources of Efficacy Information and the Principal Sources Through Which Different Modes of Treatment Operate

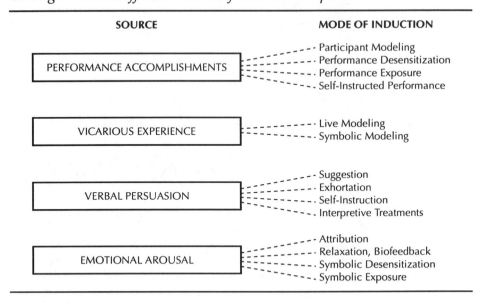

expectations influence performance and are, in turn, altered by the cumulative effects of one's efforts.

SOURCES OF EFFICACY EXPECTATIONS

In this social learning analysis, expectations of personal efficacy are based on four major sources of information: performance accomplishments, vicarious experience, verbal persuasion, and physiological states. Figure 2 presents the diverse influence procedures commonly used to reduce defensive behavior and presents the principal source through which each treatment operates to create expectations of mastery. Any given method, depending on how it is applied, may of course draw to a lesser extent on one or more other sources of efficacy information. For example,... performance-based treatments not only promote behavioral accomplishments but also extinguish fear arousal, thus authenticating self-efficacy through enactive and arousal sources of information. Other methods, however, provide fewer ways of acquiring information about one's capability for coping with threatening situations. By postulating a common mechanism of operation, this analysis provides a conceptual framework within which to study behavioral changes achieved by different modes of treatment....

... At this point a distinction must be drawn between information [that people use to judge their level of self-efficacy] contained in environmental events and information as processed and transformed by the individual. The impact of information on efficacy expectations will depend on how it is cognitively appraised. A number of contextual factors, including the social, situational, and temporal circumstances under which events occur, enter into such appraisals. For this reason, even success experiences do not necessarily create strong generalized expectations of personal efficacy. Expectations that have served self-protective functions for years are not quickly discarded. When experience contradicts firmly established expectations of self-efficacy, they may undergo little change if the conditions of performance are such as to lead one to discount the import of the experience. ...

Results of recent studies support the thesis that generalized, lasting changes in self-efficacy and behavior can best be achieved by participant methods using powerful induction procedures initially to develop capabilities, then removing external aids to verify personal efficacy, then finally using self-directed mastery to strengthen and generalize expectations of personal efficacy (Bandura et al., 1975). Independent performance can enhance efficacy expectations in several ways: (a) It creates additional exposure to former threats, which provides participants with further evidence that they are no longer aversively aroused by what they previously feared. Reduced emotional arousal confirms increased coping capabilities. (b) Self-directed mastery provides opportunities to perfect coping skills, which lessen personal vulnerability to stress. (c) Independent performance, if well executed, produces success experiences, which further reinforce expectations of self-competency.

Extensive self-directed performance of formerly threatening activities under progressively challenging conditions at a time when treatments are usually terminated could also serve to reduce susceptibility to relearning of defensive patterns of behavior. A few negative encounters among many successful experiences that have instilled a strong sense of self-efficacy will, at most, establish discriminative avoidance of realistic threats, an effect that has adaptive value. In contrast, if people have limited contact with previously feared objects after treatment, whatever expectations of self-efficacy were instated would be weaker and more vulnerable to change. Consequently, a few unfavorable experiences are likely to reestablish defensive behavior that generalizes inappropriately. ...

Just as the value of efficacy information generated enactively and vicariously depends on cognitive appraisal, so does the information arising from exhortative and emotive sources. The impact of verbal persuasion on self-efficacy may vary substantially depending on the perceived credibility of the persuaders, their prestige, trustworthiness, expertise, and assuredness. The more believable the source of the information, the more likely are efficacy expectations to change. The influence of credibility on attitudinal change has, of course, received intensive study. But its effects on perceived self-efficacy remain to be investigated.

REFERENCES

Bandura, A., Jeffery, R. W., & Gajdos, E. Generalizing change through participant modeling with self-directed mastery. *Behaviour Research and Therapy*, 1975, *13*, 141–152.

Davison, G. C., & Wilson, G. T. Processes of fear-reduction in systematic desensitization: Cognitive and social reinforcement factors in humans. *Behavior Therapy*, 1973, *4*, 1–21.

Lick, J., & Bootzin, R. Expectancy factors in the treatment of fear: Methodological and theoretical issues. *Psychological Bulletin*, 1975, *82*, 917–931.

9.3 DAVID M. BUSS

The Strategies of Human Mating

The focus of psychology has become increasingly multicultural in recent years as researchers look for universal laws of human behavior. The evolutionary approach to courtship and mate selection argues that men and women throughout the world have different reproductive strategies. David M. Buss of the University of Michigan, in collaboration with 50 other researchers around the world, surveyed over 10,000 men and women in 37 countries on their mating preferences. Buss has used the survey results to develop a theory of mate selection.

Buss received his Ph.D. in psychology from the University of California in 1981. He currently holds a position at the University of Texas at Austin, and he is director of the International Consortium of Personality and Social Psychologists. His evolutionary theory of human mate selection is detailed in his book *The Evolution of Desire: Strategies of Human Mating* (Basic Books, 1994).

This selection is from "The Strategies of Human Mating," which was published in *American Scientist* in 1994. In it, Buss outlines his theory and provides research results, obtained predominantly through surveys, that support the conclusion that, universally, men and women desire certain characteristics in a mate that are unique to each sex. How might an understanding of differences in sexual preference help men and women in their interpersonal relationships?

Key Concept: cross-cultural theory of mate selection

APA Citation: Buss, D. M. (1994). The strategies of human mating. *American Scientist, 82,* 238–249.

W hat do men and women want in a mate? Is there anything consistent about human behavior when it comes to the search for a mate? Would a Gujarati of India be attracted to the same traits in a mate as a Zulu of South Africa or a college student in the midwestern United States?

As a psychologist working in the field of human personality and mating preferences, I have come across many attempts to answer such questions and provide a coherent explanation of human mating patterns. Some theories have suggested that people search for mates who resemble archetypical images of the opposite-sex parent (à la Freud and Jung), or mates with characteristics that are either complementary or similar to one's own qualities, or mates with whom to make an equitable exchange of valuable resources.

These theories have played important roles in our understanding of human mating patterns, but few of them have provided specific predictions that can be tested. Fewer still consider the origins and functions of an individual's mating preferences. What possible function is there to mating with an individual who is an archetypical image of one's opposite-sex parent? Most theories also tend to assume that the processes that guide the mating preferences of men and women are identical, and no sex-differentiated predictions can be derived. The context of the mating behavior is also frequently ignored; the same mating tendencies are posited regardless of circumstances.

Despite the complexity of human mating behavior, it is possible to address these issues in a single, coherent theory. David Schmitt of the University of Michigan and I have recently proposed a framework for understanding the logic of human mating patterns from the standpoint of evolutionary theory. Our theory makes several predictions about the behavior of men and women in the context of their respective sexual strategies. In particular, we discuss the changes that occur when men and women shift their goals from short-term mating (casual sex) to long-term mating (a committed relationship).

Some of the studies we discuss are based on surveys of male and female college students in the United States. In these instances, the sexual attitudes of the sample population may not be reflective of the behavior of people in other cultures. In other instances, however, the results represent a much broader spectrum of the human population. In collaboration with 50 other scientists, we surveyed the mating preferences of more than 10,000 men and women in 37 countries over a six-year period spanning 1984 through 1989. Although no survey, short of canvassing the entire human population, can be considered exhaustive, our study crosses a tremendous diversity of geographic, cultural, political, ethnic, religious, racial and economic groups. It is the largest survey ever on mate preferences.

What we found is contrary to much current thinking among social scientists, which holds that the process of choosing a mate is highly culture-bound. Instead, our results are consistent with the notion that human beings, like other animals, exhibit species-typical desires when it comes to the selection of a mate. These patterns can be accounted for by our theory of human sexual strategies.

COMPETITION AND CHOICE

Sexual-strategies theory holds that patterns in mating behavior exist because they are evolutionarily advantageous. We are obviously the descendants of people who were able to mate successfully. Our theory assumes that the sexual strategies of our ancestors evolved because they permitted them to survive and produce offspring. Those people who failed to mate successfully because they did not express these strategies are not our ancestors. One simple example is the urge to mate, which is a universal desire among people in all cultures and which is undeniably evolutionary in origin.

Although the types of behavior we consider are more complicated than simply the urge to mate, a brief overview of the relevant background should be adequate to understand the evolutionary logic of human mating strategies.

As with many issues in evolutionary biology, this background begins with the work of Charles Darwin.

Darwin was the first to show that mate preferences could affect human evolution. In his seminal 1871 treatise, *The Descent of Man and Selection in Relation to Sex*, Darwin puzzled over characteristics that seemed to be perplexing when judged merely on the basis of their relative advantage for the animal's survival. How could the brilliant plumage of a male peacock evolve when it obviously increases the bird's risk of predation? Darwin's answer was sexual selection, the evolution of characteristics that confer a reproductive advantage to an organism (rather than a survival advantage). Darwin further divided sexual selection into two processes: intrasexual competition and preferential mate choice.

Intrasexual competition is the less controversial of the two processes. It involves competition between members of the same sex to gain preferential access to mating partners. Characteristics that lead to success in these same-sex competitions—such as greater strength, size, agility, confidence or cunning—can evolve simply because of the reproductive advantage gained by the victors. Darwin assumed that this is primarily a competitive interaction between males, but recent studies suggest that human females are also very competitive for access to mates.

Preferential mate choice, on the other hand, involves the desire for mating with partners that possess certain characteristics. A consensual desire affects the evolution of characteristics because it gives those possessing the desired characteristics an advantage in obtaining mates over those who do not possess the desired characteristics. Darwin assumed that preferential mate choice operates primarily through females who prefer particular males. (Indeed, he even called this component of sexual selection *female choice.*)

Darwin's theory of mate-choice selection was controversial in part because Darwin simply assumed that females desire males with certain characteristics. Darwin failed to document how such desires might have arisen and how they might be maintained in a population.

The solution to the problem was not forthcoming until 1972, when Robert Trivers, then at Harvard University, proposed that the relative parental investment of the sexes influences the two processes of sexual selection. Specifically, the sex that invests more in offspring is selected to be more discriminating in choosing a mate, whereas the sex that invests less in offspring is more competitive with members of the same sex for sexual access to the high-investing sex. Parental-investment theory accounts, in part, for both the origin and the evolutionary retention of different sexual strategies in males and females.

Consider the necessary *minimum* parental investment by a woman. After internal fertilization, the gestation period lasts about nine months and is usually followed by lactation, which in tribal societies typically can last several years. In contrast, a man's minimum parental investment can be reduced to the contribution of sperm, an effort requiring as little time as a few minutes. This disparity in parental investment means that the replacement of a child who dies (or is deserted) typically costs more (in time and energy) for women than men. Parental-investment theory predicts that women will be more choosy and selective about their mating partners. Where men can provide resources, women should desire those who are able and willing to commit those resources to her and her children.

SEXUAL STRATEGIES

Our evolutionary framework is based on three key ingredients. First, human mating is inherently strategic. These strategies exist because they solved specific problems in human evolutionary history. It is important to recognize that the manifestation of these strategies need not be through conscious psychological mechanisms. Indeed, for the most part we are completely unaware of *why* we find certain qualities attractive in a mate. A second component of our theory is that mating strategies are context-dependent. People behave differently depending on whether the situation presents itself as a short-term or long-term mating prospect. Third, men and women have faced different mating problems over the course of human evolution and, as a consequence, have evolved different strategies.

... [S]exual strategies theory consists of nine hypotheses. We can test these hypotheses by making several predictions about the behavior of men and women faced with a particular mating situation. Even though we make only a few predictions for each hypothesis, it should be clear that many more predictions can be derived to test each hypothesis. We invite the reader to devise his or her own tests of these hypotheses.

Hypothesis 1: Short-term mating is more important for men than women. This hypothesis follows from the fact that men can reduce their parental investment to the absolute minimum and still produce offspring. Consequently, short-term mating should be a key component of the sexual strategies of men, and much less so for women. We tested three predictions based on this hypothesis in a sample of 148 college students (75 men and 73 women) in the midwestern United States.

First, we predict that men will express a greater interest in seeking a short-term mate than will women. We asked the students to rate the degree to which they were currently seeking a short-term mate (defined as a one-night stand or a brief affair) and the degree to which they were currently seeking a long-term mate (defined as a marriage partner). They rated their interests on a 7-point scale, where a rating of 1 corresponds to a complete lack of interest and a 7 corresponds to a high level of interest.

We found that although the sexes do not differ in their stated proclivities for seeking a long-term mate (an average rating of about 3.4 for both sexes), men reported a significantly greater interest (an average rating of about 5) in seeking a short-term sexual partner than did women (about 3). The results also showed that at any given time men are more interested in seeking a short-term mate rather than a long-term mate, whereas women are more interested in seeking a long-term mate than a short-term mate.

Second we predict that men will desire a greater number of mates than is desired by women. We asked the same group of college students how many sexual partners they would ideally like to have during a given time interval and during their lifetimes. In this instance men consistently reported that they desired a greater number of sex partners than reported by the women for every interval of time. For example, the average man desired about eight sex partners during the next two years, whereas the average woman desired to have one sex partner. In the course of a lifetime, the average man reported the desire to have about 18 sex partners, whereas the average woman desired no more than 4 or 5 sex partners.

A third prediction that follows from this hypothesis is that men will be more willing to engage in sexual intercourse a shorter period of time after first meeting a potential sex partner. We asked the sample of 148 college students the following question: "If the conditions were right, would you consider having sexual intercourse with someone you viewed as desirable if you had known that person for *(a time period ranging from one hour to five years)*?" For each of 10 time intervals the students were asked to provide a response ranging from −3 (definitely not) to 3 (definitely yes).

After a period of 5 years, the men and women were equally likely to consent to sexual relations, each giving a score of about 2 (probably yes). For all shorter time intervals, men were consistently more likely to consider sexual intercourse. For example, after knowing a potential sex partner for only one week, the average man was still positive about the possibility of having sex, whereas women said that they were highly unlikely to have sex with someone after knowing him for only one week.

The issue was addressed in a novel way by Russell Clark and Elaine Hatfield of the University of Hawaii. They designed a study in which college students were approached by an attractive member of the opposite sex who posed one of three questions after a brief introduction: "Would you go out on a date with me tonight?" "Would you go back to my apartment with me tonight?" or "Would you have sex with me tonight?"

Of the women who were approached, 50 percent agreed to the date, 6 percent agreed to go to the apartment and none agreed to have sex. Many women found the sexual request from a virtual stranger to be odd or insulting. Of the men approached, 50 percent agreed to the date, 69 percent agreed to go back to the woman's apartment and 75 percent agreed to have sex. In contrast to women, many men found the sexual request flattering. Those few men who declined were apologetic about it, citing a fiancee or an unavoidable obligation that particular evening. Apparently, men are willing to solve the problem of partner number by agreeing to have sex with virtual strangers.

Hypotheses 2 through 9, the discussions of which are not reprinted here, are as follows.

Hypothesis 2: Men seeking a short-term mate will solve the problem of identifying women who are sexually accessible.

Hypothesis 3: Men seeking a short-term mate will minimize commitment and invest-ment.

Hypothesis 4: Men seeking a short-term mate will solve the problem of identifying fertile women.

Hypothesis 5: Men seeking a long-term mate will solve the problem of identifying reproductively valuable women.

Hypothesis 6: Men seeking a long-term mate will solve the problem of paternity confi-dence.

Hypothesis 7: Women seeking a short-term mate will prefer men willing to impart immediate resources.

Hypothesis 8: Women will be more selective than men in choosing a short-term mate.

Hypothesis 9: Women seeking a long-term mate will prefer men who can provide re-sources for her offspring.

As with Hypothesis 1, Buss makes and tests several predictions based on these hypothe-ses.—Ed.

CONCLUSION

The results of our work and that of others provide strong evidence that the traditional assumptions about mate preferences—that they are arbitrary and culture-bound—are simply wrong. Darwin's initial insights into sexual selec-tion have turned out to be scientifically profound for people, even though he understood neither their functional-adaptive nature nor the importance of rel-ative parental investment for driving the two components of sexual selection.

Men and women have evolved powerful desires for particular character-istics in a mate. These desires are not arbitrary, but are highly patterned and universal. The patterns correspond closely to the specific adaptive problems that men and women have faced during the course of human evolutionary history. These are the problems of paternity certainty, partner number and re-productive capacity for men, and the problems of willingness and ability to invest resources for women.

It turns out that a woman's physical appearance is the most powerful pre-dictor of the occupational status of the man she marries. A woman's appearance is more significant than her intelligence, her level of education or even her orig-inal socioeconomic status in determining the mate she will marry. Women who possess the qualities men prefer are most able to translate their preferences into actual mating decisions. Similarly, men possessing what women want—the ability to provide resources—are best able to mate according to their prefer-ences.

Some adaptive problems are faced by men and women equally: identify-ing mates who show a proclivity to cooperate and mates who show evidence of having good parenting skills. Men do not look at women simply as sex objects, nor do women look at men simply as success objects. One of our most robust observations was that both sexes place tremendous importance on mutual love and kindness when seeking a long-term mate.

The similarities among cultures and between sexes implies a degree of psychological unity or species typicality that transcends geographical, racial, political, ethnic and sexual diversity. Future research could fruitfully examine the ecological and historical sources of diversity, while searching for the adaptive functions of the sexual desires that are shared by all members of our species.

David M. Buss

10.1 PAUL EKMAN

Facial Expressions of Emotion: New Findings, New Questions

During the past two decades, researchers have discovered that facial expressions for a number of emotions are universally recognizable—that is, people from a wide variety of cultures will attribute certain facial expressions to the same emotions. More recently, psychologists have reported that facial muscular actions associated with specific emotions (such as frowning, which indicates sadness) cause changes in physiological arousal as well as enhance feelings of the emotion associated with the muscular movements. Paul Ekman has been at the cutting edge of research on facial expression of emotion.

Ekman (b. 1934) earned his Ph.D. from Adelphi University in 1958. He is currently a professor of psychology and the director of the Human Interaction Laboratory at the University of California at San Francisco. He has written a number of books, including *Emotion in the Human Face,* 2d ed. (Cambridge University Press, 1983) and *Telling Lies* (Berkeley, 1985).

This selection is from "Facial Expressions of Emotion: New Findings, New Questions," which was published in the American Psychological Society journal *Psychological Science* in 1992. In it, Ekman offers a glimpse of an active and relevant research program concerning observable facial expressions of emotion. In one part of the original article not included in this selection, Ekman demonstrates that there are differences among smiles and that it is possible to distinguish a smile of enjoyment from other kinds of smiling (such as a smile of embarrassment). As you read this selection, consider how easy it is to detect a person's emotions by observing his or her facial expressions. Does Ekman's evidence suggest that it is possible to modify your emotional state by exercising certain facial muscles?

Key Concept: facial expression of emotion

APA Citation: Ekman, P. (1992). Facial expressions of emotion: New findings, new questions. *Psychological Science, 3,* 34–38.

This paper focuses on the evidence and issues regarding observable facial expression of emotion.... I will focus on two new findings and one set of studies dating back 20 years. I will begin with those older studies, of universals in facial expression, because they provide the background for the newer research and also because there is renewed controversy about universals, as well as some new findings and a number of unanswered questions.

UNIVERSAL FACIAL EXPRESSIONS

From 1920 through 1960 many influential psychologists maintained that facial expressions are socially learned and culturally variable, with no fixed relationship between an expression and what it signifies. In the early 1970s there were two challenges: a critical reevaluation of the experiments which had supported that position (Ekman, Friesen, & Ellsworth, 1972) and, more important, new data. Izard and also Friesen and I conducted similar studies of literate cultures, working independently but at the same time. Izard's work and ours was influenced by Tomkins's writings on emotion (1962) and his advice on the conduct of the research we performed.

In each culture subjects chose the emotion terms which fit photographs of posed Caucasian facial expressions. Although Izard (1971) and I (Ekman, Sorenson, & Friesen, 1969) showed different photographs, gave our subjects somewhat different lists of emotion terms, and examined people in different cultures, we both obtained consistent evidence of agreement across more than a dozen Western and non-Western literate cultures in the labeling of enjoyment, anger, fear, sadness, disgust, and surprise facial expressions.

In order to rule out the possibility that such agreement could be due to members of every culture having learned expressions from a shared mass media input, Friesen and I (Ekman, 1972; Ekman & Friesen, 1971; Ekman et al., 1969) also studied a visually isolated preliterate culture in New Guinea. We replicated our findings for literate cultures, as did Heider and Rosch a few years later in another visually isolated culture in what is now West Irian. Although surprise expressions were distinguished from anger, sadness, disgust, and enjoyment expressions in both preliterate cultures, surprise was not distinguished from fear expressions in one of these cultures. Friesen and I also reversed the research design and found that when New Guineans posed facial expressions they were understandable to Western observers (Ekman & Friesen, 1971).

To reconcile these findings of universality with the many reports by cultural anthropologists of dissimilar facial expressions, we (Ekman & Friesen, 1969) postulated *display rules* to refer to what we presume each culture teaches its members about the management of expression in social contexts. Cultural differences in display rules could explain how universal expressions might be modified to create, on occasion, the appearance of culture-specific facial expressions of emotion. We tested this idea in a study comparing the spontaneous expressions shown by Japanese and Americans when they were alone, and presumably no display rules should operate, and when they were with another person (Ekman, 1972; Friesen, 1972). As predicted, there was no difference between cultures in the expressions shown in response to films of unpleasant scenes when the subjects thought they were alone. However, when an authority figure was present the Japanese more than the Americans masked negative expressions with the semblance of smile.

We, like Izard, interpreted the evidence in terms of universal facial expressions as posited by Tomkins (1962) and (much earlier) by Darwin (1872). Consistent with an evolutionary view of expression were other reports of similarities in expression in other primates and in early appearance developmentally. Recently, there have been some challenges to that interpretation. Lutz and White (1986) cited anthropologists who regard emotions as social constructions and reported cultures in which the emotions proposed as universal are neither named nor expressed. Unfortunately, such reports are not substantiated by quantitative methods nor protected against the potential for bias or error when the information is obtained by the single observer who formulated the hypothesis under study. Ortony and Turner (1990) provided a different challenge, speculating that it is only the components of expressions, not the full emotional expressions, which are universal: but see my rebuttal (Ekman, in press-a) and one by Izard (in press).

A new line of studies has found consistent evidence of cultural differences in the perception of the strength of an emotion rather than of which emotion is shown in a facial expression. Japanese make less intense attributions than do Americans (Ekman et al., 1987) regardless of whether the person showing the emotion is Japanese or American, male or female (Matsumoto & Ekman, 1989). This difference appears to be specific to the interpretation of facial expressions of emotions, since it was not found in the judgment of either nonfacial emotional stimuli or facial nonemotional stimuli (Matsumoto & Kudoh, 1991).

A number of empirical questions remain about universals in facial expression. Although there is evidence of more than one different expression for each emotion (up to five visibly different expressions for some emotions) in Western cultures, we do not know how many of those different expressions which signal a single emotion are shown universally (Ekman & Friesen, 1975, 1978). Nor is there certain knowledge about whether there are other emotions in addition to anger, fear, disgust, sadness, enjoyment, and surprise that have universal expressions. There is some evidence, although it is contradictory, for universal facial expressions for contempt, interest, shame, and guilt. Little is known also about cross-cultural differences in display rules, as a function of sex, role, age, and social context (but see recent work by Matsumoto, in press). These and other questions about universals have recently been reviewed (Ekman, 1989b).

FACIAL ACTION GENERATES EMOTION PHYSIOLOGY

Most emotion theorists emphasize the involuntary nature of emotional experience, ignoring those instances when people choose to generate an emotion through reminiscence or by adopting the physical actions associated with a particular emotion (e.g., speaking more softly to deintensify anger or smiling to generate enjoyment). Facial expression from this vantage point is seen as one of a number of emotional responses that are generated centrally when an emotion is called forth by, for example, an event, memory, or image.

A new role for facial expression was found in my collaborative study with Levenson and Friesen (Ekman, Levenson, & Friesen, 1983). Voluntarily performing certain facial muscular actions generated involuntary changes in autonomic nervous system (ANS) activity. We did not ask subjects to pose emotions, but instead to follow muscle-by-muscle instructions to create on their faces one of the expressions which had been found to be universal. For example, rather than ask a subject to pose anger we said: "Pull your eyebrows down and together; raise your upper eyelids and tighten your lower eyelids; narrow your lips and press them together." Different patterns of ANS activity occurred when subjects made the muscular movements which had been found universally for the emotions of anger, fear, sadness, and disgust.

This work has since been replicated in three more experiments (Levenson, Carstensen, Friesen, & Ekman, 1991; Levenson, Ekman, & Friesen, 1990), and a number of possible artifacts which could have been responsible for this phenomenon have been ruled out. The findings were again obtained in a very different culture—the Minangkabau of Sumatra, Indonesia, who are fundamentalist Moslem and matrilineal—suggesting that this phenomenon may be pancultural (Ekman, 1989a).

It appears that the specific patterns of ANS activity that were generated by making the different facial expressions are not unique to this task, but are the same as are found in more conventional emotion-arousing tasks. This lack of specificity confirms my proposal (Ekman, 1984, in press-b) that emotions are characterized by patterned changes in both expression and physiology, changes which are distinctive for each emotion, and which are not (in large part) specific to the means by which the emotion was aroused. This latter point is most readily noted with facial expression, which can signal that someone is angry, for example, without providing any clue as to what made the person angry.

When subjects followed our instructions to make these facial expressions, most reported not simply a physiological change but the experience of an emotion. In response to an open-ended question about what emotions, sensations, or memories they experienced, there were few reports of memories or sensations, while on 78% of the trials the subjects reported feeling an emotion. More information on this point, on the issue of generality, and on the details of the emotion-specific patterns of ANS activity can be found in... Levenson et al. (1990).

Before turning to the question of *how* voluntarily making different facial configurations generates different patterns of physiology, let me broaden our focus to consider central nervous system (CNS), not just ANS, physiology. In a study employing the same muscle-by-muscle instructions used to study ANS activity, subjects created the various facial configurations while left and right frontal, temporal, and parietal electroencephalographic (EEG) activity was measured. Different patterns of EEG activity occurred when subjects made the muscular movements which had been found universally for the emotions of happiness, anger, fear, sadness, and disgust (Davidson & Ekman, 1991; Ekman & Davidson, 1991).

In an unpublished research Friesen, Levenson, and I have formulated nine different explanations of how voluntary facial action generates emotion-specific physiology. Here I will indicate only three broad divisions among these explanations, leaving out the specific details relevant to subdistinctions within each of these divisions. The first explanation, which is the one we endorse, posits a central, hard-wired connection between the motor cortex and other areas of the brain involved in directing the physiological changes which occur during emotion. The second group of explanations proposes that such a connection is learned, not hard-wired. Such learning could be common to all members of our species or culture-specific. (Our findings in Indonesia raise questions but cannot rule out the viability of the culture-specific variation.) The third set of explanations emphasizes peripheral feedback from the facial actions themselves, rather than a central connection between the brain areas which direct those facial movements and other brain areas. This view includes variations in terms of whether feedback comes from the muscles, the skin, or temperature changes and whether it is hard-wired or requires learning. This explanation is consistent with the view of Izard (in press), Laird (Laird, 1971; Duclos et al., 1989), Tomkins (1962), and Zajonc (1985).

For now, there is no clear empirical basis for a definitive choice among these explanations. Through studies of people with facial paralysis who have no possibility of peripheral facial action or feedback we hope to challenge the third category of explanations, but this work is not yet complete, and the results may not be unambiguous....

OTHER ISSUES ABOUT EXPRESSION

In closing let me mention three major questions about observable facial expressions. Every student who examines expression itself, not its recognition, must be impressed with individual differences in the speed, magnitude, and duration of expression as well as variations in which facial expression of emotion occurs in response to a particular event. It is not known whether such differences are consistent across emotions or situations, or over time. We also do not know whether a facial activity is a necessary part of any emotional experience. Under what circumstances, and with what kinds of people, might there be evidence of physiological changes relevant to emotion and the subjective experience of emotion with no evidence of visible expression or nonvisible electromyographic facial activity? Another issue requiring study is whether personality traits, moods, and psychopathology have facial markers or are second-order inferences drawn from the occurrence of facial expressions of emotion.

REFERENCES

Darwin, C. (1972). *The expression of the emotions in man and animals.* New York: Philosophical Library.

Davidson, R. J., & Ekman, P. (1991). *Differences in regional brain activity among different emotions.* Unpublished manuscript.

Duclos, S. E., Laird, J. D., Schneider, E., Sexter, M., Stern, L., & Van Leighten, O. (1989). Emotion-specific effects of facial expressions and postures on emotional experience. *Journal of Personality and Social Psychology, 57,* 100–108.

Ekman, P. (1972). Universals and cultural differences in facial expressions of emotion. In J. Cole (Ed.), *Nebraska symposium on motivation, 1971* (pp. 207–283). Lincoln: University of Nebraska Press.

Ekman, P. (1984). Expression and the nature of emotion. In K. Scherer & P. Ekman (Eds.), *Approaches to emotion* (pp. 319–344). Hillsdale, NJ: Erlbaum.

Ekman, P. (1989a). The argument and evidence about universals in facial expressions of emotion. In H. Wagner & A. Manstead (Eds.), *Handbook of social psychophysiology* (pp. 143–164). Chichester, England: Wiley.

Ekman, P. (1989b, January). *A cross cultural study of emotional expression, language and physiology.* Symposium conducted at the annual meeting of the American Association for the Advancement of Science, San Francisco.

Ekman, P. (in press-a). Are there basic emotions? A reply to Ortony and Turner. *Psychological Review.*

Ekman, P. (in press-b). An argument for basic emotions. *Cognition and Emotion.*

Ekman, P., & Davidson, R. J. (1991). *Hemispheric activation in different types of smiles.* Unpublished manuscript.

Ekman, P., & Friesen, W. V. (1969). The repertoire of nonverbal behavior: Categories, origins, usage, and coding. *Semiotica, 1,* 49–98.

Ekman, P., & Friesen, W. V. (1971). Constants across cultures in the face and emotion. *Journal of Personality and Social Psychology, 17,* 124–129.

Ekman, P., & Friesen, W. V. (1975). *Unmasking the face: A guide to recognizing emotions from facial clues.* Englewood Cliffs, NJ: Prentice-Hall.

Ekman, P., & Friesen, W. V. (1978). *The Facial Action Coding System: A technique for the measurement of facial movement.* Palo Alto, CA: Consulting Psychologists Press.

Ekman, P., Friesen, W. V., & Ellsworth, P. (1972). *Emotion in the human face: Guidelines for research and an integration of findings.* New York: Pergamon Press.

Ekman, P., Friesen, W. V., O'Sullivan, M., Chan, A., Diacoyanni-Tarlatzis, I., Heider, K., Krause, R., LeCompte, W. A., Pitcairn, T., Ricci-Bitti, P. E., Scherer, K. R., Tomita, M., & Tzavaras, A. (1987). Universals and cultural differences in the judgments of facial expressions of emotion. *Journal of Personality and Social Psychology, 53,* 712–717.

Ekman, P., Levenson, R. W., & Friesen, W. V. (1983). Autonomic nervous system activity distinguishes between emotions. *Science, 221,* 1208–1210.

Ekman, P., Sorenson, E. R., & Friesen, W. V. (1969). Pan-cultural elements in facial displays of emotions. *Science, 164,* 86–88.

Friesen, W. V. (1972). *Cultural differences in facial expression in a social situation: An experimental test of the concept of display rules.* Unpublished doctoral dissertation, University of California, San Francisco.

Izard, C. E. (1971). *The face of emotion.* New York: Appleton-Century-Crofts.

Izard, C. E. (in press). Basic emotions, relation among emotions and emotion-cognition relation. *Psychological Review.*

Laird, J. D. (1974). Self-attribution of emotion: The effects of expressive behavior on the quality of emotional experience. *Journal of Personality and Social Psychology, 29,* 475–486.

Levenson, R. W., Carstensen, L. L., Friesen, W. V., & Ekman, P. (1991). Emotion, physiology, and expression in old age. *Psychology and Aging, 6,* 28–35.

Levenson, R. W., Ekman, P., & Friesen, W. V. (1990). Voluntary facial action generates emotion-specific autonomic nervous system activity. *Psychophysiology, 27,* 363–384.

Lutz, C., & White, G. M. (1986). The anthropology of emotions. *Annual Review of Anthropology, 15,* 405–436.

Matsumoto, D. (in press). Cultural similarities and differences in display rules. *Motivation and Emotion.*

Matsumoto, D., & Ekman, P. (1989). American-Japanese cultural differences in rating the intensity of facial expressions of emotion. *Motivation and Emotion, 13,* 143–157.

Matsumoto, D., & Kudoh, T. (1991). *Cultural differences in judgments of emotion and other personal attributes: What's in a smile?* Manuscript submitted for publication.

Ortony, A., & Turner, T. J. (1990). What's basic about basic emotions? *Psychological Review, 97,* 315–331.

Tomkins, S. S. (1962). *Affect, imagery, consciousness: Vol. 1. The positive affects.* New York: Springer.

Zajonc, R. B. (1985). Emotion and facial efference: A theory reclaimed. *Science, 228,* 15–21.

10.2 DONALD G. DUTTON AND ARTHUR P. ARON

Some Evidence for Heightened Sexual Attraction Under Conditions of High Anxiety

How do we fall in love? Researchers have suggested that we need to learn the cultural definition of love, choose an appropriate person, and experience physiological arousal. Others have suggested that we label our arousal according to our environment. In their classic study, Donald G. Dutton and Arthur P. Aron tested the notion that arousal might be interpreted as sexual attraction.

Dutton (b. 1943) received his Ph.D. in social psychology from the University of Toronto in 1970 and then accepted a position at the University of British Columbia in Vancouver, where he is currently a professor of psychology. Aron (b. 1945) earned his Ph.D. in social psychology from the University of Toronto in 1970. He taught at the University of British Columbia, Maharishi University, and the University of California at Santa Cruz before accepting his current position at State University of New York at Stony Brook.

The following selection, from "Some Evidence for Heightened Sexual Attraction Under Conditions of High Anxiety," was published in the *Journal of Personality and Social Psychology* in 1974. In it, Dutton and Aron report that after male subjects were interviewed by an attractive young woman on a precariously swaying suspension bridge, the men included more sexual imagery in stories they wrote and were more interested in calling the woman on the phone than were men who were interviewed on a solid bridge. As you read this selection, think about the influence of anxiety on perception of sexual attractiveness in everyday situations. How else might anxiety be interpreted in these situations?

Key Concept: anxiety and sexual attraction

APA Citation: Dutton, D. G., & Aron, A. P. (1974). Some evidence for heightened sexual attraction under conditions of high anxiety. *Journal of Personality and Social Psychology, 30,* 510–517.

*M*ale *passersby were contacted either on a fear-arousing suspension bridge or a non-fear-arousing bridge by an attractive female interviewer who asked them to fill out questionnaires containing Thematic Apperception Test [TAT] pictures. Sexual content of stories written by subjects on the fear-arousing bridge and tendency of these subjects to attempt postexperimental contact with the interviewer were both significantly greater. No significant differences between bridges were obtained on either measure for subjects contacted by a male interviewer....*

There is a substantial body of indirect evidence suggesting that sexual attractions occur with increased frequency during states of strong emotion. For example, heterosexual love has been observed to be associated both with hate (James, 1910; Suttie, 1935) and with pain (Ellis, 1936). A connection between "aggression" and sexual attraction is supported by Tinbergen's (1954) observations of intermixed courting and aggression behaviors in various animal species....

Aron (1970)... argued that an aggression–sexuality link exists, but it is only a special case of a more general relationship between emotional arousal of all kinds and sexual attraction. To demonstrate this point, he designed a study in which instead of anger, residual emotion from intense role playing was the independent variable. In this experiment, each of 40 male subjects role played with the same attractive female confederate in either a highly emotional or a minimally emotional situation. Subjects enacting highly emotional roles included significantly more sexual imagery in stories written in response to TAT-like stimuli ($p < .01$) and indicated significantly more desire to kiss the confederate ($p < .05$) than did subjects in the control condition. One possible explanation is suggested by Schachter's theory of emotion (Schachter, 1964; Schachter & Singer, 1962). He argued that environmental cues are used, in certain circumstances, to provide emotional labels for unexplained or ambiguous states of arousal. However, it is notable that much of the above-cited research indicates that a sexual attraction–strong emotion link may occur even when the emotions are unambiguous. Accordingly, taking into account both the Schachter position and findings from sexual attraction research in general, Aron (1970) hypothesized that strong emotions are relabeled as sexual attraction whenever an acceptable object is present, and emotion-producing circumstances do not require the full attention of the individual.

The present series of experiments is designed to test the notion that an attractive female is seen as more attractive by males who encounter her while they experience a strong emotion (fear) than by males not experiencing a strong emotion. Experiment 1 is an attempt to verify this proposed emotion–sexual attraction link in a natural setting....

Donald G. Dutton and Arthur P. Aron

EXPERIMENT 1

Method

Subjects. Subjects were males visiting either of two bridge sites who fit the following criteria: (*a*) between 18 and 35 years old and (*b*) unaccompanied by a female companion. Only one member of any group of potential subjects was contacted. A total of 85 subjects were contacted by either a male or a female interviewer.

Site. The experiment was conducted on two bridges over the Capilano River in North Vancouver, British Columbia, Canada. The "experimental" bridge was the Capilano Canyon Suspension Bridge, a five-foot-wide, 450-foot-long, bridge constructed of wooden boards attached to wire cables that ran from one side to the other of the Capilano Canyon. The bridge has many arousal-inducing features such as (*a*) a tendency to tilt, sway, and wobble, creating the impression that one is about to fall over the side; (*b*) very low handrails of wire cable which contribute to this impression; and (*c*) a 230-foot drop to rocks and shallow rapids below the bridge. The "control" bridge was a solid wood bridge further upriver. Constructed of heavy cedar, this bridge was wider and firmer than the experimental bridge, was only 10 feet above a small, shallow rivulet which ran into the main river, had high handrails, and did not tilt or sway.

Procedure. As subjects crossed either the control or experimental bridge, they were approached by the interviewer.

FEMALE INTERVIEWER The interviewer explained that she was doing a project for her psychology class on the effects of exposure to scenic attractions on creative expression. She then asked potential subjects if they would fill out a short questionnaire. The questionnaire contained six filler items such as age, education, prior visits to bridge, etc., on the first page. On the second page, subjects were instructed to write a brief, dramatic story based upon a picture of a young woman covering her face with one hand and reaching with the other. The instructions and the picture... employed were adapted from Murray's (1943) *Thematic Apperception Test Manual.*... If the subject agreed, the questionnaire was filled out on the bridge.

Stories were later scored for manifest sexual content according to a slightly modified version of the procedure employed by Barclay and Haber (1965). Scores ranged from 1 (no sexual content) to 5 (high sexual content) according to the most sexual reference in the story. Thus, for example, a story with any mention of sexual intercourse received 5 points; but if the most sexual reference was "girl friend," it received a score of 2; "kiss" counted 3; and "lover," 4.

On completion of the questionnaire, the interviewer thanked the subject and offered to explain the experiment in more detail when she had more time. At this point, the interviewer tore the corner off a sheet of paper, wrote down her name and phone number, and invited each subject to call, if he wanted to talk further. Experimental subjects were told that the interviewer's name was Gloria and control subjects, Donna, so that they could easily be classified when they called. On the assumption that curiosity about the experiment should be equal between control and experimental groups, it was felt that differential calling rates might reflect differential attraction to the interviewer.

MALE INTERVIEWER   The procedure with the male interviewer was identical to that above. Subjects were again supplied with two fictitious names so that if they phoned the interviewer, they could be classified into control or experimental groups.

Results

Check on Arousal Manipulation.   Probably the most compelling evidence for arousal on the experimental bridge is to observe people crossing the bridge. Forty percent of subjects observed crossing the bridge walked very slowly and carefully, clasping onto the handrail before taking each step. A questionnaire was administered to 30 males who fit the same criteria as the experimental subjects. Fifteen males on the experimental bridge were asked, "How fearful do you think the average person would be when he crossed this bridge?" The mean rating was 79 on a 100-point scale where 100 was equal to extremely fearful. Fifteen males on the control bridge gave a mean rating of 18 on the same scale ($t = 9.7$, $df = 28$, $p < .001$, two-tailed). In response to the question "How fearful were you while crossing the bridge?" experimental-bridge males gave a rating of 65 and control-bridge males a rating of 3 ($t = 10.6$, $p < .001$, $df = 28$, two-tailed). Hence, it can be concluded that most people are quite anxious on the experimental bridge but not on the control bridge. To prevent suspicion, no checks on the arousal of experimental subjects could be made.

Thematic Apperception Test Responses.

FEMALE INTERVIEWER   On the experimental bridge, 23 of 33 males who were approached by the female interviewer agreed to fill in the questionnaire. On the control bridge, 22 of 33 agreed. Of the 45 questionnaires completed, 7 were unusable either because they were incomplete or written in a foreign language. The remaining 38 questionnaires (20 experimental and 18 control) had their TAT stories scored for sexual imagery by two scorers who were experienced with TAT scoring. (Although both were familiar with the experimental hypothesis, questionnaires had been coded so that they were blind as to whether any given questionnaire was written by a control or experimental subject.) The interrater reliability was $+.87$.

Subjects in the experimental group obtained a mean sexual imagery score of 2.47 and those in the control group, a score of 1.41 ($t = 3.19$, $p < .01$; $df =$

36, two-tailed). Thus, the experimental hypothesis was verified by the imagery data.

Donald G. Dutton and Arthur P. Aron

MALE INTERVIEWER   Twenty-three out of 51 subjects who were approached on the experimental bridge agreed to fill in the questionnaire. On the control bridge 22 out of 42 agreed. Five of these questionnaires were unusable, leaving 20 usable in both experimental and control groups. These were rated as above. Subjects in the experimental group obtained a mean sexual imagery score of .80 and those in the control group, .61 ($t = .36$. *ns*). Hence the pattern of result obtained by the female interviewer was not reproduced by the male interviewer.

Behavioral Data.

FEMALE INTERVIEWER   In the experimental group, 18 of the 23 subjects who agreed to the interview accepted the interviewer's phone number. In the control group, 16 out of 22 accepted. A second measure of sexual attraction was the number of subjects who called the interviewer. In the experimental group 9 out of 18 called, in the control group 2 out of 16 called ($x^2 = 5.7, p < .02$). Taken in conjunction with the sexual imagery data, this finding suggests that subjects in the experimental group were more attracted to the interviewer.

MALE INTERVIEWER   In the experimental group, 7 out of 23 accepted the interviewer's phone number. In the control group, 6 out of 22 accepted. In the experimental group, 2 subjects called; in the control group, 1 subject called. Again, the pattern of results obtained by the female interviewer was not replicated by the male.

Although the results of this experiment provide prima facie support for an emotion–sexual attraction link, the experiment suffers from interpretative problems that often plague field experiments. The main problem with the study is the possibility of different subject populations on the two bridges. First, the well-advertised suspension bridge is a tourist attraction that may have attracted more out-of-town persons than did the nearby provincial park where the control bridge was located. This difference in subject populations may have affected the results in two ways. The experimental subjects may have been less able to phone the experimenter (if they were in town on a short-term tour) and less likely to hold out the possibility of further liaison with her. If this were the case, the resulting difference due to subject differences would have operated *against* the main hypothesis. Also, this difference in subject populations could not affect the sexual imagery scores unless one assumed the experimental bridge subjects to be more sexually deprived than controls. The results using the male interviewer yielded no significant differences in sexual imagery between experimental and control subjects; however, the possibility still exists that sexual deprivation could have interacted with the presence of the attractive female experimenter to produce the sexual imagery results obtained in this experiment....

The theoretical implications of these results are twofold. In the first place, they provide additional support in favor of the theoretical positions from which the original hypothesis was derived: the Schachter and Singer (1962) tradition of cognitive labeling of emotions and the Aron (1970) conceptual framework for sexual attraction processes. In the second place, these data seem to be inconsistent with (or at least unpredictable by) standard theories of interpersonal attraction. Both the reinforcement (Byrne, 1969) and the cognitive consistency (Festinger, 1957; Heider, 1958) points of view would seem to predict that a negative emotional state associated with the object would *decrease* her attractiveness; and neither theory would seem to be easily capable of explaining the arousal of a greater sexual emotion in the experimental condition of the present experiments.

REFERENCES

Aron, A. Relationship variables in human heterosexual attraction. Unpublished doctoral dissertation, University of Toronto, 1970.

Barclay, A. M., & Haber, R. N. The relation of aggressive to sexual motivation. *Journal of Personality*, 1965, **33**, 462–475.

Byrne, D. Attitudes and attraction. I. L. Berkowitz (Ed.), *Advances in experimental social psychology*. Vol 4. New York: Academic Press, 1969.

Ellis, H. *Studies in the Psychology of Sex*. New York: Random House, 1936.

Festinger, L. *A theory of cognitive dissonance*. Evanston, Ill.: Row, Peterson, 1957.

Heider, F. *The psychology of interpersonal relations*. New York: Wiley, 1958.

James, W. *The principles of psychology*. Vol. 2. New York: Holt, 1910.

Murray, H. A. *Thematic Apperception Test manual*. Cambridge, Mass.: Harvard University Press, 1943.

Schachter, S. The interaction of cognitive and physiological determinants of emotional state. In L. Berkowitz (Ed.), *Advances in experimental social psychology*. Vol. 1. New York: Academic Press, 1964.

Schachter, S., & Singer, J. E. Cognitive, social and physiological components of the emotional state. *Psychological Review*, 1962, **69**, 379–399.

Suttie, I. D. *The origins of love and hate*. London: Kegan Paul, 1935.

Tinbergen, N. The origin and evolution of courtship and threat display. In J. S. Huxley, A. C. Hardy, & E. B. Ford (Eds.), *Evolution as a process*. London: Allen & Unwin, 1954.

The Ingredients of Love

Love is one of the most important human emotions. Although it has been the subject of countless poems and works of art, it has only recently become the focus of research by psychologists. Researchers recognize that there are different kinds of love, making it difficult to generalize the results of love studies. In an attempt to make such a generalization, Yale University psychologist Robert J. Sternberg has proposed a triangular theory of love in which love consists of intimacy, passion, and decision/commitment.

Sternberg (b. 1949) earned his Ph.D. from Stanford University in 1975. He has been very influential in psychology in the cognitive area of intelligence and in the emotional area of love. The American Psychological Association awarded him the Distinguished Scientific Award for Early Career Contribution to Psychology in 1981. Sternberg has written much about his research on love, including his book *The Triangle of Love: Intimacy, Passion, and Commitment* (Basic Books, 1988).

This selection is from chapter 2, "The Ingredients of Love," of Sternberg's *Triangle of Love*. In it, Sternberg describes, in an informal, practical style, how the three ingredients intimacy, passion, and commitment combine to form eight possible kinds of love. He provides many examples, some of which should seem familiar to you. Sternberg's objective is to help you more fully understand the characteristics of love. As you read this selection, evaluate Sternberg's theory of love. Are there any other ingredients that he may have left out of his theory?

Key Concept: love

APA Citation: Sternberg, R. J. (1988). *The triangle of love.* New York: Basic Books.

A substantial body of evidence suggests that the components of intimacy, passion, and commitment play a key role in love over and above other attributes. Even before I collected the first bit of data to test my theory, I had several reasons for choosing these three components as the building blocks for it.

First, many of the other aspects of love prove, on close examination, to be either parts or manifestations of these three components. Communication, for example, is a building block of intimacy, as is caring or compassion. Were one to subdivide intimacy and passion and commitment into their own subparts, the theory would eventually contain so many elements as to become unwieldy. There is no one, solely correct fineness of division. But a division into three components works well in several ways. . . .

Second, my review of the literature on couples in the United States, as well as in other lands, suggested that, whereas some elements of love are fairly time-bound or culture-specific, the three I propose are general across time and place. The three components are not equally weighted in all cultures, but each component receives at least some weight in virtually any time or place.

Third, the three components do appear to be distinct, although, of course, they are related. You can have any one without either or both of the others. In contrast, other potential building blocks for a theory of love—for example, nurturance and caring—tend to be difficult to separate, logically as well as psychologically.

Fourth, . . . many other accounts of love seem to boil down to something similar to my own account, or a subset of it. If we take away differences in language and tone, the spirit of many other theories converges with mine.

Finally, and perhaps most important, the theory works. . . .

INTIMACY

In the context of the triangular theory, intimacy refers to those feelings in a relationship that promote closeness, bondedness, and connectedness. My research with Susan Grajek . . . indicates that intimacy includes at least ten elements:

1. *Desiring to promote the welfare of the loved one.* The lover looks out for the partner and seeks to promote his or her welfare. One may promote the other's welfare at the expense of one's own—but in the expectation that the other will reciprocate when the time comes.
2. *Experiencing happiness with the loved one.* The lover enjoys being with his or her partner. When they do things together, they have a good time and build a store of memories upon which they can draw in hard times. Furthermore, good times shared will spill over into the relationship and make it better.
3. *Holding the loved one in high regard.* The lover thinks highly of and respects his or her partner. Although the lover may recognize flaws in the partner, this recognition does not detract from the overall esteem in which the partner is held.
4. *Being able to count on the loved one in times of need.* The lover feels that the partner is there when needed. When the chips are down, the lover can call on the partner and expect that he or she will come through.

5. *Having mutual understanding with the loved one.* The lovers understand each other. They know each other's strengths and weaknesses and how to respond to each other in a way that shows genuine empathy for the loved one's emotional states. Each knows where the other is "coming from."

6. *Sharing oneself and one's possessions with the loved one.* One is willing to give of oneself and one's time, as well as one's things, to the loved one. Although all things need not be joint property, the lovers share their property as the need arises. And, most important, they share themselves.

7. *Receiving emotional support from the loved one.* The lover feels bolstered and even renewed by the loved one, especially in times of need.

8. *Giving emotional support to the loved one.* The lover supports the loved one by empathizing with, and emotionally supporting, him or her in times of need.

9. *Communicating intimately with the loved one.* The lover can communicate deeply and honestly with the loved one, sharing innermost feelings.

10. *Valuing the loved one.* The lover feels the great importance of the partner in the scheme of life.

These are only some of the possible feelings one can experience through the intimacy of love; moreover, it is not necessary to experience all of these feelings in order to experience intimacy. To the contrary, our research indicates that you experience intimacy when you sample a sufficient number of these feelings, with that number probably differing from one person and one situation to another. You do not usually experience the feelings independently, but often as one overall feeling....

Intimacy probably starts in self-disclosure. To be intimate with someone, you need to break down the walls that separate one person from another. It is well known that self-disclosure begets self-disclosure: if you want to get to know what someone else is like, let him or her learn about you. But self-disclosure is often easier in same-sex friendships than in loving relationships, probably because people see themselves as having more to lose by self-disclosure in a loving relationship. And odd as it may sound, there is actually evidence that spouses may be less symmetrical in self-disclosure than are strangers, again probably because the costs of self-disclosure can be so high in love....

Intimacy, then, is a foundation of love, but a foundation that develops slowly, through fits and starts, and is difficult to achieve. Moreover, once it starts to be attained, it may, paradoxically, start to go away because of the threat it poses. It poses a threat in terms not only of the dangers of self-disclosure but of the danger one starts to feel to one's existence as a separate, autonomous being. Few people want to be "consumed" by a relationship, yet many people start to feel as if they are being consumed when they get too close to another human being. The result is a balancing act between intimacy and autonomy which goes on throughout the lives of most couples, a balancing act in which a completely stable equilibrium is often never achieved. But this in itself is not necessarily bad: the swinging back and forth of the intimacy pendulum provides some of the excitement that keeps many relationships alive.

PASSION

The passion component of love includes what Elaine Hatfield and William Walster refer to as a "state of intense longing *for union* with the other." Passion is largely the expression of desires and needs—such as for self-esteem, nurturance, affiliation, dominance, submission, and sexual fulfillment. The strengths of these various needs vary across persons, situations, and kinds of loving relationship. For example, sexual fulfillment is likely to be a strong need in romantic relationships but not in filial ones. These needs manifest themselves through psychological and physiological arousal, which are often inseparable from each other.

Passion in love tends to interact strongly with intimacy, and often they fuel each other. For example, intimacy in a relationship may be largely a function of the extent to which the relationship meets a person's need for passion. Conversely, passion may be aroused by intimacy. In some close relationships with members of the opposite sex, for example, the passion component develops almost immediately; and intimacy, only after a while. Passion may have drawn the individuals into the relationship in the first place, but intimacy helps sustain the closeness in the relationship. In other close relationships, however, passion, especially as it applies to physical attraction, develops only after intimacy. Two close friends of the opposite sex may find themselves eventually developing a physical attraction for each other once they have achieved a certain emotional intimacy. . . .

Most people, when they think of passion, view it as sexual. But any form of psychophysiological arousal can generate the experience of passion. For example, an individual with a high need for affiliation may experience passion toward an individual who provides him or her with a unique opportunity to affiliate. For example, Debbie grew up in a broken home, with no extended family to speak of, and two parents who were constantly at war with each other and eventually divorced when she was an adolescent. Debbie felt as though she never had a family, and when she met Arthur, her passion was kindled. What he had to offer was not great sex but a large, warm, closely knit family that welcomed Debbie with open arms. Arthur was Debbie's ticket to the sense of belongingness she had never experienced but had always craved, and his ability to bring belongingness into her life aroused her passion for him. . . .

For other people, the need for submission can be the ticket to passion. . . . Social workers are often frustrated when, after months spent getting a battered woman to leave her husband, the woman ultimately goes back to the batterer. To some observers, her return may seem incomprehensible; to others, it may seem like a financial decision. But often it is neither. Such a woman has had the misfortune to identify abuse with being loved and, in going back to the abuse, is returning to what is, for her, love as she has learned it.

These patterns of response have been established through years of observation and sometimes first-hand experience, which cannot be easily undone by a social worker or anyone else in a few months. Probably the strangest learning mechanism for the buildup of passionate response is the mechanism of *intermittent reinforcement*, the periodic, sometimes random rewarding of a particular response to a stimulus. If you try to accomplish something, and sometimes are rewarded for your efforts and sometimes not, you are being intermittently reinforced. Oddly enough, intermittent reinforcement is even more powerful at developing or sustaining a given pattern of behavior than is continuous reinforcement. You are more likely to lose interest in or desire for something, and to become bored, if you are always rewarded when you seek it than if you are sometimes rewarded, but sometimes not. Put another way, sometimes the fun is in wanting something rather than in getting it. And if you are never rewarded for a given pattern of behavior, you are likely to give up on it ("extinguish," as learning theorists would say), if only because of the total frustration you experience when you act in that particular way.

Passion thrives on the intermittent reinforcement that is intense at least in the early stages of a relationship. When you want someone, sometimes you feel as if you are getting closer to him or her, and sometimes you feel you are not—an alternation that keeps the passion aroused. . . .

DECISION AND COMMITMENT

The decision/commitment component of love consists of two aspects—one short-term and one long-term. The short-term aspect is the decision to love a certain other, whereas the long-term one is the commitment to maintain that love. These two aspects of the decision/commitment component of love do not necessarily occur together. The decision to love does not necessarily imply a commitment to that love. Oddly enough, the reverse is also possible, where there is a commitment to a relationship in which you did not make the decision, as in arranged marriages. Some people are committed to loving another without ever having admitted their love. Most often, however, a decision precedes the commitment both temporally and logically. Indeed, the institution of marriage represents a legalization of the commitment to a decision to love another throughout life.

While the decision/commitment component of love may lack the "heat" or "charge" of intimacy and passion, loving relationships almost inevitably have their ups and downs, and in the latter, the decision/commitment component is what keeps a relationship together. This component can be essential for getting through hard times and for returning to better ones. In ignoring it or separating it from love, you may be missing exactly that component of a loving relationship that enables you to get through the hard times as well as the easy ones. Sometimes, you may have to trust your commitment to carry you through to the better times you hope are ahead.

The decision/commitment component of love interacts with both intimacy and passion. For most people, it results from the combination of intimate involvement and passionate arousal; however, intimate involvement or passionate arousal can follow from commitment, as in certain arranged marriages or in close relationships in which you do not have a choice of partners. For example, you do not get to choose your mother, father, siblings, aunts, uncles, or cousins. In these close relationships, you may find that whatever intimacy or passion you experience results from your cognitive commitment to the relationship, rather than the other way around. Thus, love can start off as a decision.

The expert in the study of commitment is the UCLA psychologist Harold Kelley.... For Kelley, commitment is the extent to which a person is likely to stick with something or someone and see it (or him or her) through to the finish. A person who is committed to something is expected to persist until the goal underlying the commitment is achieved. A problem for contemporary relationships is that [the] two members of a couple may have different ideas about what it means to stick with someone to the end or to the realization of a goal. These differences, moreover, may never be articulated. One person, for example, may see the "end" as that point where the relationship is no longer working, whereas the other may see the end as the ending of one of the couple's lives. In a time of changing values and notions of commitment, it is becoming increasingly common for couples to find themselves in disagreement about the exact nature and duration of their commitment to each other. When marital commitments were always and automatically assumed to be for life, divorce was clearly frowned upon. Today, divorce is clearly more acceptable than it was even fifteen years ago, in part because many people have different ideas about how durable and lasting the marital commitment need be.

Difficulties in mismatches between notions of commitment cannot always be worked out by discussing mutual definitions of it, because these may change over time and differently for the two members of a couple. Both may intend a life-long commitment at the time of marriage, for example; but one of them may have a change of mind—or heart—over time....

KINDS OF LOVING

How do people love, and what are some examples of ways in which they love? A summary of the various kinds of love captured by the triangular theory is shown in table 1.

Intimacy Alone: Liking

... Liking results when you experience only the intimacy component of love without passion or decision/commitment. The term *liking* is used here in a nontrivial sense, to describe not merely the feelings you have toward casual acquaintances and passers-by, but rather the set of feelings you experience in relationships that can truly be characterized as friendships. You feel closeness, bondedness, and warmth toward the other, without feelings of intense passion or long-term commitment. Stated another way, you feel emotionally close to the

TABLE 1

Taxonomy of Kinds of Love

Kind of Love	Intimacy	Passion	Decision/ Commitment
Non-love	-	-	-
Liking	+	-	-
Infatuated love	-	+	-
Empty love	-	-	+
Romantic love	+	+	-
Companionate love	+	-	+
Fatuous love	-	+	+
Consummate love	+	+	+

Note: + = component present; − = component absent.

friend, but the friend does not arouse your passion or make you feel that you want to spend the rest of your life with him or her.

It is possible for friendships to have elements of passionate arousal or long-term commitment, but such friendships go beyond mere liking. You can use the absence test to distinguish mere liking from love that goes beyond liking. If a typical friend whom you like goes away, even for an extended period of time, you may miss him or her but do not tend to dwell on the loss. You can pick up the friendship some years later, often in a different form, without even having thought much about the friendship during the intervening years. When a close relationship goes beyond liking, however, you actively miss the other person and tend to dwell on or be preoccupied with his or her absence. The absence has a substantial and fairly long-term effect on your life. When the absence of the other arouses strong feelings of intimacy, passion, or commitment, the relationship has gone beyond liking.

Passion Alone: Infatuated Love

Tom met Lisa at work. One look at her was enough to change his life: he fell madly in love with her. Instead of concentrating on his work, which he hated, he would think about Lisa. She was aware of this, but did not much care for Tom. When he tried to start a conversation with her, she moved on as quickly as possible....

Tom's "love at first sight" is infatuated love or, simply, infatuation. It results from the experiencing of passionate arousal without the intimacy and decision/commitment components of love. Infatuation is usually obvious, although it tends to be somewhat easier for others to spot than for the person who is experiencing it. An infatuation can arise almost instantaneously and dissipate as quickly. Infatuations generally manifest a high degree of psychophysiological arousal and bodily symptoms such as increased heartbeat or even palpitations of the heart, increased hormonal secretions, and erection of genitals. . . .

Decision/Commitment Alone: Empty Love

John and Mary had been married for twenty years, for fifteen of which Mary had been thinking about getting a divorce, but could never get herself to go through with it. . . .

Mary's kind of love emanates from the decision that you love another and are committed to that love even without having the intimacy or the passion associated with some loves. It is the love sometimes found in stagnant relationships that have been going on for years but that have lost both their original mutual emotional involvement and physical attraction. Unless the commitment to the love is very strong, such love can be close to none at all. Although in our society we see empty love generally as the final or near-final stage of a long-term relationship, in other societies empty love may be the first stage of a long-term relationship. As I have said, in societies where marriages are arranged, the marital partners start with the commitment to love each other, or to try to do so, and not much more. Here, *empty* denotes a relationship that may come to be filled with passion and intimacy, and thus marks a beginning rather than an end.

Intimacy + Passion: Romantic Love

Susan and Ralph met in their junior year of college. Their relationship started off as a good friendship, but rapidly turned into a deeply involved romantic love affair. They spent as much time together as possible, and enjoyed practically every minute of it. But Susan and Ralph were not ready to commit themselves permanently to the relationship: both felt they were too young to make any long-term decisions, and that until they at least knew where they would go after college, it was impossible to tell even how much they could be together. . . .

Ralph and Susan's relationship combines the intimacy and passion components of love. In essence, it is liking with an added element: namely, the arousal brought about by physical attraction. Therefore, in this type of love, the man and woman are not only drawn physically to each other but are also bonded emotionally. This is the view of romantic love found in classic works of literature, such as *Romeo and Juliet*. . . .

Intimacy + Commitment: Companionate Love

In their twenty years of marrige, Sam and Sara had been through some rough times. They had seen many of their friends through divorces, Sam through several jobs, and Sara through an illness that at one point had seemed as though it might be fatal. Both had friends, but there was no doubt in either of their minds that they were each other's best friend. When the going got rough, each of them knew he or she could count on the other. Neither Sam nor Sara felt any great passion in their relationship, but they had never sought out others....

Sam and Sara's kind of love evolves from a combination of the intimacy and decision/commitment components of love. It is essentially a long-term, committed friendship, the kind that frequently occurs in marriages in which physical attraction (a major source of passion) has waned....

Passion + Commitment: Fatuous Love

When Tim and Diana met at a resort in the Bahamas, they were each on the rebound. Tim's fiancé had abruptly broken off their engagement.... Diana was recently divorced, the victim of the "other woman." Each felt desperate for love, and when they met each other, they immediately saw themselves as a match made in heaven.... The manager of the resort, always on the lookout for vacation romances as good publicity, offered to marry them at the resort and to throw a lavish reception at no charge, other than cooperation in promotional materials. After thinking it over, Tim and Diana agreed....

Fatuous love, as in the case of Tim and Diana, results from the combination of passion and decision/commitment without intimacy, which takes time to develop. It is the kind of love we sometimes associate with Hollywood, or with a whirlwind courtship, in which a couple meet one day, get engaged two weeks later, and marry the next month. This love is fatuous in the sense that the couple commit themselves to one another on the basis of passion without the stabilizing element of intimate involvement. Since passion can develop almost instantaneously, and intimacy cannot, relationships based on fatuous love are not likely to last.

Intimacy + Passion + Commitment: Consummate Love

Harry and Edith seemed to all their friends to be the perfect couple. And what made them distinctive from many such "perfect couples" is that they pretty much fulfilled the notion. They felt close to each other, they continued to have great sex after fifteen years, and they could not imagine themselves happy over the long term with anyone else....

Consummate, or complete, love like Edith and Harry's results from the combination of the three components in equal measure. It is a love toward which many of us strive, especially in romantic relationships. Attaining consummate love is analogous, in at least one respect, to meeting your goal in a weight-reduction program: reaching your ideal weight is often easier than maintaining it. Attaining consummate love is no guarantee that it will last; indeed, one may become aware of the loss only after it is far gone. Consummate love, like other things of value, must be guarded carefully....

The Absence of the Components: Non-Love

Jack saw his colleague Myra at work almost every day. They interacted well in their professional relationship, but neither was particularly fond of the other. Neither felt particularly comfortable talking to the other about personal matters; and after a few tries, they decided to limit their conversations to business.

Non-love, as in the relationship of Jack and Myra, refers simply to the absence of all three components of love. Non-love characterizes many personal relationships, which are simply casual interactions that do not partake of love or even liking.

PART FIVE

Personality and Adjustment

On the Internet . . .

Sites appropriate to Part Five

This is the Personality Project site of William Revelle, director of the Graduate Program in Personality in the Department of Psychology at Northwestern University, and includes research references.

```
http://fas.psych.nwu.edu/personality.html
```

Personality Psychology Links, from Social Psychology Network, provides many links to resources on personality.

```
http://www.socialpsychology.org/person.htm
```

Personality Theories, a site maintained by C. George Boeree of Shippensburg University, provides complete descriptions of many theories of personality.

```
http://www.ship.edu/~cgboeree/
   perscontents.html
```

This Mind Tools™ site provides useful information on stress management.

```
http://www.psychwww.com/mtsite/smpage.html
```

Psych Web's psychology self-help resources on the Internet has numerous adjustment and self-help resource links.

```
http://www.psychwww.com/resource/
   selfhelp.htm
```

CHAPTER 11 Personality

11.1 JULIAN B. ROTTER

External Control and Internal Control

Psychologists do not agree on what determines personality, but many accept that reinforcement can shape behaviors that ultimately may influence personality. The social learning theory of personality suggests that behavior that is rewarded leads to the expectancy that the behavior will continue to produce rewards in the future. According to Julian B. Rotter's locus of control personality theory, which is based in the social learning theory, two personality types exist: People with an internal locus of control, who perceive that reinforcement is due to their own behavior; and people with an external locus of control, who perceive that reinforcement is independent of their behavior.

Rotter (b. 1916) earned his Ph.D. from Indiana University in 1941. He taught at several schools, including Ohio State University, before going to the University of Connecticut in 1963, where he is currently a professor of clinical psychology. Rotter's social learning theory (proposed in his 1954 book *Social Learning and Clinical Psychology*) has greatly influenced modern psychologists.

This selection is from "External Control and Internal Control," which was published in *Psychology Today* in 1971. It contains a straightforward description of Rotter's theory of personality as well as some fascinating applications. Note the development of Rotter's thinking as he describes how the idea of locus of control came to him. As you read this selection, think about the implications for people who have an internal or external locus of control. Which one, if either, do you think you have?

Key Concept: internal and external locus of control

APA Citation: Rotter, J. B. (1971). External control and internal control. *Psychology Today, 5,* 37–42; 58–59.

Some social scientists believe that the impetus behind campus unrest is youth's impatient conviction that they can control their own destinies, that they can change society for the better.

My research over the past 12 years has led me to suspect that much of the protest, outcry and agitation occurs for the opposite reason—because students feel they *cannot* change the world, that the system is too complicated and too much controlled by powerful others to be changed through the students' efforts. They feel more powerless and alienated today than they did 10 years ago, and rioting may be an expression of their hostility and resentment.

Dog

One of the most pervasive laws of animal learning is that a behavior followed by a reward tends to be repeated, and a behavior followed by a punishment tends not to be repeated. This seems to imply that reward and punishment act directly on behavior, but I think this formulation is too simplistic to account for many types of human behavior.

For example, if a dog lifts its leg at the exact moment that someone throws a bone over a fence, the dog may begin to lift its leg more often than usual when it is in the same situation—whether or not anyone is heaving a bone. Adult human beings are usually not so superstitious—a person who finds a dollar bill on the sidewalk immediately after stroking his hair is not likely to stroke his hair when he returns to the same spot.

It seemed to me that, at least with human beings who have begun to form concepts, the important factors in learning were not only the strength and frequency of rewards and punishments but also whether or not the person believed his behavior produced the reward or punishment.

According to the social-learning theory that I developed several years ago with my colleagues and students, rewarding a behavior strengthens an *expectancy* that the behavior will produce future rewards.

In animals, the expectation of reward is primarily a function of the strength and frequency of rewards. In human beings, there are other things that can influence the expectation of reward—the information others give us, our knowledge generalized from a variety of experiences, and our perceptions of causality in the situation.

Consider the ancient shell game. Suppose I place a pea under one of three shells and quickly shuffle the shells around the table. A player watches my movements carefully and then, thinking that he is using his fine perceptual skills, he tells me which shell the pea is under. If his choice is correct, he will likely choose the same shell again the next time he sees me make those particular hand movements. It looks like a simple case of rewarding a response.

But suppose I ask the subject to turn his back while I shuffle the shells. This time, even if his choice is rewarded by being correct, he is not so likely to select the same shell again, because the outcome seems to be beyond his control —just a lucky guess.

Julian B. Rotter

In 1957, E. Jerry Phares tried to find out if these intuitive differences between chance-learning and skill-learning would hold up in the laboratory. Phares would give each subject a small gray-colored chip and ask him to select one of 10 standard chips that had exactly the same shade of gray. The standards were all different but so similar in value that discrimination among them was very difficult. Phares told half of his subjects that matching the shades required great skill and that some persons were very good at it. He told the rest that the task was so difficult that success was a matter of luck. Before the experiment began, Phares arbitrarily decided which trials would be "right" and which would be "wrong"; the schedule was the same for everyone. He found that because of the difficulty of the task all subjects accepted his statements of right and wrong without question.

Phares gave each subject a stack of poker chips and asked him to bet on his accuracy before each trial as a measure of each subject's expectancy of success.

The subjects who thought that success depended on their own skills shifted and changed frequently—their bets would rise after success and drop after failure, just as reinforcement-learning theory would predict. But subjects who thought that a correct match was a matter of luck reacted differently. In fact, many of them raised their bets after failure and lowered them after success —the "gambler's fallacy." Thus, it appeared that traditional laws of learning could not explain some types of human behavior. . . .

I decided to study internal and external control (I-E), the beliefs that rewards come from one's own behavior or from external sources. The initial impetus to study internal-external control came both from an interest in individual differences and from an interest in explaining the way human beings learn complex social situations. There seemed to be a number of attitudes that would lead a person to feel that a reward was not contingent upon his own behavior, and we tried to build all of these attitudes into a measure of individual differences. A person might feel that luck or chance controlled what happened to him. He might feel that fate had preordained what would happen to him. He might feel that powerful others controlled what happened to him or he might feel that he simply could not predict the effects of this behavior because the world was too complex and confusing.

Scale

Phares first developed a test of internal-external control as part of his doctoral dissertation, and [William H.] James enlarged and improved on Phares' scale as part of his doctoral dissertation. Later scales were constructed with the important help of several of my colleagues including Liverant, Melvin Seeman and Crowne. In 1962 I developed a final 29-item version of the I-E scale and published it in *Psychological Monographs* in 1966. This is a forced-choice scale in which the subject reads a pair of statements and then indicates with which of the two statements he more strongly agrees. The scores range from zero (the consistent belief that individuals can influence the environment—that rewards

TABLE 1

Internal Control—External Control: A Sampler

Julian B. Rotter is the developer of a forced-choice 29-item scale for measuring an individual's degree of internal control and external control. This I-E test is widely used. The following are sample items taken from an earlier version of the test, but not, of course, in use in the final version. The reader can readily find for himself whether he is inclined toward internal control or toward external control, simply by adding up the choices he makes on each side.

I more strongly believe that:	*OR*
Promotions are earned through hard work and persistence.	Making a lot of money is largely a matter of getting the right breaks.
In my experience I have noticed that there is usually a direct connection between how hard I study and the grades I get.	Many times the reactions of teachers seem haphazard to me.
The number of divorces indicates that more and more people are not trying to make their marriages work.	Marriage is largely a gamble.
When I am right I can convince others.	It is silly to think that one can really change another person's basic attitudes.
In our society a man's future earning power is dependent upon his ability.	Getting promoted is really a matter of being a little luckier than the next guy.
If one knows how to deal with people they are really quite easily led.	I have little influence over the way other people behave.
In my case the grades I make are the results of my own efforts; luck has little or nothing to do with it.	Sometimes I feel that I have little to do with the grades I get.
People like me can change the course of world affairs if we make ourselves heard.	It is only wishful thinking to believe that one can really influence what happens in society at large.
I am the master of my fate.	A great deal that happens to me is probably a matter of chance.
Getting along with people is a skill that must be practiced.	It is almost impossible to figure out how to please some people.

come from *internal* forces) to 23 (the belief that all rewards come from *external* forces)....

Degree

One conclusion is clear from I-E studies: people differ in the tendency to attribute satisfactions and failures to themselves rather than to external causes, and these differences are relatively stable. For the sake of convenience most investigators divide their subjects into two groups—internals and externals—

depending on which half of the distribution a subject's score falls into. This is not meant to imply that there are two personality types and that everyone can be classified as one or the other, but that there is a continuum, and that persons have varying degrees of internality or externality.

Many studies have investigated the differences between internals and externals. For example, it has been found that lower-class children tend to be external; children from richer, better-educated families tend to have more belief in their own potential to determine what happens to them. The scores do not seem to be related to intelligence, but young children tend to become more internal as they get older.

Esther Battle and I examined the attitudes of black and white children in an industrialized Ohio city. The scale we used consisted of five comic-strip cartoons; the subjects told us what they thought one of the children in the cartoon would say. We found that middle-class blacks were only slightly more external in their beliefs than middle-class whites but that among children from lower socioeconomic levels blacks were significantly more external than whites. Herbert Lefcourt and Gordon Ladwig also found that among young prisoners in a Federal reformatory, blacks were more external than whites.

Ute

It does not seem to be socioeconomic level alone that produces externality, however. Theodore Graves, working with Richard and Shirley L. Jessor, found that Ute Indians were more external than a group of Spanish-Americans, even though the Indians had higher average living standards than the Spanish-Americans. Since Ute tradition puts great emphasis on fate and unpredictable external forces, Graves concluded that internality and externality resulted from cultural training. A group of white subjects in the same community were more internal than either the Indians or the Spanish-Americans.

A measure of internal-external control was used in the well-known Coleman Report on Equality of Educational Opportunity. The experimenters found that among disadvantaged children in the sixth, ninth and 12th grades, the students with high scores on an achievement test had more internal attitudes than did children with low achievement scores.

One might expect that internals would make active attempts to learn about their life situations. To check on this, Seeman and John Evans gave the I-E scale to patients in a tuberculosis hospital. The internal patients knew more details about their medical conditions and they questioned doctors and nurses for medical feedback more often than did the external patients. The experimenters made sure that in their study there were no differences between the internals and externals in education, occupational status or ward placement....

Bet

Highly external persons feel that they are at the mercy of the environment, that they are being manipulated by outside forces. When they *are* manipulated, externals seem to take it in stride. Internals are not so docile. For example, Crowne and Liverant set up an experiment to see how readily their subjects would go along with a crowd. In a simple ... conformity experiment in which there is one true subject plus several stooges posing as subjects, Crowne and Liverant found that neither internals nor externals were more likely to yield to an incorrect majority judgment. But when the experimenters gave money to the subjects and allowed them to bet on their own judgments, the externals yielded to the majority much more often than did the internals. When externals did vote against the majority they weren't confident about their independence —they bet less money on being right than they did when they voted along with the crowd. . . .

Suspicion

Some externals, who feel they are being manipulated by the outside world, may be highly suspicious of authorities. With Herbert Hamsher and Jesse Geller, I found that male subjects who believed that the Warren Commission Report was deliberately covering up a conspiracy were significantly more external than male subjects who accepted the report.

To some degree externality may be a defense against expected failure but internals also have their defenses. In investigating failure defenses, Jay Efran studied high-school students' memories for tasks they had completed or failed. He found that the tendency to forget failures was more common in internal subjects than in external ones. This suggests that external subjects have less need to repress past failures because they have already resigned themselves to the defensive position that failures are not their responsibility. Internals, however, are more likely to forget or repress their failures.

Today's activist student groups might lead one to assume that our universities are filled with internals—people with strong belief in their ability to improve conditions and to control their own destinies. But scores on the same I-E test involving large numbers of college students in many localities show that between 1962 and 1971 there was a large increase in externality on college campuses. Today the average score on the I-E scale is about 11. In 1962 about 80 per cent of college students had more internal scores than this. The increase in externality has been somewhat less in Midwest colleges than in universities on the coasts, but there is little doubt that, overall, college students feel more powerless to change the world and control their own destinies now than they did 10 years ago.

Clearly, we need continuing study of methods to reverse this trend. Our society has so many critical problems that it desperately needs as many active, participating internal-minded members as possible. If feelings of external control, alienation and powerlessness continue to grow, we may be heading for a society of dropouts—each person sitting back, watching the world go by.

11.2 ROBERT R. McCRAE AND PAUL T. COSTA, JR.

Validation of the Five-Factor Model of Personality Across Instruments and Observers

Over the years, there have been numerous attempts to classify personality traits. Little agreement was reached among psychologists until the five-factor model became popular. The five-factor model of personality was originally proposed in the early 1960s, but it did not become popular among psychologists until the 1980s. The five factors of this model are extraversion (sociability), agreeableness (friendliness), conscientiousness (dependability), emotional stability (versus neuroticism), and openness (liberalism). Psychologists do not all agree on the specific labels, but there is some consensus on the five areas of personality. Robert R. McCrae and Paul T. Costa, Jr., are among the leaders in the quest to understand these factors and how they can explain personality.

McCrae earned his Ph.D. from Boston University in 1976. He has since been an associate of the Gerontology Research Center of the National Institute of Aging, National Institutes of Health. Costa (b. 1942) received his Ph.D. from the University of Chicago in 1970. He is also with the National Institute on Aging, National Institutes of Health.

This selection is from "Validation of the Five-Factor Model of Personality Across Instruments and Observers," which was published in the American Psychological Association's *Journal of Personality and Social Psychology* in 1987. In it, McCrae and Costa describe the history and interpretation of each of the five factors in this model. In one part of the original article not included here, the authors report an experiment in which they used self-reports, peer ratings, and questionnaire scales to measure the five factors. The results of this study validated the five-factor model. As you read this selection, note which characteristics best describe your personality. Can you think of any other major factors of personality that might be included in this model?

Key Concept: five-factor model of personality

APA Citation: McCrae, R. R., & Costa, P. T., Jr. (1987). Validation of the five-factor model of personality across instruments and observers. *Journal of Personality and Social Psychology, 52,* 81–90.

Perhaps in response to critiques of trait models (Mischel, 1968) and to rebuttals that have called attention to common inadequacies in personality research (Block, 1977), personologists in recent years have devoted much of their attention to methodological issues.... As a body, these studies have simultaneously increased the level of methodological sophistication in personality research and restored confidence in the intelligent use of individual difference models of personality.

In contrast, there has been relatively little interest in the substance of personality—the systematic description of traits. The variables chosen as vehicles for tests of methodological hypotheses often appear arbitrary.... Indeed, Kenrick and Dantchik (1983) complained that "catalogs of convenience" have replaced meaningful taxonomies of personality traits among "most of the current generation of social/personality researchers" (p. 299).

This disregard of substance is unfortunate because substance and method are ultimately interdependent. Unless methodological studies are conducted on well-defined and meaningful traits their conclusions are dubious; unless the traits are selected from a comprehensive taxonomy, it is impossible to know how far or in what ways they can be generalized.

Fortunately, a few researchers have been concerned with the problem of structure and have recognized the need for a consensus on at least the general outlines of a trait taxonomy (H. J. Eysenck & Eysenck, 1984; Kline & Barrett, 1983; Wiggins, 1979). One particularly promising candidate has emerged. The five-factor model—comprising extraversion or surgency, agreeableness, conscientiousness, emotional stability versus neuroticism, and culture—of Tupes and Christal (1961) was replicated by Norman in 1963 and heralded by him as the basis for "an adequate taxonomy of personality." Although it was largely neglected for several years, variations on this model have recently begun to reemerge (Amelang & Borkenau, 1982; Bond, Nakazato, & Shiraishi, 1975; Conley, 1985; Digman & Takemoto-Chock, 1981; Goldberg, 1981, 1982; Hogan, 1983; Lorr & Manning, 1978; McCrae & Costa, 1985b)....

THE NATURE OF THE FIVE FACTORS

... A growing body of research has pointed to the five-factor model as a recurrent and more or less comprehensive taxonomy of personality traits. Theorists disagree, however, in precisely how to conceptualize the factors themselves. It seems useful at this point to review each of the factors and attempt to define the clear elements as well as disputed aspects....

*Robert R.
McCrae and
Paul T.
Costa, Jr.*

Neuroticism Versus Emotional Stability

There is perhaps least disagreement about neuroticism, defined here by such terms as worrying, insecure, self-conscious, and temperamental. Although adjectives describing neuroticism are relatively infrequent in English (Peabody, 1984), psychologists' concerns with psychopathology have led to the development of innumerable scales saturated with neuroticism. Indeed, neuroticism is so ubiquitous an element of personality scales that theorists sometimes take it for granted.

A provocative view of neuroticism is provided by Tellegen (in press), who views it as negative emotionality, the propensity to experience a variety of negative affects, such as anxiety, depression, anger, and embarrassment. Virtually all theorists would concur in the centrality of negative affect to neuroticism; the question is whether other features also define it. Tellegen himself (in press) pointed out that his construct of negative emotionality has behavioral and cognitive aspects. Guilford included personal relations and objectivity in his emotional health factor (Guilford, Zimmerman, & Guilford, 1976), suggesting that mistrust and self-reference form part of neuroticism. We have found that impulsive behaviors, such as tendencies to overeat, smoke, or drink excessively, form a facet of neuroticism (Costa & McCrae, 1980), and *impulse-ridden* is a definer of the neuroticism factor in self-reports, although not in ratings. Others have linked neuroticism to irrational beliefs (Teasdale & Rachman, 1983; Vestre, 1984) or to poor coping efforts (McCrae & Costa, 1986).

What these behaviors seem to share is a common origin in negative affect. Individuals high in neuroticism have more difficulty than others in quitting smoking because the distress caused by abstinence is stronger for them. They may more frequently use inappropriate coping responses like hostile reactions and wishful thinking because they must deal more often with disruptive emotions. They may adopt irrational beliefs like self-blame because these beliefs are cognitively consistent with the negative feelings they experience. Neuroticism appears to include not only negative affect, but also the disturbed thoughts and behaviors that accompany emotional distress.

Extraversion or Surgency

Sociable, fun-loving, affectionate, friendly, and talkative are the highest loading variables on the extraversion factor. This is not Jungian extraversion (see Guilford, 1977), but it does correspond to the conception of H. J. Eysenck and most other contemporary researchers, who concur with popular speech in identifying extraversion with lively sociability.

However, disputes remain about which elements are central and which are peripheral to extraversion. Most writers would agree that sociability, cheerfulness, activity level, assertiveness, and sensation seeking all covary, however

TABLE 1

80 Adjective Items from Peer Ratings

Adjectives	Adjectives
Neuroticism (N)	Agreeableness vs. antagonism (A)
Calm–worrying	Irritable–good natured
At ease–nervous	Ruthless–soft hearted
Relaxed–high-strung	Rude–courteous
Unemotional–emotional	Selfish–selfless
Even-tempered–temperamental	Uncooperative–helpful
Secure–insecure	Callous–sympathetic
Self-satisfied–self-pitying	Suspicious–trusting
Patient–impatient	Stingy–generous
Not envious–envious/jealous	Antagonistic–acquiescent
Comfortable–self-conscious	Critical–lenient
Not impulse ridden–impulse ridden	Vengeful–forgiving
Hardy–vulnerable	Narrow-minded–open-minded
Objective–subjective	Disagreeable–agreeable
	Stubborn–flexible
Extraversion (E)	Serious–cheerful
Retiring–sociable	Cynical–gullible
Sober–fun loving	Manipulative–straightforward
Reserved–affectionate	Proud–humble
Aloof–friendly	
Inhibited–spontaneous	Conscientiousness vs. undirectedness (C)
Quiet–talkative	Negligent–conscientious
Passive–active	Careless–careful
Loner–joiner	Undependable–reliable
Unfeeling–passionate	Lazy–hardworking
Cold–warm	Disorganized–well organized
Lonely–not lonely	Lax–scrupulous
Task oriented–person oriented	Weak willed–self-disciplined
Submissive–dominant	Sloppy–neat
Timid–bold	Late–punctual
	Impractical–practical
Openness (O)	Thoughtless–deliberate
Conventional–original	Aimless–ambitious
Down to earth–imaginative	Unstable–emotionally stable
Uncreative–creative	Helpless–self-reliant
Narrow interests–broad interests	Playful–businesslike
Simple–complex	Unenergetic–energetic
Uncurious–curious	Ignorant–knowledgeable
Unadventurous–daring	Quitting–persevering
Prefer routine–prefer variety	Stupid–intelligent
Conforming–independent	Unfair–fair
Unanalytical–analytical	Imperceptive–perceptive
Conservative–liberal	Uncultured–cultured
Traditional–untraditional	
Unartistic–artistic	

*Robert R.
McCrae and
Paul T.
Costa, Jr.*

loosely. But the Eysencks have at times felt the need to distinguish between sociability and what they call impulsiveness (S. B. G. Eysenck & Eysenck, 1963; Revelle, Humphreys, Simon, & Gilliland, 1980). Hogan (1983) believed that the five-factor model was improved by dividing extraversion into sociability and assertiveness factors. In Goldberg's analyses, surgency (dominance and activity) were the primary definers of extraversion, and terms like warm–cold were assigned to the agreeableness–antagonism factor. Tellegen (in press) emphasized the complementary nature of neuroticism and extraversion by labeling his extraversion factor positive emotionality.

These distinctions do seem to merge at a high enough level of analysis (H. J. Eysenck & Eysenck, 1976; McCrae & Costa, 1983a), and sociability—the enjoyment of others' company—seems to be the core. What is essential to recall, however, is that liking people does not necessarily make one likable. Salesmen, those prototypic extraverts, are generally happier to see you than you are to see them.

Openness to Experience

The reinterpretation of Norman's culture as openness to experience was the focus of some of our previous articles (McCrae & Costa, 1985a, 1985b), and the replication of results in peer ratings was one of the purposes of the present article. According to adjective-factor results, openness is best characterized by original, imaginative, broad interests, and daring. In the case of this dimension, however, questionnaires may be better than adjectives as a basis for interpretation and assessment. Many aspects of openness (e.g., openness to feelings) are not easily expressed in single adjectives, and the relative poverty of the English-language vocabulary of openness and closedness may have contributed to confusions about this domain (McCrae & Costa, 1985a). We know from questionnaire studies that openness can be manifest in fantasy, aesthetics, feelings, actions, ideas, and values (Costa & McCrae, 1978, 1980), but only ideas and values are well represented in the adjective factor. Interestingly, questionnaire measures of openness give higher validity coefficients than do adjective-factor measures. . . .

Perhaps the most important distinction to be made here is between openness and intelligence. Open individuals tend to be seen by themselves and others as somewhat more intelligent. . . . However, joint factor analyses using Army Alpha intelligence subtests and either adjectives (McCrae & Costa, 1985b) or NEO Inventory scales (McCrae & Costa, 1985a) show that intelligence scales define a factor clearly separate from openness. Intelligence may in some degree predispose the individual to openness, or openness may help develop intelligence, but the two seem best construed as separate dimensions of individual differences.

Agreeableness Versus Antagonism

As a broad dimension, agreeableness–antagonism is less familiar than extraversion or neuroticism, but some of its component traits, like trust (Stark,

1978) and Machiavellianism (Christie & Geis, 1970), have been widely researched. The essential nature of agreeableness–antagonism is perhaps best seen by examining the disagreeable pole, which we have labeled antagonism.... [A]ntagonistic people seem always to set themselves against others. Cognitively they are mistrustful and skeptical; affectively they are callous and unsympathetic; behaviorally they are uncooperative, stubborn, and rude. It would appear that their sense of attachment or bonding with their fellow human beings is defective, and in extreme cases antagonism may resemble sociopathy (cf. H. J. Eysenck & Eysenck's, 1975, psychoticism).

An insightful description of antagonism in its neurotic form is provided by Horney's account of the tendency to move against people (1945, 1950). She theorized that a struggle for mastery is the root cause of this tendency and that variations may occur, including narcissistic, perfectionistic, and arrogant vindictive types. Whereas some antagonistic persons are overtly aggressive, others may be polished manipulators. The drive for mastery and the overt or inhibited hostility of antagonistic individuals suggests a resemblance to some formulations of Type A personality (Dembroski & MacDougall, 1983), and systematic studies of the relations between agreeableness–antagonism and measures of coronary-prone behavior should be undertaken.

Unappealing as antagonism may be, it is necessary to recognize that extreme scores on the agreeable pole may also be maladaptive. The person high in agreeableness may be dependent and fawning, and agreeableness has its neurotic manifestation in Horney's self-effacing solution of moving toward people.

Antagonism is most easily confused with dominance. Amelang and Borkenau (1982), working in German and apparently unaware of the Norman taxonomy, found a factor they called *dominance*. Among its key definers, however, were Hartnäckigkeit (*stubbornness*) and Erregbarkeit (*irritability*); scales that measure agreeableness and cooperation defined the opposite pole in their questionnaire factor. Clearly, this factor corresponds to antagonism. In self-reports (McCrae & Costa, 1985b), submissive–dominant is a weak definer of extraversion; from the peers' point of view, it is a definer of antagonism. The close etymological relationship of *dominant* and *domineering* shows the basis of the confusion.

Agreeableness–antagonism and conscientiousness–undirectedness are sometimes omitted from personality systems because they may seem too value laden. Indeed, the judgment of character is made largely along these two dimensions: Is the individual well or ill intentioned? Is he or she strong or weak in carrying out those intentions? Agreeableness–antagonism, in particular, has often been assumed to be an evaluative factor of others' perceptions rather than a veridical component of personality (e.g., A. Tellegen, personal communication, March 28, 1984).

However, the fact that a trait may be judged from a moral point of view does not mean that it is not a substantive aspect of personality. The consensual validation seen among peers and between peer-reports and self-reports demonstrates that there are some observable consistencies of behavior that underlie attributions of agreeableness and conscientiousness. They may be evaluated traits, but they are not mere evaluations.

*Robert R.
McCrae and
Paul T.
Costa, Jr.*

Conscientious may mean either governed by conscience or careful and thorough (Morris, 1976), and psychologists seem to be divided about which of these meanings best characterizes the last major dimension of personality. Amelang and Borkenau (1982) labeled their factor self-control versus impulsivity, and Conley (1985) spoke of impulse control. This terminology connotes an inhibiting agent, as Cattell (Cattell, Eber, & Tatsuoka, 1970) recognized when he named his Factor G *superego strength*. A conscientious person in this sense should be dutiful, scrupulous, and perhaps moralistic.

A different picture, however, is obtained by examining the adjectives that define this factor. In addition to conscientious and scrupulous, there are a number of adjectives that suggest a more proactive stance: hardworking, ambitious, energetic, persevering. Digman and Takemoto-Chock (1981) labeled this factor *will to achieve*, and it is notable that one of the items in the questionnaire measure of conscientiousness, "He strives for excellence in all he does," comes close to the classic definition of need for achievement (McClelland, Atkinson, Clark, & Lowell, 1953).

At one time, the purposefulness and adherence to plans, schedules, and requirements suggested the word *direction* as a label for this factor, and we have retained that implication in calling the opposite pole of conscientiousness *undirectedness*. In our view, the individual low in conscientiousness is not so much uncontrolled as undirected, not so much impulse ridden as simply lazy.

It seems probable that these two meanings may be related. Certainly individuals who are well organized, habitually careful, and capable of self-discipline are more likely to be able to adhere scrupulously to a moral code if they choose to—although there is no guarantee that they will be so inclined. An undirected individual may have a demanding conscience and a pervasive sense of guilt but be unable to live up to his or her own standards for lack of self-discipline and energy. In any case, it is clear that this is a dimension worthy of a good deal more empirical attention than it has yet received. Important real-life outcomes such as alcoholism (Conley & Angelides, 1984) and academic achievement (Digman & Takemoto-Chock, 1981) are among its correlates, and a further specification of the dimension is sure to be fruitful.

Some personality theorists might object that trait ratings, in whatever form and from whatever source, need not provide the best foundation for understanding individual differences. Experimental analysis of the psychophysiological basis of personality (H. J. Eysenck & Eysenck, 1984), examination of protypic acts and act frequencies (Buss & Craik, 1983), psychodynamic formulations (Horney, 1945), or behavioral genetics (Plomin, DeFries, & McClearn, 1980) provide important alternatives. But psychophysiological, behavioral, psychodynamic, and genetic explanations must eventually be related to the traits that are universally used to describe personality, and the five-factor model can provide a framework within which these relations can be systematically examined. The minor conceptual divergences noted in this article suggest the need for additional empirical work to fine-tune the model, but the broad outlines are clear in self-reports, spouse ratings, and peer ratings; in questionnaires and adjective factors; and in English and in German (Amelang & Borkenau, 1982;

John, Goldberg, & Angleitner, 1984). Deeper causal analyses may seek to account for the structure of personality, but the structure that must be explained is, for now, best represented by the five-factor model.

REFERENCES

Amelang, M., & Borkenau, P. (1982). Über die faktorielle Struktur und externe Validität einiger Fragebogen-Skalen zur Erfassung von Dimensionen der Extraversion und emotionalen Labilität [On the factor structure and external validity of some questionnaire scales measuring dimensions of extraversion and neuroticism]. *Zeitschrift für Differentielle und Diagnostische Psychologie, 3,* 119–146.

Block J. (1977). Advancing the psychology of personality: Paradigmatic shift or improving the quality of research? In D. Magnusson & N. S. Endler (Eds.), *Personality at the cross-roads: Current issues in interactional psychology* (pp. 37–63), Hillsdale, NJ: Erlbaum.

Bond, M. H., Nakazato, H., & Shiraishi, D. (1975). Universality and distinctiveness in dimensions of Japanese person perception. *Journal of Cross-Cultural Psychology, 6,* 346–357.

Buss, D. M., & Craik, K. H. (1983). The act frequency approach to personality. *Psychological Review, 90,* 105–126.

Cattell, R. B., Eber, H. W., & Tatsuoka, M. M. (1970). *The handbook for the Sixteen Personality Factor Questionnaire.* Champaign, IL: Institute for Personality and Ability Testing.

Christie, R., & Geis, R. L. (Eds.). (1970). *Studies in Machiavellianism.* New York: Academic Press.

Conley, J. J. (1985). Longitudinal stability of personality traits: A multitrait–multimethod–multioccasion analysis. *Journal of Personality and Social Psychology, 49,* 1266–1282.

Conley, J. J., & Angelides, M. (1984). *Personality antecedents of emotional disorders and alcohol abuse in men: Results of a forty-five year prospective study.* Manuscript submitted for publication.

Costa, P. T., Jr., & McCrae, R. R. (1978). Objective personality assessment. In M. Storandt, I. C. Siegler, & M. F. Elias (Eds.), *The clinical psychology of aging* (pp. 119–143). New York: Plenum Press.

Costa, P. T., Jr., & McCrae, R. R. (1980). Still stable after all these years: Personality as a key to some issues in adulthood and old age. In P. B. Baltes & O. G. Brim, Jr. (Eds.), *Life span development and behavior* (Vol. 3, pp. 65–102). New York: Academic Press.

Dembroski, T. M., & MacDougall, J. M. (1983). Behavioral and psychophysiological perspectives on coronary-prone behavior. In T. M. Dembroski, T. H. Schmidt, & G. Blumchen (Eds.), *Biobehavioral bases of coronary heart disease* (pp. 106–129). New York: Karger.

Digman, J. M., & Takemoto-Chock, N. K. (1981). Factors in the natural language of personality: Re-analysis, comparison, and interpretation of six major studies. *Multivariate Behavioral Research, 16,* 149–170.

Eysenck, H. J., & Eysenck, M. (1984). *Personality and individual differences.* London: Plenum Press.

Eysenck, H. J., & Eysenck, S. B. G. (1967). On the unitary nature of extraversion. *Acta Psychologica, 26,* 383–390.

Eysenck, H. J., & Eysenck, S. B. G. (1975). *Manual of the Eysenck Personality Questionnaire.* San Diego, CA: EdITS.

Eysenck, S. B. G., & Eysenck, H. J. (1963). On the dual nature of extraversion. *British Journal of Social and Clinical Psychology, 2,* 46–55.

Goldberg, L. R. (1981). Language and individual differences: The search for universals in personality lexicons. In L. Wheeler (Ed.), *Review of personality and social psychology* (Vol. 2, pp. 141–165). Beverly Hills, CA: Sage.

Goldberg, L. R. (1982). From ace to zombie: Some explorations in the language of personality. In C. D. Spielberger & J. N. Butcher (Eds.), *Advances in personality assessment* (Vol. 1, pp. 203–234). Hillsdale, NJ: Erlbaum.

Guilford, J. P. (1977). Will the real factor of extraversion–introversion please stand up? A reply to Eysenck. *Psychological Bulletin, 84,* 412–416.

Guilford, J. S., Zimmerman, W. S., & Guilford, J. P. (1976). *The Guilford–Zimmerman Temperament Survey handbook: Twenty-five years of research and application.* San Diego, CA: EdITS.

Hogan, R. (1983). Socioanalytic theory of personality. In M. M. Page (Ed.), *1982 Nebraska Symposium on Motivation: Personality—current theory and research* (pp. 55–89). Lincoln: University of Nebraska Press.

Horney, K. (1945). *Our inner conflicts.* New York: Norton.

Horney, K. (1950). *Neurosis and human growth.* New York: Norton.

John, O. P., Goldberg, L. R., & Angleitner, A. (1984). Better than the alphabet: Taxonomies of personality-descriptive terms in English, Dutch, and German. In H. J. C. Bonarius, G. L. M. van Heck, & N. G. Smid (Eds.), *Personality psychology in Europe: Theoretical and empirical developments.* Lisse, Switzerland: Swets & Zeitlinger.

Kenrick, D. T., & Dantchik, A. (1983). Interactionism, idiographics, and the social psychological invasion of personality. *Journal of Personality, 51,* 286–307.

Kline, P., & Barrett, P. (1983). The factors in personality questionnaires among normal subjects. *Advances in Behaviour Research and Therapy, 5,* 141–202.

Lorr, M., & Manning, T. T. (1978). Higher-order personality factors of the ISI. *Multivariate Behavioral Research, 13,* 3–7.

McClelland, D. C., Atkinson, J. W., Clark, R. A., & Lowell, E. L. (1953). *The achievement motive.* New York: Appleton-Century-Crofts.

McCrae, R. R., & Costa, P. T., Jr. (1983a). Joint factors in self-reports and ratings: Neuroticism, extraversion, and openness to experience. *Personality and Individual Differences, 4,* 245–255.

McCrae, R. R., & Costa, P. T., Jr. (1985a). Openness to experience. In R. Hogan & W. H. Jones (Eds.), *Perspectives in personality: Theory, measurement, and interpersonal dynamics* (Vol. 1). Greenwich, CT: JAI Press.

McCrae, R. R., & Costa, P. T., Jr. (1985b). Updating Norman's "adequate taxonomy": Intelligence and personality dimensions in natural language and in questionnaires. *Journal of Personality and Social Psychology, 49,* 710–721.

McCrae, R. R., & Costa, P. T., Jr. (1986). Personality, coping, and coping effectiveness in an adult sample. *Journal of Personality, 54,* 385–405.

Mischel, W. (1968). *Personality and assessment.* New York: Wiley.

Morris, W. (Ed.). (1976). *The American Heritage dictionary of the English language.* Boston: Houghton Mifflin.

Peabody, D. (1984). Personality dimensions through trait inferences. *Journal of Personality and Social Psychology, 46*, 384–403.

Plomin, R., DeFries, J. C., & McClearn, G. E. (1980). *Behavior genetics: A primer.* San Francisco: Freeman.

Revelle, W., Humphreys, M. S., Simon, L., & Gilliland, K. (1980). The interactive effect of personality, time of day, and caffeine: A test of the arousal model. *Journal of Experimental Psychology: General, 109*, 1–31.

Stark, L., (1978). Trust. In H. London & J. E. Exner, Jr. (Eds.), *Dimensions of personality* (pp. 561–599). New York: Wiley.

Teasdale, J. D., & Rachman, S. (Eds.). (1983). Cognitions and mood: Clinical aspects and applications [Special issue]. *Advances in Behaviour Research and Therapy, 5*, 1–88.

Tellegen, A. (in press). Structures of mood and personality and their relevance to assessing anxiety, with an emphasis on self-report. In A. H. Tuma & J. D. Maser (Eds.), *Anxiety and the anxiety disorders.* Hillsdale, NJ: Erlbaum.

Tupes, E. C., & Christal, R. E. (1961). Recurrent personality factors based on trait ratings. *USAF ASD Technical Report* (No. 61–97).

Vestre, N. D. (1984). Irrational beliefs and self-reported depressed mood. *Journal of Abnormal Psychology, 93*, 239–241.

Wiggins, J. S. (1979). A psychological taxonomy of trait-descriptive terms: The interpersonal domain. *Journal of Personality and Social Psychology, 37*, 395–412.

Culture and the Self: Implications for Cognition, Emotion, and Motivation

During the past decade, psychologists have been increasingly aware of the importance of culture in determining how people define themselves. Although much knowledge has been gained through studying people in Western cultures, such as the United States, there is a great deal that we now know differs in the personality and social behavior of individuals in Eastern cultures, such as Japan. Hazel Rose Markus and Shinobu Kitayama have begun to explore some of the differences in the concept of self in individuals from different cultures.

Markus earned her Ph.D. in social psychology from the University of Michigan in 1975. She joined the University of Michigan's Research Center for Group Dynamics prior to her current position at Stanford University. Kitayama (b. 1957) received his Ph.D. in social psychology from the University of Michigan in 1987. He worked at the University of Oregon prior to accepting a position in 1992 at Japan's Kyoto University.

The following selection is from "Culture and the Self: Implications for Cognition, Emotion, and Motivation," which was published in *Psychological Review* in 1991. In it, the authors describe the independent and interdependent viewpoints of the self. The American concept of the self tends to emphasize the individual's uniqueness and independence from others. The Japanese concept of the self emphasizes interrelatedness and group harmony. In a part of the original article not included in this selection, the authors discuss the implications of the differences in the self on the individual's thinking, emotion, and motivation.

Key Concept: culture and the concept of the self

APA Citation: Markus, H. R., & Kitayama, S. (1991). Culture and the self: Implications for cognition, emotion, and motivation. *Psychological Review, 98,* 224–253.

*I*n America, "the squeaky wheel gets the grease." In Japan, "the nail that stands out gets pounded down." American parents who are trying to induce their children to eat their suppers are fond of saying "think of the starving kids in Ethiopia, and appreciate how lucky you are to be different from them." Japanese parents are likely to say "Think about the farmer who worked so hard to produce this rice for you; if you don't eat it, he will feel bad, for his efforts will have been in vain" (H. Yamada, February 16, 1989). A small Texas corporation seeking to elevate productivity told its employees to look in the mirror and say "I am beautiful" 100 times before coming to work each day. Employees of a Japanese supermarket that was recently opened in New Jersey were instructed to begin the day by holding hands and telling each other that "he" or "she is beautiful" ("A Japanese Supermarket," 1989).

Such anecdotes suggest that people in Japan and America may hold strikingly divergent construals of the self, others, and the interdependence of the two. The American examples stress attending to the self, the appreciation of one's difference from others, and the importance of asserting the self. The Japanese examples emphasize attending to and fitting in with others and the importance of harmonious interdependence with them. These construals of the self and others are tied to the implicit, normative tasks that various cultures hold for what people should be doing in their lives (cf. Cantor & Kihlstrom, 1987; Erikson, 1950; Veroff, 1983). . . .

Despite the growing body of psychological and anthropological evidence that people hold divergent views about the self, most of what psychologists currently know about human nature is based on one particular view—the so-called Western view of the individual as an independent, self-contained, autonomous entity who (a) comprises a unique configuration of internal attributes (e.g., traits, abilities, motives, and values) and (b) behaves primarily as a consequence of these internal attributes (Geertz, 1975; Sampson, 1988, 1989; Shweder & LeVine, 1984). As a result of this monocultural approach to the self (see Kennedy, Scheier, & Rogers, 1984), psychologists' understanding of those phenomena that are linked in one way or another to the self may be unnecessarily restricted (for some important exceptions, see Bond, 1986, 1988; Cousins, 1989; Fiske, in press; Maehr & Nicholls, 1980; Stevenson, Azuma, & Hakuta, 1986; Triandis, 1989; Triandis, Bontempo, Villareal, Asai, & Lucca, 1988). In this article, we suggest that construals of the self, of others, and of the relationship between the self and others may be even more powerful than previously suggested and that their influence is clearly reflected in differences among cultures. In particular, we compare an *independent* view of the self with one other, very different view, an *interdependent* view. The independent view is most clearly exemplified in some sizable segment of American culture, as well as in many Western European cultures. The interdependent view is exemplified in Japanese culture as well as in other Asian cultures. But it is also characteristic of African cultures, Latin-American cultures, and may southern European cultures. . . .

THE SELF: A DELICATE CATEGORY

Universal Aspects of the Self

In exploring the possibility of different types of self-construals, we begin with Hallowell's (1955) notion that people everywhere are likely to develop an understanding of themselves as physically distinct and separable from others. Head (192), for example, claimed the existence of a universal schema of the body that provided one with an anchor in time and space. Similarly, Allport (1937) suggested that there must exist an aspect of personality that allows one, when awakening each morning, to be sure that he or she is the same person who went to sleep the night before. Most recently, Neisser (1988) referred to this aspect of self as the *ecological self*, which he defined as "the self as perceived with respect to the physical environment: 'I' am the person here in this place, engaged in this particular activity" (p. 3). Beyond a physical or ecological sense of self, each person probably has some awareness of internal activity, such as dreams, and of the continuous flow of thoughts and feelings, which are private to the extent that they cannot be directly known by others. The awareness of this unshared experience will lead the person to some sense of an inner, private self.

Divergent Aspects of the Self

Some understanding and some representation of the private, inner aspects of the self may well be universal, but many other aspects of the self may be quite specific to particular cultures. People are capable of believing an astonishing variety of things about themselves (cf. Heelas & Lock, 1981; Marsella et al., 1985; Shweder & LeVine, 1984; Triandis, 1989). The self can be construed, framed, or conceptually represented in multiple ways. A cross-cultural survey of the self lends support to Durkheim's (1912/1968) early notion that the category of the self is primarily the product of social factors, and to Mauss's (1938/1985) claim that as a social category, the self is a "delicate" one, subject to quite substantial, if not infinite, variation.

The exact content and structure of the inner self may differ considerably by culture. Furthermore, the nature of the outer or public self that derives from one's relations with other people and social institutions may also vary markedly by culture. And, as suggested by Triandis (1989), the significance assigned to the private, inner aspects versus the public, relational aspects in regulating behavior will vary accordingly. In fact, it may not be unreasonable to suppose, as did numerous earlier anthropologists (see Allen, 1985), that in some cultures, on certain occasions, the *individual*, in the sense of a set of significant inner attributes of the person, may cease to be the primary unit of consciousness. Instead, the sense of belongingness to a social relation may become so strong that it makes better sense to think of the *relationship* as the functional unit of conscious reflection.

The current analysis focuses on just one variation in what people in different cultures can come to believe about themselves. This one variation concerns what they believe about the relationship between the self and *others* and, especially, the degree to which they see themselves as *separate* from others or as *connected* with others. We suggest that the significance and the exact functional role that the person assigns to the other when defining the self depend on the culturally shared assumptions about the separation or connectedness between the self and others.

TWO CONSTRUALS OF THE SELF: INDEPENDENT AND INTERDEPENDENT

The Independent Construal

In many Western cultures, there is a faith in the inherent separateness of distinct persons. The normative imperative of this culture is to become independent from others and to discover and express one's unique attributes (Johnson, 1985; Marsella et al., 1985; J. G. Miller, 1988; Shweder & Bourne, 1984). Achieving the cultural goal of independence requires construing oneself as an individual whose behavior is organized and made meaningful primarily by reference to one's own internal repertoire of thoughts, feelings, and action, rather than by reference to the thoughts, feelings, and actions of others. According to this construal of self, to borrow Geertz's (1975) often quoted phrase, the person is viewed as "a bounded, unique, more or less integrated motivational and cognitive universe, a dynamic center of awareness, emotion, judgment, and action organized into a distinctive whole and set contrastively both against other such wholes and against a social and natural background" (p. 48).

This view of the self derives from a belief in the wholeness and uniqueness of each person's configuration of internal attributes (Johnson, 1985; Sampson, 1985, 1988, 1989; Waterman, 1981). It gives rise to processes like "self-actualization," "realizing oneself," "expressing one's unique configuration of needs, rights, and capacities," or "developing one's distinct potential." The essential aspect of this view involves a conception of the self as an autonomous, independent person; we thus refer to it as the *independent construal of the self.* Other similar labels include *individualist, egocentric, separate, autonomous, idiocentric,* and *self-contained.* We assume that, on average, relatively more individuals in Western cultures will hold this view than will individuals in non-Western cultures. Within a given culture, however, individuals will vary in the extent to which they are good cultural representatives and construe the self in the mandated way.

The independent self must, of course, be responsive to the social environment (Fiske, in press). This responsiveness, however, is fostered not so much for the sake of the responsiveness itself. Rather, social responsiveness often, if not always, derives from the need to strategically determine the best way to express or assert the internal attributes of the self. Others, or the social situation in general, are important, but primarily as standards of reflected appraisal, or as sources that can verify and affirm the inner core of the self.

*Hazel Rose
Markus and
Shinobu
Kitayama*

The Western, independent view of the self is illustrated in Figure 1. The large circle represents the self, and the smaller circles represent specific others. The Xs are representations of the various aspects of the self or the others. In some cases, the larger circle and the small circle intersect, and there is an X in the intersection. This refers to a representation of the self-in-relation-to-others or to a particular social relation (e.g., "I am very polite in front of my professor"). An X within the self circle but outside of the intersection represents an aspect of the self perceived to be relatively independent of specific others and, thus, invariant over time and context. These self-representations usually have as their referent some individual desire, preference, attribute, or ability (e.g., "I am creative"). For those with independent construals of the self, it is these inner attributes that are most significant in regulating behavior and that are assumed, both by the actor and by the observer alike, to be diagnostic of the actor. Such representations of the inner self are thus the most elaborated in memory and the most accessible when thinking of the self (as indicated by Xs in Figure 1A). They can be called *core conceptions*, *salient identities*, or *self-schemata* (e.g., Gergen, 1968; Markus, 1977; Stryker, 1986).

The Interdependent Construal

In contrast, many non-Western cultures insist, in Kondo's (1982) terms, on the fundamental *connectedness* of human beings to each other. A normative imperative of these cultures is to maintain this interdependence among individuals (De Vos, 1985; Hsu, 1985; Miller, 1988; Shweder & Bourne, 1984). Experiencing interdependence entails seeing oneself as part of an encompassing social relationship and recognizing that one's behavior is determined, contingent on, and, to a large extent organized by what the actor perceives to be the thoughts, feelings, and actions of *others* in the relationship. The Japanese experience of the self, therefore, includes a sense of interdependence and of one's status as a participant in a larger social unit (Sampson, 1988). Within such a construal, the self becomes most meaningful and complete when it is cast in the appropriate social relationship. According to Lebra (1976) the Japanese are most fully human in the context of others.

This view of the self and the relationship between the self and others features the person not as separate from the social context but as more connected and less differentiated from others. People are motivated to find a way to fit in with relevant others, to fulfill and create obligation, and in general to become part of various interpersonal relationships. Unlike the independent self, the significant features of the self according to this construal are to be found in the interdependent and thus, in the more public components of the self. We therefore call this view the *interdependent construal of the self*. The same notion has been variously referred to, with somewhat different connotations, as *sociocentric*, *holistic*, *collective*, *allocentric*, *ensembled*, *constitutive*, *contextualist*, *connected*, and *relational*. As with the independent self, others are critical for social comparison and self-validation, yet in an interdependent formulation of the self, these others become an integral part of the setting, situation, or context to which the self is connected, fitted, and assimilated. The exact manner in which one

FIGURE 1

Conceptual Representations of the Self.
(A: Independent Construal. B: Interdependent Construal.)

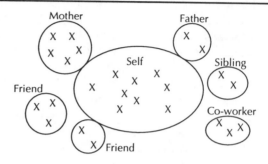

A. Independent View of Self

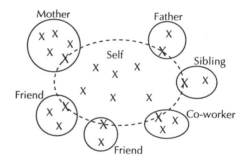

B. Interdependent View of Self

achieves the task of connection, therefore, depends crucially on the nature of the context, particularly the others present in the context. Others thus participate actively and continuously in the definition of the interdependent self.

The interdependent self also possesses and expresses a set of internal attributes, such as abilities, opinions, judgments, and personality characteristics. However, these internal attributes are understood as situation specific, and thus as sometimes elusive and unreliable. And, as such, they are unlikely to assume a powerful role in regulating overt behavior, especially if this behavior implicates significant others. In many domains of social life, one's opinions, abilities, and characteristics are assigned only secondary roles—they must instead be constantly controlled and regulated to come to terms with the primary task of interdependence. Such voluntary control of the inner attributes constitutes the core of the cultural ideal of becoming mature. The understanding of one's autonomy as secondary to, and constrained by, the primary task of interdependence distinguishes interdependent selves from independent selves, for

Hazel Rose Markus and Shinobu Kitayama

whom autonomy and its expression is often afforded primary significance. An independent behavior (e.g., asserting an opinion) exhibited by a person in an interdependent culture is likely to be based on the premise of underlying interdependence and thus may have a somewhat different significance than it has for a person from an independent culture.

The interdependent self is illustrated in Figure 1B. For those with interdependent selves, the significant self-representations (the Xs) are those in relationship to specific others. Interdependent selves certainly include representations of invariant personal attributes and abilities, and these representations can become phenomenologically quite salient, but in many circumstances they are less important in regulating observable behavior and are not assumed to be particularly diagnostic of the self. Instead, the self-knowledge that guides behavior is of the self-in-relation to specific others in particular contexts. The fundamental units of the self-system, the core conceptions, or self-schemata are thus predicated on significant interpersonal relationships.

An interdependent self cannot be properly characterized as a bounded whole, for it changes structure with the nature of the particular social context. Within each particular social situation, the self can be differently instantiated. The uniqueness of such a self derives from the specific configuration of relationships that each person has developed. What is focal and objectified in an interdependent self, then, is not the inner self, but the *relationships* of the person to other actors (Hamaguchi, 1985).

The notion of an interdependent self is linked with a monistic philosophical tradition in which the person is thought to be of the same substance as the rest of nature (see Bond, 1986; Phillips, 1976; Roland, 1988; Sass, 1988). As a consequence, the relationship between the self and other, or between subject and object, is assumed to be much closer. Thus, many non-Western cultures insist on the inseparability of basic elements (Galtung, 1981), including self and other, and person and situation. In Chinese culture, for instance, there is an emphasis on synthesizing the constituent parts of any problem or situation into an integrated or harmonious whole (Moore, 1967; Northrop, 1946). Thus, persons are only parts that when separated from the larger social whole cannot be fully understood (Phillips, 1976; Shweder, 1984). Such a holistic view is in opposition to the Cartesian, dualistic tradition that characterizes Western thinking and in which the self is separated from the object and from the natural world....

The role of the other in the interdependent self.   In an interdependent view, in contrast to an independent view, others will be assigned much more importance, will carry more weight, and will be relatively focal in one's own behavior. There are several direct consequences of an interdependent construal of the self. First, relationships, rather than being means for realizing various individual goals, will often be ends in and of themselves. Although people everywhere must maintain some relatedness with others, an appreciation and a need for people will be more important for those with an interdependent self than for those with an independent self. Second, maintaining a connection to others will mean being constantly aware of others and focusing on their needs, desires, and goals. In some cases, the goals of others may become so focal in consciousness that the goals of others may be experienced as personal goals. In other cases, fulfilling one's own goals may be quite distinct from those of others, but meeting another's goals, needs, and desires will be a necessary requirement for satisfying one's own goals, needs, and desires. The assumption is that while promoting the goals of others, one's own goals will be attended to by the person with whom one is interdependent. Hence, people may actively work to fulfill the others' goals while passively monitoring the reciprocal contributions from these others for one's own goal-fulfillment. Yamagishi (1988), in fact, suggested that the Japanese feel extremely uncomfortable, much more so than Americans, when the opportunity for such passive monitoring of others' actions is denied.

From the standpoint of an independent, "self-ish" self, one might be led to romanticize the interdependent self, who is ever attuned to the concerns of others. Yet in many cases, responsive and cooperative actions are exercised only when there is a reasonable assurance of the "good-intentions" of others, namely their commitment to continue to engage in reciprocal interaction and mutual support. Clearly, interdependent selves do not attend to the needs, desires, and goals of *all* others. Attention to others is not indiscriminate; it is highly selective and will be most characteristic of relationships with "in-group" members. These are others with whom one shares a common fate, such as family members or members of the same lasting social group, such as the work group. Out-group members are typically treated quite differently and are unlikely to experience either the advantages or disadvantages of interdependence. Independent selves are also selective in their association with others but not to the extent of inter-dependent selves because much less of their behavior is directly contingent on the actions of others. Given the importance of others in constructing reality and regulating behavior, the in-group–out-group distinction is a vital one for inter-dependent selves, and the subjective boundary of one's "in-group" may tend to be narrower for the interdependent selves than for the independent selves (Triandis, 1989).

To illustrate the reciprocal nature of interaction among those with interde-pendent views, imagine that one has a friend over for lunch and has decided to make a sandwich for him. The conversation might be: "Hey, Tom, what do you want in your sandwich? I have turkey, salami, and cheese." Tom responds, "Oh, I like turkey." Note that the friend is given a choice because the host assumes that friend has a right, if not a duty, to make a choice reflecting his inner at-tributes, such as preferences or desires. And the friend makes his choice exactly because of the belief in the same assumption. This script is "natural," however, only within the independent view of self. What would happen if the friend were a visitor from Japan? A likely response to the question "Hey, Tomio, what do you want?" would be a little moment of bewilderment and then a noncommital utterance like "I don't know." This happens because under the assumptions of an interdependent self, it is the responsibility of the host to be able to "read" the mind of the friend and offer what the host perceives to be the best for the friend. And the duty of the guest, on the other hand, is to receive the favor with grace and to be prepared to return the favor in the near future, if not right at the next moment. A likely interdependent script for the same situation would be: "Hey, Tomio, I made you a turkey sandwich because I remember that last week you said you like turkey more than beef." And Tomio will respond, "Oh, thank you, I really like turkey."

*Hazel Rose
Markus and
Shinobu
Kitayama*

The reciprocal interdependence with others that is the sign of the interdependent self seems to require constant engagement of what Mead (1934) meant by taking the role of the other. It involves the willingness and ability to feel and think what others are feeling and thinking, to absorb this information without being told, and then to help others satisfy their wishes and realize their goals. Maintaining connection requires inhibiting the "I" perspective and processing instead from the "thou" perspective (Hsu, 1981). The requirement is to "read" the other's mind and thus to know what the other is thinking or feeling. In contrast, with an independent self, it is the individual's responsibility to "say what's on one's mind" if one expects to be attended to or understood.

REFERENCES

Allen, N. J. (1985). The category of the person: A reading of Mauss's last essay. In M. Carrithers, S. Collins, & S. Lukes (Eds.), *The category of the person: Anthropology, philosophy, history* (pp. 26–35). Cambridge, England: Cambridge University Press.

Allport, G. W. (1937). *Personality: A psychological interpretation.* New York: Holt.

Bond, M. H. (1986). *The psychology of the Chinese people.* New York: Oxford University Press.

Bond, M. H. (Eds.), (1988). *The cross-cultural challenge to social psychology.* Beverly Hills, CA: Sage.

Cantor, N., & Kihlstrom, J. (1987). *Personality and social intelligence.* Englewood Cliffs, NJ: Prentice-Hall.

Cousins, S. (1989). Culture and selfhood in Japan and the U.S. *Journal of Personality and Social Psychology, 56,* 124–131.

De Vos, G. (1985). Dimensions of the self in Japanese culture. In A. Marsella, G. De Vos, & F. L. K. Hsu (Eds.), *Culture and self* (pp. 149–184). London: Tavistock.

Durkheim, E. (1968). *Les formes elementaires de la vie religieuse* [Basic forms of religious belief] (6th ed.). Paris: Presses Universitarires de France. (Original work published 1912)

Erikson, E. (1950). Identification as the basis for a theory of motivation. *American Psychological Review, 26,* 14–21.

Fiske, A. P. (in press). *Making up society: The four elementary relational structures.* New York: Free Press.

Galtung, J. (1981). Structure, culture, and intellectual style: An essay comparing Saxonic, Teutonic, Gallic and Nipponic approaches. *Social Science Information, 20,* 817–856.

Geertz, C. (1975). On the nature of anthropological understanding. *American Scientist, 63,* 47–53.

Gergen, K. J. (1968). Personal consistency and the presentation of self. In C. Gordon & K. J. Gergen (Eds.), *The self in social interaction: Classic and contemporary perspectives* (Vol. 1, pp. 299–308). New York: Wiley.

Hallowell, A. I. (1955). *Culture and experience.* Philadelphia: University of Pennsylvania Press.

Hamaguchi, E. (1985). A contextual model of the Japanese: Toward a methodological innovation in Japan studies. *Journal of Japanese Studies, 11,* 289–321.

Head, H. (1920). *Studies in neurology.* London: Oxford University Press.

Heelas, P. L. F., & Lock, A. J. (Eds.). (1981). *Indigenous psychologies: The anthropology of the self.* London: Academic Press.

Hsu, F. L. K. (1981). *American and Chinese: Passage to differences.* Honolulu: University of Hawaii Press.

Hsu, F. L. K. (1985). The self in cross-cultural perspective. In A. J. Marsella, G. De Vos, & F. L. K. Hsu (Eds.), *Culture and self* (pp. 24–55). London: Tavistock.

Johnson, F. (1985). The Western concept of self. In A. Marsella, G. De Vos, & F. L. K. Hsu (Eds.), *Culture and self.* London: Tavistock.

Kennedy, S., Scheier, J., & Rogers, A. (1984). The price of success: Our monocultural science. *American Psychologist, 39,* 996–997.

Kondo, D. (1982). *Work, family and the self: A cultural analysis of Japanese family enterprise.* Unpublished doctoral dissertation, Harvard University.

Lebra, T. S. (1976). *Japanese patterns of behavior.* Honolulu: University of Hawaii Press.

Maehr, M., & Nicholls, J. (1980). Culture and achievement motivation: A second look. In N. Warren (Ed.), *Studies in cross-cultural psychology* (Vol. 2, pp. 221–267). New York: Academic Press.

Markus, H. (1977). Self-schemas and processing information about the self. *Journal of Personality and Social Psychology, 35,* 63–78.

Marsella, A., De Vos, G., & Hsu, F. L. K. (Eds.). (1985). *Culture and self.* London: Tavistock.

Mauss, M. (1985). A category of the human mind: The notion of person; the notion of self (W. D. Halls, Trans.). In M. Carrithers, S. Collins, & S. Lukes (Eds.), *The category of the person: Anthropology, philosophy, history* (pp. 1–25). Cambridge, England: Cambridge University Press. (Original work published 1938)

Mead, G. H. (1934). *Mind, self and society.* Chicago: University of Chicago Press.

Miller, J. G. (1988). Bridging the content-structure dichotomy: Culture and the self. In M. H. Bond (Ed.), *The cross-cultural challenge to social psychology* (pp. 266–281). Beverly Hills, CA: Sage.

Moore, C. A. (Ed.). (1967). Introduction: The humanistic Chinese mind. In *The Chinese mind: Essentials of Chinese philosophy and culture* (pp. 1–10). Honolulu: University of Hawaii Press.

Neisser, U. (1988). Five kinds of self-knowledge. *Philosophical Psychology, 1,* 35–59.

Northrop, F. S. C. (1946). *The meeting of East and West.* New York: Macmillan.

Phillips, D. C. (1976). *Holistic thought in social science.* Stanford, CA: Stanford University Press.

Roland, A. (1988). *In search of self in India and Japan: Toward a cross-cultural psychology.* Princeton, NJ: Princeton University Press.

Sampson, E. E. (1985). The decentralization of identity: Toward a revised concept of personal and social order. *American Psychologist, 40,* 1203–1211.

Sampson, E. E. (1988). The debate on individualism: Indigenous psychologies of the individual and their role in personal and societal functioning. *American Psychologist, 43,* 15–22.

Sampson, E. E. (1989). The challenge of social change for psychology: Globalization and psychology's theory of the person. *American Psychologist, 44,* 914–921.

Sass, L. A. (1988). The self and its vicissitudes: An "archaeological" study of the psychoanalytic avant-garde. *Social Research, 55,* 551–607.

Shweder, R. A. (1984). Preview: A colloquy of culture theorists. In R. A. Shweder & R. A. LeVine (Eds.), *Culture theory: Essays on mind, self, and emotion* (pp. 1–24). Cambridge, England: Cambridge University Press.

Shweder, R. A., & Bourne, E. J. (1984). Does the concept of the person vary cross-culturally? In R. A. Shweder & R. A. LeVine (Eds.), *Culture theory: Essays on mind, self, and emotion* (pp. 158–199). Cambridge, England: Cambridge University Press.

Shweder, R. A., & LeVine, R. A. (Eds.). (1984). *Culture theory: Essays on mind, self, and emotion.* Cambridge, England: Cambridge University Press.

Stevenson, H., Azuma, H., & Hakuta, K. (1986). *Child development and education in Japan.* New York: Freeman.

Stryker, S. (1986). Identity theory: Developments and extensions. In K. Yardley & T. Honess (Eds.), *Self and identity* (pp. 89–104). New York: Wiley.

Triandis, H. C. (1989). The self and social behavior in differing cultural contexts. *Psychological Review, 96,* 506–520.

Triandis, H. C., Bontempo, R., Villareal, M J., Asai, M., & Lucca, N. (1988). Individualism and collectivism: Cross-cultural perspectives on self-ingroup relationships. *Journal of Personality and Social Psychology, 54,* 323–338.

Veroff, J. (1983). Contextual determinants of personality. *Personality and Social Psychology Bulletin, 9,* 331–344.

Waterman, A. S. (1981). Individualism and interdependence. *American Psychologist, 36,* 762–773.

Yamagishi, T. (1988). Exit from the group as an individualistic solution to the free-rider problem in the United States and Japan. *Journal of Experimental Social Psychology, 24,* 530–542.

CHAPTER 12 Stress, Adjustment, and Health

12.1 HANS SELYE

The Evolution of the Stress Concept

Only in the past couple of decades have psychologists become convinced that psychological as well as physiological variables can produce stress. However, as far back as the 1930s, Canadian physiologist Hans Selye was studying stress through the general adaptation syndrome (GAS). The general adaptation syndrome, first identified by Selye, is a consistent series of bodily reactions to stress that can be divided into three stages: the alarm reaction stage, the stage of resistance, and the stage of exhaustion. The GAS serves as a model for investigating the long-term effects of stress on the body.

Selye (1907–1982) received his D.Sc. from McGill University in 1942 and later earned a Ph.D. and an M.D. He spent most of his professional career at the Institute of Experimental Medicine and Surgery at the University of Montreal. As an endocrinologist, he dedicated his life to understanding the hormonal reactions in the stress syndrome. Selye wrote over 30 books on stress, including *The Stress of Life* (1976) and *Stress Without Distress* (1974).

This selection is from "The Evolution of the Stress Concept," which was published in *American Scientist* in 1973. In it, Selye provides the history behind his famous general adaptation syndrome model of stress. Note how Selye's discoveries occurred in steps as he encountered different situations.

As you read this selection, consider the definition of stress and how you measure the effects of stress in your life.

Hans Selye

Key Concept: stress and the general adaptation syndrome

APA Citation: Selye, H. (1973). The evolution of the stress concept. *American Scientist, 61,* 692–699.

Everybody knows what stress is and nobody knows what it is. The word *stress*, like *success, failure,* or *happiness,* means different things to different people and, except for a few specialized scientists, no one has really tried to define it although it has become part of our daily vocabulary....

Yet, how are we to cope with the stress of life if we cannot even define it? The businessman who is under constant pressure from his clients and employees alike, the air traffic controller who knows that a moment of distraction may mean death to hundreds of people, the athlete who desperately wants to win a race, and the husband who helplessly watches his wife slowly and painfully die of cancer—all suffer from stress. The problems they face are totally different, but medical research has shown that in many respects their bodies respond in a stereotyped manner with identical biochemical changes, meant fundamentally to cope with any type of increased demand upon the human machinery. The stress-producing factors—technically called *stressors*—are different, and yet they all produce essentially the same biologic stress response. This distinction between stressor and stress was perhaps the first important step in the scientific analysis of that most common biologic phenomenon that we all know only too well from personal experience.

But if we want to use what the laboratory has taught us about stress in formulating our own philosophy of life, if we want to avoid its bad effects and yet be able to enjoy the pleasures of accomplishment, we have to learn more about the nature and mechanism of stress. To succeed in this, we must concentrate on the fundamental technical data which the laboratory has given us as a basis for a scientific philosophy of conduct. Examination of the data seems to be the only way of finding purpose in life without having to fall back upon traditional beliefs whose acceptance depends primarily on indoctrination (1).

WHAT IS STRESS?

Stress is the nonspecific response of the body to any demand made upon it. In order to understand this definition we must first comprehend what is meant by "nonspecific." Each demand made upon our body is in a sense unique, that is, specific. When exposed to cold we shiver to produce more heat, and the blood vessels in our skin contract to diminish loss of heat from the body surface. When exposed to heat we sweat, because evaporation of perspiration from the surface of our skin has a cooling effect. When we eat so much sugar that the blood-sugar level rises above normal, we excrete some of it and try to activate chemical reactions which will enable us to store or burn up the rest so that the blood sugar may return to normal. A great muscular effort, such as running up many flights of stairs at full speed, makes increased demands upon our musculature and cardiovascular system: the muscles will need more energy to perform this unusual work; hence, the heart will beat more rapidly and strongly, and the blood pressure will rise to accelerate delivery of blood to the musculature.

Each drug and hormone has such specific actions: diuretics increase urine production; adrenalin augments the pulse rate and blood pressure, simultaneously increasing blood sugar, whereas insulin decreases blood sugar. Yet, no matter what kind of derangement is produced, all these agents have one thing in common: they also make an increased demand upon the body to readjust itself. This demand is nonspecific; it requires adaptation to a problem, regardless of what that problem may be. That is to say, in addition to their specific actions, all agents to which we are exposed produce a nonspecific increase in the need to perform certain adaptive functions and then to reestablish normalcy, which is independent of the specific activity that caused the rise in requirements. This nonspecific demand for activity as such is the essence of stress.

From the point of view of its stress-producing, or stressor, activity, it is even immaterial whether the agent or situation we face is pleasant or unpleasant; all that counts is the intensity of the demand for readjustment or adaptation. The mother who is suddenly told that her only son died in battle suffers a terrible mental shock; if years later it turns out that the news was false, and the son unexpectedly walks into her room alive and well, she experiences extreme joy. The *specific* results of the two events, sorrow and joy, are completely different, in fact, opposite to each other; yet their stressor effect—the *nonspecific* demand to readjust to an entirely new situation—may be the same.

It is difficult to see how such essentially different things as cold, heat, drugs, hormones, sorrow, and joy could provoke an identical biochemical reaction in the organism. Yet this is the case; it can now be demonstrated by highly objective quantitative biochemical determinations that certain reactions of the body are totally nonspecific and common to all types of exposure....

WHAT STRESS IS NOT

Since the term stress has been used quite loosely, many confusing and often contradictory definitions have been formulated; hence, it will be useful to add a few remarks stating clearly what it is *not*. Stress is not simply nervous tension; stress reactions do occur in lower animals, which have no nervous system, and even in plants. Stress is not the nonspecific result of damage. We have seen that it is immaterial whether an agent is pleasant or unpleasant; its stressor effect depends merely on the intensity of the demand made upon the adaptive work of the body. As I have explained elsewhere (2), "normal activities—a game of tennis or even a passionate kiss—can produce considerable stress without causing conspicuous damage."

Stress is not something to be avoided. In fact, it is evident from the definition given earlier that it cannot be avoided; no matter what you do or what happens to you, there arises a demand to provide the necessary energy to perform the tasks required to maintain life and to resist and adapt to the changing external influences. Even while fully relaxed and asleep, you are under some stress: your heart must continue to pump blood, your intestines to digest last night's dinner, your muscles to move your chest to permit respiration; even your brain is not at complete rest while you are dreaming.

Complete freedom from stress is death. Contrary to public opinion, we must not—and indeed cannot—avoid stress, but we can meet it efficiently and enjoy it by learning more about its mechanism and adjusting our philosophy of life accordingly (1).

HISTORIC DEVELOPMENT

The concept of stress is very old; it must have occurred even to prehistoric man that the loss of vigor and feeling of exhaustion that overcame him after hard labor, prolonged exposure to cold or heat, loss of blood, agonizing fear, or any kind of disease had something in common. He may not have been consciously aware of this similarity in his response to anything that was just too much for him, but when the feeling came he must have realized that he had exceeded the limits of what he could reasonably handle, in other words that "he had had it."

Man soon must have discovered also that whenever faced with a prolonged and unaccustomed strenuous task—be it swimming in cold water, lifting rocks, or going without food—he passes through three stages: at first the experience is a hardship, then one gets used to it, and finally one cannot stand it any longer....

How could different agents produce the same result? Is there a nonspecific adaptive reaction to change as such? In 1926, as a second-year medical student, I first came across this problem of a stereotyped response to any exacting task. I began to wonder why patients suffering from the most diverse diseases have so many signs and symptoms in common. Whether a man suffers from severe loss of blood, an infectious disease, or advanced cancer, he loses his appetite, his muscular strength, and his ambition to accomplish anything; usually the patient also loses weight, and even his facial expression betrays that he is ill. What is the scientific basis of what I thought of at the time as the "syndrome of just being sick"? Could the mechanism of this syndrome be analyzed by modern scientific techniques? Could it be reduced to its elements and expressed in the precise terms of biochemistry, biophysics, and morphology? Could this reaction be subject to scientific analysis?

It was not until 1936 that the problem presented itself again, now under conditions more suited to analysis. At that time, I was working in the biochemistry department of McGill University, trying to find a new hormone in extracts of cattle ovaries. I injected the extracts into rats to see if their organs would show unpredictable changes that could not be attributed to any known hormone. Much to my satisfaction, the first and most impure extracts changed the rats in three ways: (1) the adrenal cortex became enlarged, (2) the thymus, spleen, lymph nodes, and all other lymphatic structures shrank, and (3) deep, bleeding ulcers appeared in the stomach and in the upper gut. Because the three types of change were closely interdependent they formed a definite syndrome. The changes varied from slight to pronounced, depending on the amount of extract I injected.

At first, I ascribed all these changes to a new sex hormone in the extract. But soon I found that all toxic substances—extracts of kidney, spleen, or even a toxin not derived from living tissue—produced the same syndrome. Gradually, my classroom concept of the "syndrome of just being sick" came back to me. I realized that the reaction I had produced with my impure extracts and toxic drugs was an experimental replica of this syndrome. Adrenal enlargement, gastrointestinal ulcers, and thymicolymphatic shrinkage were the omnipresent signs of damage to the body when under disease attack. The three changes thus became the objective indexes of stress and the basis for the development of the entire stress concept.

The reaction was first described in *Nature* (4 July 1936) as "A Syndrome Produced by Various Nocuous Agents" and, subsequently, it became known as the General Adaptation Syndrome (GAS) or biologic stress syndrome. In the same paper I also suggested the name *alarm reaction* for the initial response, arguing that it probably represents the somatic expression of a generalized "call to arms" of the body's defensive forces.

THE GENERAL ADAPTATION SYNDROME

The alarm reaction, however, was evidently not the entire response. Upon continued exposure to any noxious agent capable of eliciting this reaction, a stage of adaptation or resistance ensues. In other words, no organism can be maintained continuously in a state of alarm. If the agent is so drastic that continued exposure becomes incompatible with life, the animal dies during the alarm reaction within the first hours or days. If it can survive, this initial reaction is necessarily followed by the "stage of resistance." The manifestations of this second phase are quite different from—in many instances, the exact opposite of —those which characterize the alarm reaction. For example, during the alarm reaction, the cells of the adrenal cortex discharge their secretory granules into the bloodstream and thus become depleted of corticoid-containing lipid storage material; in the stage of resistance, on the other hand, the cortex becomes particularly rich in secretory granules. Whereas in the alarm reaction, there is hemoconcentration, hypochloremia, and general tissue catabolism, during the stage of resistance, there is hemodilution, hyperchloremia, and anabolism, with a return toward normal body weight.

Curiously, after still more exposure to the noxious agent, the acquired adaptation is lost again. The animal enters into a third phase, the "stage of exhaustion," which inexorably follows as long as the stressor is severe enough and applied for a sufficient length of time. Because of its great practical importance, it should be pointed out that the triphasic nature of the GAS gave us the first indication that the body's adaptability, or "adaptation energy," is finite since, under constant stress, exhaustion eventually ensues. We still do not know precisely what is lost, except that it is not merely caloric energy, since food intake is normal during the stage of resistance. Hence, one would think that once adaptation has occurred and ample energy is available, resistance should go on indefinitely. But just as any inanimate machine gradually wears out, so does the human machine sooner or later become the victim of constant wear and tear.

REFERENCES

1. H. Selye. In preparation. *Stress without Distress.* New York, Philadelphia: Lippincott.
2. H. Selye. 1956. *The Stress of Life.* New York: McGraw-Hill.

Little Hassles Can Be Hazardous to Health

There is no doubt that stress is harmful to mental and physical health. The common belief that major life changes cause the most severe stress was challenged in the early 1980s by Richard S. Lazarus, who emphasized the concept of daily hassles.

Lazarus (b. 1922) earned his Ph.D. in experimental psychology from the University of Pittsburgh in 1948. He taught at Johns Hopkins University and Clark University before accepting a position at the University of California, Berkeley in 1957, where he is currently a professor emeritus. Much of his professional career has focused on emotions and stress, as evidenced by his recent book *Emotion and Adaptation* (Oxford University Press, 1991).

This selection is from "Little Hassles Can Be Hazardous to Health," which was published in *Psychology Today* in 1981. In it, Lazarus defines *hassles* as the irritating or frustrating little incidents that happen every day, like spilling a drink, losing your car keys, having an argument, or being caught in a long line. He also discusses the pleasant uplifts that can occur. Note that the uplifts have a different effect on men and women. As you read this selection, think about your daily hassles and uplifts. How do you generally respond to hassles in your life? How do you think you *should* respond?

Key Concept: hassles and stress

APA Citation: Lazarus, R. S. (1981). Little hassles can be hazardous to health. *Psychology Today, 15,* 58–62.

Modern research on the effects of stress has concentrated on the dramatic events of life: the death of a spouse or a friend, divorce, marriage, retirement, being fired. This research has largely ignored the effect of the minor but more frequent daily events that might be best described as hassles. Hassles, as I define them, are the irritating, frustrating, or distressing incidents that occur in our everyday transactions with the environment. They can take the form of disagreements, disappointments, accidents, or unpleasant surprises. They range from getting stuck in a traffic jam to losing a wallet; from an argument with a teenage son to a dispute with a superior or a subordinate at work.

I recently completed a year-long study of the effects of daily hassles with a group of my colleagues at the University of California at Berkeley: Allen Kanner, James Coyne, Catherine Schaefer, Anita DeLongis, and Gayle Dakof. We discovered that daily hassles are more closely linked to and may have a greater effect on our moods and our health than the major misfortunes of life. By keeping track of the accumulation of hassles, we found that their effects varied according to their frequency, intensity, and the reactions people had to them. We also kept track of the daily uplifts in the lives of our participants to see if pleasant or satisfying moments can counter the negative effects of daily hassles. To our surprise, we found that uplifts seemed to have a different effect on men and women.

THE TOP TEN HASSLES AND UPLIFTS

HASSLES
1. Concern about weight
2. Health of a family member
3. Rising prices of common goods
4. Home maintenance
5. Too many things to do
6. Misplacing or losing things
7. Yard work or outside home maintenance
8. Property, investment, or taxes
9. Crime
10. Physical appearance

UPLIFTS
1. Relating well with your spouse or lover
2. Relating well with friends
3. Completing a task
4. Feeling healthy
5. Getting enough sleep
6. Eating out
7. Meeting responsibilities
8. Visiting, phoning, or writing someone
9. Spending time with family
10. Home pleasing to you

While our findings may seem obvious to some readers, our work marks a significant shift in stress research. Most previous work in the field has operated under the premise that all major life changes—whether positive or negative—produce stress and that the more a person endures, the greater the potential for physical and mental illness. Our study raises serious doubts about that premise.

The preoccupation with major life events began in the mid-1960s with the pioneering work of Thomas Holmes and Richard Rahe at the University of Washington. Using interviews and health histories of several thousand people, Holmes and Rahe found a statistically significant relationship between the major events in their lives and their physical condition within the next year or two. The effect seemed to be cumulative: the more life changes, the greater the likelihood of a later illness. This finding applied both to positive events like marriage or promotion and to negative events like divorce or getting fired.

Holmes and Rahe developed a 43-item checklist of "recent life events" and gave each one a numerical value in "life change units" based on its estimated impact as a stressor. Death of a spouse, for example, they rates at 100 units; death of a close friend, at 37; a minor violation of the law, 11. People who have accumulated more than 300 life change units in the previous two years are supposedly more likely than others to suffer serious health problems.

- The particular events in the checklist may not be the most relevant ones for certain groups of people, such as students, working mothers, the poor, or the elderly.
- Simply adding up the life change units of major events fails to take into account the particular context of the changes, how the individual appraises them, and how well or how poorly he or she copes with them.
- The statistical correlation between life events scores and health outcomes, though positive, is relatively weak.
- The life events approach provides no clues to the specific processes by which the events have an impact on health; it tells us nothing about how the events are translated into the stresses of day-to-day living.
- Life events are built solely around the idea of change; yet much stress arises from chronic or repeated conditions of living—boredom, continuing tension in a family relationship, lack of occupational progress, isolation and loneliness, absence of meaning and commitment.

The impact of hassles on our physical and mental health depends to a great extent on their frequency, duration, and intensity. A person's response to a given hassle depends on a variety of other factors: personality, coping style, other resources, and how the rest of the day has gone. When someone is under pressure, petty problems that otherwise might be ignored—a broken shoelace, for example—can have a much greater effect than if they had occurred at less anxious times.

For that reason, the particular hassles cited by the people we surveyed are less important than their overall intensity and the individual reactions to them. And though our data do not yet allow us to say this, we suspect that some of the impact of hassles stems from their personal meaning and significance or from our ineptness in coping with certain interpersonal difficulties. As I pointed out in an interview with *Psychology Today* ("Positive Denial: The Case for Not Facing Reality," November 1979), "Psychological stress resides neither in the situation nor the person; it depends on a transaction between the two. It arises from how the person appraises an event and adapts to it."

The kind of hassles that affect a person's overall psychological economy have several possible sources. Major life events, in addition to their obvious or immediate impact, can create continuing hassles—a kind of "ripple effect." Divorce, for example, might force a man inexperienced at such tasks to make his own meals, do the laundry, or clean the house; it might force a woman to handle household finances or repair a leaky faucet for the first time.

Some hassles may recur because of a permanent but not always harmonious relationship in marriage or at work, such as sexual incompatibility with a spouse or personality conflict with a coworker. (There continuing hassles create the "chronic role strains" studied by Leonard Pearlin and Morton Lieberman at the University of Chicago.) Other hassles may occur not as a result of any major life change or permanent relationship, but from a momentary situation—an unexpected phone call, an uninvited guest, a flat tire.

Assessing the effect of daily hassles led us to consider the effect of uplifts, their positive psychological counterparts: pleasant, happy, or satisfying experiences like hearing good news, getting a good night's rest, solving a difficult problem. Just as negative stressors or hassles can cause physical and psychological changes that may result in illness, we think that uplifts may serve as emotional buffers against the same disorders.

There are several ways in which uplifts may help people cope with daily hassles. They may serve as breathers, sustainers, or restorers when psychological resources have been run down during stressful periods. They may help us recover from the effects of harm or loss. They may act as psychological protection against the effects of hassles or major life changes.

A group of us compiled a list of daily hassles and uplifts by citing common annoyances and pleasures that occur at work, among family and friends, or in other contexts. We got additional suggestions from patients enrolled in a regional group health insurance program. We converted our list into a hassles questionnaire. The questionnaire does not have a fixed or final form, for there are undoubtedly many common examples that could or should be on our list; and the list itself may not be appropriate for certain groups like young parents or the elderly.

We selected our research sample of 100 people (48 men and 52 women), ages 45 to 64, from a much larger survey population in Alameda County, California. Our subjects were mainly white, middle-aged, middle-class, and Protestant, with above-average incomes and education. Most were married (86 percent) and relatively stable in employment history and residence. While we know that our sample is not representative of the general population, at this preliminary stage of our research we want to test our notions on a relatively small and homogeneous group. We hope to study more diverse groups in the future.

Participants in the study filled out a variety of questionnaires over the course of a year. At the beginning and end of the year they filled out a 24-item life events scale comparable to the Homes-Rahe scale. Each month they also filled out a 117-item hassle checklist and a 135-item uplift checklist. They marked the items that had occurred that month and rated the frequency and severity of the items on a 3-point scale.

To measure the effect of the hassles and uplifts, we had each person fill out physical- and mental-health questionnaires at the beginning and end of the year. We used a health-status questionnaire that covers a wide variety of chronic illnesses, like hypertension, and specific symptoms, like chest pains and measures of energy level. We also used the Hopkins Symptom Checklist, a 58-item psychological questionnaire that asks how often people have headaches, bad dreams, worries, poor appetite, crying spells, and so on. Each month, to measure fluctuations in mood, everyone filled out the Bradburn Morale Scale, a widely used index of emotions which asks whether a person is feeling lonely, angry, excited, pleased, bored, proud, restless, uneasy, and so on. Each month, the participants also kept a daily log of their emotions for four consecutive days.

As we expected, hassles turned out to be much better predictors of psychological and physical health than life events. The more frequent and intense the hassles people reported, the poorer their overall mental and physical health. While we found no significant relationship between life events that occurred during the study and the health of the participants at its end, we did find a moderate relationship between life events that occurred during the two and a half years *before* the study and people's health at the end. In short, we found that major events do have some long-term effects, but in the short term, hassles seem to have a much stronger impact on mental and physical health. . . .

When we added the information from the mood scales and daily logs of emotions to the data on hassles, we found that particularly for men, the more hassles and the more negative emotions, the worse a person's subsequent health. Our results strongly suggest that hassles trigger unpleasant emotions, which, in turn or in combination, have an adverse effect on health.

Contrary to our expectation, uplifts did not seem to have much buffer effect on the impact of hassles in this study. In fact, for women, uplifts seemed to have a negative effect on emotions and on psychological health.

At such an early stage in our research, we have no explanation that we can support with data for these surprising findings. In future studies we will continue to search for the positive functions that we still believe uplifts play in a person's psychological economy.

12.3 SHELLEY E. TAYLOR

Adjustment to Threatening Events: A Theory of Cognitive Adaptation

Health psychologists focus on topics such as the promotion of health, the role of psychological factors in illness, the management of stress, and the improvement of health care. University of California psychologist Shelley E. Taylor has been a leader in studying how people adapt to events that threaten their health.

Taylor (b. 1946) earned her Ph.D. in social psychology from Yale University in 1972. She taught at Harvard University before accepting her current position as a professor of psychology at the University of California at Los Angeles in 1979. She has written several books, including *Health Psychology* (McGraw-Hill, 1999).

The following selection, from "Adjustment to Threatening Events: A Theory of Cognitive Adaptation," was published in *American Psychologist* in 1983. Taylor's theory suggests that adjustment to threatening events (such as cancer) focuses on three processes: searching for meaning, regaining mastery, and restoring self-esteem. As you read this selection, think about how you adapt to health problems. What other social psychological processes are involved in a person's adaptation to health-related threats?

Key Concept: cognitive adaptation theory in health psychology

APA Citation: Taylor, S. E. (1983). Adjustment to threatening events: A theory of cognitive adaptation. *American Psychologist, 38,* 1161–1173.

One of the most impressive qualities of the human psyche is its ability to withstand severe personal tragedy successfully. Despite serious setbacks such as personal illness or the death of a family member, the majority of people facing such blows achieve a quality of life or level of happiness equivalent to or even exceeding their prior level of satisfaction. Not everyone readjusts, of course (Silver & Wortman, 1980), but most do, and furthermore they do so substantially on their own. That is, typically people do not seek professional help in dealing with personal problems. They use their social networks and individual resources, and their apparent cure rate, if self-reports of satisfaction are to be trusted, is impressive even by professional standards (Gurin, Veroff, & Feld, 1960; Wills, 1982).

These self-curing abilities are a formidable resource, and our recent work with cancer patients, cardiac patients, rape victims, and other individuals facing life-threatening events has explored them. The consequence of these investigations is a theory of cognitive adaptation. I will argue that when an individual has experienced a personally threatening event, the readjustment process focuses around three themes: a search for meaning in the experience, an attempt to regain mastery over the event in particular and over one's life more generally, and an effort to enhance one's self-esteem—to feel good about oneself again despite the personal setback. . . .

The following analysis draws heavily on the responses of 78 women with breast cancer and many of their family members whom Rosemary Lichtman, Joanne Wood, and I have intensively interviewed during the past two years (Taylor, Lichtman, & Wood, 1982). Some of the women have good prognoses, others do not. Some have achieved a high quality of life following their illness (although it may have taken them several years to do so), others have not. But virtually all of them have shown some attempt to resolve the three issues of meaning, mastery, and self-enhancement. . . .

THE SEARCH FOR MEANING

The search for meaning involves the need to understand why a crisis occurred and what its impact has been. One of the ways in which meaning is addressed is through causal attributions. Attribution theory (Heider, 1958; Kelley, 1967) maintains that following a threatening or dramatic event, people will make attributions so as to understand, predict, and control their environment (Wong & Weiner, 1981). By understanding the cause of an event, one may also begin to understand the significance of the event and what it symbolizes about one's life. In the case of cancer, of course, no one knows the true cause or causes. There are a number of known causes, such as heredity, diet, or specific carcinogens, but a search for the cause of cancer on the part of a patient would seem to be a fruitless endeavor.

Nonetheless, cancer patients do try to understand why they developed cancer. Ninety-five percent of our respondents offered some explanation for why their cancer occurred. In an effort to have some comparison group against which to judge this rate, we also asked the spouses of these patients whether they had any theory about the cause of their partner's cancer. One would also expect spouses' rates of making attributions to be inflated, relative to an uninvolved person, since they, like the patients, have been strongly affected by the cancer experience. Nonetheless, their rate of making causal attributions was significantly less (63%), suggesting that the need for an explanation was more insistent among the patients themselves.

Does any particular form of the attributional explanation meet the search for meaning better than others? This question can be partially addressed by looking at the specific content of the cancer patients' explanations and then relating those explanations to overall psychological adjustment. The largest number (41%) attributed their cancer either to general stress or to a particular type of stress. When a particular stressor was mentioned, it was often either an ongoing problematic marriage or a recent divorce. Thirty-two percent of the sample attributed their cancer to some particular carcinogen, including ingested substances such as birth control pills, DES, or primarin (which is an estrogen replenisher prescribed for menopausal women) or to environmental carcinogens such as having lived near a chemical dump, a nuclear testing site, or a copper mine. Twenty-six percent of the women attributed their cancer to hereditary factors. Another 17% attributed it to diet (usually to a diet high in protein and fat and low in vegetables), and 10% blamed some blow to the breast such as an automobile accident, a fall, or in one case, being hit in the breast by a frisbee. (The numbers exceed 100% because a number of people had multiple theories.) It is noteworthy that with the exception of heredity, all of these causes are either past, rather than ongoing events, or they are events over which one currently has some control, such as stress or diet. This fact anticipates a point to be made shortly—that meaning and mastery may often be intertwined.

When one relates these specific attributions to overall psychological adjustment to the cancer, no single attribution stands out as more functional than any other. All are uncorrelated with adjustment. It would be premature to conclude from this information that these attributional explanations are functionally interchangeable. However, the high frequency of making attributions, coupled with the fact that no specific attribution produces better adjustment, suggests that causal meaning itself is the goal of the attributional search rather than the specific form through which it is realized.

The search for meaning involves not only understanding why the event occurred, but what its implications for one's life are now. Slightly over half of our respondents reported that the cancer experience had caused them to reappraise their lives. Here is one example from a 61-year-old woman:

> You can take a picture of what someone has done, but when you frame it, it becomes significant. I feel as if I were for the first time really conscious. My life is framed in a certain amount of time. I always knew it. But I can see it, and it's made better by the knowledge....

To summarize, the attempt to find meaning in the cancer experience takes at least two forms: a causal analysis that provides an answer to the question of why it happened and a rethinking of one's attitudes and priorities to restructure one's life along more satisfying lines, changes that are prompted by and attributed to the cancer.

GAINING A SENSE OF MASTERY

A sudden threatening event like cancer can easily undermine one's sense of control over one's body and one's life generally (e.g., Leventhal, 1975). Accordingly, a second theme of the adjustment process is gaining a feeling of control over the threatening event so as to manage it or keep it from occurring again. This theme of mastery is exemplified by beliefs about personal control.

Many cancer patients seem to solve the issue of mastery by believing that they personally can keep the cancer from coming back. Two thirds of the patients we interviewed believed they had at least some control over the course of or recurrence of their cancer, and 37% believed they had a lot of control. Some of the remaining one third believed that although they personally had no control over the cancer, it could be controlled by the doctor or by continued treatments. Hence, belief in direct control of the cancer is quite strong. Again, using the significant others as a comparison population, belief in both the patient's ability to control the cancer and the physician's ability to control the cancer are less strong, suggesting that mastery needs are greater among patients. Significantly, both the belief that one can control one's own cancer and the belief that the physician or treatments can control it are strongly associated with overall positive adjustment, and both together are even better.

Many of the patients' efforts at control were mental. One of the most common manifestations was a belief that a positive attitude would keep the cancer from coming back:

> I believe that if you're a positive person, your attitude has a lot to do with it. I definitely feel I will never get it again.

> My mental attitude, I think, is the biggest control over it I have. I want to feel there is something I can do, that there is some way I can control it.

> I think that if you feel you are in control of it, you can control it up to a point. I absolutely refuse to have any more cancer.

A substantial number attempted to control their cancer by using specific techniques of psychological control. These techniques included meditation, imaging, self-hypnosis, positive thinking, or a combination of factors. Many had read the Simonton and Simonton (1975) work suggesting that people can control their own cancers using these kinds of methods, and they saw no harm in trying them on their own; a number had great faith in them....

Although many patients have regained a sense of mastery by thinking about their cancer differently, others adopt direct behavioral efforts to keep the cancer from coming back. In a number of cases, patients made changes in their lives that both enabled them to reduce the likelihood of recurrence (they believed) and gave them something to control now. For some, these were dietary changes; a full 49% of our sample had changed their diet since the cancer bout, usually in the direction of adding fresh fruit and vegetables and cutting down on red meats and fats. For others, eliminating the medications they had taken like birth control pills or estrogen replenishers fulfilled the same function....

Attempting to control the side effects of one's treatments represents another effort at mastery. For example, 92% of the patients who received chemotherapy did something to control its side effects. For slightly under half, this involved simply medications or sleep, but the remaining half used a combination of mental efforts at control. These included imaging, self-hypnosis, distraction, and meditation. Similar efforts were made to control the less debilitating but still unpleasant side effects of radiation therapy. For example, one woman who was undergoing radiation therapy would imagine that there was a protective shield keeping her body from being burned by the radiation. Another woman imaged her chemotherapy as powerful cannons which blasted away pieces of the dragon, cancer. One 61-year-old woman simply focused her attention on healing with the instruction to her body, "Body, cut this... out."

A sense of mastery, then, can be achieved by believing that one can control the cancer by taking active steps that are perceived as directly controlling the cancer or by assuming control over related aspects of one's cancer, such as treatment. This belief in mastery and its relationship to adjustment ties in with a large body of literature indicating that manipulated feelings of control enhance coping with short-term aversive events (Averill, 1973; see Thompson, 1981, for a... review). The cancer patients' experiences suggest that self-generated feelings of control over a chronic condition can achieve the same beneficial effects.

THE PROCESS OF SELF-ENHANCEMENT

The third theme identified in our patients' adjustment process was an effort to enhance the self and restore self-esteem. Researchers exploring a range of threatening events from the death of one's child (Chodoff, Friedman, & Hamburg, 1964) to going on welfare (Briar, 1966) have documented the toll such events can take on self-regard. Even when the events can be legitimately attributed to external forces beyond the individual's control, there is often a precipitous drop in self-esteem. After experiencing such a drop, however, many individuals then initiate cognitive efforts to pull themselves back out of their low self-regard.

In some cases, esteem-enhancing cognitions are quite direct. During our interviews, we asked our respondents to describe any changes that had occurred in their lives since the cancer incident. To digress momentarily, I think people are always curious about how others change their lives when they have had a life-threatening experience. Popular images would have patients changing jobs, changing spouses, moving, or squandering all their money on a series of self-indulgent adventures. In fact, these major changes are fairly rare, and when they do occur, they are associated with unsuccessful overall adjustment. Frequently, a couple will have one "binge" such as taking a cruise or buying a Cadillac, but otherwise there are typically few overt dramatic changes. After people reported the changes they had experienced in their lives since cancer, we asked them to indicate whether those changes were positive or negative. Only 17% reported *any* negative changes in their lives. Fifty-three percent reported only positive changes; the remainder reported no changes. We also asked our patients to rate their emotional adjustment before any signs of cancer, at various points during the cancer bout, and at the time of the interview. Not only did patients see themselves as generally well adjusted at the time of the interview and as better adjusted than they were during the cancer bout, they also saw themselves as better adjusted than before they had any signs of cancer! When you consider that these women usually had had disfiguring surgery, had often had painful follow-up care, and had been seriously frightened and lived under the shadow of possible recurrence, this is a remarkable ability to construe personal benefit from potential tragedy.

Some of the most intriguing illusions that contribute to self-enhancement are generated by social comparisons (Festinger, 1954; Latané, 1966; Suls & Miller, 1977). Drawing on some provocative suggestions by Wortman and Dunkel-Schetter (1979) concerning cancer patients' needs for social comparison, we hypothesized that if we could identify the women's objects of comparison we could predict who would perceive themselves as coping well or badly. The media highlight people who are models of good adjustment to crises. With respect to breast cancer, women such as Betty Ford, Shirley Temple Black, or Marvella Bayh come to mind. We reasoned that such models might demoralize normal women by making them feel they were not doing well by comparison (Taylor & Levin, 1976). In contrast, comparisons with average women who might be experiencing a number of more negative reactions to cancer should yield more favorable self-evaluations. An alternative prediction derived from Festinger's (1954) social comparison theory (Wheeler, 1966) is that people will compare themselves with someone doing slightly better than they are—in other words, make upward comparisons in order to learn how to cope more effectively.

What we found conformed neither to our analysis nor to the upward comparison prediction (Wood, Taylor, & Lichtman, 1982). Instead, virtually all the women we interviewed thought they were doing as well as or somewhat better than other women coping with the same crisis. Only two said they were doing somewhat worse. If we had an unusually well-adjusted sample, of course, these perceptions could be vertical, but we know from other information that this was not true. These results suggest that these women are making downward comparisons, comparing themselves with women who were as fortunate or less fortunate than they. These results tie in with a more general body of literature recently brought together by Wills (1981) indicating that when faced with threat, individuals will usually make self-enhancing comparisons in an apparent effort to bolster self-esteem. Downward comparisons, then, would seem to be a fairly robust method of self-protection against threat.

In some cases, these downward comparisons were drawn explicitly. For example, one woman took great glee from the fact that her Reach to Recovery volunteer (the woman sent in by the American Cancer Society to serve as a model of good adjustment) seemed to be more poorly adjusted than she was. Despite some direct comparisons, however, many of the social comparisons seem to be made against hypothetical women.... It seems, then, that the need to come out of the comparison process appearing better off drives the process itself; the process does not determine the outcome. If a comparison person who makes one appear well adjusted is not available from personal experience, such a person may be manufactured.

Choice of comparison target is not the only way that social comparison processes can operate to enhance self-esteem. One must also consider the dimensions selected for evaluation. Conceivably, one could select a dimension that would make one appear more advantaged than others or one could select a dimension for evaluation that would put one at a disadvantage. . . .

In our study, several women with lumpectomies compared themselves favorably to women with mastectomies; no woman with a mastectomy ever evaluated herself against a woman with a lumpectomy. Older women considered themselves better off than younger women; no younger woman expressed the wish that she had been older. Married women pitied the single woman; no single woman pointed out that it would have been easier if she'd been married. The women who were the worst off consoled themselves with the fact that they were not dying or were not in pain. The amount of self-enhancement in these dimensional comparisons is striking. Not only choice of comparison target, then, but also choice of comparison dimension is important for restoring self-enhancement in the face of threat. The issue of dimension selection in social comparisons is one that has been almost entirely ignored in the social comparison literature. This would seem to be an important oversight, particularly for research that examines social comparisons made under threat (Taylor, Wood, & Lichtman, in press).

The fact that social comparison processes can be used to enhance oneself is important, because it meshes social psychological processes with clinically significant outcomes. However, these social comparisons appear to serve important functions other than just self-enhancement. Several researchers (e.g., Fazio, 1979; Singer, 1966) have made a distinction between social comparisons that are made to validate one's self-impression versus social comparisons that are drawn to construct self-impressions. The results just described can be construed as efforts to validate a favorable self-image. However, one can also see evidence of constructive social comparisons among the respondents. Specifically, some of the comparisons involved instances in which women selected as comparison objects other women who were worse off physically (such as women with nodal involvement, women with metastatic cancer, or women with double mastectomies) but who were coping very well. Such comparisons are self-enhancing, but they are also instructive and motivating. That is, the fact that women worse off are coping well seems to inspire the person drawing the comparison to try to do as well and to pattern her own behavior after the comparison person. These comparisons are particularly important because self-enhancement, and indeed cognitive illusion generally, is often written off as defensive and dysfunctional. Instead, these illusions may have multiple functions. In addition to self-enhancement, they can instill motivation and provide information, as these downward comparisons apparently did for some of our respondents (see Brickman & Bulman, 1977). . . .

What, then, can be learned from the analysis of cancer patients' comparative processes? These women made downward comparisons instead of upward ones, and appear to have selected their comparison persons to enhance their self-esteem rather than letting their self-esteem be determined by who was available for comparison. If other appropriate persons were not readily available for comparison, they manufactured a norm that other women were worse off than they were. The dimensions singled out for comparison were ones on which they appeared better, rather than worse, off. Physically disadvantaged but successful copers also were selected as models. One, then, has the best of both worlds: The comparisons enable one to feel better about oneself, but one does not lose the advantage of having a successful model on which to pattern one's efforts at adjustment....

CONCLUSION

... As a theoretical and empirical venture, cognitive adaptation theory is still in its infancy. It suggests a general strategy for studying adaptation to threatening events by focusing on multiple cognitively adaptive efforts simultaneously, rather than upon the adaptive value of particular cognitions in isolation. It also takes a stand against laboratory-based examinations of reactions to threat that fail to acknowledge the relation of particular cognitions to overriding goals or values. More specifically, the theory points to some directions for beginning research. Systematically documenting the themes of meaning, mastery, and self-enhancement in adjustment to threatening events other than cancer is an important empirical step. In this context, it is encouraging to note that evidence for each of the three themes—meaning (Chodoff et al., 1964; Frankl, 1963; Mechanic, 1977; Visotsky et al., 1961; Weisman & Worden, 1975), mastery (Bulman & Wortman, 1977; Janoff-Bulman, 1979; Rothbaum et al., 1982), and self-enhancement (Pearlin & Schooler, 1978; Wills, 1981)—has already been reported by investigators exploring misfortunes as varied as economic difficulty, marital problems, rape, and physical illness other than cancer. A second beginning line of research stems from the different predictions that cognitive adaptation theory generates for reactions to disconfirmation of cognitions, as compared with reactance or learned helplessness theory. The theory suggests, for example, that in field settings where people have multiple response options at their disposal, they will turn their frustrated efforts at control, understanding, or self-enhancement to tasks on which they are more likely to be successful....

My biologist acquaintances frequently note that the more they know about the human body, the more, not less, miraculous it seems. The recuperative powers of the mind merit similar awe. The process of cognitive adaptation to threat, though often time-consuming and not always successful, nonetheless restores many people to their prior level of functioning and inspires others to find new meaning in their lives. For this reason, cognitive adaptation occupies a special place in the roster of human capabilities.

REFERENCES

Averill, J. R. Personal control over aversive stimuli and its relationship to stress. *Psychological Bulletin*, 1973, *80*, 286–303.

Briar, S. Welfare from below: Recipient's views of the public welfare system. *California Law Review*, 1966, *54*, 370–385.

Brickman, P., & Bulman, R. J. Pleasure and pain in social comparison. In J. M. Suls & R. L. Miller (Eds.), *Social comparison processes: Theoretical and empirical perspectives*. Washington, D.C.: Hemisphere, 1977.

Bulman, R. J., & Wortman, C. B. Attributions of blame and coping in the "real world": Severe accident victims react to their lot. *Journal of Personality and Social Psychology*, 1977, *35*, 351–363.

Chodoff, P., Friedman, P. B., & Hamburg, D. A. Stress, defenses and coping behavior: Observations in parents of children with malignant disease. *American Journal of Psychiatry*, 1964, *120*, 743–749.

Fazio, R. H. Motives for social comparison: The construction-validation distinction. *Journal of Personality and Social Psychology*, 1979, *37*, 1683–1698.

Festinger, L. A theory of social comparison processes. *Human Relations*, 1954, *7*, 117–140.

Frankl, V. E. *Man's search for meaning*. New York: Washginton Square Press, 1963.

Gurin, G., Veroff, J., & Feld, S. *Americans view their mental health*. New York: Basic Books, 1960.

Heider, F. *The psychology of interpersonal relations*. New York: Wiley, 1958.

Janoff-Bulman, R. Characterological versus behavioral self-blame: Inquiries into depression and rape. *Journal of Personality and Social Psychology*, 1979, *37*, 1798–1809.

Kelley, H. H. Attribution theory in social psychology. In D. Levine (Ed.), *Nebraska Symposium on Motivation* (Vol. 15). Lincoln: University of Nebraska Press, 1967.

Latané, B. Studies in social comparison: Introduction and overview. *Journal of Experimental Social Psychology*, 1966, *Supplement 1*, 1–5.

Leventhal, H. The consequences of depersonalization during illness and treatment. In J. Howard & A. Strauss (Eds.), *Humanizing health care*. New York: Wiley, 1975.

Mechanic, D. Illness behavior, social adaptation, and the management of illness. *Journal of Nervous and Mental Disease*, 1977, *165*, 79–87.

Perlin, L. I., & Schooler, C. The structure of coping. *Journal of Health and Social Behavior*, 1978, *19*, 2–21.

Rothbaum, F., Weisz, J. R., & Snyder, S. S. Changing the world and changing the self: A two-process model of perceived control. *Journal of Personality and Social Psychology*, 1982, *42*, 5–37.

Silver, R. L., & Wortman, C. B. Coping with undesirable life events. In J. Garber & M. E. P. Seligman (Eds.), *Human helplessness: Theory and applications*. New York: Academic Press, 1980.

Simonton, O. C., & Simonton, S. Belief systems and management of the emotional aspects of malignancy. *Journal of Transpersonal Psychology*, 1975, *7*, 29–48.

Singer, J. E. Social comparison: Progress and issues. *Journal of Experimental Social Psychology*, 1966, *Supplement 1*, 103–110.

Suls, J. M., & Miller, R. L. M. *Social comparison processes: Theoretical and empirical perspectives*. New York: Wiley, 1977.

Taylor, S. E., & Levin, S. *The psychological impact of breast cancer: Theory and practice.* San Francisco: West Coast Cancer Foundation, 1976.

Taylor, S. E., Lichtman, R. R., & Wood, J. V., *Adjustment to breast cancer: Physical, socio-demographic, and psychological predictors,* Manuscript submitted for publication, 1982.

Taylor, S. E., Wood, J. V., & Lichtman, R. R. It could be worse: Selective evaluation as a response to victimization. *Journal of Social Issues,* in press.

Thompson, S. C. Will it hurt less if I can control it? A complex answer to a simple question. *Psychological Bulletin,* 1981, *90,* 89–101.

Visotsky, H. M., Hamburg, D. A., Goss, M. E., & Lebovits, B. Z. Coping behavior under extreme stress. *Archives of General Psychiatry,* 1961, *5,* 423–448.

Weisman, A. D., & Worden, J. W. Psychological analysis of cancer deaths. *Omega,* 1975, *6,* 61–75.

Wheeler, L. Motivation as a determinant of upward comparison. *Journal of Experimental Social Psychology,* 1966, *Supplement 1,* 27–31.

Wills, T. A. Downward comparison principles in social psychology. *Psychological Bulletin,* 1981, *90,* 245–271.

Wills, T. A. Social comparison and help-seeking. In B. M. DePaulo, A. Nadler, & J. D. Fisher (Eds.), *New directions in helping: Vol. 2. Help-seeking.* New York: Academic Press, 1982.

Wong, P. T. P., & Weiner, B. When people ask "why" questions, and the heuristics of attributional search. *Journal of Personality and Social Psychology,* 1981, *40,* 650–663.

Wortman, C. B., & Dunkel-Schetter, C. Interpersonal relationships and cancer: A theoretical analysis. *Journal of Social Issues,* 1979, *35,* 120–155.

Wood, J. V., Taylor, S. E., & Lichtman, R. R. *Social comparison processes in adjustment to cancer.* Manuscript submitted for publication, 1982.

PART SIX

Psychological Disorders

On the Internet . . .

Sites appropriate to Part Six

The Mental Health Infosource site provides information on a variety of psychological disorders.

    http://www.mhsource.com/disorders/

The American Psychological Association's HelpCenter site presents information on getting help with personal problems.

    http://helping.apa.org

The Freud Online Exhibition from the Library of Congress presents information on Sigmund Freud and his ideas.

    http://lcweb.loc.gov/exhibits/freud/
       preview.html

The About Humanistic Psychology site provides information and resources on humanistic psychologists, including Carl Rogers and Abraham Maslow.

    http://www.ahpweb.org/aboutahp/whatis.html

CHAPTER 13 Abnormal Behavior

13.1 D. L. ROSENHAN

On Being Sane in Insane Places

Mental health workers have devised various classification schemes to help them diagnose abnormal behaviors. Although this may be beneficial in the vast majority of cases, some psychologists worry that misdiagnosis can result in inappropriate treatments or stigmatization and that mental health workers therefore need to be extremely careful about labeling mental patients. Social psychologist David L. Rosenhan is a leading critic of the method in which patients are labeled in mental hospitals.

Rosenhan (b. 1929) earned his Ph.D. from Columbia University in 1958. He is currently a professor emeritus of psychology at Stanford University. Among his books is *Abnormal Psychology,* coauthored with Martin Seligman (W. W. Norton, 1995).

This selection is from "On Being Sane in Insane Places," which was published in *Science* in 1973. In it, Rosenhan describes his and others' experiences as pseudopatients (healthy people who secretly gained admission to mental hospitals as patients), and he discusses the implications of labeling mental patients as insane or as mentally ill. Rosenhan's article encouraged debate among mental health providers on diagnosis in clinical psychology that is still going on today. A readable article, it provides a good inside look at mental institutions as well as the labeling process. Although Rosenhan's research successfully persuaded psychologists to discuss the problems that come with diagnosing mental patients, some people have criticized the study as unethical. As you read this selection, consider what it must be like for mental patients to live in an institution.

Key Concept: labeling and the diagnosis of abnormal behavior

APA Citation: Rosenhan, D. L. (1973). On being sane in insane places. *Science, 179,* 250–258.

*I*f sanity and insanity exist, how shall we know them?

The question is neither capricious nor itself insane. However much we may be personally convinced that we can tell the normal from the abnormal, the evidence is simply not compelling. It is commonplace, for example, to read about murder trials wherein eminent psychiatrists for the defense are contradicted by equally eminent psychiatrists for the prosecution on the matter of the defendant's sanity. More generally, there are a great deal of conflicting data on the reliability, utility, and meaning of such terms as "sanity," "insanity," "mental illness," and "schizophrenia." Finally, as early as 1934, Benedict suggested that normality and abnormality are not universal (1). What is viewed as normal in one culture may be seen as quite aberrant in another. Thus, notions of normality and abnormality may not be quite as accurate as people believe they are.

To raise questions regarding normality and abnormality is in no way to question the fact that some behaviors are deviant or odd. Murder is deviant. So, too, are hallucinations. Nor does raising such questions deny the existence of the personal anguish that is often associated with "mental illness." Anxiety and depression exist. Psychological suffering exists. But normality and abnormality, sanity and insanity, and the diagnoses that flow from them may be less substantive than many believe them to be.

At its heart, the question of whether the sane can be distinguished from the insane (and whether degrees of insanity can be distinguished from each other) is a simple matter: do the salient characteristics that lead to diagnoses reside in the patients themselves or in the environments and contexts in which observers find them? . . . [T]he belief has been strong that patients present symptoms, that those symptoms can be categorized, and, implicitly, that the sane are distinguishable from the insane. More recently, however, this belief has been questioned. Based in part on theoretical and anthropological considerations, but also on philosophical, legal, and therapeutic ones, the view has grown that psychological categorization of mental illness is useless at best and downright harmful, misleading, and pejorative at worst. Psychiatric diagnoses, in this view, are in the minds of the observers and are not valid summaries of characteristics displayed by the observed.

Gains can be made in deciding which of these is more nearly accurate by getting normal people (that is, people who do not have, and have never suffered, symptoms of serious psychiatric disorders) admitted to psychiatric hospitals and then determining whether they were discovered to be sane and, if so, how. If the sanity of such pseudopatients were always detected, there would be prima facie evidence that a sane individual can be distinguished from the insane context in which he is found. Normality (and presumably abnormality) is distinct enough that it can be recognized wherever it occurs, for it is carried within the person. If, on the other hand, the sanity of the pseudopatients were never discovered, serious difficulties would arise for those who support traditional modes of psychiatric diagnosis. Given that the hospital staff was not incompetent, that the pseudopatient had been behaving as sanely as he had been outside of the hospital, and that it had never been previously suggested that he belonged in a psychiatric hospital, such an unlikely outcome would support the view that psychiatric diagnosis betrays little about the patient but much about the environment in which an observer finds him.

This article describes such an experiment. Eight sane people gained secret admission to 12 different hospitals. Their diagnostic experiences constitute the data of the first part of this article; the remainder is devoted to a description of their experiences in psychiatric institutions. Too few psychiatrists and psychologists, even those who have worked in such hospitals, know what the experience is like. They rarely talk about it with former patients, perhaps because they distrust information coming from the previously insane. Those who have worked in psychiatric hospitals are likely to have adapted so thoroughly to the settings that they are insensitive to the impact of the experience. And while there have been occasional reports of researchers who submitted themselves to psychiatric hospitalization (3), these researchers have commonly remained in the hospitals for short periods of time, often with the knowledge of the hospital staff. It is difficult to know the extent to which they were treated like patients or like research colleagues. Nevertheless, their reports about the inside of the psychiatric hospital have been valuable. This article extends those efforts.

PSEUDOPATIENTS AND THEIR SETTINGS

The eight pseudopatients were a varied group. One was a psychology graduate student in his 20's. The remaining seven were older and "established." Among them were three psychologists, a pediatrician, a psychiatrist, a painter, and a housewife. Three pseudopatients were women, five were men. All of them employed pseudonyms, lest their alleged diagnoses embarrass them later. Those who were in mental health professions alleged another occupation in order to avoid the special attentions that might be accorded by staff, as a matter of courtesy or caution, to ailing colleagues. With the exception of myself (I was the first pseudopatient and my presence was known to the hospital administrator and chief psychologist and, so far as I can tell, to them alone), the presence of pseudopatients and the nature of the research program was not known to the hospital staffs.

The settings were similarly varied. In order to generalize the findings, admission into a variety of hospitals was sought. The 12 hospitals in the sample are located in five different states on the East and West coasts. Some were old and shabby, some were quite new. Some were research-oriented, others not. Some had good staff-patient ratios, others were quite understaffed. Only one was a strictly private hospital. All the others were supported by state or federal funds or, in one instance, by university funds.

After calling the hospital for an appointment, the pseudopatient arrived at the admissions office complaining that he had been hearing voices. Asked what the voices said, he replied that they were often unclear, but as far as he could tell they said "empty," "hollow," and "thud." The voices were unfamiliar and were of the same sex as the pseudopatient. The choice of these symptoms was occasioned by their apparent similarity to existential symptoms. Such symptoms were alleged to arise from painful concerns about the perceived meaninglessness of one's life. It is as if the hallucinating person were saying, "My life is empty and hollow." The choice of these symptoms was also determined by the *absence* of a single report of existential psychoses in the literature.

Beyond alleging the symptoms and falsifying name, vocation, and employment, no further alterations of person, history, or circumstances were made. The significant events of the pseudopatient's life history were presented as they had actually occurred. Relationships with parents and siblings, with spouse and children, with people at work and in school, consistent with the aforementioned exceptions, were described as they were or had been. Frustrations and upsets were described along with joys and satisfactions. These facts are important to remember. If anything, they strongly biased the subsequent results in favor of detecting sanity, since none of their histories or current behaviors were seriously pathological in any way.

Immediately upon admission to the psychiatric ward, the pseudopatient ceased simulating *any* symptoms of abnormality. In some cases, there was a brief period of mild nervousness and anxiety, since none of the pseudopatients really believed that they would be admitted so easily. Indeed their shared fear was that they would be immediately exposed as frauds and greatly embarrassed. Moreover, many of them had never visited a psychiatric ward; even those who had, nevertheless, had some genuine fears about what might happen to them. Their nervousness, then, was quite appropriate to the novelty of the hospital setting, and it abated rapidly.

Apart from that short-lived nervousness, the pseudopatient behaved on the ward as he "normally" behaved. The pseudopatient spoke to patients and staff as he might ordinarily. Because there is uncommonly little to do on a psychiatric ward, he attempted to engage others in conversation. When asked by staff how he was feeling, he indicated that he was fine, that he no longer experienced symptoms. He responded to instructions from attendants, to calls for medication (which was not swallowed), and to dining-hall instructions. Beyond such activities as were available to him on the admissions ward, he spent his time writing down his observations about the ward, its patients, and the staff. Initially these notes were written "secretly," but as it soon became clear that no one much cared, they were subsequently written on standard tablets of paper in such public places as the dayroom. No secret was made of these activities.

The pseudopatient, very much as a true psychiatric patient, entered a hospital with no foreknowledge of when he would be discharged. Each was told that he would have to get out by his own devices, essentially by convincing the staff that he was sane. The psychological stresses associated with hospitalization were considerable, and all but one of the pseudopatients desired to be discharged almost immediately after being admitted. They were, therefore, motivated not only to behave sanely, but to be paragons of cooperation. That their behavior was in no way disruptive is confirmed by nursing reports, which have been obtained on most of the patients. These reports uniformly indicate that the patients were "friendly," "cooperative," and "exhibited no abnormal indications."

THE NORMAL ARE NOT DETECTABLY SANE

Despite their public "show" of sanity, the pseudopatients were never detected. Admitted, except in one case, with a diagnosis of schizophrenia, each was discharged with a diagnosis of schizophrenia "in remission." The label "in remission" should in no way be dismissed as a formality, for at no time during any hospitalization had any question been raised about any pseudopatient's simulation. Nor are there any indications in the hospital records that the pseudopatient's status was suspect. Rather, the evidence is strong that, once labeled schizophrenic, the pseudopatient was stuck with that label. If the pseudopatient was to be discharged, he must naturally be "in remission"; but he was not sane, nor, in the institution's view, had he ever been sane.

The uniform failure to recognize sanity cannot be attributed to the quality of the hospitals, for, although there were considerable variations among them, several are considered excellent. Nor can it be alleged that there was simply not enough time to observe the pseudopatients. Length of hospitalization ranged from 7 to 52 days, with an average of 19 days. The pseudopatients were not, in fact, carefully observed, but this failure clearly speaks more to traditions within psychiatric hospitals than to lack of opportunity.

Finally, it cannot be said that the failure to recognize the pseudopatients' sanity was due to the fact that they were not behaving sanely. While there was clearly some tension present in all of them, their daily visitors could detect no serious behavioral consequences—nor, indeed, could other patients. It was quite common for the patients to "detect" the pseudopatients' sanity. During the first three hospitalizations, when accurate counts were kept, 35 of a total of 118 patients on the admissions ward voiced their suspicions, some vigorously. "You're not crazy. You're a journalist, or a professor [referring to the continual note-taking]. You're checking up on the hospital." While most of the patients were reassured by the pseudopatient's insistence that he had been sick before he came in but was fine now, some continued to believe that the pseudopatient was sane throughout his hospitalization. The fact that the patients often recognized normality when staff did not raises important questions.

Failure to detect sanity during the course of hospitalization may be due to the fact that physicians operate with a strong bias toward what statisticians call the type 2 error (2). This is to say that physicians are more inclined to call a healthy person sick (a false positive, type 2) than a sick person healthy (a false negative, type 1). The reasons for this are not hard to find: it is clearly more dangerous to misdiagnose illness than health. Better to err on the side of caution, to suspect illness even among the healthy.

But what holds for medicine does not hold equally well for psychiatry. Medical illnesses, while unfortunate, are not commonly pejorative. Psychiatric diagnoses, on the contrary, carry with them personal, legal, and social stigmas (4)....

THE STICKINESS OF PSYCHODIAGNOSTIC LABELS

Beyond the tendency to call the healthy sick—a tendency that accounts better for diagnostic behavior on admission than it does for such behavior after a lengthy period of exposure—the data speak to the massive role of labeling in psychiatric assessment. Having once been labeled schizophrenic, there is nothing the pseudopatient can do to overcome this tag. The tag profoundly colors others' perceptions of him and his behavior....

Once a person is designated abnormal, all of his other behaviors and characteristics are colored by that label. Indeed, that label is so powerful that many of the pseudopatients' normal behaviors were overlooked entirely or profoundly misinterpreted....

All pseudopatients took extensive notes publicly. Under ordinary circumstances, such behavior would have raised questions in the minds of observers, as, in fact, it did among patients. Indeed, it seemed so certain that the notes would elicit suspicion that elaborate precautions were taken to remove them from the ward each day. But the precautions proved needless. The closest any staff member came to questioning these notes occurred when one pseudopatient asked his physician what kind of medication he was receiving and began to write down the response. "You needn't write it," he was told gently. "If you have trouble remembering, just ask me again."

If no questions were asked of the pseudopatients, how was their writing interpreted? Nursing records for three patients indicate that the writing was seen as an aspect of their pathological behavior. "Patient engages in writing behavior" was the daily nursing comment on one of the pseudopatients who was never questioned about his writing. Given that the patient is in the hospital, he must be psychologically disturbed. And given that he is disturbed, continuous writing must be a behavioral manifestation of that disturbance, perhaps a subset of the compulsive behaviors that are sometimes correlated with schizophrenia....

A psychiatric label has a life and an influence of its own. Once the impression has been formed that the patient is schizophrenic, the expectation is that he will continue to be schizophrenic. When a sufficient amount of time has passed, during which the patient has done nothing bizarre, he is considered to be in remission and available for discharge. But the label endures beyond discharge, with the unconfirmed expectation that he will behave as a schizophrenic again. Such labels, conferred by mental health professionals, are as influential on the patient as they are on his relatives and friends, and it should not surprise anyone that the diagnosis acts on all of them as a self-fulfilling prophecy. Eventually, the patient himself accepts the diagnosis, with all of its surplus meanings and expectations, and behaves accordingly (5).... If it makes no sense to label ourselves permanently depressed on the basis of an occasional depression, then it takes better evidence than is presently available to label all patients insane or schizophrenic on the basis of bizarre behaviors or cognitions. It seems more useful, as Mischel (5) has pointed out, to limit our discussions to *behaviors*, the stimuli that provoke them, and their correlates.... I may hallucinate because I am sleeping, or I may hallucinate because I have ingested a peculiar drug. These are termed sleep-induced hallucinations, or dreams, and drug-induced hallucinations, respectively. But when the stimuli to my hallucinations are unknown, that is called craziness, or schizophrenia—as if that inference were somehow as illuminating as the others....

SUMMARY AND CONCLUSIONS

It is clear that we cannot distinguish the sane from the insane in psychiatric hospitals. The hospital itself imposes a special environment in which the meanings of behavior can easily be misunderstood. The consequences to patients hospitalized in such an environment—the powerlessness, depersonalization, segregation, mortification, and self-labeling—seem undoubtedly countertherapeutic.

I do not, even now, understand this problem well enough to perceive solutions. But two matters seem to have some promise. The first concerns the proliferation of community mental health facilities, of crisis intervention centers, of the human potential movement, and of behavior therapies that, for all of their own problems, tend to avoid psychiatric labels, to focus on specific problems and behaviors, and to retain the individual in a relatively nonpejorative environment. Clearly, to the extent that we refrain from sending the distressed to insane places, our impressions of them are less likely to be distorted. (The risk of distorted perceptions, it seems to me, is always present, since we are much more sensitive to an individual's behaviors and verbalizations than we are to the subtle contextual stimuli that often promote them. At issue here is a matter of magnitude. And, as I have shown, the magnitude of distortion is exceedingly high in the extreme context that is a psychiatric hospital).

The second matter that might prove promising speaks to the need to increase the sensitivity of mental health workers and researchers to the *Catch 22* position of psychiatric patients. Simply reading materials in this area will be of help to some such workers and researchers. For others, directly experiencing the impact of psychiatric hospitalization will be of enormous use. Clearly, further research into the social psychology of such total institutions will both facilitate treatment and deepen understanding.

NOTES

1. R. Benedict, *J. Gen. Psychol.* **10**, 59 (1934).

2. T. J. Scheff, *Being Mentally Ill: A Sociological Theory* (Aldine, Chicago, 1966).

3. A. Barry, *Bellevue Is a State of Mind* (Harcourt Brace Jovanovich, New York, 1971); . . .

4. J. Cumming and E. Cumming, *Community Ment. Health* **1**, 135 (1965); . . .

5. W. Mischel, *Personality and Assessment* (Wiley, New York, 1968).

13.2 SIGMUND FREUD

Inhibitions, Symptoms and Anxiety

Anxiety is a part of everyone's life. Much of what psychologists know about anxiety has been shaped by the views of Sigmund Freud. Freud developed the psychoanalytic approach to psychological disorders, and anxiety was one of his cornerstones.

Freud (1856–1939), an Austrian neurologist, obtained his M.D. in 1881 from the University of Vienna. Through his medical practice, he began to study patients' mental disorders. In doing so, he employed his theory of psychoanalysis, which emphasizes past experiences and unconscious motivations as the determinants of personality.

This selection is from Freud's book *Inhibitions, Symptoms and Anxiety* (W. W. Norton, 1926). In it, Freud describes the symptoms of anxiety and discusses the functions of anxiety. He argues that anxiety is a reaction to danger and occurs whenever one perceives danger. Notice how he focuses on early experiences (e.g., birth) to explain the origins of anxiety. As you read this selection, think about what causes anxiety in your life. What do you think the function of anxiety might be?

Key Concept: anxiety disorders

APA Citation: Freud, S. (1926). *Inhibitions, symptoms, and anxiety.* New York: Norton. (c 1959 Norton Trans. by Alix Strachey)

*A*nxiety . . . is in the first place something that is felt. We call it an affective state, although we are also ignorant of what an affect is. As a feeling, anxiety has a very marked character of unpleasure. But that is not the whole of its quality. Not every unpleasure can be called anxiety, for there are other feelings, such as tension, pain or mourning, which have the character of unpleasure. Thus anxiety must have other distinctive features besides this quality of unpleasure. Can we succeed in understanding the differences between these various unpleasurable affects?

We can at any rate note one or two things about the feeling of anxiety. Its unpleasurable character seems to have a note of its own—something not very obvious, whose presence is difficult to prove yet which is in all likelihood there. But besides having this special feature which is difficult to isolate, we notice that anxiety is accompanied by fairly definite physical sensations which can be referred to particular organs of the body. As we are not concerned here with the physiology of anxiety, we shall content ourselves with mentioning a few representatives of these sensations. The clearest and most frequent ones are those connected with the respiratory organs and with the heart. They provide evidence that motor innervations—that is, processes of discharge—play a part in the general phenomenon of anxiety.

Analysis of anxiety-states therefore reveals the existence of (1) a specific character of unpleasure, (2) acts of discharge and (3) perceptions of those acts. The two last points indicate at once a difference between states of anxiety and other similar states, like those of mourning and pain. The latter do not have any motor manifestation; or if they have, the manifestation is not an integral part of the whole state but is distinct from it as being a result of it or a reaction to it. Anxiety, then, is a special state of unpleasure with acts of discharge along particular paths. In accordance with our general views we should be inclined to think that anxiety is based upon an increase of excitation which on the one hand produces the character of unpleasure and on the other finds relief through the acts of discharge already mentioned. But a purely physiological account of this sort will scarcely satisfy us. We are tempted to assume the presence of a historical factor which binds the sensations of anxiety and its innervations firmly together. We assume, in other words, that an anxiety-state is the reproduction of some experience which contained the necessary conditions for such an increase of excitation and a discharge along particular paths, and that from this circumstance the unpleasure of anxiety receives its specific character. In man, birth provides a prototypic experience of this kind, and we are therefore inclined to regard anxiety-states as a reproduction of the trauma of birth.

This does not imply that anxiety occupies an exceptional position among the affective states. In my opinion the other affects are also reproductions of very early, perhaps even pre-individual, experiences of vital importance; and I should be inclined to regard them as universal, typical and innate hysterical attacks, as compared to the recently and individually acquired attacks which occur in hysterical neuroses and whose origin and significance as mnemic symbols have been revealed by analysis. It would be very desirable, of course, to be able to demonstrate the truth of this view in a number of such affects—a thing which is still very far from being the case.

The view that anxiety goes back to the event of birth raises immediate objections which have to be met. It may be argued that anxiety is a reaction which, in all probability, is common to every organism, certainly every organism of a higher order, whereas birth is only experienced by the mammals; and it is doubtful whether in all of them, even, birth has the significance of a trauma. Therefore there can be anxiety without the prototype of birth. But this objection takes us beyond the barrier that divides psychology from biology. It may be that, precisely because anxiety has an indispensable biological function to fulfil as a reaction to a state of danger, it is differently contrived in different organisms. We do not know, besides, whether anxiety involves the same sensations and innervations in organisms far removed from man as it does in man himself.

Thus there is no good argument here against the view that, in man, anxiety is modelled upon the process of birth.

If the structure and origin of anxiety are as described, the next question is: what is the function of anxiety and on what occasions is it reproduced? The answer seems to be obvious and convincing: anxiety arose originally as a reaction to a state of *danger* and it is reproduced whenever a state of that kind recurs.

This answer, however, raises further considerations. The innervations involved in the original state of anxiety probably had a meaning and purpose, in just the same way as the muscular movements which accompany a first hysterical attack. In order to understand a hysterical attack, all one has to do is to look for the situation in which the movements in question formed part of an appropriate and expedient action. Thus at birth it is probable that the innervation, in being directed to the respiratory organs, is preparing the way for the activity of the lungs, and, in accelerating the heartbeat, is helping to keep the blood free from toxic substances. Naturally, when the anxiety-state is reproduced later as an affect it will be lacking in any such expediency, just as are the repetitions of a hysterical attack. When the individual is placed in a new situation of danger it may well be quite inexpedient for him to respond with an anxiety-state (which is a reaction to an earlier danger) instead of initiating a reaction appropriate to the current danger. But his behavior may become expedient once more if the danger-situation is recognized as it approaches and is signalled by an outbreak of anxiety. In that case he can at once get rid of his anxiety by having recourse to more suitable measures. Thus we see that there are two ways in which anxiety can emerge: in an inexpedient way, when a new situation of danger has occurred, or in an expedient way in order to give a signal and prevent such a situation from occurring.

But what is a 'danger'? In the act of birth there is a real danger to life. We know what this means objectively; but in a psychological sense it says nothing at all to us. The danger of birth has as yet no psychical content. We cannot possibly suppose that the foetus has any sort of knowledge that there is a possibility of its life being destroyed. It can only be aware of some vast disturbance in the economy of its narcissistic libido. Large sums of excitation crowd in upon it, giving rise to new kinds of feelings of unpleasure, and some organs acquire an increased cathexis, thus foreshadowing the object-cathexis which will soon set in. What elements in all this will be made use of as the sign of a 'danger-situation'?

Unfortunately far too little is known about the mental make-up of a newborn baby to make a direct answer possible. I cannot even vouch for the validity of the description I have just given. It is easy to say that the baby will repeat its affect of anxiety in every situation which recalls the event of birth. The important thing to know is what recalls the event and what it is that is recalled.

All we can do is to examine the occasions on which infants in arms or somewhat older children show readiness to produce anxiety. In his book on the trauma of birth, Rank (1924) has made a determined attempt to establish a relationship between the earliest phobias of children and the impressions made on them by the event of birth. But I do not think he has been successful. His theory is open to two objections. In the first place, he assumes that the infant has received certain sensory impressions, in particular of a visual kind, at the time of birth, the renewal of which can recall to its memory the trauma of birth and thus evoke a reaction of anxiety. This assumption is quite unfounded and extremely improbable. It is not credible that a child should retain any but tactile and general sensations relating to the process of birth. If, later on, children show fear of small animals that disappear into holes or emerge from them, this reaction, according to Rank, is due to their perceiving an analogy. But it is an analogy of which they cannot be aware. In the second place, in considering these later anxiety-situations Rank dwells, as suits him best, now on the child's recollection of its happy intra-uterine existence, now on its recollection of the traumatic disturbance which interrupted that existence—which leaves the door wide open for arbitrary interpretation. There are, moreover, certain examples of childhood anxiety which directly traverse his theory. When, for instance, a child is left alone in the dark one would expect it, according to his view, to welcome the re-establishment of the intra-uterine situation; yet it is precisely on such occasions that the child reacts with anxiety. And if this is explained by saying that the child is being reminded of the interruption which the event of birth made in its intra-uterine happiness, it becomes impossible to shut one's eyes any longer to the far-fetched character of such explanations.

I am driven to the conclusion that the earliest phobias of infancy cannot be directly traced back to impressions of the act of birth and that so far they have not been explained. A certain preparedness for anxiety is undoubtedly present in the infant in arms. But this preparedness for anxiety, instead of being at its maximum immediately after birth and then slowly decreasing, does not emerge till later, as mental development proceeds, and lasts over a certain period of childhood. If these early phobias persist beyond that period one is inclined to suspect the presence of a neurotic disturbance, although it is not at all clear what their relation is to the undoubted neuroses that appear later on in childhood.

Only a few of the manifestations of anxiety in children are comprehensible to us, and we must confine our attention to them. They occur, for instance, when a child is alone, or in the dark, or when it finds itself with an unknown person instead of one to whom it is used—such as its mother. These three instances can be reduced to a single condition—namely, that of missing someone who is loved and longed for. But here, I think, we have the key to an understanding of anxiety and to a reconciliation of the contradictions that seem to beset it.

The child's mnemic image of the person longed for is no doubt intensely cathected, probably in a hallucinatory way at first. But this has no effect; and now it seems as though the longing turns into anxiety. This anxiety has all the appearance of being an expression of the child's feeling at its wits' end, as though in its still very undeveloped state it did not know how better to cope with its cathexis of longing. Here anxiety appears as a reaction to the felt loss of the object; and we are at once reminded of the fact that castration anxiety, too, is a fear of being separated from a highly valued object, and that the earliest anxiety of all—the 'primal anxiety' of birth—is brought about on the occasion of a separation from the mother.

But a moment's reflection takes us beyond this question of loss of object. The reason why the infant in arms wants to perceive the presence of its mother is only because it already knows by experience that she satisfies all its needs without delay. The situation, then, which it regards as a 'danger' and against which it wants to be safeguarded is that of non-satisfaction, of a *growing tension due to need*, against which it is helpless. I think that if we adopt this view all the facts fall into place. The situation of non-satisfaction in which the amounts of stimulation rise to an unpleasurable height without its being possible for them to be mastered psychically or discharged must for the infant be analogous to the experience of being born—must be a repetition of the situation of danger. What both situations have in common is the economic disturbance caused by an accumulation of amounts of stimulation which require to be disposed of. It is this factor, then, which is the real essence of the 'danger'. In both cases the reaction of anxiety sets in. (This reaction is still an expedient one in the infant in arms, for the discharge, being directed into the respiratory and vocal muscular apparatus, now calls its mother to it, just as it activated the lungs of the new-born baby to get rid of the internal stimuli.) It is unnecessary to suppose that the child carries anything more with it from the time of its birth than this way of indicating the presence of danger.

When the infant has found out by experience that an external, perceptible object can put an end to the dangerous situation which is reminiscent of birth, the content of the danger it fears is displaced from the economic situation on to the condition which determined that situation, viz., the loss of object. It is the absence of the mother that is now the danger; and as soon as that danger arises the infant gives the signal of anxiety, before the dreaded economic situation has set in. This change constitutes a first great step forward in the provision made by the infant for its self-preservation, and at the same time represents a transition from the automatic and involuntary fresh appearance of anxiety to the intentional reproduction of anxiety as a signal of danger.

Depression

Depression is a very serious mental disorder, and a number of different the-oretical explanations of depression have been proposed. In the mid-1970s, Martin E. P. Seligman proposed the learned helplessness model of depression. This theory suggests that when people come to feel that they have no control over a situation, they feel helpless and tend to give up; they passively accept adverse stimuli. This helplessness can lead to depression.

Seligman (b. 1942) received his Ph.D. in psychology in 1967 from the University of Pennsylvania, where he is currently a professor of psychology. In addition to depression, Seligman has also had an impact on psychology in the areas of learning theory, phobias, and personality and adjustment.

This selection is from chapter 5, "Depression," of Seligman's *Helplessness: On Depression, Development, and Death* (W. H. Freeman, 1975). In it, Seligman describes the causes of, consequences of, and treatments for learned helplessness. Note the emphasis Seligman places on common, everyday occurrences and their role in inducing helplessness. As you read this selection, consider how you react to frustrating situations.

Key Concept: learned helplessness

APA Citation: Seligman, M. E. P. (1975). *Helplessness.* San Francisco: Freeman.

*L*earned helplessness is caused by learning that responding is independent of reinforcement; so the model suggests that the cause of depression is the belief that action is futile. What kind of events set off reactive depressions? Failure at work and school, death of a loved one, rejection or separation from friends and loved ones, physical disease, financial difficulty, being faced with insoluble problems, and growing old. There are many others, but this list captures the flavor.

I believe that what links these experiences and lies at the heart of depression is unitary: the depressed patient believes or has learned that he cannot control those elements of his life that relieve suffering, bring gratification, or provide nurture—in short, he believes that he is helpless. Consider a few of the precipitating events: What is the meaning of job failure or incompetence at school? Often it means that all of a person's efforts have been in vain, that his responses have failed to achieve his desires. When an individual is rejected by someone he loves, he can no longer control this significant source of gratification and support. When a parent or lover dies, the bereaved is powerless to elicit love from the dead person. Physical disease and growing old are helpless conditions par excellence; the person finds his own responses ineffective and is thrown upon the care of others.

Endogenous depressions [caused by internal factors], while not set off by an explicit helplessness-inducing event, also may involve the belief in helplessness. I suspect that a continuum of susceptibility to this belief may underlie the endogenous-reactive continuum. At the extreme endogenous end, the slightest obstacle will trigger in the depressive a vicious circle of beliefs in how ineffective he is. At the extreme reactive ends, a sequence of disastrous events in which a person is actually helpless is necessary to force the belief that responding is useless. . . .

Is depression a cognitive or an emotional disorder? Neither and both. Clearly, cognitions of helplessness lower mood, and a lowered mood, which may be brought about physiologically, increases susceptibility to cognitions of helplessness; indeed, this is the most insidious vicious circle in depression. In the end, I believe that the cognition-emotion distinction in depression will be untenable. Cognition and emotion need not be separable entities in nature simply because our language separates them. When depression is observed close up, the exquisite interdependence of feelings and thought is undeniable: one does not *feel* depressed without depressing thoughts, nor does one have depressing thoughts without feeling depressed. I suggest that it is a failure of language, not a failure of understanding, that has fostered the confusion about whether depression is a cognitive or an emotional disorder. . . .

In the last few years, many of my students have come to tell me that they felt depressed. Often they attributed their depression to their belief that life had no intrinsic meaning, that the Vietnam war would never end, that the poor and the black are oppressed, or that our leaders are corrupt. These are legitimate concerns and to devote so much thought and energy to them is certainly justifiable. But was the feeling, the actual depression, caused directly by these issues? Clearly, for a poor person, a black, or a student about to be drafted, these propositions could directly cause depression. But most of those I saw were neither poor, nor black, nor about to be drafted; these propositions were remote from their daily lives. Yet they said they were depressed about them—not just concerned or angry, but depressed. To me, this meant that they were feeling bad about something much closer to home, bad about themselves, their capacities, and their daily lives. Such existential depressions are rampant today, I daresay much more than when I was a student ten years ago.

At first it seems paradoxical. More of the good things of life are available now than ever before: more sex, more records, more intellectual stimulation, more books, more buying power. On the other hand, there have always been wars, oppression, corruption, and absurdity; the human condition has been pretty stable along these lines. Why should this particularly fortunate generation find itself especially depressed?

I think the answer may lie in the lack of contingency between the actions of these students and the good things, as well as the negative events, that came their way. These reinforcers came about less through the efforts of the young individuals who benefited from them, than because our society is affluent. They have experienced a minimum of hard work followed by reward. From where does one get a sense of power, worth, and self-esteem? Not from what he owns, but from long experience watching his own actions change the world.

I am claiming, then, that not only trauma occurring independently of response, but noncontingent *positive* events, can produce helplessness and depression. After all, what is the evolutionary significance of mood? Presumably sentient organisms could just as well be constructed without mood—complex computers are. What selective pressure produced feeling and affect? It may be that the hedonic [pleasure] system evolved to goad and fuel instrumental action. I suggest that joy accompanies and motivates effective responding; and that in the absence of effective responding, an aversive state arises, which organisms seek to avoid. It is called depression. It is highly significant that when rats and pigeons are given a choice between getting free food and getting the same food for making responses, they choose to work. Infants smile at a mobile whose movements are contingent on their responses, but not at a noncontingent mobile. Do hunters hunt from a lust to kill or mountain climbers scale peaks for glory? I think not. These activities, because they entail effective instrumental responding, produce joy.

Dysphoria [a state of feeling unwell or unhappy] produced by the cessation of effective responding may explain "success depression." Not infrequently, when a person finally achieves a goal toward which he has been striving for years, depression ensues. Officials elected to public office after arduous campaigns, presidents of the American Psychological Association, successful novelists, and even men who land on the moon can become severely depressed soon after achieving the pinnacle. For a theory of depression by loss of reinforcers, these depressions are paradoxical, since successful individuals continue to receive most of their old reinforcers, plus more new reinforcers than ever before.

This phenomenon is not a paradox for the theory of helplessness. Depressed, successful people tell you that they are now rewarded not for what they're doing, but for who they are or what they *have* done. Having achieved the goal that they strove for, their rewards now come independently of any ongoing instrumental activity. . . .

In summary, I suggest that what produces self-esteem and a sense of competence, and protects against depression, is not only the absolute quality of experience, but the perception that one's own actions controlled the experience. To the degree that uncontrollable events occur, either traumatic or positive, depression will be predisposed and ego strength undermined. To the degree that controllable events occur, a sense of mastery and resistance to depression will result.

Forced exposure to the fact that responding produces reinforcement is the most effective way of breaking up learned helplessness. Helplessness also dissipates in *time*. Furthermore, two physiological therapies seem to have an effect: electroconvulsive shock (ECS) broke up helplessness in three out of six dogs, and atropine cannulated to the septum broke it up in cats.

There is no scientifically established panacea for depression. Left alone, depression often dissipates in a few weeks or months; but there are therapies that are reported to alleviate depression and that are consistent with the theory of learned helplessness. According to this view, the central goal in successful therapy should be to have the patient come to believe that his responses produce the gratification he desires—that he is, in short, an effective human being. ....

A. T. Beck's (1970, 1971) cognitive therapy is aimed at similar goals. In his view, successful manipulations change the negative cognitive set to a more positive one: he argues that the primary task of the therapist is to change the negative expectation of the depressed patient to a more optimistic one, in which the patient comes to believe that his responses will produce the outcomes he wants. ....

Other therapies are claimed to be successful in alleviating depression and providing the patient with control over important outcomes. The "Tuscaloosa Plan" of a Veterans Administration hospital in Alabama puts severely depressed patients in an "anti-depression room." In this room the patient is subjected to an attitude of "kind firmness": He is told to sand a block of wood, and then reprimanded when he sands against the grain. He then sands with the grain, only to be reprimanded for that. Alternatively, he is told to begin counting about a million little seashells scattered about the room. This systematic harassment continues until the depressed patient finally tells the guard "Get off my back!" or says something like "I've counted my last seashell." He is then promptly let out of the room with apologies. The patient has been forced to emit one of the most powerful responses people have for controlling others—anger, and when this response is dragged out of his depleted repertoire, he is powerfully reinforced. This breaks up depression—lastingly.

Gradual exposure to the response-reinforcement contingencies of work reinforces active behaviors, and may be effective against depression. In a graded-task treatment of depression, E. P. Burgess (1968) first had her patients emit some minimal bit of behavior, like making a telephone call. She emphasizes that it is crucial that the patient succeed, rather than just start and give up. The task requirements were then increased, and the patient was reinforced for successfully completing the tasks by the attention and interest of the therapist. ....

Individuals often adopt their own strategies for dealing with their own minor depressions. Asking for help and getting it or helping someone else (even caring for a pet) are two strategies that entail gaining control and may alleviate minor depressions. ....

Many therapies... claim to be able to cure depression. But we do not yet have sufficient evidence from well-controlled studies to evaluate the effectiveness of any form of psychotherapy for depression. The evidence I have presented is selected: only those treatments that seem compatible with helplessness were discussed. It is possible that when other therapies work it is because they, too, restore the patient's sense of efficacy. What is needed now is experimental evidence isolating the effective variable in the psychological treatment of depression. It is also essential that untreated control groups be run, since depression dissipates in time, of its own accord.

PREVENTION OF DEPRESSION AND LEARNED HELPLESSNESS

Learned helplessness can be prevented if the subject first masters outcomes before being exposed to their uncontrollability. Can depression be prevented? Almost everyone loses control over some of the outcomes that are significant to him: parents die, loved ones reject him, failure occurs. Everyone becomes at least mildly and transiently depressed in the wake of such events, but why are some people hospitalized by depression for long periods, and others so resilient?...

The life histories of those individuals who are particularly resistant to depression, or resilient from depression, may have been filled with mastery; these people may have had extensive experience controlling and manipulating the sources of reinforcement in their lives, and may therefore see the future optimistically. Those people who are particularly susceptible to depression may have had lives relatively devoid of mastery; their lives may have been full of situations in which they were helpless to influence their sources of suffering and relief....

A caveat is in order here, however. While it seems reasonable that extended experience with controllable outcomes will make a person more resilient from depression, how about the person who has met only with success? Is a person whose responses have always succeeded especially susceptible to depression when confronted with situations beyond his control? We all know of people who were stunningly successful in high school, but who collapsed on encountering their first failure in college. Everyone eventually confronts failure and anxiety; too much success with controlling reinforcers, just like too little, might not allow the development and use of responses for coping with failure.

Successful therapy should be preventative. Therapy must not focus just on undoing past problems; it should also arm the patient against future depressions. Would therapy for depression be more successful if it strove explicitly to provide the patient with a wide repertoire of coping responses that he could use at times when he found his usual responses ineffective?

CHAPTER 14 Therapy

14.1 CARL R. ROGERS

Some Hypotheses Regarding the Facilitation of Personal Growth

Insight therapy is designed to help people gain an understanding of who they are and why they feel the way they do. One popular type of insight therapy is person-centered therapy (formerly called "client-centered therapy"), which was founded by Carl R. Rogers. The main assumption of person-centered therapy is that everyone has the capacity to be psychologically healthy. The therapist's role is to provide a warm, nondirective atmosphere, to draw out the client's thoughts and feelings, and to help the client accept his or her true self.

Rogers (1902–1987), who helped develop the humanistic approach to psychology, earned his Ph.D. in clinical psychology from Columbia University in 1931. He taught at Ohio State University, the University of Chicago, and the University of Wisconsin before establishing the Center for Studies of the Person in La Jolla, California. Rogers wrote numerous books, including *Client-Centered Therapy* (Houghton Mifflin, 1951) and *A Way of Being* (Houghton Mifflin, 1980).

This selection is from chapter 2, "Some Hypotheses Regarding the Facilitation of Personal Growth," of *On Becoming a Person: A Therapist's View of Psychotherapy* (Houghton Mifflin, 1961). In this chapter, which is based on a talk he gave at Oberlin College in Ohio in 1954, Rogers presents the core characteristics of the person-centered approach to therapy and he tries to present his approach in an understandable fashion. As you read this selection, consider how the core characteristics of the person-centered relationship might be used to help foster personal growth in normal individuals.

Key Concept: person-centered therapy

APA Citation: Rogers, C. R. (1961). *On becoming a person.* Boston: Houghton Mifflin.

*T*o be faced by a troubled, conflicted person who is seeking and expecting help, has always constituted a great challenge to me. Do I have the knowledge, the resources, the psychological strength, the skill—do I have whatever it takes to be of help to such an individual?

For more than twenty-five years I have been trying to meet this kind of challenge. It has caused me to draw upon every element of my professional background: the rigorous methods of personality measurement which I first learned at Teachers' College, Columbia; the Freudian psychoanalytic insights and methods of the Institute for Child Guidance where I worked as interne; the continuing developments in the field of clinical psychology, with which I have been closely associated; the briefer exposure to the work of Otto Rank, to the methods of psychiatric social work, and other resources too numerous to mention. But most of all it has meant a continual learning from my own experience and that of my colleagues at the Counseling Center as we have endeavored to discover for ourselves effective means of working with people in distress. Gradually I have developed a way of working which grows out of that experience, and which can be tested, refined, and reshaped by further experience and by research.

A GENERAL HYPOTHESIS

One brief way of describing the change which has taken place in me is to say that in my early professional years I was asking the question, How can I treat, or cure, or change this person? Now I would phrase the question in this way: How can I provide a relationship which this person may use for his own personal growth?

It is as I have come to put the question in this second way that I realize that whatever I have learned is applicable to all of my human relationships, not just to working with clients with problems. It is for this reason that I feel it is possible that the learnings which have had meaning for me in my experience may have some meaning for you in your experience, since all of us are involved in human relationships.

Perhaps I should start with a negative learning. It has gradually been driven home to me that I cannot be of help to this troubled person by means of any intellectual or training procedure. No approach which relies upon knowledge upon training, upon the acceptance of something that is *taught*, is of any use. These approaches seem so tempting and direct that I have, in the past, tried a great many of them. It is possible to explain a person to himself, to prescribe steps which should lead him forward, to train him in knowledge about a more satisfying mode of life. But such methods are, in my experience, futile and inconsequential. The most they can accomplish is some temporary change, which soon disappears, leaving the individual more than ever convinced of his inadequacy.

The failure of any such approach through the intellect has forced me to recognize that change appears to come about through experience in a relationship. So I am going to try to state very briefly and informally, some of the essential hypotheses regarding a helping relationship which have seemed to gain increasing confirmation both from experience and research.

I can state the overall hypothesis in one sentence, as follows. If I can provide a certain type of relationship, the other person will discover within himself the capacity to use that relationship for growth, and change and personal development will occur.

THE RELATIONSHIP

But what meaning do these terms have? Let me take separately the three major phrases in this sentence and indicate something of the meaning they have for me. What is this certain type of relationship I would like to provide?

I have found that the more that I can be genuine in the relationship, the more helpful it will be. This means that I need to be aware of my own feelings, in so far as possible, rather than presenting an outward façade of one attitude, while actually holding another attitude at a deeper or unconscious level. Being genuine also involves the willingness to be and to express, in my words and my behavior, the various feelings and attitudes which exist in me. It is only in this way that the relationship can have *reality*, and reality seems deeply important as a first condition. It is only by providing the genuine reality which is in me, that the other person can successfully seek for the reality in him. I have found this to be true even when the attitudes I feel are not attitudes with which I am pleased, or attitudes which seem conducive to a good relationship. It seems extremely important to be *real*.

As a second condition, I find that the more acceptance and liking I feel toward this individual, the more I will be creating a relationship which he can use. By acceptance I mean a warm regard for him as a person of unconditional self-worth—of value no matter what his condition, his behavior, or his feelings. It means a respect and liking for him as a separate person, a willingness for him to possess his own feelings in his own way. It means an acceptance of and regard for his attitudes of the moment, no matter how negative or positive, no matter how much they may contradict other attitudes he has held in the past. This acceptance of each fluctuating aspect of this other person makes it for him a relationship of warmth and safety, and the safety of being liked and prized as a person seems a highly important element in a helping relationship.

I also find that the relationship is significant to the extent that I feel a continuing desire to understand—a sensitive empathy with each of the client's feelings and communications as they seem to him at that moment. Acceptance does not mean much until it involves understanding. It is only as I *understand* the feelings and thoughts which seem so horrible to you, or so weak, or so sentimental, or so bizarre—it is only as I see them as you see them, and accept them and you, that you feel really free to explore all the hidden nooks and frightening crannies of your inner and often buried experience. This *freedom* is an important condition of the relationship. There is implied here a freedom to explore oneself at both conscious and unconscious levels, as rapidly as one can dare to embark on this dangerous quest. There is also a complete freedom from any type of moral or diagnostic evaluation, since all such evaluations are, I believe, always threatening.

Thus the relationship which I have found helpful is characterized by a sort of transparency on my part, in which my real feelings are evident; by an acceptance of this other person as a separate person with value in his own right; and by a deep empathic understanding which enables me to see his private world through his eyes. When these conditions are achieved, I become a companion to my client, accompanying him in the frightening search for himself, which he now feels free to undertake.

I am by no means always able to achieve this kind of relationship with another, and sometimes, even when I feel I have achieved it in myself, he may be too frightened to perceive what is being offered to him. But I would say that when I hold in myself the kind of attitudes I have described, and when the other person can to some degree experience these attitudes, then I believe that change and constructive personal development will *invariably* occur—and I include the word "invariably" only after long and careful consideration.

THE MOTIVATION FOR CHANGE

So much for the relationship. The second phrase in my overall hypothesis was that the individual will discover within himself the capacity to use this relationship for growth. I will try to indicate something of the meaning which that phrase has for me. Gradually my experience has forced me to conclude that the individual has within himself the capacity and the tendency, latent if not evident, to move forward toward maturity. In a suitable psychological climate this tendency is released, and becomes actual rather than potential. It is evident in the capacity of the individual to understand those aspects of his life and of himself which are causing him pain and dissatisfaction, an understanding which probes beneath his conscious knowledge of himself into those experiences which he has hidden from himself because of their threatening nature. It shows itself in the tendency to reorganize his personality and his relationship to life in ways which are regarded as more mature. Whether one calls it a growth tendency, a drive toward self-actualization, or a forward-moving directional tendency, it is the mainspring of life, and is, in the last analysis, the tendency upon which all psychotherapy depends. It is the urge which is evident in all organic and human life—to expand, extend, become autonomous, develop, mature—the tendency to express and activate all the capacities of the organism, to the extent that such activation enhances the organism or the self. This tendency may become deeply buried under layer after layer of encrusted psychological defenses; it may be hidden behind elaborate façades which deny its existence; but it is my belief that it exists in every individual, and awaits only the proper conditions to be released and expressed.

THE OUTCOMES

I have attempted to describe the relationship which is basic to constructive personality change. I have tried to put into words the type of capacity which the individual brings to such a relationship. The third phrase of my general statement was that change and personal development would occur. It is my hypothesis that in such a relationship the individual will reorganize himself at both the conscious and deeper levels of his personality in such a manner as to cope with life more constructively, more intelligently, and in a more socialized as well as a more satisfying way.

Here I can depart from speculation and bring in the steadily increasing body of solid research knowledge which is accumulating. We know now that individuals who live in such a relationship even for a relatively limited number of hours show profound and significant changes in personality, attitudes, and behavior, changes that do not occur in matched control groups. In such a relationship the individual becomes more integrated, more effective. He shows fewer of the characteristics which are usually termed neurotic or psychotic, and more of the characteristics of the healthy, well-functioning person. He changes his perception of himself, becoming more realistic in his views of self. He becomes more like the person he wishes to be. He values himself more highly. He is more self-confident and self-directing. He has a better understanding of himself, becomes more open to his experience, denies or represses less of his experience. He becomes more accepting in his attitudes toward others, seeing others as more similar to himself.

In his behavior he shows similar changes. He is less frustrated by stress, and recovers from stress more quickly. He becomes more mature in his everyday behavior as this is observed by friends. He is less defensive, more adaptive, more able to meet situations creatively.

These are some of the changes which we now know come about in individuals who have completed a series of counseling interviews in which the psychological atmosphere approximates the relationship I described. Each of the statements made is based upon objective evidence. Much more research needs to be done, but there can no longer be any doubt as to the effectiveness of such a relationship in producing personality change.

Principles of Cognitive Therapy

Aaron T. Beck developed cognitive therapy to help people with psychological disorders caused by negative, self-defeating thoughts and feelings. Cognitive therapists attempt to restructure these negative thoughts and modify the way people view the world. Beck originally developed cognitive therapy to treat depression, but recently he has extended it to the treatment of anxiety disorders.

Beck (b. 1921) earned his M.D. from the Yale University School of Medicine in 1946. He is currently a professor of psychiatry at the University of Pennsylvania. Beck's theories of depression and cognitive therapy have had a significant impact on clinical psychology. He has written a number of books in this area, including *Depression: Clinical, Experimental, and Theoretical Aspects* (1967) and *Anxiety Disorders and Phobias: A Cognitive Perspective* (Basic Books, 1985), coauthored with Gary Emery.

This selection is from chapter 9, "Principles of Cognitive Therapy," of Beck's *Cognitive Therapy and the Emotional Disorders* (International Universities Press, 1976). In it, Beck presents the basic concepts of cognitive therapy, and he provides several examples of how therapists apply these concepts in treating depressed patients. Note that cognitive therapy is effective only for those who are able to think and reason about their problems. Do you think the principles of cognitive therapy can be applied to everyday problems as well as to more serious psychological disorders?

Key Concept: cognitive therapy

APA Citation: Beck, A. T. (1976). *Cognitive therapy and the emotional disorders.* New York: International Universities Press.

We have seen that the common psychological disorders center around certain aberrations in thinking. The challenge to psychotherapy is to offer the patient effective techniques for overcoming his blindspots, his blurred perceptions, and his self-deceptions. A promising lead is provided by the observation that a person responds realistically and effectively to situations not related to his neurosis. His judgments and behavior in areas of experience beyond the boundaries of his specific vulnerability often reflect a high level of functioning. Furthermore, prior to the onset of illness, the neurotic frequently shows adequate development of his conceptual tools for dealing with the problems of living.

Psychological skills (integrating, labeling, and interpreting experience) can be applied to correcting the psychological aberrations. Since the central psychological problem and the psychological *remedy* are both concerned with the patient's thinking (or cognitions), we call this form of help cognitive therapy.

In the broadest sense, cognitive therapy consists of all the approaches that alleviate psychological distress through the medium of correcting faulty conceptions and self-signals. The emphasis on thinking, however, should not obscure the importance of the emotional reactions which are generally the immediate source of distress. It simply means that we get to the person's emotions through his cognitions. By correcting erroneous beliefs, we can damp down or alter excessive, inappropriate emotional reactions.

Many methods of helping a patient make more realistic appraisals of himself and his world are available. The "intellectual" approach consists of identifying the misconceptions, testing their validity, and substituting more appropriate concepts. Often the need for broad attitudinal change emerges with the patient's recognition that the rules he has relied on to guide his thinking and behavior have served to deceive and to defeat him.

The "experiential" approach exposes the patient to experiences that are in themselves powerful enough to change misconceptions. The interactions with other people in certain organized situations, such as encounter groups or conventional psychotherapy, may help a person to perceive others more realistically and consequently to modify his inappropriate maladaptive responses to them. In encounter groups, the interpersonal experiences may cut through maladaptive attitudes blocking the expression of intimate feelings. Similarly, a patient, in response to his psychotherapist's warmth and acceptance, often modifies his stereotyped conception of authority figures. Such a change has been labeled "corrective emotional experience" (Alexander, 1950). Sometimes the effectiveness of psychotherapy is implemented by motivating a patient to enter situations he had previously avoided because of his misconceptions.

The "behavioral" approach encourages the development of specific forms of behavior that lead to more general changes in the way the patient views himself and the real world. Practicing techniques for dealing with people who frighten him, as in "assertive training," not only enables him to regard other people more realistically but enhances his self-confidence....

TARGETS OF COGNITIVE THERAPY

Cognitive techniques are most appropriate for people who have the capacity for introspection and for reflecting about their own thoughts and fantasies. This approach is essentially an extension and a refinement of what people have done to varying degrees since the early stages of their intellectual development.

The particular techniques such as labeling objects and situations, setting up hypotheses, and weeding out and testing the hypotheses are based on skills that people apply automatically without being cognizant of the operations involved.

This kind of intellectual function is analogous to the formation of speech in which rules of pronunciation and grammatical construction are applied without consciousness of the rules or of their application. When an adult has to correct a speech disorder or attempts to learn a new language, then he has to concentrate on the formation of words and sentences. Similarly, when he has a problem in interpreting certain aspects of reality, it may be useful for him to focus on the rules he applies in making judgments. In examining a problem area, he finds that the rule is incorrect or that he has been applying it incorrectly.

Since making the incorrect judgments has probably become a deeply ingrained habit, which he may not be conscious of, several steps are required to correct it. First, he has to become aware of what he is thinking. Second, he needs to recognize what thoughts are awry. Then he has to substitute accurate for inaccurate judgments. Finally, he needs feedback to inform him whether his changes are correct. The same kind of sequence is necessary for making behavioral changes, such as improving form in a sport, correcting faults in playing an instrument, or perfecting techniques of persuasion.

To illustrate the process of cognitive change, let us take as a rather gross example a person who is afraid of all strangers. When we explore his reactions, we may find that he is operating under the rule, "All strangers are unfriendly or hostile." In this case, the rule is wrong. On the other hand, he may realize that strangers vary, but he may not have learned to discriminate among friendly strangers, neutral strangers, and unfriendly strangers. In such a case, his trouble is in applying the rule, that is, in converting the available information in a given situation into an appropriate judgment.

It is obvious that not all people who think erroneously need or want to get their thinking straightened out. When a person's erroneous ideation disrupts his life or makes him feel miserable, then he becomes a candidate for some form of help.

The troubles or problems that stimulate a person to seek help may be manifested by distress of a subjective nature (such as anxiety or depression), a difficulty in his overt behavior (such as disabling inhibition or overaggressiveness), or a deficiency in his responses (for example, inability to experience or express warm feelings). The kinds of thinking that underlie these problems may be summarized as follows.

Direct, Tangible Distortions of Reality

Distortions familiar to everybody are the thoughts of a paranoid patient who indiscriminately concludes when he sees other people (even people who are obviously friendly toward him): "Those people want to harm me." Or, as one patient once told me, "I killed President Kennedy."

Less obvious distortions of reality occur in all neuroses. For example, a depressed patient may say, "I have lost my ability to type, to read, to drive a car." However, when he becomes involved in the task, he may find his performance is still adequate. A depressed businessman complains that he is on the verge of bankruptcy, yet examination of his accounts indicates that he is completely solvent and, in fact, is prospering. The label "distortion of reality" is justified because an objective appraisal of the situation contradicts his appraisal.

Other examples of distortions that are relatively simple to check are ideas such as, "I am getting fat" or "I am a burden to my family." Some judgments require greater work to authenticate; for example, "Nobody likes me." The therapeutic sessions, particularly when the patient has been trained to report his automatic thoughts, provide an excellent laboratory for exposing distortions. The therapist may readily identify certain distortions, for instance, when a patient toward whom he has warm feelings reports the thought that he believes the therapist dislikes him.

Illogical Thinking

The patient's appraisal of reality may not be distorted, but his system of making inferences or drawing conclusions from his observations is at fault: He hears distant noise and concludes someone has fired a gun at him. In such instances, the basic premises may be erroneous or the logical processes may be faulty. A depressed patient observed that a faucet was leaking in a bathroom, that the pilot light was out in the stove, and that one of the steps in the staircase was broken. He concluded, "The whole house is deteriorating." The house was in excellent condition (except for these minor problems); he had made a massive overgeneralization. In the same way, patients who have difficulties as a result of their overt behavior often start from inaccurate premises. Someone who consistently alienates potential friends because of his overaggressiveness may operate according to the rule, "If I don't push people around, they will push me around." A timid, inhibited person may be indiscriminately applying the principle, "If I open my mouth, everybody will jump on me."

THE THERAPEUTIC COLLABORATION

Certain factors are important in practically all forms of psychotherapy, but are crucial in cognitive therapy. An obvious primary component of effective psychotherapy is genuine collaboration between the therapist and patient. Moving blindly in separate directions, as sometimes happens, frustrates the therapist and distresses the patient. It is important to realize that the dispenser of the service (the therapist) and the recipient (the patient) may envision the therapeutic relationship quite differently. The patient, for instance, may visualize therapy as a molding of a lump of clay by an omnipotent and omniscient God figure. To minimize such hazards, the patient and therapist should reach a consensus regarding what problem requires help, the goal of therapy, and how they plan to reach that goal. Agreement regarding the nature and duration of therapy is important in determining the outcome. One study has shown, for instance, that a discrepancy between the patient's expectations and the kind of therapy he actually receives militates against a successful outcome. On the other hand, preliminary coaching of the patient about the type of therapy selected appeared to enhance its effectiveness (Orne and Wender, 1968).

Furthermore, the therapist needs to be tuned in to the vicissitudes of the patient's problems from session to session. Patients frequently formulate an "agenda" of topics they want to discuss at a particular session; if the therapist disregards this, he may impose an unnecessary strain on the relationship. For instance, a patient who is disturbed by a recent altercation with his wife may be alienated by the therapist's rigid adherence to a predetermined format such as desensitizing him to his subway phobia.

It is useful to conceive of the patient-therapist relationship as a joint effort. It is not the therapist's function to try to reform the patient; rather, his role is working with the patient against "*it*," the patient's problem. Placing the emphasis on solving problems, rather than his presumed defects or bad habits, helps the patient to examine his difficulties with more detachment and makes him less prone to experience shame, a sense of inferiority, and defensiveness. The partnership concept helps the therapist to obtain valuable "feedback" about the efficacy of therapeutic techniques and further detailed information about the patient's thoughts and feelings. In employing systematic desensitization, for instance, I customarily ask for a detailed description of each image. The patient's report is often very informative and, on many occasions, reveals new problems that had not previously been identified. The partnership arrangement also reduces the patient's tendency to cast the therapist in the role of a superman. Investigators (Rogers, 1951; Truax, 1963) have found that if the therapist shows the following characteristics, a successful outcome is facilitated: genuine warmth, acceptance, and accurate empathy. By working with the patient as a collaborator, the therapist is more likely to show these characteristics than if he assumes a Godlike role.

ESTABLISHING CREDIBILITY

Problems often arise with regard to the suggestions and formulations offered by the therapist. Patients who view the therapist as a kind of superman are likely to accept his interpretations and suggestions as sacred pronouncements. Such bland ingestion of the therapist's hypotheses deprives the therapy of the corrective effect of critical evaluation by the patient.

A different type of problem is presented by patients who automatically react to the therapist's statements with suspicion or skepticism. Such a reaction is most pronounced in paranoid and severely depressed patients. In attempting to expose the distortions of reality, the therapist may become mired in the patient's deeply entrenched belief system. The therapist, therefore, must establish some common ground, find some point of agreement, and then attempt to extend the area of consensus from there. Depressed patients are often concerned that their emotional disorder will persist or get worse, and that they will not respond to therapy. If the therapist assumes a hearty optimistic attitude, the patient may decide that the therapist is either faking, doesn't really understand the gravity of the disorder, or is simply a fool. Similarly, trying to talk a paranoid patient out of his distorted views of reality may drive him to stronger belief in his paranoid ideas. Also, if the paranoid patient begins to regard the therapist as a member of the "opposition," he may assign the therapist a key role in his delusional system.

A more appropriate approach in establishing credibility is to convey a message such as: "You have certain ideas that upset you. They may or they may not be correct. Now let us examine some of them." By assuming a neutral stance, the therapist may then encourage the patient to express his distorted ideas and listen to them attentively. Later he sends up some "trial balloons" to determine whether the patient is ready to examine the evidence regarding these distortions....

Many patients appear to agree with the therapist because of their fears of challenging him and their need to please him. A clue to such superficial consensus is provided by the patient who says, "I agree with you intellectually but not emotionally." Such a statement generally indicates that the therapist's comments or interpretations may seem logical to the patient, but that they do not penetrate the patient's basic belief system (Ellis, 1962). The patient continues to operate according to his faulty ideas. Moreover, strongly authoritative remarks that appeal to the patient's yearning for explanations for his misery may set the stage for disillusionment when the patient finds loopholes in the therapist's formulations. The therapist's confidence in his role as an expert requires a strong admixture of humility. Psychotherapy often involves a good deal of trial-and-error, experimenting with several approaches or formulations to determine which fit the best....

In less extreme cases, it is possible to deal more directly with the irrational ideas. However, the therapist must assess the "latitude of acceptance" of the patient for statements challenging his distorted concepts. Being told that his ideas are wrong might antagonize the patient; but, he might respond favorably to a question such as "Is there another way of interpreting your wife's behavior?" As long as the therapist's attempts at clarification are within an acceptable range, the problem of a credibility gap is minimized.

PROBLEM REDUCTION

Many patients come to the therapist with a host of symptoms or problems. To solve each one of the problems in isolation from the others might very well take a lifetime. A patient may seek help for a variety of ailments such as headaches, insomnia, and anxiety, in addition to interpersonal problems. Identifying problems with similar causes and grouping them together is termed "problem reduction." Once the multifarious difficulties are condensed, the therapist can select the appropriate techniques for each group of problems.

Let us take as an example the patient with multiple phobias. A woman... was greatly handicapped by a fear of elevators, tunnels, hills, closed spaces, riding in an open car, riding in an airplane, swimming, walking fast or running, strong winds, and hot, muggy days. Treating each phobia separately with the technique of systematic desensitization might have required innumerable therapeutic sessions, However, it was possible to find a common denominator for her symptoms: an overriding fear of suffocation. She believed that each of the phobic situations presented substantial risk of deprivation of air and consequent suffocation. The therapy was focused directly on this central fear.

The principle of problem reduction is also applicable to a constellation of symptoms that comprise a specific disorder such as depression. By concentrating on certain key components of the disorder, such as low self-esteem or negative expectations, the therapy can produce improvement in mood, overt behavior, appetite, and sleeping pattern. One patient, for instance, revealed that whenever he was in a gratifying situation, he would get some kind of "killjoy" thought: When he began to feel pleasure from listening to music, he would think, "This record will be over soon," and his pleasure would disappear. When he discovered that he was enjoying a movie, a date with a girl, or just walking, he would think: "This will end soon," and immediately his satisfaction was squelched. In this case, a thought pattern that he could not enjoy things because they would end became the focus of the therapy.

In another case the main focus was the patient's overabsorption in the negative aspects of her life and her selective inattention to positive occurrences. The therapy consisted of having her write down and report back positive experiences. She was surprised to find how many positive, gratifying experiences she had had and subsequently forgotten about.

Another form of problem reduction is the identification of the first link in a chain of symptoms. An interesting feature is that the first link may be a relatively small and easily eradicable problem that leads to consequences that are disabling. For analogy, a person may writhe with pain and be unable to walk, eat, talk at length, or perform minimal constructive activities—because of a speck in the eye. The "speck in the eye" syndrome probably occurs more frequently among psychiatric patients than is generally realized. Because of delay in identifying and dealing with the initial problem, however, the ensuing difficulties become deeply entrenched. A mother who was afraid to leave her children at home with a babysitter continued to be housebound long after the children reached maturity. . . .

LEARNING TO LEARN

. . . [I]t is not necessary for a psychotherapist to help a patient solve every problem that troubles him. Nor is it necessary to anticipate all the problems that may occur after the termination of therapy and to try to work them out in advance. The kind of therapeutic collaboration previously described is conducive to the patient's developing new ways to learn from his experiences and to solve problems. In a sense the patient is "learning to learn." This process has been labeled deutero-learning (Bateson, 1942).

The problem-solving approach to psychotherapy removes much of the responsibility from the therapist and engages the patient more actively in working on his difficulties. By reducing the patient's dependency on the therapist, this approach increases the patient's self-confidence and self-esteem. More important, perhaps, is the fact that the patient's active participation in defining the problem and considering various options yields more ample information than would otherwise be available. His participation in making the decision helps him implement it.

I have explained the problem-solving concept to patients in somewhat the following way: "One of the goals of therapy is to help you learn new ways of approaching problems. Then, as problems come up, you can apply the formulas that you have already learned. For instance, in learning arithmetic you simply learned the fundamental rules. It was not necessary to learn every single possible addition and subtraction. Once you had learned the operations, you could apply them to any arithmetic problem."

To illustrate "learning to learn," let us consider the practical and interpersonal problems that contribute to a patient's various symptoms. A woman, for instance, discovered she was constantly plagued with headaches, feelings of tension, abdominal pain, and insomnia. By focusing on her problems at work and at home, the patient was able to find some solutions for them and became less prone to experience symptoms. As was hoped, she was able to generalize these practical lessons to solving other problems of living, so that it was not necessary for us to work on all her problems in therapy....

"Learning to learn" consists of much more than the patient's adopting a few techniques that can be used in a wide variety of situations. Basically, this approach attempts to remove obstacles that have prevented the patient from profiting from experience and from developing adequate ways of dealing with their internal and external problems. Most of the patients have been blocked in their psychosocial development by certain maladaptive attitudes and patterns of behavior. For instance, the woman with the numerous problems at work and at home had a characteristic response when she was confronted with sensitive interpersonal relations or new practical problems: "I don't know what to do." As a result of therapy, each successful experience tended to erode this negative attitude. Consequently, she was enabled to draw on her ingenuity in meeting and mastering completely different situations.

Patients generally try to avoid situations that cause them uneasiness. Consequently, they do not develop the trial-and-error techniques that are prerequisite to solving many problems. Or by staying out of difficult situations, they do not learn how to rid themselves of their tendency to distort or exaggerate. A person who stays close to home because he fears strangers does not learn how to test the validity of his fears or to discriminate between "safe" strangers and "dangerous" strangers. Through therapy he can learn to "reality-test" not only these fears but other fears as well.

The sense of mastery from solving one problem frequently inspires the patient to approach and solve other problems that he has long avoided. Thus, a bonus of successful therapy is not only freedom from the original problems, but a thorough psychological change that prepares him to meet new challenges.

REFERENCES

Alexander, F. (1950). *Psychosomatic medicine: Its principles and applications.* New York: W. W. Norton.

Bateson, G. (1942). Social planning and the concept of deutero-learning in relation to the democratic way of life. In: *Science, philosophy, and religion* (2nd Symposium). New York: Harper.

Ellis, A. (1962). *Reason and emotion in psychotherapy.* New York: Lyle Stuart.

Orne, M. T., & Wender, P. H. (1968). Anticipatory socialization for psychotherapy: Method and rationale. *American Journal of Psychiatry, 124,* 1202–1212.

Rogers, C. R. (1951). *Client-centered therapy: Its current practice, implications, and theory.* Boston: Houghton Mifflin.

Truat, C. B. (1963). Effective ingredients in psychotherapy: an approach to unraveling the patient-therapist interaction. *Journal of Counseling Psychology, 10,* 256–263.

The Effectiveness of Psychotherapy: The Consumer Reports Study

The evaluation of the effectiveness of psychotherapy is a major concern of psychologists. Obviously if one approach to therapy is vastly superior, it should be the preferred treatment. An even more basic concern is the degree to which any type of psychotherapy is effective. Martin E. P. Seligman served as a consultant to a study by *Consumer Reports* that measured the effectiveness of various types of psychotherapy.

Seligman was born in Albany, New York, in 1942. He attended Princeton University as an undergraduate and received his Ph.D. in psychology from the University of Pennsylvania in 1967, where he is currently a professor of psychology. He served as president of the American Psychological Association in 1998. He has written 13 books, including *Learned Optimism* (Knopf, 1991) and *What You Can Change and What You Can't* (Knopf, 1993).

The following selection is from "The Effectiveness of Psychotherapy: The *Consumer Reports* Study", which was published in *American Psychologist* in 1995. In it, Seligman reviews survey results that indicate that psychotherapy is indeed effective. As you read this selection, note the distinction between efficacy studies and effectiveness studies. It is important to remember that the information was obtained through survey results.

Key Concept: evaluation of psychotherapy

APA Citation: Seligman, M. E. P. (1995). The effectiveness of therapy: The *Consumer Reports* study. *American Psychologist, 50*, 965–974.

Consumer Reports (1995, November) published an article which concluded that patients benefited very substantially from psychotherapy, that long-term treatment did considerably better than short-term treatment, and that psychotherapy alone did not differ in effectiveness from medication plus psychotherapy. Furthermore, no specific modality of psychotherapy did better than any other for any disorder; psychologists, psychiatrists, and social workers did not differ in their effectiveness as treaters; and all did better than marriage counselors and long-term family doctoring. Patients whose length of therapy or choice of therapist was limited by insurance or managed care did worse. The methodological virtues and drawbacks of this large-scale survey are examined and contrasted with the more traditional efficacy study, in which patients are randomized into a manualized, fixed duration treatment or into control groups. I conclude that the *Consumer Reports* survey complements the efficacy method, and that the best features of these two methods can be combined into a more ideal method that will best provide empirical validation of psychotherapy.

How do we find out whether psychotherapy works? To answer this, two methods have arisen: the *efficacy study* and the *effectiveness study*. An efficacy study is the more popular method. It contrasts some kind of therapy to a comparison group under well-controlled conditions. But there is much more to an efficacy study than just a control group, and such studies have become a high-paradigm endeavor with sophisticated methodology. In the ideal efficacy study, all of the following niceties are found:

1. The patients are randomly assigned to treatment and control conditions.
2. The controls are rigorous: Not only are patients included who receive no treatment at all, but placebos containing potentially therapeutic ingredients credible to both the patient and the therapist are used in order to control for such influences as rapport, expectation of gain, and sympathetic attention (dubbed *nonspecifics*).
3. The treatments are manualized, with highly detailed scripting of therapy made explicit. Fidelity to the manual is assessed using videotaped sessions, and wayward implementers are corrected.
4. Patients are seen for a fixed number of sessions.
5. The target outcomes are well operationalized (e.g., clinician-diagnosed DSM–IV disorder, number of reported orgasms, self-reports of panic attacks, percentage of fluent utterances).
6. Raters and diagnosticians are blind to which group the patient comes from. (Contrary to the "double-blind" method of drug studies, efficacy studies of psychotherapy can be at most "single-blind," since the patient and therapist both know what the treatment is. Whenever you hear someone demanding the double-blind study of psychotherapy, hold onto your wallet.)
7. The patients meet criteria for a single diagnosed disorder, and patients with multiple disorders are typically excluded.
8. The patients are followed for a fixed period after termination of treatment with a thorough assessment battery.

So when an efficacy study demonstrates a difference between a form of psychotherapy and controls, academic clinicians and researchers take this modality seriously indeed. In spite of how expensive and time-consuming they are, hundreds of efficacy studies of both psychotherapy and drugs now exist—

many of them well done. These studies show, among many other things, that cognitive therapy, interpersonal therapy, and medications all provide moderate relief from unipolar depressive disorder; that exposure and clomipramine both relieve the symptoms of obsessive–compulsive disorder moderately well but that exposure has more lasting benefits; that cognitive therapy works very well in panic disorder; that systematic desensitization relieves specific phobias; that "applied tension" virtually cures blood and injury phobia; that transcendental meditation relieves anxiety; that aversion therapy produces only marginal improvement with sexual offenders; that disulfram (Antabuse) does not provide lasting relief from alcoholism; that flooding plus medication does better in the treatment of agoraphobia than either alone; and that cognitive therapy provides significant relief of bulimia, outperforming medications alone (see Seligman, 1991, for a review).

The high praise "empirically validated" is now virtually synonymous with positive results in efficacy studies, and many investigators have come to think that an efficacy study is the "gold standard" for measuring whether a treatment works.

I also had come to that opinion when I wrote *What You Can Change & What You Can't* (Seligman, 1994). In trying to summarize what was known about the effects of the panoply of drugs and psychotherapies for each major disorder, I read hundreds of efficacy studies and came to appreciate the genre. At minimum I was convinced that an efficacy study may be the best scientific instrument for telling us whether a novel treatment is *likely* to work on a given disorder when the treatment is exported from controlled conditions into the field. Because treatment in efficacy studies is delivered under tightly controlled conditions to carefully screened patients, sensitivity is maximized and efficacy studies are very useful for deciding whether one treatment is better than another treatment for a given disorder.

But my belief has changed about what counts as a "gold standard." And it was a study by *Consumer Reports* (1995, November) that singlehandedly shook my belief. I came to see that deciding whether one treatment, under highly controlled conditions, works better than another treatment or a control group is a different question from deciding what works in the field (Muñoz, Hollon, McGrath, Rehm, & VandenBos, 1994). I no longer believe that efficacy studies are the only, or even the best, way of finding out what treatments actually work in the field. I have come to believe that the "effectiveness" study of how patients fare under the actual conditions of treatment in the field, can yield useful and credible "empirical validation" of psychotherapy and medication. This is the method that *Consumer Reports* pioneered.

WHAT EFFICACY STUDIES LEAVE OUT

It is easy to assume that, if some form of treatment is not listed among the many which have been "empirically validated," the treatment must be inert, rather than just "untested" given the existing method of validation. I will dub this the *inertness assumption.* The inertness assumption is a challenge to practitioners, since long-term dynamic treatment, family therapy, and more generally, eclectic psychotherapy, are not on the list of treatments empirically validated by efficacy studies, and these modalities probably make up most of what is actually practiced. I want to look closely at the inertness assumption, since the effectiveness strategy of empirical validation follows from what is wrong with the assumption.

The usual argument against the inertness assumption is that long-term dynamic therapy, family therapy, and eclectic therapy cannot be tested in efficacy studies, and thus we have no hard evidence one way or another. They cannot be tested because they are too cumbersome for the efficacy study paradigm. Imagine, for example, what a decent efficacy study of long-term dynamic therapy would require: control groups receiving no treatment for several years; an equally credible comparison treatment of the same duration that has the same "nonspecifics"—rapport, attention, and expectation of gain—but is actually inert; a step-by-step manual covering hundreds of sessions; and the random assignment of patients to treatments which last a year or more. The ethical and scientific problems of such research are daunting, to say nothing of how much such a study would cost.

While this argument cannot be gainsaid, it still leaves the average psychotherapist in an uncomfortable position, with a substantial body of literature validating a panoply of short-term therapies the psychotherapist does not perform, and with the long-term, eclectic therapy he or she does perform unproven.

But there is a much better argument against the inertness assumption: *The efficacy study is the wrong method for empirically validating psychotherapy as it is actually done, because it omits too many crucial elements of what is done in the field.*

The five properties that follow characterize psychotherapy as it is done in the field. Each of these properties are absent from an efficacy study done under controlled conditions. If these properties are important to patients' getting better, efficacy studies will underestimate or even miss altogether the value of psychotherapy done in the field.

1. Psychotherapy (like other health treatments) in the field is *not of fixed duration.* It usually keeps going until the patient is markedly improved or until he or she quits. In contrast, the intervention in efficacy studies stops after a limited number of sessions—usually about 12—regardless of how well or how poorly the patient is doing.

2. Psychotherapy (again, like other health treatments) in the field is *self-correcting.* If one technique is not working, another technique—or even another modality—is usually tried. In contrast, the intervention in efficacy studies is confined to a small number of techniques, all within one modality and manualized to be delivered in a fixed order.

3. Patients in psychotherapy in the field often get there by *active* shopping, entering a kind of treatment they actively sought with a therapist they screened and chose. This is especially true of patients who work with independent practitioners, and somewhat less so of patients who go to outpatient clinics or have managed care. In contrast, patients enter

efficacy studies by the *passive* process of random assignment to treatment and acquiescence with who and what happens to be offered in the study (Howard, Orlinsky, & Lueger, 1994).

4. Patients in psychotherapy in the field usually have *multiple problems,* and psychotherapy is geared to relieving parallel and interacting difficulties. Patients in efficacy studies are selected to have but one diagnosis (except when two conditions are highly comorbid) by a long set of exclusion and inclusion criteria.

5. Psychotherapy in the field is almost always concerned with *improvement in the general functioning* of patients, as well as amelioration of a disorder and relief of specific, presenting symptoms. Efficacy studies usually focus only on specific symptom reduction and whether the disorder ends.

It is hard to imagine how one could ever do a scientifically compelling efficacy study of a treatment which had variable duration and self-correcting improvisations and was aimed at improved quality of life as well as symptom relief, with patients who were not randomly assigned and had multiple problems. But this does not mean that the effectiveness of treatment so delivered cannot be empirically validated. Indeed it can, but it requires a different method: a survey of large numbers of people who have gone through such treatments. So let us explore the virtues and drawbacks of a well-done effectiveness study, the *Consumer Reports* (1995) one, in contrast to an efficacy study.

Consumer Reports *Survey*

Consumer Reports (CR) included a supplementary survey about psychotherapy and drugs in one version of its 1994 annual questionnaire, along with its customary inquiries about appliances and services. *CR*'s 180,000 readers received this version, which included approximately 100 questions about automobiles and about mental health. *CR* asked readers to fill out the mental health section "if at any time over the past three years you experienced stress or other emotional problems for which you sought help from any of the following: friends, relatives, or a member of the clergy; a mental health professional like a psychologist or a psychiatrist; your family doctor; or a support group." Twenty-two thousand readers responded. Of these, approximately 7,000 subscribers responded to the mental health questions. Of these 7,000, about 3,000 had just talked to friends, relatives, or clergy, and 4,100 went to some combination of mental health professionals, family doctors, and support groups. Of these 4,100, 2,900 saw a mental health professional: Psychologists (37%) were the most frequently seen mental health professional, followed by psychiatrists (22%), social workers (14%), and marriage counselors (9%). Other mental health professionals made up 18%. In addition, 1,300 joined self-help groups, and about 1,000 saw family physicians. The respondents as a whole were highly educated, predominantly middle class; about half were women, and the median age was 46.

Twenty-six questions were asked about mental health professionals, and parallel but less detailed questions were asked about physicians, medications, and self-help groups:

- What kind of therapist
- What presenting problem (e.g., general anxiety, panic, phobia, depression, low mood, alcohol or drugs, grief, weight, eating disorders, marital or sexual problems, children or family, work, stress)
- Emotional state at outset (from *very poor* to *very good*)
- Emotional state now (from *very poor* to *very good*)
- Group versus individual therapy
- Duration and frequency of therapy
- Modality (psychodynamic, behavioral, cognitive, feminist)
- Cost
- Health care plan and limitations on coverage
- Therapist competence
- How much therapy helped (from *made things a lot better* to *made things a lot worse*) and in what areas (specific problem that led to therapy, relations to others, productivity, coping with stress, enjoying life more, growth and insight, self-esteem and confidence, raising low mood)
- Satisfaction with therapy
- Reasons for termination (problems resolved or more manageable, felt further treatment wouldn't help, therapist recommended termination, a new therapist, concerns about therapist's competence, cost, and problems with insurance coverage)

The data set is thus a rich one, probably uniquely rich, and the data analysis was sophisticated. Because I was privileged to be a consultant to this study and thus privy to the entire data set, much of what I now present will be new to you—even if you have read the *CR* article carefully. *CR*'s analysts decided that no single measure of therapy effectiveness would do and so created a multivariate measure. This composite had three subscales, consisting of:

1. Specific improvement ("How much did treatment help with the specific problem that led you to therapy?" *made no difference; made things somewhat worse; made things a lot worse; not sure*);
2. Satisfaction ("Overall how satisfied were you with this therapist's treatment of your problems?" *completely satisfied; very satisfied; fairly well satisfied; somewhat satisfied; very dissatisfied; completely dissatisfied*); and
3. Global improvement (how respondents described their "overall emotional state" at the time of the survey compared with the start of treatment: "*very poor:* I barely managed to deal with things; *fairly poor:* Life was usually pretty tough for me; *so-so:* I had my ups and downs; *quite good:* I had no serious complaints; *very good:* Life was much the way I liked it to be").

Each of the three subscales was transformed and weighted equally on a 0–100 scale, resulting in a 0–300 scale for effectiveness. The statistical analysis was largely multiple regression, with initial severity and duration of treatment (the two biggest effects) partialed out. Stringent levels of statistical significance were used.

There were a number of clear-cut results, among them:

- Treatment by a mental health professional usually worked. Most respondents got a lot better. Averaged over all mental health professionals, of the 426 people who were feeling *very poor* when they began therapy, 87% were feeling *very good, good,* or at least *so-so* by the time of the survey. Of the 786 people who were feeling *fairly poor* at the outset, 92% were feeling *very good, good,* or at least *so-so* by the time of the survey. These findings converge with meta-analyses of efficacy (Lipsey & Wilson, 1993; Shapiro & Shapiro, 1982; Smith, Miller, & Glass, 1980).
- Long-term therapy produced more improvement than short-term therapy. This result was very robust, and held up over all statistical models.... This "dose–response curve" held for patients in both psychotherapy alone and in psychotherapy plus medication (see Howard, Kopta, Krause, & Orlinsky, 1986, for parallel dose–response findings for psychotherapy).
- There was no difference between psychotherapy alone and psychotherapy plus medication for any disorder (very few respondents reported that they had medication with no psychotherapy at all).
- While all mental health professionals appeared to help their patients, psychologists, psychiatrists, and social workers did equally well and better than marriage counselors. Their patients' overall improvement scores (0–300 scale) were 220, 226, 225 (not significantly different from each other), and 208 (significantly worse than the first three), respectively.
- Family doctors did just as well as mental health professionals in the short term, but worse in the long term. Some patients saw both family doctors and mental health professionals, and those who saw both had more severe problems. For patients who relied solely on family doctors, their overall improvement scores when treated for up to six months was 213, and it remained at that level (212) for those treated longer than six months. In contrast, the overall improvement scores for patients of mental health professionals was 211 up to six months, but climbed to 232 when treatment went on for more than six months. The advantages of long-term treatment by a mental health professional held not only for the specific problems that led to treatment, but for a variety of general functioning scores as well: ability to relate to others, coping with everyday stress, enjoying life more, personal growth and understanding, self-esteem and confidence.
- Alcoholics Anonymous (AA) did especially well, with an average improvement score of 251, significantly bettering mental health professionals. People who went to non-AA groups had less severe problems and did not do as well as those who went to AA (average score = 215).
- Active shoppers and active clients did better in treatment than passive recipients (determined by responses to "Was it mostly your idea to seek

therapy? When choosing this therapist, did you discuss qualifications, therapist's experience, discuss frequency, duration, and cost, speak to someone who was treated by this therapist, check out other therapists? During therapy, did you try to be as open as possible, ask for explanation of diagnosis and unclear terms, do homework, not cancel sessions often, discuss negative feelings toward therapist?").

- No specific modality of psychotherapy did any better than any other for any problem. These results confirm the "dodo bird" hypothesis, that all forms of psychotherapies do about equally well (Luborsky, Singer, & Luborsky, 1975). They come as a rude shock to efficacy researchers, since the main theme of efficacy studies has been the demonstration of the usefulness of specific techniques for specific disorders.

- Respondents whose choice of therapist or duration of care was limited by their insurance coverage did worse... (determined by responses to "Did limitations on your insurance coverage affect any of the following choices you made? Type of therapist I chose; How often I met with my therapist; How long I stayed in therapy")....

The Ideal Study

The CR study, then, is to be taken seriously—not only for its results and its credible source, but for its method. It is large-scale; it samples treatment as it is actually delivered in the field; it samples without obvious bias those who seek out treatment; it measures multiple outcomes including specific improvement and more global gains such as growth, insight, productivity, mood, enjoyment of life, and interpersonal relations; it is statistically stringent and finds clinically meaningful results. Furthermore, it is highly cost-effective.

Its major advantage over the efficacy method for studying the effectiveness of psychotherapy and medications is that it captures how and to whom treatment is actually delivered and toward what end. At the very least, the CR study and its underlying survey method provides a powerful addition to what we know about the effectiveness of psychotherapy and a pioneering way of finding out more.

The study is not without flaws, the chief one being the limited meaning of its answer to the question "Can psychotherapy help?" This question has three possible kinds of answers. The first is that psychotherapy does better than something else, such as talking to friends, going to church, or doing nothing at all. Because it lacks comparison groups, the CR study only answers this question indirectly. The second possible answer is that psychotherapy returns people to normality or more liberally to within, say, two standard deviations of the average. The CR study, lacking an untroubled group and lacking measures of how people were before they became troubled, does not answer this question. The third answer is "Do people have fewer symptoms and a better life after therapy than they did before?" This is the question that the CR study answers with a clear "yes."

The CR study can be improved upon, allowing it to speak to all three senses of "psychotherapy works." These improvements would combine several of the best features of efficacy studies with the realism of the survey method. First, the survey could be done prospectively: A large sample of those who seek treatment could be given an assessment battery before and after treatment, while still preserving progress-contingent treatment duration, self-correction, multiple problems, and self-selection of treatment. Second, the assessment battery could include well-normed questionnaires as well as detailed, behavioral information in addition to more global improvement information, thus increasing its sensitivity and allowing it to answer the return-to-normal question. Third, blind diagnostic workups could be included, adding multiple perspectives to self-report.

At any rate, *Consumer Reports* has provided empirical validation of the effectiveness of psychotherapy. Prospective and diagnostically sophisticated surveys, combined with the well-normed and detailed assessment used in efficacy studies, would bolster this pioneering study. They would be expensive, but, in my opinion, very much worth doing.

REFERENCES

Consumer Reports. (1995, November). Mental health: Does therapy help? pp. 734–739.

Howard, K., Kopta, S., Krause, M., & Orlinsky, D. (1986). The dose-effect relationship in psychotherapy. *American Psychologist, 41,* 159–164.

Howard, K., Orlinsky, D., & Lueger, R. (1994). Clinically relevant outcome research in individual psychotherapy. *British Journal of Psychiatry, 165,* 4–8.

Lipsey, M., & Wilson, D. (1993). The efficacy of psychological, educational, and behavioral treatment: Confirmation from meta-analysis. *American Psychologist, 48,* 1181–1209.

Luborsky, L., Singer, B., & Luborsky, L. (1975). Comparative studies of psychotherapies. *Archives of General Psychiatry, 32,* 995–1008.

Muñoz, R., Hollon, S., McGrath, E., Rehm, L., & VandenBos, G. (1994). On the AHCPR guidelines: Further considerations for practitioners. *American Psychologist, 49,* 42–61.

Seligman, M. (1991). *Learned optimism.* New York: Knopf.

Seligman, M. (1994). *What you can change & what you can't.* New York: Knopf.

Shapiro, D., & Shapiro, D. (1982). Meta-analysis of comparative therapy outcome studies: A replication and refinement. *Psychological Bulletin, 92,* 581–604.

Smith, M., Glass, G., & Miller, T. (1980). *The benefit of psychotherapy.* Baltimore: Johns Hopkins University Press.

PART SEVEN

Social Processes

On the Internet . . .

Sites appropriate to Part Seven

The Social Psychology Network is maintained by Scott Plous of Wesleyan University, and provides a vast array of resources and links to information on social psychology.

    http://www.social psychology.org

Resources for Diversity is a site that contains many links to resources in areas of ethnicity, culture, disability, gender, sexuality, and religion.

    http://alabanza.com/kabacoff/Inter-Links/
       diversity.html

The Stanley Milgram Page includes biographical information as well as information on his theories and research.

    http://muskingum.edu/~psychology/psycweb/
       history/milgram.htm

The National Institute on Media and the Family site provides information on the effects of media violence on children. Other media topics are presented, as well.

    http://www.mediaandthefamily.org/home.html

CHAPTER 15 Social Psychology

15.1 LEON FESTINGER

An Introduction to the Theory of Dissonance

Psychologists have studied attitude development and attitude change for many years. In the late 1950s, Leon Festinger proposed a somewhat radical view (at the time) of attitude change. According to his theory of cognitive dissonance, people experience tension when they hold two inconsistent ideas, and this state creates a drive to reduce the dissonance, or tension.

Festinger (1919–1989) obtained his Ph.D. in psychology from the State University of Iowa in 1942. He taught at several universities, including Stanford University, before going to the New School for Social Research in New York City in 1968. Although Festinger contributed numerous theories to social psychology, none has had greater impact than his theory of cognitive dissonance.

This selection is from chapter 1, "An Introduction to the Theory of Dissonance," of Festinger's *A Theory of Cognitive Dissonance* (Stanford University Press, 1957). As well as providing a readable introduction to the development of dissonance, Festinger offers some possible techniques for reducing dissonance in everyday situations. As you read this selection, think about what variables influence cognitive dissonance in your daily life.

Key Concept: cognitive dissonance

APA Citation: Festinger, L. A. (1957). *A theory of cognitive dissonance.* Stanford, CA: Stanford University Press.

*I*t has frequently been implied, and sometimes even pointed out, that the individual strives toward consistency within himself. His opinions and attitudes, for example, tend to exist in clusters that are internally consistent. Certainly one may find exceptions.... [S]omeone may think little children should be quiet and unobtrusive and yet may be quite proud when his child aggressively captures the attention of his adult guests. When such inconsistencies are found to exist, they may be quite dramatic, but they capture our interest primarily because they stand out in sharp contrast against a background of consistency. It is still overwhelmingly true that related opinions or attitudes are consistent with one another. Study after study reports such consistency among one person's political attitudes, social attitudes, and many others.

There is the same kind of consistency between what a person knows or believes and what he does. A person who believes a college education is a good thing will very likely encourage his children to go to college; a child who knows he will be severely punished for some misdemeanor will not commit it or at least will try not to be caught doing it. This is not surprising, of course; it is so much the rule that we take it for granted. Again what captures our attention are the exceptions to otherwise consistent behavior. A person may know that smoking is bad for him and yet continue to smoke; many persons commit crimes even though they know the high probability of being caught and the punishment that awaits them.

Granting that consistency is the usual thing, perhaps overwhelmingly so, what about these exceptions which come to mind so readily? Only rarely, if ever, are they accepted psychologically *as inconsistencies* by the person involved. Usually more or less successful attempts are made to rationalize them. Thus, the person who continues to smoke, knowing that it is bad for his health, may also feel (*a*) he enjoys smoking so much it is worth it; (*b*) the chances of his health suffering are not as serious as some would make out; (*c*) he can't always avoid every possible dangerous contingency and still live; and (*d*) perhaps even if he stopped smoking he would put on weight which is equally bad for his health. So, continuing to smoke is, after all, consistent with his ideas about smoking.

But persons are not always successful in explaining away or in rationalizing inconsistencies to themselves. For one reason or another, attempts to achieve consistency may fail. The inconsistency then simply continues to exist. Under such circumstances—that is, in the presence of an inconsistency—there is psychological discomfort.

The basic hypotheses... can now be stated. First, I will replace the word "inconsistency" with a term which has less of a logical connotation, namely, *dissonance*. I will likewise replace the word "consistency" with a more neutral term, namely, *consonance*. A more formal definition of these terms will be given shortly; for the moment, let us try to get along with the implicit meaning they have acquired as a result of the preceding discussion.

The basic hypotheses I wish to state are as follows:

1. The existence of dissonance, being psychologically uncomfortable, will motivate the person to try to reduce the dissonance and achieve consonance.

2. When dissonance is present, in addition to trying to reduce it, the person will actively avoid situations and information which would likely increase the dissonance.

Before proceeding to develop this theory of dissonance and the pressures to reduce it, it would be well to clarify the nature of dissonance, what kind of a concept it is, and where the theory concerning it will lead. The two hypotheses stated above provide a good starting point for this clarification. While they refer here specifically to dissonance, they are in fact very general hypotheses. In place of "dissonance" one can substitute other notions similar in nature, such as "hunger," "frustration," or "disequilibrium," and the hypotheses would still make perfectly good sense.

In short, I am proposing that dissonance, that is, the existence of nonfitting relations among cognitions, is a motivating factor in its own right. By the term *cognition* ... I mean any knowledge, opinion, or belief about the environment, about oneself, or about one's behavior. Cognitive dissonance can be seen as an antecedent condition which leads to activity oriented toward dissonance reduction just as hunger leads to activity oriented toward hunger reduction. It is a very different motivation from what psychologists are used to dealing with but, as we shall see, nonetheless powerful. ...

THE OCCURRENCE AND PERSISTENCE OF DISSONANCE

Why and how does dissonance ever arise? How does it happen that persons sometimes find themselves doing things that do not fit with what they know, or having opinions that do not fit with other opinions they hold? An answer to this question may be found in discussing two of the more common situations in which dissonance may occur.

1. New events may happen or new information may become known to a person, creating at least a momentary dissonance with existing knowledge, opinion, or cognition concerning behavior. Since a person does not have complete and perfect control over the information that reaches him and over events that can happen in his environment, such dissonances may easily arise. Thus, for example, a person may plan to go on a picnic with complete confidence that the weather will be warm and sunny. Nevertheless, just before he is due to start, it may begin to rain. The knowledge that it is now raining is dissonant with his confidence in a sunny day and with his planning to go to a picnic. Or, as another example, a person who is quite certain in his knowledge that automatic transmissions on automobiles are inefficient may accidentally come across an article praising automatic transmissions. Again, at least a momentary dissonance is created.

2. Even in the absence of new, unforeseen events or information, the existence of dissonance is undoubtedly an everyday condition. Very few things are all black or all white; very few situations are clear-cut enough so that opinions or behaviors are not to some extent a mixture of contradictions. Thus, a

midwestern farmer who is a Republican may be opposed to his party's position on farm price supports; a person buying a new car may prefer the economy of one model but the design of another; a person deciding on how to invest his money may know that the outcome of his investment depends upon economic conditions beyond his control. Where an opinion must be formed or a decision taken, some dissonance is almost unavoidably created between the cognition of the action taken and those opinions or knowledges which tend to point to a different action.

There is, then, a fairly wide variety of situations in which dissonance is nearly unavoidable.... If the hypotheses stated above are correct, then as soon as dissonance occurs there will be pressures to reduce it.

THE REDUCTION OF DISSONANCE

The presence of dissonance gives rise to pressures to reduce or eliminate the dissonance. The strength of the pressures to reduce the dissonance is a function of the magnitude of the dissonance. In other words, dissonance acts in the same way as a state of drive or need or tension. The presence of dissonance leads to action to reduce it just as, for example, the presence of hunger leads to action to reduce the hunger. Also, similar to the action of a drive, the greater the dissonance, the greater will be the intensity of the action to reduce the dissonance and the greater the avoidance of situations that would increase the dissonance.

In order to be specific about how the pressure to reduce dissonance would manifest itself, it is necessary to examine the possible ways in which existing dissonance can be reduced or eliminated. In general, if dissonance exists between two elements, this dissonance can be eliminated by changing one of those elements. The important thing is how these changes may be brought about....

Changing a Behavioral Cognitive Element

When the dissonance under consideration is between an element corresponding to some knowledge concerning environment (environmental element) and a behavioral element, the dissonance can, of course, be eliminated by changing the behavioral cognitive element in such a way that it is consonant with the environmental element.... This method of reducing or eliminating dissonance is a very frequent occurrence. Our behavior and feelings are frequently modified in accordance with new information. If a person starts out on a picnic and notices that it has begun to rain, he may very well turn around and go home. There are many persons who do stop smoking if and when they discover it is bad for their health.

It may not always be possible, however, to eliminate dissonance or even to reduce it materially by changing one's action or feeling. The difficulty of changing the behavior may be too great, or the change, while eliminating some dissonances, may create a whole host of new ones.

Leon Festinger

Just as it is possible to change a behavioral cognitive element by changing the behavior which this element mirrors, it is sometimes possible to change an *environmental* cognitive element by changing the situation to which that element corresponds. This, of course, is much more difficult than changing one's behavior, for one must have a sufficient degree of control over one's environment—a relatively rare occurrence.

Changing the environment itself in order to reduce dissonance is more feasible when the social environment is in question than when the physical environment is involved....

Whenever there is sufficient control over the environment, this method of reducing dissonance may be employed. For example, a person who is habitually very hostile toward other people may surround himself with persons who provoke hostility. His cognitions about the persons with whom he associates are then consonant with the cognitions corresponding to his hostile behavior. The possibilities of manipulating the environment are limited, however, and most endeavors to change a cognitive element will follow other lines....

Adding New Cognitive Elements

It is clear that in order to eliminate a dissonance completely, some cognitive element must be changed. It is also clear that this is not always possible. But even if it is impossible to eliminate a dissonance, it is possible to reduce the total magnitude of dissonance by adding new cognitive elements. Thus, for example, if dissonance existed between some cognitive elements concerning the effects of smoking and cognition concerning the behavior of continuing to smoke, the total dissonance could be reduced by adding new cognitive elements that are consonant with the fact of smoking. In the presence of such dissonance, then, a person might be expected to actively seek new information that would reduce the total dissonance and, at the same time, to avoid new information that might increase the existing dissonance. Thus, to pursue the example, the person might seek out and avidly read any material critical of the research which purported to show that smoking was bad for one's health. At the same time he would avoid reading material that praised this research. (If he unavoidably came in contact with the latter type of material, his reading would be critical indeed.)

Actually, the possibilities for adding new elements which would reduce the existing dissonances are broad. Our smoker, for example, could find out all about accidents and death rates in automobiles. Having then added the cognition that the danger from smoking is negligible compared to the danger he runs driving a car, his dissonance would also have been somewhat reduced. Here the total dissonance is reduced by reducing the *importance* of the existing dissonance....

Before moving on, it is worthwhile to emphasize again that the presence of pressures to reduce dissonance, or even activity directed toward such reduction, does not guarantee that the dissonance will be reduced. A person may not be able to find the social support needed to change a cognitive element, or he may not be able to find new elements which reduce the total dissonance. In fact, it is quite conceivable that in the process of trying to reduce dissonance, it might even be increased. This will depend upon what the person encounters while attempting to reduce the dissonance. The important point to be made so far is that in the presence of a dissonance, one will be able to observe the *attempts* to reduce it. If attempts to reduce dissonance fail, one should be able to observe symptoms of psychological discomfort, provided the dissonance is appreciable enough so that the discomfort is clearly and overtly manifested....

AVOIDANCE OF DISSONANCE

The discussion thus far has focused on the tendencies to reduce or eliminate dissonance and the problems involved in achieving such reduction. Under certain circumstances there are also strong and important tendencies to avoid increases of dissonance or to avoid the occurrence of dissonance altogether. Let us now turn our attention to a consideration of these circumstances and the manifestations of the avoidance tendencies which we might expect to observe.

The avoidance of an increase in dissonance comes about, of course, as a result of the existence of dissonance. This avoidance is especially important where, in the process of attempting to reduce dissonance, support is sought for a new cognitive element to replace an existing one or where new cognitive elements are to be added. In both these circumstances, the seeking of support and the seeking of new information must be done in a highly selective manner. A person would initiate discussion with someone he thought would agree with the new cognitive element but would avoid discussion with someone who might agree with the element that he was trying to change. A person would expose himself to sources of information which he expected would add new elements which would increase consonance but would certainly avoid sources which would increase dissonance....

The operation of a fear of dissonance may also lead to a reluctance to commit oneself behaviorally. There is a large class of actions that, once taken, are difficult to change. Hence, it is possible for dissonances to arise and to mount in intensity. A fear of dissonance would lead to a reluctance to take action—a reluctance to commit oneself. Where decision and action cannot be indefinitely delayed, the taking of action may be accompanied by a cognitive negation of the action. Thus, for example, a person who buys a new car and is very afraid of dissonance may, immediately following the purchase, announce his conviction that he did the wrong thing. Such strong fear of dissonance is probably relatively rare, but it does occur. Personality differences with respect to fear of dissonance and the effectiveness with which one is able to reduce dissonance are undoubtedly important in determining whether or not such avoidance of dissonance is likely to happen.

15.2 JOHN F. DOVIDIO AND SAMUEL L. GAERTNER

Affirmative Action, Unintentional Racial Biases, and Intergroup Relations

It is unfortunate that despite the efforts of psychologists to understand and reduce prejudice, it continues to be present in our society. The traditional form of prejudice was direct; however, more recent forms of prejudice are more subtle. John F. Dovidio and Samuel L. Gaertner have been working toward understanding modern aversive prejudice.

Dovidio (b. 1951) earned his Ph.D. in social psychology from the University of Delaware in 1977. He then accepted a position at Colgate University, where he is currently a professor of psychology. Gaertner (b. 1942) earned his Ph.D. in social psychology from the City University of New York in 1970. He then joined the University of Delaware, where he is presently a professor of psychology. Dovidio and Gaertner coedited the book *Prejudice, Discrimination, and Racism* (Academic Press, 1986).

The following selection is from "Affirmative Action, Unintentional Racial Biases, and Intergroup Relations," which was published in the *Journal of Social Issues* in 1996. In it, the authors describe modern aversive racism and review research studies that demonstrate racism's effects in various settings. As you read this selection, consider how a program might be developed to reduce the level of aversive prejudice.

Key Concept: prejudice

APA Citation: Dovidio, J. F., & Gaertner, S. L. (1996). Affirmative action, unintentional racial biases, and intergroup relations. *Journal of Social Issues, 52,* 51–75.

CONTEMPORARY RACIAL ATTITUDES

The nature of prejudice appears to have changed. Whereas traditional forms of prejudice are direct and overt, contemporary forms are indirect and subtle. Aversive racism (see Dovidio & Gaertner, 1991; Dovidio, Mann, & Gaertner, 1989; Gaertner & Dovidio, 1986; Kovel, 1970) has been identified as a modern form of prejudice that characterizes the racial attitudes of many Whites who endorse egalitarian values, who regard themselves as nonprejudiced, but who discriminate in subtle, rationalizable ways. Most of the work on aversive racism that will be discussed here involves Whites' attitudes toward Blacks. Elsewhere we have demonstrated the generalizability of these processes to attitudes toward Latinos (Dovidio, Gaertner, Anastasio, & Sanitioso, 1992) and women (Dovidio & Gaertner, 1983).

According to the aversive racism perspective, many people who consciously and sincerely support egalitarian principles and believe themselves to be nonprejudiced also unconsciously harbor negative feelings and beliefs about Blacks. These feelings and beliefs, which may be based in part on almost unavoidable cognitive (e.g., informational processing biases that result when people are categorized into ingroups and outgroups; see Hamilton & Trolier, 1986), motivational (e.g., personal or group interest), and sociocultural processes (e.g., social learning; see Gaertner & Dovidio, 1986).

The feelings of aversive racists toward Blacks are characterized by mildly negative feelings, such as fear, disgust, and uneasiness, that tend to motivate avoidance rather than intentionally destructive or hostile behavior, which is more likely to characterize the traditional, old-fashioned form of racism. Relative to the more overt, traditional racists (see Kovel, 1970), aversive racists do not represent the open flame of racial hatred nor do they usually *intend* to act out of bigoted beliefs or feelings. Instead, that bias is expressed in subtle and indirect ways that do not threaten the aversive racist's nonprejudiced self-image. When a negative response can be rationalized on the basis of some factor other than race, bias against Blacks is likely to occur; when these rationalizations are less available, bias is less likely to be manifested. In addition, whereas aversive racists may be very guarded about behaving in anti-Black ways, their biases may be more likely unintentionally manifested in pro-White behaviors (i.e., ingroup favoritism rather than outgroup derogation).

Consistent with the aversive racism perspective, other theories of contemporary racism and sexism also hypothesize that bias is currently expressed more subtly than in the past. One such approach is symbolic racism theory (Kinder & Sears, 1981; McConahay & Hough, 1976; Sears, 1988; Sears, Citrin, & van Laar, 1995; Sears, Hensler, & Speer, 1979; Sears & Allen, 1984) or modern racism (McConahay, 1986) theory. Work on symbolic (Sears, 1988) and modern (McConahay, 1986) racism evolved from the conceptual and practical problems that arose from the weak relationships between traditional self-report prejudice items and racially relevant behaviors, such as voting intentions, that were being obtained in survey data. According to symbolic racism theory, negative feelings toward Blacks that Whites acquire early in life persist into adulthood but are expressed indirectly and symbolically, in terms of opposition to busing or resistance to preferential treatment, rather than directly or overtly, as in support

*John F. Dovidio
and Samuel L.
Gaertner*

for segregation. The items and theory that were developed focused on "the expression in terms of abstract ideological symbols and symbolic behaviors of the feeling that blacks are violating cherished values and making illegitimate demands for changes in the *status quo*" (McConahay & Hough, 1976, p. 23). These "cherished values" were those, such as personal freedom, that were associated with a politically conservative ideology.

McConahay's (1986) theory of modern racism accepted the basic tenets of symbolic racism but amplified the definition "to add the belief that discrimination no longer exists and that the cherished values are those associated with 'equality' or 'equality of opportunity'" (pp. 95–96). McConahay (1986) further proposed that because modern racism involves the rejection of traditional racist beliefs and the displacement of anti-Black feelings onto more abstract social and political issues, modern racists, like aversive racists, are relatively unaware of their racist feelings. Swim, Aikin, Hall, and Hunter (1995) have extended these notions to contemporary prejudice toward women.

Whereas symbolic and modern racism are subtle forms of contemporary racism that seem to exist among political conservatives, aversive racism is more strongly associated with liberals. In addition, we have proposed that because of the sensitivity of aversive racists to race-related issues, it may not be possible to assess individual differences in aversive racism using self-report measures of prejudice (Gaertner & Dovidio, 1986). Kleinpenning and Hagendoorn (1993), believing otherwise however, have suggested that aversive racism can be assessed through self-reports of how pleasant or unpleasant social interactions (e.g., as classmates) or intimate relations (e.g., as marriage partners) with members of other groups would be. They conceptualize forms of racism on a continuum, beginning with aversive racism (which they regard as the mildest form), and followed by symbolic racism and then old-fashioned racism. Kleinpenning and Hagendoorn (1993) conclude that prejudice is a cumulative dimension that begins with avoidance of minorities in private contexts (aversive prejudice) and runs through beliefs that minority groups receive more social and economic benefits than they deserve (symbolic prejudice) to full-blown racist ideologies portraying minorities as being genetically inferior (old-fashioned prejudice).

EMPIRICAL EVIDENCE

Although contemporary forms of bias may be expressed subtly and often unintentionally, the effects may be profound. Across a number of paradigms, we have found consistent evidence of the impact of aversive racism in Whites' responses to Blacks (see Gaertner & Dovidio, 1986). For example, one of our early studies (Gaertner & Dovidio, 1977) demonstrated its influence in an emergency situation.

In one early test of the aversive racism perspective, we investigated whether or not high and low prejudice-scoring White students would help Black or White victims in emergency situations depending upon the clarity of norms regarding intervention (Gaertner & Dovidio, 1977). White subjects were led to believe they were the only bystanders or were among three witnesses (all White) to an emergency involving a Black or White victim. According to Darley and Latané (1968), the normatively appropriate behavior, helping, is clearly defined when a bystander is the only witness to an emergency. In contrast, the appropriate response when other bystanders are believed to be present is less clear and obvious: The presumed presence of other bystanders allows bystanders to diffuse responsibility (Darley & Latané, 1968), to relieve feelings of obligation to help by coming to the conclusion that someone else will act.

Gaertner and Dovidio (1977) found that the White bystanders who believed they were the only witnesses to the emergency were as likely to help Black victims as White victims. When other White bystanders were present, however, Whites were more likely to diffuse responsibility and less likely to intervene to aid the Black victim than the White victim—here they helped the Black victim *half as often* as they helped the White victim. Thus, in the situation in which socially appropriate behavior was clearly defined, White subjects behaved in accordance with their generally nonprejudiced self-images and did not discriminate against the Black victim; when witnesses could rationalize nonintervention, White bystanders discriminated against Black victims. Whereas the situational context was a strong predictor of bias, traditional measures of racial attitudes were not. Neither self-report of prejudice nor authoritarianism correlated overall with responses to the Black victim when bystanders were alone or in the presence of others.

The impact of aversive racism continues to persist today. Its consequences are evident in more considered, deliberative judgments as well as in spontaneous expression of behavior.

Evaluative Judgments

The principles and processes associated with aversive racism may be manifested in situations involving personnel selection. For instance, in a recent study (Dovidio, 1995), White students were recruited ostensibly to help select resident (dormitory) advisors, highly prestigious and competitive student positions, for the coming semester. When the information provided about candidates was unambiguous (i.e., uniformly positive or uniformly negative), Black and White applicants were treated equivalently. However, when the candidate's record was more ambiguous—involving a combination of positive and negative information—White applicants were endorsed more strongly than Black applicants. As in the emergency helping study, contextual ambiguity, not self-reported racial attitudes, predicted whether or not discrimination against Blacks would occur. . . .

Even when equal access for employment is provided in principle, subtle, perhaps unconscious, expressions of bias related to aversive racism, like more blatant forms, may limit opportunities for Blacks and other minorities in practice. We have hypothesized that aversive racism is more intensely manifested in situations in which Whites may be directly or symbolically threatened by the advancement of Blacks to positions of status and control.

Acceptance of Competence

In one study, for instance, we investigated the relationship between status and bias in the context of a decision with implications for participants—making admissions decisions for their university (Kline & Dovidio, 1982). Applicant qualifications were systematically varied: Participants evaluated a poorly qualified applicant, a moderately qualified candidate, or a highly qualified applicant. In addition, the race of the applicant was manipulated by a photograph attached to the file. The central question concerned how this picture would affect participants' admissions decisions.

Discrimination against the Black applicant occurred, but, as expected, it did not occur equally in all conditions. Students rated the poorly qualified Black and White applicants equally low. They showed some bias when they evaluated the moderately qualified White applicant slightly higher than the comparable African-American candidate. Discrimination against the Black applicant was most apparent, however, when the applicants were *highly* qualified. This bias can also be interpreted as a pro-White manifestation of aversive racism (Gaertner et al., 1996). Although White students evaluated the highly qualified African-American applicant very positively, they judged the highly qualified White applicant—with exactly the same credentials—as even better. Thus, a situation that appears to offer equal opportunity to very well-qualified applicants still favors Whites over Blacks because of subtle and pervasive biases.

This study also included individual items that contributed to the overall evaluative score—scaled according to how directly they related to the information presented in the applicant's transcript. The less directly related the item was to the transcript information, the greater the bias ($r = .69$). These results are consistent with the finding that Whites tend to evaluate Blacks less favorably than Whites on subjective dimensions of work performance (Kraiger & Ford, 1985) and support Goddard's (1986) observation in applied settings that "vague, ill-defined, subjective criteria lend themselves to all kinds of biased judgments" (p. 34).

Maintaining the Status Quo

Whereas blatant racial and ethnic prejudices relate to support for policies that unconditionally restrict the rights and opportunities of minority groups, subtle racism is associated with support for the *status quo* or for restrictions when other justifications (e.g., lack of credentials) are available (Pettigrew &

Meertens, 1995). Thus, in other research we investigated the possibility that the generally articulated issue of relative competence is a rationalization in which a nonracial factor, competence, is used by Whites to object to the advancement of Blacks in ways that increase the likelihood that Whites will be subordinated to minority groups.

This reasoning also has relevance to reactions to affirmative action. Consistent with the aversive racism framework, resistance to affirmative action is not commonly expressed directly, but rather mainly as concerns about individual freedom or about unfair distribution of rewards. Nevertheless, although common protests by Whites regarding affirmative action seem to express mainly the concern that *qualified* Whites will be disadvantaged relative to *less qualified* Blacks, it is possible that the reversal of the traditional role relationship, in which Whites occupied positions of superior status, represents the primary threat to Whites.

The results of two separate studies comparing the reactions of White male and female participants to a Black male partner (Dovidio & Gaertner, 1981) and a White female partner (Dovidio & Gaertner, 1983) relative to a White male partner produced convergent findings. Specifically, relative status, rather than relative ability, was the primary determinant of positive behaviors toward Black male and White female partners. Regardless of their competence, Black male and White female supervisors were responded to *less favorably* than were Black male or White female subordinates. In contrast, in both studies White male supervisors were responded to somewhat *more positively* than were White male subordinates.

How could participants in these experiments rationalize not responding as positively to competent Black and female supervisors? Participants' post-experimental evaluations of their partners revealed that their behaviors may have been mediated by perceptions of *relative* intelligence (competence). Although participants' ratings indicated that they accepted high-ability White male partners as being somewhat more intelligent than themselves, participants described even high-ability Black partners as significantly less intelligent than themselves and high-ability female partners as no more intelligent than themselves. To the extent that majority group members are reluctant to believe Blacks and women are higher or equal in competence compared to themselves, they are likely to perceive programs that foster the advancement of members of these groups over themselves and members of their group as unfair preferential treatment. This biased perception of relative competence also decreases the likelihood that passive equal employment opportunity programs can insure truly equitable treatment of disadvantaged groups by the majority group.

Subtle Bias and the Glass Ceiling

Aversive racism and contemporary forms of sexism are difficult to identify definitively in complex organizations because they are subtle and other explanations are usually possible. In fact, aversive racism is generally manifested *only* when other explanations that can rationalize bias are present. Thus, we cannot say that simply because disparities exist in organizations, racism is the cause.

But, where racism exists, disparities will exist. These disparities generally reflect the patterns we have discovered in the laboratory. Across organizations as diverse as the armed forces, federal government, and Fortune 1000 companies, greater racial disparities occur at higher status levels. In addition, these patterns have persisted over the past decade.

Across the different branches of the military in 1988, African Americans who were identified as qualified for officer promotions succeeded at significantly lower rates than did White candidates. Consistent with our laboratory demonstrations, disparities in promotion rates tended to increase with higher ranks. Within the Navy, for example, in 1988 African Americans represented 13% of the force, but only 5% of the officers and 1.5% of the admirals. We have also examined patterns of disparities for various segments of federal employees and found similar evidence: Blacks are generally less well represented in higher grades (e.g., GS 16–18) than in lower grades. Furthermore, these disparities have remained relatively stable across time as well.

A recent Department of Labor survey of Fortune 1000 companies provides independent evidence of the "glass ceiling effect" for Blacks and other minorities in industry. Representations of minorities consistently declined with higher occupational status. A Department of Commerce survey further confirmed substantial income disparities between African-American and White men. In 1989, African-American men with a high school education earned $6230 less per year than White men with comparable education ($20,280 vs. $26,510). The gap was even larger ($9710) between college-educated African-American and White men ($31,380 vs. $41,090).

Thus, across a range of settings we see consistent patterns of disparities in occupational advancement and income. We acknowledge that the "glass ceiling effect" can occur for a wide range of reasons and that the leap from laboratory to organizations is a large one. Nevertheless, the pattern of disparities that we see in organizations conforms to our predictions.

REFERENCES

Darley, J. M., & Latané, B. (1968). Bystander intervention in emergencies: Diffusion of responsibility. *Journal of Personality and Social Psychology, 8*, 377–383.

Dovidio, J. F. (1995). *Bias in evaluative judgments and personnel selection: The role of ambiguity.* Unpublished manuscript. Department of Psychology, Colgate University, Hamilton, NY.

Dovidio, J. F., & Gaertner, S. L. (1981). The effects of race, status, and ability on helping behavior. *Social Psychology Quarterly, 44*, 192–203.

Dovidio, J. F., & Gaertner, S. L. (1983). The effects of sex, status, and ability on helping behavior. *Journal of Applied Social Psychology, 13*, 191–205.

Dovidio, J. F., & Gaertner, S. L. (1991). Changes in the nature and expression of racial prejudice. In H. Knopke, J. Norrell, & R. Rogers (Eds.), *Opening doors: An appraisal of race relations in contemporary America* (pp. 201–241). Tuscaloosa, AL: University of Alabama Press.

Dovidio, J. F., Gaertner, S. L., Anastasio, P. A., & Sanitioso, R. (1992). Cognitive and motivational bases of bias: The implications of aversive racism for attitudes toward Hispanics. In S. Knouse, P. Rosenfeld, & A. Culbertson (Eds.). *Hispanics in the workplace* (pp. 75–106). Newbury Park, CA: Sage.

Dovidio, J. F., Mann, J. A., & Gaertner, S. L. (1989). Resistance to affirmative action: The implication of aversive racism. In F. A. Blanchard & F. J. Crosby (Eds.), *Affirmative action in perspective* (pp. 83–102). New York: Springer-Verlag.

Gaertner, S. L., & Dovidio, J. F. (1977). The subtlety of White racism, arousal, and helping behavior. *Journal of Personality and Social Psychology, 35,* 691–707.

Gaertner, S. L., & Dovidio, J. F. (1986). The aversive form of racism. In J. F. Dovidio & S. L. Gaertner (Eds.), *Prejudice, discrimination, and racism* (pp. 61–89). Orlando, FL: Academic Press.

Gaertner, S. L., Dovidio, J. F., Banker, B., Rust, M., Nier, J., Mottola, G., & Ward, C. (1996). Does racism necessarily mean anti-Blackness? Aversive racism and pro-Whiteness. In M. Fine, L. Powell, L. Weis, & M. Wong (Eds.), *Off White* (pp. 167–178). London: Routledge.

Goddard, R. W. (1986, October). Post-employment: The changing current in discrimination charges. *Personnel Journal, 65,* 34–40.

Hamilton, D. L., & Trolier, T. K. (1986). Stereotypes and stereotyping: An overview of the cognitive approach. In J. F. Dovidio & S. L. Gaertner (Eds.), *Prejudice, discrimination, and racism* (pp. 127–163). Orlando, FL: Academic Press.

Kinder, D. R., & Sears, D. O. (1981). Prejudice and politics: Symbolic racism versus threats to "the good life." *Journal of Personality and Social Psychology, 40,* 414–431.

Kleinpenning, G., & Hagendoorn, L. (1993). Forms of racism and the cumulative dimension of ethnic attitudes. *Social Psychology Quarterly, 56,* 21–36.

Kline, B. B., & Dovidio, J. F. (1982, April). *Effects of race, sex, and qualifications on predictions of a college applicant's performance.* Paper presented at the annual meeting of the Eastern Psychological Association, Baltimore, MD.

Kovel, J. (1970). *White racism: A psychohistory.* New York: Pantheon.

Kraiger, K., & Ford, J. K. (1985). A meta-analysis of ratee effects in performance ratings. *Journal of Applied Psychology, 70,* 56–65.

McConahay, J. B. (1986). Modern racism, ambivalence, and the modern racism scale. In J. F. Dovidio & S. L. Gaertner (Eds.), *Prejudice, discrimination, and racism* (pp. 91–125). Orlando, FL: Academic Press.

McConahay, J. B., & Hough, J. C. (1976). Symbolic racism. *Journal of Social Issues, 32(2),* 23–45.

Pettigrew, T. F., & Meertens, R. W. (1995). Subtle and blatant prejudice in Western Europe. *European Journal of Social Psychology, 25,* 57–76.

Sears, D. O. (1988). Symbolic racism. In P. A. Katz & D. A. Taylor (Eds.), *Eliminating racism: Profiles in controversy* (pp. 53–84). New York: Plenum Press.

Sears, D. O., & Allen, H. M., Jr. (1984). The trajectory of local desegregation controversies and Whites' opposition to busing. In M. B. Brewer & N. Miller (Eds.), *Groups in contact: The psychology of desegregation* (pp. 123–151). New York: Academic Press.

Sears, D. O., Citrin, J., & van Laar, C. (1995, September). *Black exceptionalism in a multicultural society.* Paper presented at the joint meeting of the Society for Experimental Psychology and the European Association of Experimental Social Psychology, Washington, DC.

Sears, D. O., Hensler, C. P., & Speer, L. K. (1979). Whites' opposition to "busing": Self-interest or symbolic politics? *American Political Science Review, 73,* 369–384.

Swim, J. K., Aikin, K. J., Hall, W. S., & Hunter, B. A. (1995). Sexism and racism: Old-fashioned and modern prejudices. *Journal of Personality and Social Psychology, 68,* 199–214.

John F. Dovidio and Samuel L. Gaertner

Behavioral Study of Obedience

Obedience is a type of social influence in which an individual exhibits the behavior required by a command from someone else. We are taught as children to obey parents and teachers, and as we grow up we learn to obey employers, law enforcement officers, and a variety of other authority figures. One of the best-known studies on obedience was performed by Stanley Milgram at Yale University.

Milgram (1933–1984) studied under social psychologist Solomon E. Asch and earned his Ph.D. from Harvard University in 1960. He taught at Yale University and Harvard University before accepting a position at the Graduate Center of the City University of New York in 1967. Milgram, a very creative social psychologist, studied social communication, prejudice, interpersonal relationships, and obedience.

This selection is from "Behavioral Study of Obedience," which was published in *Journal of Abnormal and Social Psychology* in 1963. It presents the results of the first in a series of Milgram's obedience experiments, in which a large percentage of his subjects delivered what they believed to be the maximum level of electric shocks to "learners" (Milgram's confederates), despite the learners' screaming protests, because an authority figure told them to do so. This study has been a subject of controversy during the past three decades because of its ethical considerations as well as its social implications. As you read this selection, consider the extent to which you obey in today's society.

Key Concept: obedience

APA Citation: Milgram, S. (1963). Behavioral study of obedience. *Journal of Abnormal and Social Psychology, 67,* 371–378.

Obedience is as basic an element in the structure of social life as one can point to. Some system of authority is a requirement of all communal living, and it is only the man dwelling in isolation who is not forced to respond, through defiance or submission, to the commands of others. Obedience, as a determinant of behavior, is of particular relevance to our time. It has been reliably established that from 1933–45 millions of innocent persons were systematically slaughtered on command. Gas chambers were built, death camps were guarded, daily quotas of corpses were produced with the same efficiency as the manufacture of appliances. These inhumane policies may have originated in the mind of a single person, but they could only be carried out on a massive scale if a very large number of persons obeyed orders....

General Procedure

A procedure was devised which seems useful as a tool for studying obedience (Milgram, 1961). It consists of ordering a naive subject to administer electric shock to a victim. A simulated shock generator is used, with 30 clearly marked voltage levels that range from 15 to 450 volts. The instrument bears verbal designations that range from Slight Shock to Danger: Severe Shock. The responses of the victim, who is a trained confederate of the experimenter, are standardized. The orders to administer shocks are given to the naive subject in the context of a "learning experiment" ostensibly set up to study the effects of punishment on memory. As the experiment proceeds the naive subject is commanded to administer increasingly more intense shocks to the victim, even to a point of reaching the level marked Danger: Severe Shock. Internal resistances become stronger, and at a certain point the subject refuses to go on with the experiment. Behavior prior to this rupture is considered "obedience," in that the subject complies with the commands of the experimenter. The point of rupture is the act of disobedience. A quantitative value is assigned to the subject's performance based on the maximum intensity shock he is willing to administer before he refuses to participate further. Thus for any particular subject and for any particular experimental condition the degree of obedience may be specified with a numerical value. The crux of the study is to systematically vary the factors believed to alter the degree of obedience to the experimental commands....

METHOD

Subjects

The subjects were 40 males between the ages of 20 and 50, drawn from New Haven and surrounding communities. Subjects were obtained by a newspaper advertisement and direct mail solicitation. Those who responded to the appeal believed they were to participate in a study of memory and learning at Yale University. A wide range of occupations is represented in the sample. Typical subjects were postal clerks, high school teachers, salesmen, engineers, and laborers. Subjects ranged in educational level from one who had not finished elementary school, to those who had doctorate and other professional degrees. They were paid $4.50 for their participation in the experiment.

However, subjects were told that payment was simply for coming to the laboratory, and that the money was theirs no matter what happened after they arrived....

PERSONNEL AND LOCALE

The experiment was conducted on the grounds of Yale University in the elegant interaction laboratory. (This detail is relevant to the perceived legitimacy of the experiment. In further variations, the experiment was dissociated from the university, with consequences for performance.) The role of experimenter was played by a 31-year-old high school teacher of biology. His manner was impassive, and his appearance somewhat stern throughout the experiment. He was dressed in a gray technician's coat. The victim was played by a 47-year-old accountant, trained for the role; he was of Irish-American stock, whom most observers found mild-mannered and likeable.

Procedure

One naive subject and one victim (an accomplice) performed in each experiment. A pretext had to be devised that would justify the administration of electric shock by the naive subject. This was effectively accomplished by the cover story. After a general introduction on the presumed relation between punishment and learning, subjects were told:

> But actually, we know *very little* about the effect of punishment on learning, because almost no truly scientific studies have been made of it in human beings.
>
> For instance, we don't know how *much* punishment is best for learning—and we don't know how much difference it makes as to who is giving the punishment, whether an adult learns best from a younger or an older person than himself —or many things of that sort.
>
> So in this study we are bringing together a number of adults of different occupations and ages. And we're asking some of them to be teachers and some of them to be learners.
>
> We want to find out just what effect different people have on each other as teachers and learners, and also what effect *punishment* will have on learning in this situation.
>
> Therefore, I'm going to ask one of you to be the teacher here tonight and the other one to be the learner.
>
> Does either of you have a preference?

Subjects then drew slips of paper from a hat to determine who would be the teacher and who would be the learner in the experiment. The drawing was rigged so that the naive subject was always the teacher and the accomplice always the learner. (Both slips contained the word "Teacher.") Immediately after the drawing, the teacher and learner were taken to an adjacent room and the learner was strapped into an "electric chair" apparatus.

The experimenter explained that the straps were to prevent excessive movement while the learner was being shocked. The effect was to make it impossible for him to escape from the situation. An electrode was attached to the learner's wrist, and electrode paste was applied "to avoid blisters and burns." Subjects were told that the electrode was attached to the shock generator in the adjoining room.

In order to improve credibility the experimenter declared, in response to a question by the learner: "Although the shocks can be extremely painful, they cause no permanent tissue damage."

Learning task. The lesson administered by the subject was a paired-associate learning task. The subject read a series of word pairs to the learner, and then read the first word of the pair along with four terms. The learner was to indicate which of the four terms had originally been paired with the first word. He communicated his answer by pressing one of four switches in front of him, which in turn lit up one of four numbered quadrants in a answer-box located atop the shock generator.

Shock generator. The instrument panel consists of 30 lever switches set in a horizontal line. Each switch is clearly labeled with a voltage designation that ranges from 15 to 450 volts. There is a 15-volt increment from one switch to the next going from left to right. In addition, the following verbal designations are clearly indicated for groups of four switches going from left to right: Slight Shock, Moderate Shock, Strong Shock, Intense Shock, Extremely Intense Shock, Danger: Severe Shock. (Two switches after this last designation are simply marked XXX.)

Upon depressing a switch: a pilot light corresponding to each switch is illuminated in bright red; an electric buzzing is heard; an electric blue light, labeled "voltage energizer," flashes; the dial on the voltage meter swings to the right; various relay clicks are sounded.

The upper left-hand corner of the generator is labeled Shock generator, Type ZLB, Dyson Instrument Company, Waltham, Mass. Output 15 Volts–450 Volts.

Details of the instrument were carefully handled to insure an appearance of authenticity. The panel was engraved by precision industrial engravers, and all components were of high quality. No subject in the experiment suspected that the instrument was merely a simulated shock generator.

Sample shock. Each naive subject is given a sample shock on the shock generator, prior to beginning his run as teacher. This shock is always 45 volts, and is applied by pressing the third switch of the generator. The shock is applied to the wrist of the naive subject, and has its source in a 45-volt battery wired into the generator. This further convinces the subject of the authenticity of the generator.

Shock instructions. The subject is told to administer a shock to the learner each time he gives a wrong response. Moreover—and this is the key command —the subject is instructed to "move one level higher on the shock generator each time the learner flashes a wrong answer." He is also instructed to announce the voltage level before administering a shock. This serves to continually remind subjects of the increasing intensity of shocks administered to the learner.

Preliminary and regular run. Pretests revealed that the procedure of reading words and administering shocks requires some practice before it can be handled smoothly. Therefore, immediately preceding the regular run, the teacher is given a preliminary series of 10 words to read to the learner. There are 3 neutral words in the practice series (i.e., words that the learner answers correctly), so that shocks are administered for 7 of the words, with the maximum shock of 105 volts (moderate shock). Almost all subjects master the procedure by the time the preliminary run is over.

Subjects are then presented with a second list, and are told that the procedure is the same as for the first list; the experimenter adds however:

> When you get to the bottom of the list, repeat it over again, and continue giving shocks, until the learner has learned all the pairs correctly.

The experimenter instructs the subject to,

> start from 15 volts and increase the shock level one step each time the learner gives a wrong answer.

Feedback from the victim. In all conditions the learner gives a predetermined set of responses to the word pair test, based on a schedule of approximately three wrong answers to one correct answer. In the present experimental condition no vocal response or other sign of protest is heard from the learner until Shock Level 300 is reached. When the 300-volt shock is administered, the learner pounds on the wall of the room in which he is bound to the electric chair. The pounding can be heard by the subject. From this point on, the learner's answers no longer appear on the four-way panel.

At this juncture, subjects ordinarily turn to the experimenter for guidance. The experimenter instructs the subject to treat absence of a response as a wrong answer, and to shock the subject according to the usual schedule. He advises the subjects to allow 5–10 seconds before considering no response as a wrong answer, and to increase the shock level one step each time the learner fails to respond correctly. The learner's pounding is repeated after the 315-volt shock is administered; afterwards he is not heard from, nor do his answers reappear on the four-way signal box.

Experimenter feedback. At various points in the experiment the subject may turn to the experimenter for advice on whether he should continue to administer shocks. Or he may indicate that he does not wish to go on. It was important to standardize the experimenter's responses to these inquiries and reactions.

If the subject indicated his unwillingness to go on, the experimenter responded with a sequence of "prods," using as many as necessary to bring the subject into line.

Prod 1: Please continue. *or* Please go on.

Prod 2: The experiment requires that you continue.

Prod 3: It is absolutely essential that you continue.

Prod 4: You have no other choice, you *must* go on.

The prods were always made in sequence: Only if Prod 1 had been unsuccessful, could Prod 2 be used. If the subject still refused to obey the experimenter after Prod 4, the experiment was terminated. The experimenter's tone of voice was at all times firm, but not impolite. The sequence was begun anew on each occasion that the subject balked or showed reluctance to follow orders.

Special prods. If the subject asked if the learner was liable to suffer permanent physical injury, the experimenter said:

Although the shocks may be painful, there is no permanent tissue damage, so please go on. [Followed by Prods 2, 3, and 4 if necessary.]

If the subject said that the learner did not want to go on, the experimenter replied:

Whether the learner likes it or not, you must go on until he has learned all the word pairs correctly. So please go on. [Followed by Prods 2, 3, and 4 if necessary.]

Dependent Measures

The primary dependent measure for any subject is the maximum shock he administers before he refuses to go any further. In principle this may vary from 0 (for a subject who refuses to administer even the first shock) to 30 (for a subject who administers the highest shock on the generator). A subject who breaks off the experiment at any point prior to administering the thirtieth shock level is termed a *defiant subject*. One who complies with experimental command fully, and proceeds to administer all shock levels commanded, is termed an *obedient subject*. . . .

Interview and dehoax.   Following the experiment, subjects were interviewed; open-ended questions, projective measures, and attitude scales were employed. After the interview, procedures were undertaken to assure that the subject would leave the laboratory in a state of well being. A friendly reconciliation was arranged between the subject and the victim, and an effort was made to reduce any tensions that arose as a result of the experiment.

RESULTS

Preliminary Notions

Before giving an account of the experimental results, it is instructive to consider how persons predict others will perform when commanded to administer powerful shocks to another person. Fourteen Yale seniors, all psychology majors, were provided with a detailed description of the experimental situation. They were asked to reflect carefully on it, and to predict the behavior of 100 hypothetical subjects. More specifically, they were instructed to plot the distribution of obedience of "100 Americans of diverse occupations, and ranging in age from 20 to 50 years," who were placed in the experimental situation.

There was considerable agreement among the respondents on the expected behavior of hypothetical subjects. All respondents predicted that only an insignificant minority would go through to the end of the shock series. (The estimates ranged from 0 to 3%; i.e, the most "pessimistic" member of the class predicted that of 100 persons, 3 would continue through to the most potent shock available on the shock generator—450 volts.) The class mean was 1.2%. The question was also posed informally to colleagues of the author, and the most general feeling was that few if any subjects would go beyond the designation Very Strong Shock.

Result of Experiment I

Subjects accept situation.   With few exceptions subjects were convinced of the reality of the experimental situation, that they were administering shocks to another person, and the most potent shocks were extremely painful. In the post-experimental interview subjects were asked: "How painful to the learner were the last few shocks that you administered to him?" Subjects were instructed to indicate their answers on a printed 14-point scale ranging from "Not at all painful" to "Extremely painful." The modal response was 14 (Extremely painful) with the mean at 13.42.

Signs of extreme tension.   Many subjects showed signs of nervousness in the experimental situation, and especially upon administering the more powerful shocks. In a large number of cases the degree of tension reached extremes that are rarely seen in sociopsychological laboratory studies. Subjects were observed to sweat, tremble, stutter, bite their lips, groan, and dig their fingernails into their flesh. These were characteristic rather than exceptional responses to the experiment.

One sign of tension was the regular occurrence of nervous laughing fits. Fourteen of the 40 subjects showed definite signs of nervous laughter and smiling. The laughter seemed entirely out of place, even bizarre. Full-blown, uncontrollable seizures were observed for 3 subjects. On one occasion we observed a seizure so violently convulsive that it was necessary to call a halt to the experiment. The subject, a 46-year-old encyclopedia salesman, was seriously embarrassed by his untoward and uncontrollable behavior. In the post-experimental interviews subjects took such pains to point out that they were not sadistic types, and that the laughter did not mean they enjoyed shocking the victim.

Distribution of scores.   It had been conjectured that persons would not, in general, agree to administer shocks beyond the level designated Very Strong Shock. The distribution of maximum shocks for this experiment is shown in Table 1. The obtained distribution of scores deviates radically from the prediction.

Upon command of the experimenter, each of the 40 subjects went beyond the expected breakoff point. No subject stopped prior to administering Shock Level 20. (At this level—300 volts—the victim kicks on the wall and no longer provides answers to the teacher's multiple-choice questions.)

Of the 40 subjects, 5 refused to obey the experimental commands beyond the 300-volt level. Four more subjects administered one further shock, and then refused to go on. Two broke off at the 330-volt level, and 1 each at 345, 360, and 375 volts. Thus a total of 14 subjects defied the experimenter. It is instructive to reprint their remarks at the point of defiance, as transcribed from the tape recordings:

> [0124] I think he's trying to communicate, he's knocking.... Well it's not fair to shock the guy... these are terrific volts. I don't think this is very humane.... Oh, I can't go on with this; no this isn't right. It's a hell of an experiment. The guy is suffering in there. No, I don't want to go on. This is crazy. [Subject refused to administer more shocks.]

> [0123] He's banging in there. I'm gonna chicken out. I'd like to continue, but I can't do that to a man.... I'm sorry I can't do that to a man. I'll hurt his heart. You take your check.... No really, I couldn't do it.

These subjects were frequently in a highly agitated and even angered state. Sometimes, verbal protest was at a minimum, and the subject simply got up from his chair in front of the shock generator, and indicated that he wished to leave the laboratory.

Of the 40 subjects, 26 obeyed the orders of the experimenter to the end, proceeding to punish the victim until they reached the most potent shock available on the shock generator. At that point, the experimenter called a halt to the sessions. (The maximum shock is labeled 450 volts, and is two steps beyond the designation: Danger: Severe Shock.) Although obedient subjects continued to administer shocks, they often did so under extreme stress. Some expressed reluctance to administer shocks beyond the 300-volt level, and displayed fears similar to those who defied the experimenter; yet they obeyed.

After the maximum shocks had been delivered, and the experimenter called a halt to the proceedings, many obedient subjects heaved sighs of relief, mopped their brows, rubbed their fingers over their eyes, or nervously fumbled cigarettes. Some shook their heads, apparently in regret. Some subjects had remained calm throughout the experiment, and displayed only minimal signs of tension from beginning to end.

TABLE 1

Distribution of Breakoff Points

Verbal designation and voltage indication	*Number of subjects for whom this was maximum shock*
Slight Shock	
15	0
30	0
45	0
60	0
Moderate Shock	
75	0
90	0
105	0
120	0
Strong Shock	
135	0
150	0
165	0
180	0
Very Strong Shock	
195	0
210	0
225	0
240	0
Intense Shock	
255	0
270	0
285	0
300	5
Extreme Intensity Shock	
315	4
330	2
345	1
360	1
Danger: Severe Shock	
375	1
390	0
405	0
420	0
XXX	
435	0
450	26

DISCUSSION

The experiment yielded two findings that were surprising. The first finding concerns the sheer strength of obedient tendencies manifested in this situation. Subjects have learned from childhood that it is a fundamental breach of moral conduct to hurt another person against his will. Yet, 26 subjects abandon this tenet in following the instructions of an authority who has no special powers to enforce his commands. To disobey would bring no material loss to the subject; no punishment would ensue. It is clear from the remarks and outward behavior of many participants that in punishing the victim they are often acting against their own values. Subjects often expressed deep disapproval of shocking a man in the face of his objections, and others denounced it as stupid and senseless. Yet the majority complied with the experimental commands. This outcome was surprising from two perspectives: first, from the standpoint of predictions made in the questionnaire described earlier. (Here, however, it is possible that the remoteness of the respondents from the actual situation, and the difficulty of conveying to them the concrete details of the experiment, could account for the serious underestimation of obedience.)

But the results were also unexpected to persons who observed the experiment in progress, through one-way mirrors. Observers often uttered expressions of disbelief upon seeing a subject administer more powerful shocks to the victim. These persons had a full acquaintance with the details of the situation, and yet systematically underestimated the amount of obedience that subjects would display.

The second unanticipated effect was the extraordinary tension generated by the procedures. One might suppose that a subject would simply break off or continue as his conscience dictated. Yet, this is very far from what happened. There were striking reactions of tension and emotional strain.

REFERENCES

Milgram, S. Dynamics of obedience. Washington: National Science Foundation, 25 January 1961. (Mimeo)

15.4 ALBERT BANDURA, DOROTHEA ROSS, AND SHEILA A. ROSS

Imitation of Film-Mediated Aggressive Models

Rising levels of crime and destructive aggression have been studied by psychologists for decades. One ongoing debate has focused on whether or not observation and imitation is a problem with regard to aggression that occurs in the media. Do children imitate the aggressive acts they observe in movies and on television? Through a series of studies, Albert Bandura and his colleagues have begun to answer this question.

Bandura (b. 1925), a leading theorist in observational learning, received his Ph.D. from the University of Iowa in 1952. Shortly afterward, he began his academic career at Stanford University, where he has remained. He has written many books, including *Aggression: A Social Learning Analysis* (Prentice Hall, 1973) and *Social Learning Theory* (Prentice Hall, 1977). Dorothea Ross and Sheila A. Ross both earned a Ph.D. in developmental psychology from Stanford University. Ross and Ross specialized in children's health and cognitive development prior to their retirement.

This selection is from "Imitation of Film-Mediated Aggressive Models," which was published in *Journal of Abnormal and Social Psychology* in 1963. It details Bandura et al.'s classic study on aggression imitation in standard research article format. Note the care with which the procedure was carried out. An important point for understanding the statistical results is that a probability (p) level less than .05 is significant and indicates a real difference among experimental conditions. Bandura et al.'s findings go against most of the research reported prior to the study, which maintained that film-mediated aggression reduces aggressive drives through a cathartic process. The research reported in this selection suggests that filmed aggression can facilitate aggression in children. What are the implications of this study for aggression and violence in movies and on television today?

Key Concept: observation learning of aggression

APA Citation: Bandura, A., Ross, D., & Ross, S. (1963). Imitation of film-mediated aggressive models. *Journal of Abnormal and Social Psychology, 66*, 3–11.

*I*n a test of the hypothesis that exposure of children to film-mediated aggressive models would increase the probability of Ss' [Subjects—i.e., children] aggression to subsequent frustration, 1 group of experimental Ss observed real-life aggressive models, a 2nd observed these same models portraying aggression on film, while a 3rd group viewed a film depicting an aggressive cartoon character. Following the exposure treatment, Ss were mildly frustrated and tested for the amount of imitative and nonimitative aggression in a different experimental setting. The overall results provide evidence for both the facilitating and the modeling influence of film-mediated aggressive stimulation. In addition, the findings reveal that the effects of such exposure are to some extent a function of the sex of the model, sex of the child, and the reality cues of the model....

*Albert Bandura
et al.*

A recent incident (San Francisco Chronicle, 1961) in which a boy was seriously knifed during a re-enactment of a switchblade knife fight the boys had seen the previous evening on a televised rerun of the James Dean movie, *Rebel Without a Cause*, is a dramatic illustration of the possible imitative influence of film stimulation. Indeed, anecdotal data suggest that portrayal of aggression through pictorial media may be more influential in shaping the form aggression will take when a person is instigated on later occasions, than in altering the level of instigation to aggression.

In an earlier experiment (Bandura & Huston, 1961), it was shown that children readily imitated aggressive behavior exhibited by a model in the presence of the model. A succeeding investigation (Bandura, Ross, & Ross, 1961), demonstrated that children exposed to aggressive models generalized aggressive responses to a new setting in which the model was absent. The present study sought to determine the extent to which film-mediated aggressive models may serve as an important source of imitative behavior.

Aggressive models can be ordered on a reality-fictional stimulus dimension with real-life models located at the realty end of the continuum, nonhuman cartoon characters at the fictional end, and films portraying human models occupying an intermediate position. It was predicted, on the basis of saliency and similarity of cues, that the more remote the model was from reality, the weaker would be the tendency for subjects to imitate the behavior of the model....

To the extent that observation of adults displaying aggression conveys a certain degree of permissiveness for aggressive behavior, it may be assumed that such exposure not only facilitates the learning of new aggressive responses but also weakens competing inhibitory responses in subjects and thereby increases the probability of occurrence of previously learned patterns of aggression. It was predicted, therefore, that subjects who observed aggressive models would display significantly more aggression when subsequently frustrated than subjects who were equally frustrated but who had no prior exposure to models exhibiting aggression.

METHOD

The subjects were 48 boys and 48 girls enrolled in the Stanford University Nursery School. They ranged in age from 35 to 69 months, with a mean age of 52 months.

Two adults, a male and a female, served in the role of models both in the real-life and the human film-aggression condition, and one female experimenter conducted the study for all 96 children.

General Procedure

Subjects were divided into three experimental groups and one control group of 24 subjects each. One group of experimental subjects observed real-life aggressive models, a second group observed these same models portraying aggression on film, while a third group viewed a film depicting an aggressive cartoon character. The experimental groups were further subdivided into male and female subjects so that half the subjects in the two conditions involving human models were exposed to same-sex models, while the remaining subjects viewed models of the opposite sex.

Following the exposure experience, subjects were tested for the amount of imitative and nonimitative aggression in a different experimental setting in the absence of the models.

The control group subjects had no exposure to the aggressive models and were tested only in the generalization situation.

Subjects in the experimental and control groups were matched individually on the basis of ratings of their aggressive behavior in social interactions in the nursery school. The experimenter and a nursery school teacher rated the subjects on four five-point rating scales which measured the extent to which subjects displayed physical aggression, verbal aggression, aggression toward inanimate objects, and aggression inhibition. The latter scale, which dealt with the subjects' tendency to inhibit aggressive reactions in the face of high instigation, provided the measure of aggression anxiety. Seventy-one percent of the subjects were rated independently by both judges so as to permit an assessment of interrater agreement. The reliability of the composite aggression score, estimated by means of the Pearson product-moment correlation, was .80. . . .

Experimental Conditions

Subjects in the Real-Life Aggressive condition were brought individually by the experimenter to the experimental room and the model, who was in the hallway outside the room, was invited by the experimenter to come and join in the game. The subject was then escorted to one corner of the room and seated at a small table which contained potato prints, multicolor picture stickers, and colored paper. After demonstrating how the subject could design pictures with the materials provided, the experimenter escorted the model to the opposite corner of the room which contained a small table and chair, a tinker toy set, a mallet, and a 5-foot inflated Bobo doll. The experimenter explained that this was the model's play area and after the model was seated, the experimenter left the experimental room.

The model began the session by assembling the tinker toys but after approximately a minute had elapsed, the model turned to the Bobo doll and spent the remainder of the period aggressing toward it with highly novel responses which are unlikely to be performed by children independently of the observation of the model's behavior. Thus, in addition to punching the Bobo doll, the model exhibited the following distinctive aggressive acts which were to be scored as imitative responses:

The model sat on the Bobo doll and punched it repeatedly in the nose.

The model then raised the Bobo doll and pommeled it on the head with a mallet.

Following the mallet aggression, the model tossed the doll up in the air aggressively and kicked it about the room. This sequence of physically aggressive acts was repeated approximately three times, interspersed with verbally aggressive responses such as, "Sock him in the nose... ," "Hit him down... ," "Throw him in the air... ," "Kick him... ," and "Pow."

Subjects in the Human Film-Aggression condition were brought by the experimenter to the semi-darkened experimental room, introduced to the picture materials, and informed that while the subjects worked on potato prints, a movie would be shown on a screen, positioned approximately 6 feet from the subject's table. The movie projector was located in a distant corner of the room and was screened from the subject's view by large wooden panels.

The color movie and a tape recording of the sound track was begun by a male projectionist as soon as the experimenter left the experimental room and was shown for a duration of 10 minutes. The models in the film presentations were the same adult males and females who participated in the Real-Life condition of the experiment. Similarly, the aggressive behavior they portrayed in the film was identical with their real-life performances.

For subjects in the Cartoon Film-Aggression condition, after seating the subject at the table with the picture construction material, the experimenter walked over to a television console approximately 3 feet in front of the subject's table, remarked, "I guess I'll turn on the color TV," and ostensibly tuned in a cartoon program. The experimenter then left the experimental room. The cartoon was shown on a glass lens screen in the television set by means of a rear projection arrangement screened from the subject's view by large panels....

In both film conditions, at the conclusion of the movie the experimenter entered the room and then escorted the subject to the test room.

Aggression Instigation

In order to differentiate clearly the exposure and test situations subjects were tested for the amount of imitative learning in a different experimental room which was set off from the main nursery school building.

The degree to which a child has learned aggressive patterns of behavior through imitation becomes most evident when the child is instigated to aggression on later occasions. Thus, for example, the effects of viewing the movie,

Rebel Without a Cause, were not evident until the boys were instigated to aggression the following day, at which time they re-enacted the televised switchblade knife fight in considerable detail. For this reason, the children in the experiment, both those in the control group, and those who were exposed to the aggressive models, were mildly frustrated before they were brought to the test room.

Following the exposure experience, the experimenter brought the subject to an anteroom which contained a varied array of highly attractive toys. The experimenter explained that the toys were for the subject to play with, but, as soon as the subject became sufficiently involved with the play material, the experimenter remarked that these were her very best toys, that she did not let just anyone play with them, and that she had decided to reserve these toys for some other children. However, the subject could play with any of the toys in the next room. The experimenter and the subject then entered the adjoining experimental room. . . .

Test for Delayed Imitation

The experimental room contained a variety of toys, some of which could be used in imitative or nonimitative aggression, and others which tended to elicit predominantly nonaggressive forms of behavior. The aggressive toys included a 3-foot Bobo doll, a mallet and peg board, two dart guns, and a tether ball with a face painted on it which hung from the ceiling. The nonaggressive toys, on the other hand, included a tea set, crayons and coloring paper, a ball, two dolls, three bears, cars and trucks, and plastic farm animals. . . .

The subject spent 20 minutes in the experimental room during which time his behavior was rated in terms of predetermined response categories by judges who observed the session through a one-way mirror in an adjoining observation room. The 20-minute session was divided in 5-second intervals by means of an electric interval timer, thus yielding a total number of 240 response units for each subject. . . .

RESULTS

The mean imitative and nonimitative aggression scores for subjects in the various experimental and control groups are presented in Table 1.

Since the distributions of scores departed from normality and the assumption of homogeneity of variance could not be made for most of the measures, the Freidman two-way analysis of variance by ranks was employed for testing the significance of the obtained differences.

Total Aggression

The mean total aggression scores for subjects in the real-life, human film, cartoon film, and the control groups are 83, 92, 99, and 54 respectively. The results of the analysis of variance performed on these scores reveal that the

TABLE 1

*Mean Aggression Scores for Subgroups
of Experimental and Control Subjects*

Response category	Experimental groups					
	Real-life aggressive		Human film aggressive		Cartoon film aggressive	Control group
	F Model	M Model	F Model	M Model		
Total aggression						
Girls	65.8	57.3	87.0	79.5	80.9	36.4
Boys	76.8	131.8	114.5	85.0	117.2	72.2
Imitative aggression						
Girls	19.2	9.2	10.0	8.0	7.8	1.8
Boys	18.4	38.4	34.3	13.3	16.2	3.9
Mallet aggression						
Girls	17.2	18.7	49.2	19.5	36.8	13.1
Boys	15.5	28.8	20.5	16.3	12.5	13.5
Sits on Bobo doll[a]						
Girls	10.4	5.6	10.3	4.5	15.3	3.3
Boys	1.3	0.7	7.7	0.0	5.6	0.6
Nonimitative aggression						
Girls	27.6	24.9	24.0	34.3	27.5	17.8
Boys	35.5	48.6	46.8	31.8	71.8	40.4
Aggressive gun play						
Girls	1.8	4.5	3.8	17.6	8.8	3.7
Boys	7.3	15.9	12.8	23.7	16.6	14.3

[a] This response category was not included in the total aggression score.

main effect of treatment conditions is significant ($Xr^2 = p < .05$), confirming the prediction that exposure of subjects to aggressive models increases the probability that subjects will respond aggressively when instigated on later occasions. Further analyses of pairs of scores by means of the Wilcoxon matched-pairs signed-ranks test show that subjects who viewed the real-life models and the film-mediated models do not differ from each other in total aggressiveness but all three experimental groups expressed significantly more aggressive behavior than the control subjects....

Influence of Sex of Model and Sex of Child

In order to determine the influence of sex of model and sex of child on the expression of imitative and nonimitative aggression, the data from the experimental groups were combined and the significance of the differences between groups was assessed by *t* tests for uncorrelated means. In statistical comparisons involving relatively skewed distributions of scores the Mann-Whitney *U* test was employed.

Sex of subjects had a highly significant effect on both the learning and the performance of aggression. Boys, in relation to girls, exhibited significantly more total aggression ($t = 2.69$, $p < .01$), more imitative aggression ($t = 2.82$, $p < .005$), more aggressive gun play ($z = 3.38$, $p < .001$), and more nonimitative aggressive behavior ($t = 2.98$, $p < .005$). Girls, on the other hand, were more inclined than boys to sit on the Bobo doll but refrained from punching it ($z = 3.47$, $p < .001$).

The analyses also disclosed some influences of the sex of the model. Subjects exposed to the male model, as compared to the female model, expressed significantly more aggressive gun play ($z = 2.83$, $p < .005$). The most marked differences in aggressive gun play ($U = 9.5$, $p < .001$), however, were found between girls exposed to the female model ($M = 2.9$) and males who observed the male model ($M = 19.8$). Although the overall model difference in partially imitative behavior, Sits on Bobo, was not significant, Sex x Model subgroup comparisons yielded some interesting results. Boys who observed the aggressive female model, for example, were more likely to sit on the Bobo doll without punching it than boys who viewed the male model ($U = 33$, $p < .05$). Girls reproduced the nonaggressive component of the male model's aggressive pattern of behavior (i.e., sat on the doll without punching it) with considerably higher frequency than did boys who observed the same model ($U = 21.5$, $p < .02$). The highest incidence of partially imitative responses was yielded by the group of girls who viewed the aggressive female model ($M = 10.4$), and the lowest values by the boys who were exposed to the male model ($M = 0.3$). This difference was significant beyond the .05 significance level. These findings, along with the sex of child and sex of model differences reported in the preceding sections, provide further support for the view that the influence of models in promoting social learning is determined, in part, by the sex appropriateness of the model's behavior (Bandura et al., 1961). . . .

DISCUSSION

The results of the present study provide strong evidence that exposure to filmed aggression heightens aggressive reactions in children. Subjects who viewed the aggressive human and cartoon models on film exhibited nearly twice as much aggression than did subjects in the control group who were not exposed to the aggressive film content. . . .

Filmed aggression, not only facilitated the expression of aggression, but also effectively shaped the form of the subjects' aggressive behavior. The finding that children modeled their behavior to some extent after the film characters suggests that pictorial mass media, particularly television, may serve as an important source of social behavior. In fact, a possible generalization of responses originally learned in the television situation to the experimental film may account for the significantly greater amount of aggressive gun play displayed by subjects in the film condition as compared to subjects in the real-life and control groups. It is unfortunate that the qualitative features of the gun behavior were not scored since subjects in the film condition, unlike those in the other two groups, developed interesting elaborations in gun play (for example, stalking the imaginary opponent, quick drawing, and rapid firing), characteristic of the Western gun fighter.

REFERENCES

Bandura, A., & Huston, Aletha C. Identification as a process of incidental learning. *J. abnorm. soc. Psychol.*, 1961, **63,** 311–318.

Bandura, A., Ross, Dorothea, & Ross, Sheila A. Transmission of aggression through imitation of aggressive models. *J. abnorm. soc. Psychol.*, 1961, **63,** 575–582.

San Francisco Chronicle. "James Dean" knifing in South City. *San Francisco Chron.*, March 1, 1961, 6.

ACKNOWLEDGMENTS

1.1 From *The Principles of Psychology* (Vol. 1, pp. 1, 4-8) by W. James, 1950. New York: Dover Publications. (Original work published 1890.) Notes omitted.

1.2 From "Psychology as the Behaviorist Views It" by J. B. Watson, 1913, *Psychological Review, 20*, pp. 158–177.

1.3 From "Experimental Psychology at Wellesley College" by M. W. Calkins, 1892, *American Journal of Psychology, 5*, pp. 464-468.

1.4 From "Fragmentation of Psychology?" by G. H. Bower, 1993, *American Psychologist, 48*, pp. 905-907. Copyright © 1993 by The American Psychological Association. Reprinted by permission.

2.1 From "Hemisphere Deconnection and Unity in Conscious Awareness" by R. W. Sperry, 1968, *American Psychologist, 23*, pp. 723-733. Copyright © 1968 by The American Psychological Association. Reprinted by permission.

2.2 From "The Localization of a Simple Type of Learning and Memory: The Cerebellum and Classical Eyeblink Conditioning" by J. E. Steinmetz, 1998, *Current Directions in Psychological Science, 7*, pp. 72-77. Copyright © 1998 by American Psychological Society. Reprinted by permission of Blackwell Publishers. Notes omitted.

2.3 From "Serotonin, Motor Activity and Depression-Related Disorders" by B. L. Jacobs, 1994, *American Scientist, 82*, pp. 456, 458–459, 461–463. Copyright © 1994 by Sigma Xi. Reprinted by permission. Bibliography omitted.

2.4 From "Environment and Genes: Determinants of Behavior" by R. Plomin, 1989, *American Psychologist, 44*, pp. 105-108, 110-111. Copyright © 1989 by The American Psychological Association. Reprinted by permission.

3.1 From "The Stages of the Intellectual Development of the Child" by J. Piaget, 1962, *Bulletin of the Menninger Clinic, 26*, pp. 120-128. Copyright © 1962 by The Guilford Press. Reprinted by permission of Guilford Publications, Inc.

3.2 From "Infant–Mother Attachment" by M. D. S. Ainsworth, 1979, *American Psychologist, 34*, pp. 932–937. Copyright © 1979 by Mary D. Salter Ainsworth. Reprinted by permission.

3.3 From "The Child as a Moral Philosopher" by L. Kohlberg, 1968, *Psychology Today, 214*, pp. 25-26, 28-30. Copyright © 1968 by Sussex Publishers, Inc. Reprinted by permission of *Psychology Today*.

3.4 From "Gender and Relationships: A Developmental Account" by E. E. Maccoby, 1990, *American Psychologist, 45*, pp. 513-517, 519-520. Copyright © 1990 by The American Psychological Association. Reprinted by permission.

4.1 From "The 'Visual Cliff'" by E. J. Gibson and R. D. Walk, 1960, *Scientific American, 202*, pp. 67-71. Copyright © 1960 by Scientific American, Inc. Reprinted by permission.

4.2 From "Exploration of the Primary Visual Cortex" by D. H. Hubel, 1982, *Nature, 299*, pp. 515-524. Copyright © 1982 by Macmillan Journals Ltd.

5.1 From "Weapon Against Pain: Hypnosis Is No Mirage" by E.R. Hilgard, 1974, *Psychology Today*, pp. 121-122, 126, 128. Copyright © 1974 by Sussex Publishers, Inc. Reprinted by permission of *Psychology Today*.

5.2 From *The Interpretation of Dreams* (pp. 33–43) by S. Freud, 1950 (A. A. Brill, Trans.). New York: Random House. (Original work published 1900.) Translation originally copyrighted © 1938; copyright renewed 1965 in *The Basic Writings of Sigmund Freud*. New York: Modern Library. Reprinted by permission. Notes omitted.

6.1 From *Conditioned Reflexes: An Investigation of the Physiological Activity of the Cerebral Cortex* (pp. 20-29) by I. P. Pavlov, 1927 (G. V. Anrer, Trans.). New York: Dover Publications.

6.2 From "Conditioned Emotional Reactions" by J. B. Watson and R. Rayner, 1920, *Journal of Experimental Psychology, 3*, pp. 1-7, 10, 13-14. Notes omitted.

6.3 From *Science and Human Behavior* (pp. 91-93, 98-104) by B. F. Skinner, 1953. New York: Free Press. Copyright © 1953 by Prentice-Hall, Inc., Upper Saddle River, NJ. Reprinted by permission.

7.1 From "Storage and Retrieval Processes in Long-Term Memory" by R. M. Shiffrin and R. C. Atkinson, 1969, *Psychological Review, 76*, pp. 179-183, 187-193. Copyright © 1969 by The American Psychological Association. Adapted with permission.

7.2 From "What Is Episodic Memory" by E. Tulving, 1993, *Current Directions in Psychological Science, 2*, pp. 67-70. Copyright © 1993 by The American Psychological Society. Reprinted by permission.

7.3 From "Leading Questions and the Eyewitness Report" by E. F. Loftus, 1972, *Cognitive Psychology, 7*, pp. 560-567, 569, 572. Copyright © 1972 by Academic Press, Inc. Reprinted by permission.

8.1 From "Creativity: Its Nature and Assessment" by R. J. Sternberg and T. I. Lubart, 1992, *School Psychology International, 13*, pp. 243-249, 252-253. Copyright © 1992 by Sage Publications Ltd. Reprinted by permission. Notes omitted.

8.2 From "Teachers' Expectancies: Determinants of Pupils' IQ Gains" by R. Rosenthal and L. Jacobson, 1966, *Psychological Reports, 19*, pp. 115–118. Copyright © 1966 by Southern Universities Press. Reprinted by permission.

8.3 From "Listening to Speech in the First Year of Life: Experiential Influences on Phoneme Perception" by J. F. Werker and R. N. Desjardins, 1995, *Current Directions in Psychological Science, 4*, pp. 76-78, 80-81. Copyright © 1995 by The American Psychological Society. Reprinted by permission of Blackwell Publishers.

9.1 From "A Theory of Human Motivation" by A. H. Maslow, 1943, *Psychological Review, 50*, pp. 371-396. Notes omitted.

9.2 From "Self-Efficacy: Toward a Unifying Theory of Behavioral Change" by A. Bandura, 1977, *Psychological Review, 84*, pp. 193–195, 200, 202, 213–215. Copyright © 1977 by The American Psychological Association. Reprinted by permission.

9.3 From "The Strategies of Human Mating" by D. M. Buss, 1994, *American Scientist, 82*, pp. 238-242, 249. Copyright © 1994 by *American Scientist*. Reprinted by permission. Bibliography omitted.

10.1 From "Facial Expressions of Emotion: New Findings, New Questions" by P. Ekman, 1992, *Psychological Science, 3*, pp. 34–38. Copyright © 1992 by The American Psychological Society. Reprinted by permission of Blackwell Publishers. Some references omitted. A large section on smiling has been omitted for this volume.

10.2 From "Some Evidence for Heightened Sexual Attraction Under Conditions of High Anxiety" by D. G. Dutton and A. P. Aron, 1974, *Journal of Personality and Social Psychology, 30*, pp. 510–513, 516–517. Copyright © 1974 by The American Psychological Association. Reprinted by permission. Notes omitted.

356

Acknowledgments

10.3   From *Triangle of Love: Intimacy, Passion, Commitment* (pp. 37-48, 51-61) by R. J. Sternberg, 1988. New York: Basic Books. Copyright © 1988 by Basic Books, Inc. Reprinted by permission of Basic Books, a member of Perseus Books, LLC.

11.1   From "External Control and Internal Control" by J. B. Rotter, 1971, *Psychology Today, 5*, pp. 37–38, 42, 58–59. Copyright © 1971 by Sussex Publishers, Inc. Reprinted by permission of *Psychology Today.*

11.2   From "Validation of the Five-Factor Model of Personality Across Instruments and Observers" by R. R. McCrae and P. T. Costa, Jr., 1987, *Journal of Personality and Social Psychology, 52*, pp. 81, 85-90.

11.3   From "Culture and the Self: Implications for Cognition, Emotion, and Motivation" by H. R. Markus and S. Kitayama, 1991, *Psychological Review, 98*, pp. 224–227, 229. Copyright © 1991 by The American Psychological Association. Reprinted by permission.

12.1   From "The Evolution of the Stress Concept" by H. Selye, 1973, *American Scientist, 61*, pp. 692–699. Copyright © 1973 by *American Scientist.* Reprinted by permission.

12.2   From "Little Hassles Can Be Hazardous to Health" by R. S. Lazarus, 1981, *Psychology Today*, pp. 58, 60–62. Copyright © 1981 by Sussex Publishers, Inc. Reprinted by permission of *Psychology Today.*

12.3   From "Adjustment to Threatening Events: A Theory of Cognitive Adaptation" by S. E. Taylor, 1983, *American Psychologist, 38*, pp. 1161–1166, 1171–1173. Copyright © 1983 by The American Psychological Association. Reprinted by permission. Notes omitted.

13.1   From "On Being Sane in Insane Places" by D. L. Rosenhan, 1973, *Science, 179*, pp. 250-258. Copyright © 1973 by The American Association for the Advancement of Science. Reprinted by permission. Some notes omitted.

13.2   From *Inhibitions, Symptoms, and Anxiety* (pp. 60–67) by S. Freud, 1926 (A. Strachey, Trans.). New York: W. W. Norton. Translation copyright © 1959 by Alix Strachey. Reprinted by permission of W. W. Norton & Company, Inc. and by arrangement with Mark Paterson and Associates, Colchester, England. Notes and references omitted.

13.3   From *Helplessness: On Depression, Development, and Death* (pp. 93-95, 97-105) by M. E. P. Seligman, 1975. New York: W. H. Freeman. Copyright © 1975 by Martin E. P. Seligman; copyright renewed 1992 by Martin E. P. Seligman. Reprinted by permission of W. H. Freeman and Company. Notes omitted.

14.1   From *On Becoming a Person: A Therapist's View of Psychotherapy* (pp. 31, 33-36) by C. R. Rogers, 1961. Boston: Houghton Mifflin. Copyright © 1961 by Carl R. Rogers. Reprinted by permission of Houghton Mifflin Company.

14.2   From *Cognitive Therapy and the Emotional Disorders* (pp. 213–227, 229–232) by A. T. Beck, 1976. Madison, CT: International Universities Press. Copyright © 1976 by Aaron T. Beck. Reprinted by permission of International Universities Press, Inc. References omitted.

14.3   From "The Effectiveness of Psychotherapy: The Consumer Reports Study" by M. E. P. Seligman, 1995, *American Psychologist, 50*, pp. 965-969, 974. Copyright © 1995 by The American Psychological Association. Adapted by permission.

15.1   From *A Theory of Cognitive Dissonance* (pp. 1-5, 18-24, 29-31) by L. Festinger, 1957. Stanford, CA: Stanford University Press. Copyright © 1957 by Leon Festinger. Reprinted by permission of Stanford University Press.

15.2   From "Affirmative Action, Unintentional Racial Biases, and Intergroup Relations" by J. F. Dovidio and S. L. Gaertner, 1996, *Journal of Social Issues, 52*, pp. 51, 53-60, 71-75. Copyright © 1996 by The Society for the Psychological Study of Social Issues. Reprinted by permission of Blackwell Publishers.

15.3   From "Behavioral Study of Obedience" by S. Milgram, 1963, *Journal of Abnormal and Social Psychology, 67*, pp. 371-378. Copyright © 1963 by Stanley Milgram. Reprinted by permission of Alexandra Milgram, literary executor.

15.4   From "Imitation of Film-Mediated Aggressive Models" by A. Bandura, D. Ross, and S. A. Ross, 1963, *Journal of Abnormal and Social Psychology, 66*, pp. 3-11. Copyright © 1963 by The American Psychological Association. Reprinted by permission.

Index